Dream Worlds

View of the second landing on the grand staircase, Dufayel's credit establishment, Paris. (From *Architectural Record*, vol. 12, no. 4, September, 1902: 441. Courtesy of *Architectural Record*.)

Dream Worlds

Mass Consumption in
Late Nineteenth-Century France

Rosalind H. Williams

University of California Press
Berkeley · Los Angeles · London

University of California Press
Berkeley and Los Angeles, California

University of California Press, Ltd.
London, England

© 1982 by
The Regents of the University of California

Printed in the United States of America

1 2 3 4 5 6 7 8 9

Library of Congress Cataloging in Publication Data

Williams, Rosalind H.
  Dream worlds: Mass consumption in late nineteenth-century France.

  Bibliography: p.
  Includes index.
  1. Consumers—France—History.   I.   Title.
HC280.C6W54   381′.3′0944   81-4689
ISBN 0-520-04355-3   AACR2

To Gary

The consumer . . . has yet to find a historian.
Theodore Zeldin, France 1848–1945

Contents

Illustrations

Acknowledgments

In considering the debts I have accumulated in composing this book, I have rediscovered a couple of simple truths about human helpfulness. The first is that it is impossible to draw definite limits around influence and assistance, and consequently around gratitude. Because this project originated as a doctoral dissertation, my most immediate and obvious debt is to my dissertation committee: William M. Johnston, Charles Rearick, and Patrick Eagan. But my appreciation extends to other members of the History Department at the University of Massachusetts, as well as to Michael Wolff in the English Department, who helped make my graduate work at once stimulating and pleasant. From there the circle of indebtedness keeps widening to include many other teachers at the University of California at Berkeley, Harvard College, and Wellesley College, who have in a less direct but still important way imparted ideas and training which have been incorporated in this book. The fact that they are too numerous to mention by name should not at all minimize their contribution.

In a similar way I am indebted to members of the Science, Technology, and Society Program at the Massachusetts Institute of Technology for helping me bring this project to completion. As a Research Fellow with the STS Program during 1980–1982, I enjoyed exchanging ideas with my colleagues, especially with Leo Marx, and I was also afforded time and resources which enabled me to prepare the manuscript for publication. In particular I would like to thank Merrill Smith of MIT's Rotch Visual Collection for her generous assistance in collecting illustrations to accompany the text.

The second lesson I have relearned is the difficulty of disentangling intellectual from moral support. The two merge to create the confidence that is vitally necessary for anyone embarked on a long writing project. William Johnston, chairman of my dissertation committee, gave me constant encouragement along with scholarly and practical advice. Friends who read the manuscript, or who listened to my efforts to explain some of its themes, bolstered my morale more than they knew. For the same reason, thanking my family is by no means a matter of form. My parents provided enthusiasm, sympathy, and time; my children, amusement and cooperation; and my husband, all of these and infinitely more in the way of ideas, criticism, and encouragement—which is why the book is dedicated to him.

1 The Implications of the Consumer Revolution

The Advent of Mass Consumption – In the 1860s, twenty-year-old Denise Baudu and her two younger brothers, recent orphans, emigrated from a provincial French village to Paris, to live with their uncle. Arriving at daybreak after a sleepless night on the hard benches of a third-class railway car, they set out in search of their uncle's fabric store. The unfamiliar streets opened onto a tumultuous square where they halted abruptly, awestruck by the sight of a building more impressive than any they had ever seen: a department store. "Look," Denise murmured to her brothers. "Now *there* is a store!" This monument was immeasurably grander than her village's quiet variety shop, in which she had worked. She felt her heart rise within her and forgot her fatigue, her fright, everything except this vision. Directly in front of her, over the central doorway, two allegorical figures of laughing women flaunted a sign proclaiming the store's name, "Au Bonheur des Dames" ("To the Happiness of the Ladies"). Through the door could be seen a landslide of gloves, scarves, and hats tumbling from racks and counters, while in the distance display windows unrolled along the street.

Entranced, the three youngsters walked slowly along, gazing at the displays. In one window an intricate arrangement of umbrellas formed the roof of a rustic cabin, while in another a dazzling rainbow of silks, satins, and velvets arched high above them. At the last display of ready-to-wear clothing, a snowfall of expensive laces cascaded in the background, and before them pirouetted three elegant mannequins, one draped in a velvet coat trimmed with silver fox, another in a white cashmere opera cloak, the third in an overcoat edged with feathers. The heads of the mannequins had been removed and been replaced by large price tags. On either side of the display, mirrors endlessly multiplied the images of these strange and seductive creatures, half-human and half-merchandise, until they seemed to people the street.

Denise awoke from her reverie. She and her brothers still had to locate their uncle. Asking directions, they discovered they were on the very block where he kept his shop. It was housed in a moldering building on the opposite side of the street, where its three dark, empty windows grimly confronted the brilliant displays of Au Bonheur des Dames. Inside Denise glimpsed a dim showroom with a low ceiling, greenish woodwork, and tables cluttered with dusty bolts of cloth. She felt as if she were staring into the dank shadows of a primeval cave.

Denise is the heroine of Émile Zola's novel *Au Bonheur des Dames* (1884), which opens with this account of her arrival in Paris. Her initial encounter with a department store dramatizes the way nineteenth-century society as a whole suddenly found itself confronting a style of consumption radically different from any previously known. The quantity of consumer goods available to most people had been drastically limited: a few kitchen utensils used to prepare a sparse and monotonous diet, several well-worn pieces of furniture (bed, chest, table, perhaps a stool or bench), bedding, shoes or clogs, a shirt and trousers or a dress (and sometimes one outfit for special occasions), some essential tools. That was all. Moreover, these goods were obtained mainly through barter and self-production, so that the activity of consumption was closely linked with that of production. Money was rarely used by the average person and credit was haphazard and scarce. Only the better-off spent much time in stores; for most, the activity of shopping was restricted to occasional fairs.

In the past century these ancient and universal patterns have been shattered by the advent of mass consumption. Its characteristics are a radical division between the activities of production and of consumption, the prevalence of standardized merchandise sold in large volume, the ceaseless introduction of new products, widespread reliance on money and credit, and ubiquitous publicity. This fabulous prospect of a vast and permanent fair, which transfixed Denise, has since charmed millions of others as it has reached out from the largest cities to ever smaller ones, and from the richest countries to poorer ones. The merchandise itself is by no means available to all, but the *vision* of a seemingly unlimited profusion of commodities is available, is, indeed, nearly unavoidable. In the wealthier societies the manifestations of mass consumption—department stores, discount houses, supermarkets, chain stores, mail-order houses, and perpetual advertising in newspapers and magazines and on television, radio, and billboards—are so pervasive that we hardly realize how recently and how thoroughly both private and collective life have been transformed into a medium where people habitually interact with merchandise.

The advent of mass consumption represents a pivotal historical moment. Once people enjoy discretionary income and choice of products, once they glimpse the vision of commodities in profusion, they do not easily return to traditional modes of consumption. Having gazed upon the delights of a department store, Denise would never again be satisfied with the plain, unadorned virtues of Uncle Baudu's shop. The hackneyed plot of the young innocent in the big city receives a specifically modern twist, for now the seduction is commercial. We who have tasted the fruits of the consumer revolution have lost our innocence.

The Moral Implications of Mass Consumption – Although such moralistic language is not usually applied to consumer affairs, it is appropriate. The implications of the consumer revolution extend far beyond economic statistics and technological innovations to intensely felt, deeply troubling conflicts in personal and social values. Before the nineteenth century, when only a tiny fraction of the population had any choice in this realm, consumption was dictated for most by natural scarcity and unquestioned social tradition. Where there is no freedom, there is no moral dilemma. But now, for the first time in history, many people have considerable choice in what to consume, how, and how much, and in addition have the leisure, education, and health to ponder these questions. The consumer revolution brought both the opportunity and the need to reassess values, but this reassessment has been incomplete and only partly conscious. While the unprecedented expansion of goods and time has obvious blessings, it has also brought a weight of remorse and guilt, craving and envy, anxiety and, above all, uneasy conscience, as we sense that we have too much, yet keep wanting more. We resent our own tendency to judge ourselves and others according to trival differences in consumption habits.

If mass consumption has altered the patterns of personal and social consciousness, these new attitudes have in turn had profound material effects. The population explosion, the hunger crisis, the energy shortage, the environmental crisis, chronic inflation—all these central concerns of the present originate in our values and habits as consumers. The great hope of the nineteenth century was that production could be expanded indefinitely to meet rising consumption everywhere. We are now coming to terms with the fallacies of that expectation, by recognizing material limits as a permanent condition of human life. While the expansion of production can be regarded primarily as a technical problem, the acceptance of limits on consumption involves not so much technological know-how as political imagination, personal will, and social morality, with an intellectual understanding of all of these. Such an understanding is now lacking. Decisions are made in response to concrete problems which, pressing as they may be, will only keep accumulating unless our consumer values are clarified.

Such clarification has to begin with a fuller appreciation of just what we mean by *consumption*. The word is often defined in a vague (and pejorative) sense as "using up something in order to maintain life." Another common view is that consumption is the opposite of production. Hannah Arendt has remarked that these two definitions are contradictory, since consumption cannot be the converse of production when the two together form a reciprocal and interdependent cycle necessary to sustain life. She further suggests that impermanent "consumer goods," having as their purpose the maintenance of life, should be distinguished from "use objects," intended to create a world of durable things serving as a familiar home for man in the midst of non-human nature. According to Arendt, the activities and objects we lump together as involving consumption really include two distinct groups, one related to life sustenance, the other to giving meaning to life.[1]

Something like this distinction may be found by comparing the two Latin expressions that serve as sources for the single word *consumption* in modern Romance languages. The English word comes from the Latin root *consumere*—a conjunction of *cum* and *sumere*, the latter meaning "to take," so that the expression as a whole signifies "to take away with" or "to use up entirely." With this derivation, it is logical for the English term *consumption* to refer not only to the use of commodities but also to the wasting away of the body (specifically, in tuberculosis), for in both cases the process involves the destruction of matter. That destruction may be active and rapid, as in the case of consumer goods like food or fuel, or gradual and passive, as in the case of use objects like chairs or works of art, which are repaired in an attempt to resist the process of deterioration. But in either case consumption is considered equivalent to destruction, waste, decay—in short, to a death-directed process. The unfavorable connotation of the term lingered when, beginning in the mid-eighteenth century, it became increasingly used as a specialized term in political economy, a linguistic evolution that accompanied the evolution of an organized capitalist market system.[2]

The second Latin root suggests a much more positive appreciation of the human relation to material things. This is *consummare*, from *cum summa*, "to make the sum" or "to sum up," as in arithmetic—to carry to completion, to terminate in perfection. The Latin translation of Jesus' last words on the cross is "Consummatum est." The usual English translation of his cry ("It is finished") implies only termination and fails to convey the meaning of a life summed up and perfected in the moment of death. A more adequate and more typical English translation of *consummare* is "to consummate," which does suggest an understanding of death, and therefore of life, as achievement despite and, indeed, through the inevitable destruction of animate and inanimate matter.

This second Latin root is the source of the French terms—the verb *consommer* and its related noun *la consommation*—which are translated into English as "to consume" and "consumption." The difference in linguistic origins means that the French expressions have implications not conveyed by the English equivalent. For example, the rich broth the French call a *consommé* is not so named because it is used up as a food but because it represents the distilled essence of bouillon. The French also have a word *consumer*, from the first Latin root, *consumere*, which is properly reserved for specific actions of destruction such as those of fire, corrosion, or wasting disease. In popular usage, however, the two French words *consommer* and *consumer* have long been confused—an instructive confusion, contravening as it does national pride in linguistic precision. It suggests the ambiguity of consumption itself, its mingled nature as achievement and destruction, as submission to entropy and triumph over it. A part of us craves the rewards of "using up" the good things of life, while another part is aware of moving ever closer to the point of death, which will "sum up" our lives in a way that has nothing to do with transient pleasures. The fundamental ambivalence in values lies not in the words but in ourselves.

The Relevance of French History – In attempting to understand the implications of mass consumption, Americans today habitually turn to social scientists such as the sociologist Vance Packard or the economist J. K. Galbraith, who are among the best-known writers on the subject.[3] The current prestige of the social sciences is such that this response is a natural, almost an automatic, reflex, but such responses are not always entirely beneficial ones. At the least there is ample room for a variety of approaches to understanding a subject of such import. This book seeks that understanding in the past.

Consumer society is the product of a long historical evolution, at once material and mental. Its material evolution deserves far more study than it has yet received from economic and social historians. In this book, however, the mental evolution is the primary concern. As much as do our economic and political institutions, our attitudes have a history, and examination of their origins may be equally helpful in assessing contemporary life. To explore the emergence of the consumer mentality requires the techniques of cultural and intellectual history, techniques which are humanistic without being unscientific. They include an alertness to figurative language, to allusions and overtones, to how people express themselves as well as what they express, in order to discern patterns of response that have a collective validity. Such techniques are sometimes frowned upon in the social sciences today, especially in those branches which seek quantifiable evidence. However, as we shall see, one value of the historical approach is that it uncovers alternative modes of social science, advanced at the time the profession was taking shape, which could be more helpful in understanding modern consumption than many of the prevailing modes.

Another reflex impels most Americans to assume that if history can indeed be a powerful aid in understanding the present, our own national history must be the most helpful of all. Again this is a natural response, not only because of national pride, but even more because the United States has become a paradigm of modern consumer society. The idea of studying a paradigmatic national model is basically commendable. It provides a focus for an inquiry which, if viewed on an international scale, would be hopelessly unwieldy, and it still leaves room to suggest how the general phenomenon transcends national boundaries.

In fact, however, the history of France, even more than that of the United States, most illuminates the nature and dilemmas of modern consumption. This is because, in the first place, the French have long prided themselves on furnishing a universally valid model of enlightened consumption. By the eighteenth century the way of life enjoyed by the French aristocracy and wealthy bourgeoisie had established itself as a prototype admired and imitated by upper classes throughout Europe. Princes and kings constructed miniature versions of Versailles; their courtiers admired paintings by Watteau and danced the gavotte to the music of Rameau; and rich bourgeois hired French tutors for their children, instructed their chefs to prepare dishes à la française, and bought chairs designed in the style of Louis XV. This prototype was also adopted by the upper classes in the American colonies, who imported from Europe their manners, card games, liquors, fashions in clothing, and furniture.

These consumer habits, together with less tangible patterns of taste and manners, of reason and feeling, comprised *civilisation*, understood by the French as an absolute standard worthy of emulation by all other peoples. The concept of *civilisation* provided an authoritative guide for the consumer—in an age when only a small fraction of the population were consumers in the sense of enjoying discretionary spending—by positing a humanistic ideal capable of giving consumption a meaning and purpose. In the nineteenth century, however, the humanistic ideal of *civilisation* tended to evaporate, leaving behind a residue of material possessions which by themselves claimed prestige for their owners. By the end of that century the model of consumption that had originated in prerevolutionary court life had become degraded to the level of the heavy velour curtains, crystal chandeliers, ornate mirrors, and imitation Louis XV divans in the cramped salons of aspiring tradesmen. They can be seen in living rooms even today; such is the tenacity of the forms of courtly life and, in a far more elusive way, of the ideal of *civilisation* they were intended to embody.

The development of this ideal and these forms in France is the subject of the next chapter. Chapter III will examine the consequences of the consumer revolution, which opened up the pleasures of discretionary consumption to the masses and challenged the authority of the courtly model of consumption. Although the concept of a consumer revolution is far less familiar than that of the industrial revolution, they are really two facets of a single upheaval that decisively altered the material basis of human life. Mass consumption inevitably accompanied mass production. A transformation of such magnitude cannot be dated precisely, but the tempo of change was at its swiftest in the nineteenth century. In France, the critical period runs from about 1850 to the outbreak of World War I. Between those dates there was for the first time a steady (if not unbroken) increase in purchasing power—the basic economic fact upon which all the rest depended. A Parisian worker who had 100 francs to spend in 1850 had the equivalent of 165 francs by the early years of the twentieth century. This increase in discretionary income meant that he was able to buy more staples like fuel, fabrics, and, above all, food. Even more significantly, Frenchmen could purchase more nonessentials. For example, they continued to eat about the same amount of potatoes and bread from 1850 to 1914 but consumed far more wine, meat, sugar, coffee, and cheese. Furthermore, the percentage of income spent on all foods kept falling, from an average of nearly 80 percent for a working-class family in 1850 to about 60 percent by 1905. As disposable income rose, banking systems were overhauled to facilitate payment greatly, especially by the introduction of the ordinary bank check. The increasing availability of credit was particularly significant in France, where before 1860 credit and deposit banking for individuals and small businesses was almost nonexistent.[4]

These economic transformations are one mainspring of the consumer revolution. The second (and the two are wholly interdependent) consists of a torrent of technological changes that simultaneously lowered the cost of existing consumer goods and provided entirely new ones. The enormous gains in productivity made available both more goods and more money with which to buy them. Steam, the productive force in the early days of industrialization, was supplanted by the internal combustion engine and by electricity, forms of power that could be transported more easily and could be reduced in scale for use by individual consumers. The distinctive inventions of early industrialization were machines of production, especially for the production of textiles, which consequently led the way in the revolution of mass-marketed, cheaper goods. After 1850 many notable inventions were consumer products themselves—the bicycle, the automobile, chemical dyes, the telephone, electric lighting, photography, the phonograph. Never before or since has there been such a concentration of technological change affecting the ordinary consumer. What he ate, what he ate with, where he lived, what he wore, how he moved around—all these daily activities and more were being altered simultaneously.

The advent of the consumer revolution in the French

provinces was more gradual than in the cities but was still decisive. In the 1860s there were still large regional differences in provincial consumer habits: in Provence a peasant ate wheat bread; in the north he ate potatoes and rye bread; and in the center of the country, he ate chestnuts and potatoes. By 1900, they all ate wheat bread. In the 1860s the dress of peasant and also of working-class women was noticeably darker and cruder than the complicated trains, trailing skirts, laces, and ribbons of wealthier women. By the 1890s everyone wore shorter, simpler, more colorful clothes. Mass consumption means that similar merchandise reaches to all regions and all classes, and by the turn of the century this uniform market was expanding in France.[5]

The consumer revolution introduced a style of consumption unlike the model that had originated in the courts and had gradually spread among the wealthy bourgeoisie. The upper classes had assumed that the kind of luxuries they preferred would permeate the lower levels of society in time. The future was expected to bring, in the popular phrase, "the democratization of luxury." The future held a rude surprise. The luxury that was democratized was quite different in character from the upper-class paradigm. And in creating this new style of mass consumption the French were nearly as preeminent in the nineteenth century as they had been in developing the courtly model in earlier times. France pioneered in retailing and advertising, the twin pillars of modern consumer life. Its capital city became a sort of pilot plant of mass consumption. The period of its most rapid change was just beginning when Denise Baudu is supposed to have disembarked there. By the time she reached middle age, a quarter of a century later, she would have seen the transmutation of Paris from the cramped city of Victor Hugo to a modern capital of consumption, a city of boulevards, cafés, electric lights, apartments, advertising posters, the Métro, cinemas, restaurants, and parks, with production largely exiled to an outer belt while the heart of the city was devoted to commerce. If the North of England is the landscape that symbolizes the industrial revolution, the Île de France can well claim to serve as the emblem of the consumer revolution.

French initiative in creating the new style of mass consumption was crowned by the Paris expositions of 1889 and 1900. There was revealed for the first time a planned environment of mass consumption; there thoughtful observers realized, in a confused and uneasy way, that they were immersed in a strange new world of consumer behavior. They saw crowds milling around displays of luxurious automobiles and around glass cages displaying couturier-clothed mannequins; taking imaginary voyages via cinematic techniques to the floor of the sea or the craters of the moon; and, at night, staring at displays of lighted fountains or at voluptuous belly dancers wriggling in a reproduction of a Cairo nightspot. The expositions and similar environments (such as department stores and automobile trade shows) displayed a novel and crucial juxtaposition of imagination and merchandise, of dreams and commerce, of collective consciousness and economic fact. In mass consumption the needs of the imagination play as large a role as those of the body. Both are exploited by commerce, which appeals to consumers by inviting them into a fantasy world of pleasure, comfort, and amusement.

The Relevance of French Thought—Now it is possible to understand why French thinkers around the turn of the century were peculiarly sensitive to the impact of the consumer revolution—and this is the final reason why the French experience is uniquely illuminating. They were witnessing an historical collision as longstanding cultural traditions of enlightened consumption slammed into material and social changes that directly challenged those traditions. They sensed that they lived in an age of transition from which there could be no return to the former state of things—a situation that aroused both great hopes and great apprehensions. New combinations of thought and feeling were ventured and new values enunciated, since inherited ones were for the most part inadequate to deal with changing social reality. The generations of the 1880s and, especially, of the 1890s were richly inventive in what we would now call consumer lifestyles. In those decades emerged at least two major modes of consumption that provided alternatives to the courtly and mass models already described. The first alternative, elitist in spirit and derived from the dandy tradition, attempted to transcend the supposed vulgarity of ordinary consumption through a uniquely individual arrangement of commodities serving lofty spiritual and aesthetic ideals (Chapter IV). The second lifestyle, inspired by democratic principles, embodied the ideal of social reform by reforming the design of everyday consumer items (Chapter V).

Both the elitist and the democratic modes of consumption have proved durable. Their contemporary equivalents are all around us, and, together with upper-class and mass consumption, they make up an interdependent system of lifestyles that still endures. But in France some of the innovators who helped define these styles of consumption became acutely aware of the frustrations that result from placing such emphasis on merchandise as a means of personal and social self-definition, no matter how idealistic the motives for this emphasis may be. The accumulating sense that the consumer revolution had caused a moral crisis which could not be resolved by multiplying lifestyles led to a reconsideration of the moral implications of modern consumption.

French thinkers were particularly well prepared to undertake this reconsideration because they had behind them the intellectual tradition of the *moraliste*—an untranslatable term suggesting a thinker with a broadly philosophical and historical outlook and a bent toward cultural criticism and social commentary. The closest exemplars in the English-speaking world are the great Victorian social prophets like Thomas Carlyle or John Ruskin. In France the tradition is especially old and well-established (Michel de Montaigne, who wrote in the sixteenth century, is a famous early example), and it still retains considerable respectability (Albert Camus is a twentieth-century example). Most of the *moralistes* to be discussed here are less famous than these but were no less molded by an outlook that encourages them to consider social and economic changes with an awareness of their ethical implications. They are well-educated, well-informed, intelligent commentators, not necessarily the central geniuses of their day but hardly representative of mass opinion. In many cases they occupy a strategic middle ground between the world of ideas and that of ongoing political, social, and artistic activities.

In trying to assess the implications of the consumer revolution, some of these thinkers revived the venerable concept of luxury and tried to update traditional arguments about its morality to apply to the new "democratized" luxury. Their debate revealed a profound division between desire to consume and guilt about that desire, and this ambivalence formed a serious fault line in bourgeois culture. The desire was justified by the scientific authority of evolutionary theory, which equated moral and material progress; the guilt derived from religious and philosophical teachings of great antiquity, which upheld the virtues of austerity. Although modern science and traditional ethics were both respected authorities, in regard to consumption they offered conflicting and ultimately irreconcilable advice (Chapter VI).

The late nineteenth-century debate about luxury never got beyond this deadlock. Only when the moral problems of modern consumption were posed in different terms was real progress made in solving them. The concept of solidarity above all others suggested the kinds of values most appropriate to post-consumer revolution society. Charles Gide applied the concept of solidarity to economics, calling for consumers to unite and cast off their subservience to producers. More than this, Gide put his ideas into practice by helping found some of the first important consumer organizations, which eventually joined forces with consumer cooperatives begun by socialists (Chapter VII). Émile Durkheim and Gabriel Tarde applied solidarity to social thought and suggested ways in which mass consumption might give rise to new systems of social values (Chapter VIII). All these thinkers of the 1890s and early 1900s advocated means for consumption to serve social values rather than imposing its own material values upon society.

World War I cut short this era of intellectual experimentation. Not only did its destruction of productive capacity sharply reduce opportunities to consume but its slaughter made the subject of consumer ethics seem frivolous. Intellectuals who had been concerned with the social effects of technological change instead became preoccupied with the implications of mechanized warfare. Now that production has more than recovered from the effects of two world wars, we have come to realize that, along with our military technologies, our technologies of consumption may pose a threat to world peace and even to human survival.

In coming to terms with that realization, we may be helped by reexamining ideas raised in France during the consumer revolution. French intellectuals of that time were prophetically aware that consumption would have to be restricted at some point, that the endless multiplication of merchandise Denise saw in the department-store window was only a mirage. While no one can solve our dilemmas for us, these social critics raised issues we now confront; they defined problems, pointed out dead ends, and provided a starting point for further inquiry. By examining their contributions, we may arrive at a fuller appreciation of what was unquestionably one of the great creative periods in French culture. Even more importantly, this act of historical recovery may increase our understanding of the social ethics of consumption and enable us to create a viable moral code of our own.

Part One

The Development
of Consumer Lifestyles

*Today, as always, the authentic language
of fashion is worth listening to.*

Tom Wolfe
Mauve Gloves & Madmen

2 The Closed World of Courtly Consumption

The Consumer Class of the Renaissance Courts–Finding the origins of modern consumer society requires a journey in the reverse direction from Denise's migration, a journey away from the dazzle of city department stores, back to the French countryside. The Loire valley southwest of Paris is a tranquil, pleasant region where one-street villages of lopsided stucco houses surrounded by vegetable gardens sit among wheatfields and vineyards. The villages recall a centuries-old rural way of life, so that a visit to the Loire countryside begins to assume the quality of a journey back in time, especially when one glimpses castle ruins straggling down the high ground overlooking the river. Some of the earliest stone castles in Europe were built here around 1000 A.D., at a time when both these strongholds and the unfortified village settlements were engulfed by dark and threatening forest. Most of the trees in the Loire valley have long since been cut, but even today some roadways are lined by thick woods and dotted with signs warning motorists to watch out for game.

Far down such a road, at the distant edge of the woods, appears a vision as unexpected and dreamlike to a modern traveler as the sight of Au Bonheur des Dames must have been to a nineteenth-century peasant girl: a white stone palace, bedecked with intricately carved staircases, portals, pillars, and turrets, rising from the mists of surrounding gardens and pools. Everything about this vision of a Loire château testifies that its inhabitants, unlike the castle-dwellers of the Middle Ages, valued elegance over safety. If the château is set next to water (or, in the case of Chenonceaux, across a river), it is to furnish not a defensible moat but a flattering mirror. Inside these splendid structures is further evidence that their builders had acquired complicated and costly desires for material possessions. Room after room is filled with tapestries and draperies, with frescoes and stuccoes and worked leather, with elaborately carved chests and tables, all indicating that the people who lived here loved to acquire things, to ornament their surroundings, to express their mentality through a choice of material objects. They were consumers.

The châteaux of the Loire were constructed by French aristocrats during the Renaissance, and especially by the courtly circle during the reign of King Francis I (1515–1547). This group formed the consumer class at a time when that class encompassed only a small fraction of the total population. The enjoyments of the tiny consumer class were directly dependent on the exploitation of the peasant masses; this brute social fact was concretely visible in the contrast between the accumulated wealth of the châteaux and the poverty of the huts inhabited by those who worked the soil. The peasants were also consumers in the sense that they used food, fuel, clothing, and so forth to survive, but both the level and the type of consumption they practiced were dictated by a rigidly constricting combination of natural limits and social traditions. They cannot be said to have composed a consumer class, in the sense of a group that exercises discretion in what and how much it consumes.

The sixteenth-century aristocracy was nearly homogeneous in its consumer tastes, because the ladies and gentlemen of the court acknowledged the king as "the first gentleman of the kingdom." This social prestige of the monarch reflects the consolidation of royal economic and political power since the Middle Ages. By the time of Francis I, the nobles were rapidly losing their medieval independence as local magnates and were being transformed from a feudal nobility of free knights and lords into a royal nobility dependent on the king. Instead of fighting against Francis I, they fought for him in his invasions of Italy, indulging his territorial and dynastic ambitions. And when the king returned from these wars passionately fond of the Italo-Antique style in consumer goods, the entire court followed suit. They all brought back Italian statues and paintings, as well as Italian decorators and architects—Francis himself lured Leonardo da Vinci, who died shortly after his arrival in France and was buried at the royal château of Amboise in the Loire valley. The uniformity of taste among this consumer class is evident in the Italianate loggias, staircases, and façades of its châteaux; its preference for the fashionable rather than the utilitarian is evident in the inappropriateness for the colder French climate of many of these Italian features. The appearance of the Loire châteaux therefore reflects faithfully a social system where discretionary consumption was restricted to a small group which in turn acknowledged the authority—social as well as economic and political—of one individual, the king.

That aristocracy and monarchy disappeared nearly two centuries ago, but the prestige of the courtly style of consumption survives tenaciously to this day. When in the late nineteenth century alternative models of consumption—alternative lifestyles, to use contemporary parlance—arose, they supplanted rather than replaced the aristocratic model. Succeeding chapters will trace the late nineteenth-century origins of these alternatives that have replaced one homogeneous consumer style, derived from a single source of authority, with a diversity of styles based on a multiplicity of authorities. The subject of this chapter is the evolution of the courtly model which was for so long the only lifestyle, so to speak. Only against this background can the magnitude of the late-nineteenth-century changes be appreciated. Within the court itself, the historical evolution was in the direction of ever more rigid and extravagant forms of consumption that eventually contributed to the downfall of this consumer class. At the same time, however, the aristocratic model of consumption was being diffused to other social groups outside the confines of the court. By the time of the French Revolution, when the monarchy and aristocracy fell, the prestige of the courtly model had spread so widely that it not only survived but enlarged its embrace to include the new consumer classes of the early nineteenth century.

Consumption and Civilization–The tenacious hold of the external forms of château life—the carved buffets, upholstered chairs, porticoes, columns, and gold leaf found in the homes of the well-to-do even today—should not distract us from seeing that a far more crucial element of courtly consumption did not survive the overthrow of the aristocracy: the conviction that possession of these amenities was justified by the place of the aristocracy in a divinely ordered social hierarchy. A consumer class is identified not only by its privilege of discretion in consumption, but also, and even more, by its understanding of how that privilege is merited. Today, when authorities and standards in consumption have become complex and varied, our rationales and justifications have similarly become confused and diverse. The situation was much simpler in the sixteenth century, when the consumer class was largely coextensive with the aristocratic class. To question the right of the nobility to live differently from the peasantry would have seemed as absurd as asking a peacock why it deserved plumage more brilliant than that of the sparrow. God had decreed these differences. He had ordained that mankind be divided into three orders, or estates, each serving a distinct purpose: nobility, clergy, and commoners, or those who fight, those who pray, and those who work. As God had chosen the Bourbons to serve as kings of France, so He had chosen noble families to aid the monarch honorably and loyally with their swords and counsel.

This explanation of aristocratic prerogative is based on a religious understanding of society accepted as self-evident and self-sufficient in the Middle Ages. During the Renaissance, however, another sort of reasoning was advanced to explain the privileges of the consumer class. This was a secular justification which still retains some persuasiveness, unlike the medieval religious explanation, which now seems meaningless. The secular argument, in brief, is that consumption fosters civilization—an overarching ideal that simultaneously includes the nurture of art, science, and learning in society at large and the development of courteous, restrained behavior in the individual. This ideal incorporates a material component which it surpasses but cannot eliminate. Peasants living at the margin of subsistence could not have the leisure and discretionary income to pursue the civilizing ideal; only the consumer class could do this. At a time when social wealth was inadequate to allow a comfortable standard of life for all, the enjoyment of a level of consumption far above the ordinary was regarded as a means to the end of preserving and extending civilization. In a particularly splendid room at his château at Fontainebleau, Francis I commissioned an Italian decorator to portray in painting and sculpture the mythical battle between the Lapiths and Centaurs, between Greeks and the half-man, half-beast marauders from the mountains. In these heroic images of civilized men writhing in ferocious combat with coarse animality, the Renaissance court saw a representation of its own consciousness.

The process by which higher standards of civilization and of consumption evolved together in European courtly circles has been described in the remarkable book *The Civilizing Process* (1939) by the German sociologist and historian, Norbert Elias. Elias's topic is the evolution of manners as codified in etiquette manuals from the Renaissance to modern times. This "civilizing process" originated in the courts—for example, the court of Francis I adopted Italian refinements of etiquette as readily as it copied Italian architectural styles—and from there it slowly disseminated to bourgeois society. Over the centuries this process involved the suppression of aggressive and instinctual behavior, an increased self-consciousness about the perception of one's actions by others, and a greater emphasis on politeness, restraint, and refinement as ideals of conduct. Although Elias does not particularly stress the point, his research shows clearly that the development of civilization in this sense is intimately related to an increase in standards of consumption. "The civilizing process" is an evolution at once material and behavioral, for as etiquette becomes more complex so do material needs. Table manners provide the most obvious example. In the Middle Ages a person needed only a sharp knife to hack away at the common joint of meat. He shared a common plate and cup, and used his sleeve to wipe his hands and face. By the sixteenth century forks and napkins began to be used, and from then on plates and cups and other implements for individual use began to accumulate, until by the nineteenth century each person had a whole battery of objects to use in the process of eating. Also beginning in the sixteenth century, "civilized" people began to use handkerchiefs instead of wiping their noses on sleeves. Somewhat later commenced the habits of wearing special clothes to bed (instead of going naked or wearing daytime clothes) and of using a spittoon rather than the ground.

"The civilizing process" implies a transference of attention from the expression of personal feelings to the exhibition of impersonal objects. The more behavior is watched over and passions curbed, the more consumer objects are complicated and the more they proliferate. Elias's study avoids the common failing whereby the psychology of consumption is examined on the level of individual mentality, devoid of any social context. Instead, he traces a collective historical phenomenon that suggests how people's relationship to other people evolves along with their relationship to consumer objects. If changes in modes of social interaction are an integral part of changes in modes of consumption, this relationship is of vital importance in understanding consumption, both past and present. Elias is always reminding us to view consumption in these historical terms, to see it as a process proceeding through time rather than as a static behavioral pattern.

From this perspective the process was not far advanced at the time of the Renaissance. The savagery and untamed instincts of the Middle Ages could still be discerned in the court of Francis I; the brilliant life of the châteaux did not escape the shadow cast by the surrounding dark forest. The courtiers may have been consumers, but they were also warriors and hunters. In bands of hundreds, for weeks on end, lords and ladies chased the game that abounded in the valley. They got sunburned, ate outdoors, and slept outdoors if necessary. Jousting was their other favorite pastime. Francis's successor, Henri II, was accidentally killed in a tournament, and the unlucky knight who drove a lance through the king's eye was promptly executed. Barbarity on a far larger scale erupted in the religious wars following the death of Henri II, when atrocities, bloodshed, and famine afflicted nobles and commoners alike. Against this background the survival, let alone the triumph, of civilized behavior was by no means assured. Only from the vantage point of the twentieth century can we see that despite enormous setbacks the ideal of civilization did endure over the preceding five hundred years. The essential ambiguity of the civilizing ideal is that it inevitably includes a material component; its potential tragedy is that the material forms can survive and even flourish while the vitality of the ideal withers. If barbarism is the enemy without, decadence is the enemy within. At the court of Louis XIV (1638–1715), the development of civilization reached a point where the glut of materiality overwhelmed the ideal.

Louis XIV, the Consumer King–Today few people can recall any important military, religious, or political event of the reign of Louis XIV, but everyone remembers that he lived in staggering splendor at Versailles. In sheer scale this palace far surpassed earlier standards of royal pomp. The hunting lodge constructed by Louis XIV's father on the site still stands, but it is dwarfed by the building Louis began to erect in 1661 and is today hardly discernible behind an elaborate façade at the back of the mammoth central courtyard. In its interior appointments, too, Versailles proclaimed a new standard of consumption. The Hall of Mirrors alone—a single room in a palace housing five thousand people—displayed wealth beyond the resources of the Renaissance kings. One wall is lined with seventeen massive mirrors, each requiring years of labor to make; from the ceiling, painted by Le Brun, hung thirty-two silver chandeliers; and the floor was covered with exquisite handmade carpets on which were placed flowers and orange trees planted in silver tubs.

What made the cost of Versailles even more crushing was the fact that its furnishings were continually being changed. Upholstery and curtains in all rooms were altered according to the season—red and green velvet in the winter, silks of all colors and brocades trimmed with gold and silver in the summer—and the building itself was always being remodeled. One disgruntled courtier complained, "There isn't a part of Versailles which hasn't been modified at least ten times, and often not for the better."[1]

Louis XIV was too restless and ambitious a consumer to remain satisfied with renovation. He built Versailles in the first place rather than remodel the Louvre in Paris, as his ministers had advised, and as soon as Versailles was habitable he began the Grand Trianon palace nearby as a retreat with a more relaxed atmosphere. Still his appetite for construction was unsatisfied. At a somewhat greater distance from Versailles he built Marly, to provide even more intimate and relaxing surroundings. At Marly were gardens where rare imported birds warbled among hundreds of thousands of tulips, where trees arched over walkways lined with marble statues, where pools of water, ringed with gold-leafed balustrades, were filled with the finest specimens of gold, silver, and blue carp. Some contemporaries guessed that Marly cost more than Versailles itself; they were probably wrong, but not far wrong.

The character of Louis XIV beautifully illustrates the thesis that the civilizing process entails simultaneously an elaboration of objects and the exercise of restraint in spontaneity and instinctual response. The self-control of the king was remarked by all. His reserve, formality, and impeccable manners created an aura of immense dignity. Although he was a man of strong emotions and appetites, and although he vented his passions and angers in the private chambers of Mme. de Maintenon (his second, and secret, wife), Louis XIV maintained his composure in public even under the most trying circumstances. The formality and rigidity of his nature were evident above all in the way each act of his daily life was ritualized—his rising in the morning, including his rubdown, shaving, prayers, and dressing (*lever*), his attendance at Mass, his walks, his meals, and his retirement at night (*coucher*). Observance of the *lever* and *coucher* had begun in the reign of Henri II, but in far less elaborate form. By the reign of the Sun King, the ceremonies had become so fixed and complicated that Saint-Simon, one of the most distinguished members of the court, referred to them as *le mécanique* ("the mechanism") of Versailles. The metaphor is appropriate for a mode of consumption which, for all its extravagance, was highly programmed and predictable. If Louis XIV was a grand consumer, he was an absolutely methodical one, and he subjected the entire court to the same discipline. A detailed code of etiquette determined which courtiers could attend the *lever* or *coucher*, which ones could stand and which ones could sit while they watched the king devour prodigious amounts of food at the royal table, which ones enjoyed the coveted privilege of handing the king a candle or article of clothing when he retired.

The sumptuous style of life at Versailles provided little personal pleasure either for the king or for his courtiers. That was not its purpose. The ceremonies of consumption, the feasts and *fêtes,* the balls and parties, were all part of a calculated system that had as its aim not individual gratification but enhancement of political authority. Louis XIV transformed consumption into a method of rule. The theory that the nobility gathered at court to serve the monarch with their swords and advice may have had some validity in the time of Francis I, but by the late seventeenth century the reason nobles flocked to Versailles was because only there could they obtain immensely lucrative royal favors, pensions, benefits, and positions in the church, army, and bureaucracy. These were the rewards dangled before the four or five thousand nobles whose lineage was ancient enough to gain them admittance to court (out of a total of perhaps half a million aristocrats, who composed about two percent of the population of France at that time). Few could resist the temptation: they knew that exclusion from court meant exclusion from great wealth and prestige. "To be away from you, Sire," one courtier told Louis XIV, "one is not only unhappy, one is ridiculous."[2] It was a flattering remark but also an accurate one.

Once admitted to the charmed circle of the court, however, a noble had to spend ruinously to stay there. He needed clothes embroidered with gold and silver threads and brilliant jewels to wear to the balls; a stable of horses and kennel of dogs for hunting; carriages with velvet upholstery and painted panels so that he could accompany the king on migrations to other palaces; houses and furnishings so that he could provide dances and dinners for the court; and dozens of valets and servants and stablehands, to make all the rest possible. With rare exceptions, courtiers ran up stupendous debts. Although compelled by overwhelming pressure to perpetual imitation of the royal lifestyle, they had nothing like the king's income because they lacked power to tax. Accordingly, courtiers were driven to the monarch for financial help. The royal treasury supported not only the lavish living of Louis XIV but also, indirectly, that of the entire court, through loans and pensions which sometimes ran to several hundreds of thousands of livres annually at a time when three thousand livres was considered a comfortable yearly income for a bourgeois.[3] State spending increased astronomically. In return for this expenditure, the monarchy gained a dependent nobility which gathered at court because royal power was concentrated there, only to find themselves committed to a level of consumption which further enhanced that power.

Furthermore, the attention of the nobility was diverted from matters of political substance to matters of style. While Louis XIV distributed ministerial posts and other important offices to lower nobles or bourgeois ineligible for presentation at court, the courtiers themselves bickered over points of precedence. The elaborate ceremonies of consumption, at which their presence was required, provided myriad opportunities for quarrels over minutiae. Whether one marched fifth or eighth in a procession, whether one was admitted to the intimate *petit lever* when the king first arose or relegated to the crowd of hundreds attending the subsequent *grand lever*—such were the subjects of endless disputes and conflicts. These were not entirely empty arguments, for proximity to the king on a point of etiquette could enable a courtier to gain royal attention to ask for a favor. To be one of the twenty or thirty persons admitted to the *petit lever* afforded a splendid opportunity to request a pension or to whisper, "Sire, Marly" (the dream of every courtier was to be a guest there). Thus the refinement and ritualization of court life in every way focused attention on the king, just as its extravagance enhanced royal power over the nobility. In the adroit hands of the Sun King, vanity became a means of government, and the nobles were tamed by turning them into insatiable consumers.

The novelist Stendhal (1783–1842), mourning the decay of the genuine aristocratic ideal, remarked sadly that "the masterpiece of Louis XIV was to create an *ennui* like exile" among his courtiers.[4] *Ennui* is usually translated as "boredom," but in French the word implies much more than boredom, suggesting, rather, a chronic sense of vacuity, frustration, aimlessness, and futility. The many amusements of the court—hunting, dancing, practical jokes, gambling, billiards, chess, plays, word games, music, parties—came and went according to the vagaries of fashion, but they never amounted to much more than listless attempts to fill time. The routine of the court demonstrates how a system of consumption can develop its own imperatives, which bear little relation to the attainment of individual happiness or even pleasure.

What was more ominous, the system distracted not only the courtiers but also the king himself from events, outside Versailles, of substantial significance to national life. In the latter years of Louis XIV's reign, these events began to intrude upon courtly life. Military defeat followed defeat. France was invaded, and the court almost had to flee to Chambord in the Loire valley for safety. Humiliating peace treaties were signed. Louis's attempts to secure the Spanish throne for his grandson crumbled. Taxes kept mounting. The winter of 1709 was so severe that people froze to death all over France, and a dreadful famine followed in the fall. Lords and ladies who ventured out of Versailles were trailed by packs of starving peasants. The king pawned his jewels and melted his silver furniture and tableware, and ordered his courtiers to do the same. The increasing influence of the sober and devout Mme. de Maintenon (she was called "the old fright" behind her back) made life at Versailles far more somber than it had been. Louis's grandson, heir to the throne, died in 1712, and his wife died shortly thereafter, leaving their small sickly son as the last direct representative of the Bourbon line. Despite all this, Louis kept his reserve and dignity, insisting on ceremonies which must have seemed hollow to him. There is a kind of stoic fortitude in his refusal to submit to the futility of the grandeur he had created. Despite everything, "despite the gloom at the defeats and famines, . . . the king remains Louis the Great, because he is king of Versailles."[5]

Bourgeois Consumption Habits–Grandeur, unquestionably; but is this civilization? No more than in the time of Francis I did the court doubt that its boundaries were coextensive with those of civilized manners. As far as the courtiers of Louis XIV were concerned, outside of *ce pays-ci*, "this country," as they called Versailles, lay social wilderness. The emaciated peasants who crowded around their carriages during the famine of 1709 must have seemed to them like centaurs, half-beast, dirty, ignorant, and dangerous. The radical distinction between the way of life of the courtly elite and that of the masses was as great as it had been in the sixteenth century.

In another respect, though, the composition of society had changed significantly. By the eighteenth century there was a group of considerable size, perhaps ten percent of the total population, which was outside the court but which could still claim to be civilized. This was the bourgeoisie. While nobles quarreled about precedence in the little "country" of Versailles, in the great country outside another hierarchy of social and economic standing had been forming. The division of society into three orders, a theory that had made some sense in medieval times when society was poor, had ceased to correspond to reality in the relatively wealthy eighteenth century. No longer were those who worked, with few exceptions, working the land. Cities now offered alternative opportunities for employment and even for acquisition of wealth. Even before the age of Francis I, the peasant inhabiting the flat, open countryside lived at a different pace from those clustered in *bourgs* protected by walls closed at night. Over the centuries some of these towns grew until they took on a rhythm of their own, distinctive but not divorced from the surrounding countryside, with their own modes of production and consumption, their own scales of wealth and poverty, their own gradations of power ranging from an oligarchy running the town government to miserable laborers-for-hire.

The familiar phrase "the rise of the bourgeoisie" may be expressed more aptly as the slow shift in dominance from countryside to town. That shift is visible within the ranks of the aristocracy itself, as nobles increasingly preferred to acquire a town residence so they could live part of the year, at least, in the city. By the eighteenth century the social life of any noble without a town house [*hôtel*] in a provincial capital or, ideally, in Paris, was stultifying. With few exceptions, nobles continued to derive most of their income from land rents, but the general shift in economic power from country to town meant that land was no longer the only important source of revenue. Urban production of goods (especially luxury items made by skilled craftsmen), trade, finance, and professions like law, accounting, and medicine all provided alternative sources of income. In defining the bourgeoisie, this matter of origin of income is a significant criterion. By the eighteenth century, not everyone living in a town was considered a bourgeois, but only those supporting themselves by business, the professions, or skilled craftsmanship (as opposed to routine manual labor). Moreover, the income had to be fairly generous for someone to be considered a bourgeois. It was the discretionary income, whether a lot or a little, that distinguished the bourgeois from town dwellers living at subsistence level.

But no matter how comfortable, the bourgeois almost invariably yearned for more, for the legal status of nobility. There were practical reasons for this craving, since nobility entailed specific financial privileges, most notably freedom from taxation and access to certain offices in the government, army, and church. More than that, to be part of the aristocracy meant enormous social prestige which no bourgeois, no matter how wealthy, could hope to approach. Such was that prestige that numerous daughters of well-to-do bourgeois families were married off to impecunious aristocrats so that their children could assume a title. There were other ways a bourgeois family could elevate itself to the rank of the nobility. A commoner could purchase land from a hard-pressed aristocrat and gradually accumulate an estate; eventually he might acquire a title or simply start adding the particle *de* to the family name, indicating noble status. Bourgeois could also purchase high government offices carrying aristocratic rank. Many such positions in the army, church, and municipal or national government were sold to whoever could afford them, and could be passed on with the rest of an estate. Consequently, the concept of aristocracy, which in the Middle Ages signified gentle birth and service to the crown, became more and more equivalent to wealth. The rich could buy nobility, and nobles had privileges that helped make them rich. Social contact between aristocrats and wealthy commoners was fairly frequent, at least compared to Germany, where the nobility was almost a closed caste. Still, many more bourgeois wanted noble status than were able to buy their way in. The overwhelming prestige of the aristocracy resulted in intense envy among the bourgeois, who felt dissatisfied with their social standing no matter how many material comforts they accumulated.

Envy may not be an attractive emotion, but it is one that is highly effective in promoting social similarity. Just as the taste of the court was homogeneous because everyone there imitated the model of the king, so the taste of the bourgeoisie faithfully reflected the aristocratic model. Just as the court fell under the spell of the king, the bourgeoisie was hypnotized by the prestige of the nobility. One result was that bourgeois standards of civilized behavior—that is, rules of etiquette and habits of politeness—were by the eighteenth century very nearly identical to courtly standards. Furthermore, the consumption habits of the bourgeoisie mimicked those of the nobility. The bourgeois household had a salon, a room set aside for receiving guests, which was carefully furnished like similar rooms in a *hôtel* or château, albeit on a thriftier scale—rugs, mirrors, draperies, paintings, knickknacks, upholstered furniture, maybe even tapestries.

An even more striking indication of the bourgeois propensity to imitate the aristocratic model is less visible, and this is its reverence for leisure. Once his household was outfitted with reasonable comfort and dignity—once he had acquired a "standard package" of consumer goods, to use contemporary sociological terms—the typical bourgeois preferred to buy time rather than things. The reason for this preference was his envy of the nobility for its ability to live off rents rather than earning an income in daily work. The bourgeois too wanted to "live nobly," meaning to retire from his business or profession, live off unearned income, and pass on this privilege to his children. He therefore shunned investment in industry or trade, which might prove highly profitable but which was riskier and less prestigious than purchasing real estate or an honorific government position furnishing a secure and adequate income. As a consumer the bourgeois could "live nobly" even though he was not a noble. Although tangible furnishings and investments were not the same as the intangible glory of ennoblement, they came as close as money could buy. The consumer habits of the bourgeois expressed their aspiration to be something other than what they were. As consumers they could in their material environment construct an approximation of their dreams.

Yet bourgeois imitation of the aristocratic model was not total. It could not be, since the bourgeois had to live within his income. For the free-spending aristocrat, money arrived providentially from rents, gambling wins, and royal whims. If it did not arrive, there was no shame attached to going into debt, for the only shame lay in failure to spend in the style of the court. The bourgeois, on the other hand, had no access to royal credit; bank credit for individuals was nonexistent, and moneylenders were expensive. In other ways, too, the objective conditions of bourgeois life encouraged a restraint in consumption which did not operate in courtly circles. The emphasis on preserving a family inheritance distinguished the bourgeois outlook as much as anything, for nobles who automatically passed on power and prestige with their title were less concerned about passing on a block of capital. In general, the bourgeois emphasis on attaining and preserving social rank meant that they pursued a finite goal, unlike the goals of wealth and power, which could be, and often were, pursued indefinitely at court.

Finally, the clear distinction in bourgeois life between family privacy and public display meant that only a portion of a family's consumption was intended to impress others. The family could practice relative austerity in private with no humiliation, and in fact the family did often economize in order to cultivate the public aspect of consumption. For everyday meals, they ate plain food in the kitchen, using earthenware or porcelain plates; only when guests were present would delicacies be served in the salon on fine china and silver. The bourgeois household practiced a private form of consumption as well as a public one, and the private form was modest but comfortable. In the extended social household of the court, however, not only the king but to a lesser extent all the courtiers lived almost entirely in public. The contrast between the magnificent ceremonial rooms at Versailles and the wretched living quarters, with their bugs, stench, filth, and cold—conditions even the grandest dukes and duchesses endured—indicates the predominance there of public consumption and the relative insignificance of private comfort.

In all these ways, then, bourgeois values in consumption differed from aristocratic ones, and bourgeois envy of the nobility was mingled with resentment of its profligacy and moral laxness. The two groups had different ethics of consumption because they inhabited two different environments of consumption—the one being the private home, the other the public court. By the end of Louis XIV's reign, however, the values of the two groups were growing increasingly similar. All the time the bourgeoisie had been absorbing the aristocratic lifestyle, the nobility had been taking on bourgeois traits. The continual entry of commoners into noble ranks meant a slow infiltration of habits of economy and sobriety. Even more significant as an agent of social similarity was the attraction of city life. Nobles spent more and more time in their *hôtels* and developed a taste for urban forms of sociability which, unlike the traditional aristocratic recreation of hunting, could be shared with commoners. The salon provided an environment of consumption that united the brilliance of the court with the intimacy of the home. In the seventeenth century the word *salon* came to signify not only a reception room, such as finer homes had long had, but also a specific type of event held there, a regularly scheduled reception where guests were welcomed for conversation and light food and drink.

This social invention, so important in "the civilizing process," owes its origin and development neither to the horse-loving noble nor to the account-keeping merchant but to their wives and mistresses. The first salons emerged during the reign of Henri IV (1553–1610), who finally restored royal power after the savage religious wars that followed the accidental death of Henri II. Once again the nobility was free to enjoy a social life, but Henri IV himself was a straightforward military man and his court adopted the same character of rugged masculinity. The young marquise de Rambouillet (1588–1665), dissatisfied with the lack of refinement at court, left its precincts and began holding receptions in her Paris *hôtel*. These were intimate events, numbering perhaps twenty people and including among the nobles a number of men of letters who could converse with particular wit and gaiety.

Toward the end of the seventeenth century other host-esses, both aristocratic and bourgeois, began to copy the style of entertainment initiated by Mme. de Rambouillet. The habitués of the salons, although not forgetting differences in wealth and rank, did value agreeable behavior and conversational dexterity along with money and birth. A common classical education allowed them to exchange ideas on topics that had nothing to do with their profession; indeed, subjects of specialized interest were tacitly forbidden, although by the eighteenth century some salons tended toward talk about politics, art, or literature, depending on the leadership of the hostess. By then not only in Paris but also in provincial centers like Strasbourg, Dijon, Toulouse, and Bordeaux, salons were being established by shopkeepers, lawyers, bankers, and aristocrats. As a setting for social exchanges, salons did much to promote similarity in manners, ideas, taste, and attitudes between nobles and bourgeois, two groups separated by legal distinctions and social origins but united by economic privilege. Both in Paris and in smaller cities, these two groups were slowly consolidating into a united upper class, largely because they came to share a common environment of consumption.

Civilization and Consumption: Voltaire–Was the environment of salon society, then, civilization? The word itself, *civilisation* as an abstract noun, originated and became a key concept in French thought in the mid-eighteenth century, just when salons were proliferating and growing in size. The use of the term suggests the idea that all society, not just an elite, might be civilized, that vulgarity might be not only kept out of courtly circles but might be eliminated altogether. The goal of civilization is a social state where manners are gentle, education broadly distributed, laws rationalized, and art and science cultivated. This ideal is opposed on the one hand to barbaric survivals from the past—abject poverty, torture, religious intolerance—and on the other to decadent, excessively refined manners. Since the monarchy and court could be accused of both archaic dogmatism and decadent extravagance, the ideal of civilization implied a double criticism of the existing government, and this was indeed the political overtone when progressive bourgeois and even some like-minded nobles appealed to the concept. To be sure, their criticism was mild and reformist, but the appeal to civilization was undeniably a call for change.

The consumption habits of the well-to-do must be viewed in this ideological context. To many enlightened thinkers of the eighteenth century, it seemed self-evident that enlightened consumption—patronage of the arts, the vivacious conversation of the salons, collection of paintings and books—was a necessary means to the advancement of civilization. With little mental effort the habitués of the salons could equate their concrete social pleasures with the highest and most abstract social goals. The nature of "the civilizing process" remained mixed and ambiguous, a blend of idealism and materialism. In the eighteenth century the idea of civilization referred both to a general social and political ideal and, more narrowly, to a comfortable way of life reserved for the upper classes.

Voltaire was the most irrepressible and convincing spokesman for civilization in both senses. His family origins encapsulate the consolidation of aristocratic and bourgeois traditions, for his mother came from a noble family and his father was a prosperous Parisian notary. Thanks to family and school connections Voltaire had easy access to salon society, beginning with libertine literary circles and then moving upward to grander, titled society. As he ascended the social ladder Voltaire's mischievous and sardonic nature earned him many enemies, but the handsome fortune he gathered through clever speculations won him as many adherents. He spent his money lavishly, first in Parisian society and then, after 1735, at Cirey, an estate in Champagne, where he retreated to surround himself with the comforts of a woman both loving and philosophizing (Mme. du Châtelet, his "darling Emily"), a library, wine cellar, carpets, paintings, mirrors, silver, statues, and gardens complete with fish-filled ponds and secluded grottoes.

In this little Versailles Voltaire composed his poem "Le Mondain" ("The Man of the World") (1736) in celebration of the consumer pleasures he was enjoying. The poem describes a socialite who lives in a comfortable town house decorated (like Cirey) with delicate drawings signed by Poussin and framed in gold, Gobelins tapestries, and finely worked silverplate. Leaving his house in a comfortable chariot, "like a house on wheels," this man-about-town goes first to amorous rendezvous with young ladies, then to the opera, and finally to a supper prepared by a "divinely inspired" chef where laughter rings and excellent wine flows freely. This taste for luxury, ornaments, and the arts—and Voltaire equates them—is shared, in the opinion of the poet, by every right-thinking person. Greek and Roman poets mistakenly praise the life before civilization for its simplicity, but this life was in truth harsh and uncomfortable. "Was it virtue? It was pure ignorance." As usual, Voltaire is especially hard on Christian apologists, in this case those who describe the simple life of the Garden of Eden as Paradise on earth. In truth Adam and Eve must have been hideous creatures having long black nails and sunburned leathery skin, living off water and acorns, sleeping on the cold ground. The true "terrestrial Paradise," Voltaire concludes at the end of the poem, "is where I am."[6]

How could this philosopher reconcile his vigorous defense of aristocratic consumption habits (Nietzsche referred to Voltaire as "the consummation of courtly taste")[7] with his equally lively denunciations of aristocratic privilege and political tyranny? It was from luxurious surroundings oozing aristocratic and monarchical tradition that he hurled his cry "Écrasez l'infâme," that is, crush all the irrational and repressive dogmatisms of the past. As a crusader for the abstract ideal of civilization, Voltaire was keenly aware that most Frenchmen in his day were victims of a system of economic and political inequity which helped to keep them in a state similar to that he ascribes to Adam and Eve—a state of ignorance, nakedness, hunger, and dirt. The problem is to reconcile this awareness with his praise of civilization in the more limited sense of an upper-class lifestyle.

More significant than the way Voltaire achieved this reconciliation is the fact that he and others like him felt the need to justify themselves at all. In the eighteenth century privilege in consumption begins to need explanation: this is a major change in historical consciousness from the time when noble birth in itself justified exalted living standards. In the Age of Enlightenment noble birth was more and more seen as an arbitrary and irrational accident rather than as a divinely ordained gift. Moreover, bourgeois were well aware that they, rather than the aristocrats, were performing much of the real service to the crown. Besides, many who were now tasting the delights of luxury were, like Voltaire, not noble at all. How could one commoner defend privileges others failed to attain?

Voltaire's response was that civilization defined as upper-class luxury is necessary to foster civilization defined as general social progress. He had lived in London from 1726 to 1729, when Bernard de Mandeville's *Fable of the Bees* was the talk of the town. Voltaire was impressed by its ingenious argument that private vices result in public benefits, that pride, envy, and vanity in individual "bees" paradoxically maximize the welfare of the social "hive" by stimulating industry. At about the same time, William Petty and other English mercantile economists were dispersing similar ideas in both France and England, justifying private luxury by pointing to its public utility. In "Le Mondain" Voltaire develops this argument by lauding "The superfluous, this very necessary thing," as the stimulus behind the vast increase in trade which had united the hemispheres and raised living standards everywhere. In other writings he expands upon the theme that luxury stimulates enterprise by rousing men from the natural laziness which always threatens to let society slip back to barbarism. Luxury also provides employment, since those who live well are the best clients of workers and merchants. The moral code calling for suppression of needs (and here again Voltaire attacks ancient philosophers and the Church Fathers) might have been appropriate for a poor society, but now it would be a mistake "To call virtue what is poverty."[8] In modern times living well is a virtue. As long as outright immorality and perversity are shunned, the consumer is acting ethically in enjoying the superfluities available to him according to his resources. Both decadent sensuality and barbaric austerity are enemies of civilization; the enlightened consumer is its friend.

Civilization and Consumption: Rousseau – Voltaire represents an important vein of thought about consumer ethics in the eighteenth century—an attitude at once sensual and rational, skeptical and serious, critical of traditional morality yet moralistic—but this ethical viewpoint did not go unchallenged. Throughout the century the question of luxury was vigorously debated, and in its fundamental terms this debate represents the first sustained attempt to frame a modern ethic of consumption.[9]

The opponents of luxury as much as proponents like Voltaire appealed to rationality and social utility to justify their arguments; they tacitly accepted the Voltairean axiom that the moral codes and religious dogmas of the past were no longer sufficient authorities. The Enlightenment debate about luxury was conducted in the language of economic welfare and social benefit, not of personal salvation or philosophical detachment from gross materiality. For example, a group of French economists, the Physiocrats, who opposed the English mercantile economists publicized by the Anglophile Voltaire, used the social argument that too much monetary wealth would banish "industry and the arts, so casting states into poverty and depopulation."[10] Often derided then and now for their seemingly reactionary preference for the value of land over that of commerce and industry—a preference which seems more sensible if it is interpreted as a general concern for the preservation and development of natural resources—the Physiocrats questioned the identification of luxury and civilization. The wealth of precious metals, they suggested, was a sterile and deceptive wealth, whereas agricultural goods represented genuinely usable, renewable, honest wealth, the basis of true civilization. Although the Physiocrats met with little success in England, in France their views were adopted by important bourgeois reformers in the government bureaucracy. It is an indication that the French upper classes were by no means unanimous on the definition of civilization.

The most famous opponent of luxury, however, was not from the ranks of the respectable at all: he was the perpetual outsider Jean-Jacques Rousseau. Born of French Protestant parents in Calvinist Geneva, his father a watchmaker and his mother the daughter of a minister, Rousseau spent his youth wandering in the hinterlands of France, working fitfully—as a servant, music teacher, tutor, and lover—all the while entertaining notions of writing. In 1749 Rousseau noticed an announcement that the Dijon Academy (one of many provincial organizations devoted to the cultivation of learning) was offering a prize for the best essay on the topic "Whether restoration of the sciences and arts has tended to purify morals." By paradoxically arguing that this restoration had corrupted morals, and that the state of barbarism was preferable to that of civilization, Rousseau won both the prize and fame. His essay brought a counterattack from Voltaire himself, and the ensuing debate, in which many other joined, lasted intensively for three years and in a more subdued form to the end of Rousseau's life.

The basic issue was whether luxury in consumption fostered civilization or weakened it. Rousseau's definition of civilization was opposite to that of Voltaire. The wanderer from Geneva uncompromisingly condemned luxury, and he was radical enough to insist that the arts and sciences be classed as such, along with such obvious examples as diamond necklaces. One weakness in Rousseau's position, as Voltaire quickly perceived, was his attempt to ground his moral viewpoint in historical events, to demonstrate that material simplicity and social harmony had been facts in the distant past. Voltaire's description of Adam and Eve probably has more historical accuracy as a description of primitive times than Rousseau's reveries of a golden age. But Rousseau was on firm ground in enumerating the contemporary consequences of luxurious consumption:

> Princes always view with pleasure the spread among their subjects of the taste for the arts and for superfluities. . . . For, besides fostering that spiritual pettiness so appropriate to slavery, they know well that the needs that people create for themselves are like chains binding them. . . . The sciences, letters, and arts . . . wind garlands of flowers around the iron chains that bind them [the people], stifle in them the feeling of that original liberty for which they seemed to have been born, make them love their slavery, and turn them into what is called civilized people.[11]

Voltaire praises luxury as an abstract level of social activity; Rousseau disdains it as a concrete tool of political tyranny. Voltaire defines liberty as the individual's freedom to grasp whatever superfluities he can afford, but Rousseau sees this grasping as slavery to the instincts and submission to the powers that be. Where Voltaire accepts and, indeed, praises inequality as the basis of general welfare, since the rich consume what the poor produce, Rousseau affirms that consumption can be conducive to virtue only when all share its benefits equally. For Rousseau, wealth and poverty are relative terms that become significant only when the natural equality of the primitive state has been destroyed. He had no illusions that this original state could be restored; instead, he affirmed that the community could overcome present corruption and inequality only by being based on the general, or popular, will rather than on the enslaving desires of individual wills.

Rousseau could be the most self-contradictory of men: he abandoned four children to foundling homes and later wrote a book tenderly depicting the ideal education of a child and lauding domestic affection. However, in the matter of consumption there was little discrepancy between his private life and his publicly espoused principles. Rousseau stubbornly, even perversely, refused to accept financial security or personal comforts. The year after his prize essay was published, one of his operas was performed before the court of Louis XV with such success that the next day the composer was ordered to be presented to the king. This honor meant the bestowal of a royal pension, but Rousseau refused to go. Soon afterward he sold his valuables, quit his job as a cashier, and announced that henceforth he would earn his living by copying music.

Rousseau's motives may have been less exalted than he claimed: his criticism of luxury may be interpreted as a defense of his own position as a quarrelsome, unstable eccentric without the wealth, well-placed friends, or cleverness that Voltaire enjoyed. Yet Rousseau's denunciations of luxury should no more be dismissed as the querulous plaint of a neurotic than Voltaire's praise of luxury should be written off as the self-justification of a bon vivant. The viewpoints they adopted represent a critical juncture in historical *conscience*—in French the word combines the meanings of "consciousness" and "conscience." It was a time when the upper classes were developing an unprecedented consciousness of their privileged position as consumers and were also developing a sense of uneasy conscience about their privileges, a discomfort which Voltaire expressed by justifying luxury and Rousseau by rejecting it. The fact of inequity in consumption was not new. What was new was the fact that those who enjoyed luxury were so aware of their distinction and troubled by it. Henceforth "the civilizing process" would be a dialectical one, with the moral appeal of the simple life evolving side by side with the appeal of ever higher material standards.

The growing cultural importance of nostalgia for simplicity could be observed even at court, the heart of privileged consumption. During the eighteenth century the grandeur of Versailles as it had been under Louis XIV was continuously modified in the direction of greater informality and intimacy. Under Louis XV palace furniture became smaller and more comfortable, and ornate *fêtes* gave way to picnics. Louis XV constructed the Petit Trianon as a retreat for his wife; while supremely elegant, it is smaller and simpler than the Grand Trianon and Marly, which Louis XIV used for similar purposes. Louis XVI's queen, Marie Antoinette, was even more extravagant in her taste for simplicity. She supervised the construction of a "little hamlet" near the Petit Trianon as a sort of life-sized play farm with stables, ponds, dovecotes, haylofts, and cabbage patches, where she could pretend to be a peasant or shepherdess. Such games represent a high degree of civilization. The courtiers of Francis I were too close to the realities of peasant life to play at it, but by the later eighteenth century there was a strong desire to retrieve spiritual freedom through material divestiture. That desire must be taken seriously even when expressed in Rousseau's sentimentalism or Marie Antoinette's silliness, just as the appeal of material pleasures associated with urban life must be taken seriously even when expressed in the strident self-righteousness of *le mondain*. Despite these deficiencies in expression, each tendency offers a fundamental and lasting appeal to the modern consumer, and in their conflict emerges his ambivalent *conscience*.

The French Revolution and Its Aftermath – In 1788 Louis XVI convoked a meeting of the Estates General, the national parliament of France, which had not met since 1614. He did so to bail himself out of imminent bankruptcy. Ruinous debts are a common enough fate for a big spender, but in this case the debtor was a king and his creditors were a nation. The eventual consequences of his need for money were of a magnitude no one had foreseen. When the Estates General convened in the spring of 1789, not only did it vote new taxes but transformed itself into a constitutional assembly intending to reform the entire structure of government. The nation grew restless. In July a Parisian crowd tore down the Bastille. Disorders spread through the countryside until, on the night of August 4, in one tumultuous session, the assembly scrapped feudal rights which had been in force for centuries. Not long after this, it proclaimed the Declaration of the Rights of Man. The French government was destined to be reformed, but most reformers still assumed their work would proceed while the king remained on the throne.

On the night of October 3, amid rumors, plots, famine, international intrigue, and popular unrest, a banquet was held at Versailles to honor the soldiers loyally guarding the royal family in those troubled times. The scene had taken place countless times before in those brilliant halls: lords and ladies, glittering jewels, songs, blazing chandeliers, laden tables, wine in crystal goblets. But this time, when the news of the banquet reached Paris, an enormous crowd, mainly women struggling to find scraps of bread to feed their own families, started marching with the national guard to Versailles to protest the festivities there. When the crowd arrived, Louis XVI was just returning from a hunting expedition. Before the palace gates, blocking his entrance, he found a swarm of uninvited guests, starved, frenzied. He tried to speak to them, without success. There ensued confusion, threats, struggle, bloodshed: the result was that Louis and his queen were virtual prisoners of the people. They had to consent to leave Versailles and go to Paris. There, four years later, they were guillotined.

The royal executions came during the Jacobin phase of the revolution, when the guillotine claimed, among victims from all classes, many well-born representatives of the courtly concept of civilization. It was then that the revolution came closest to fulfilling the opposite ideal of civilization as moral purity and material simplicity. The leading Jacobin, Maximilien Robespierre, worshipped Rousseau. His own austere, "sea-green integrity" was legendary, and his ideal of consumption was a daily bowl of lentils for each citizen. Although this egalitarian asceticism had its day, it did not last for long. In 1794 the coup of Thermidor deposed Robespierre, who was himself led to the guillotine, and the Jacobin phase of the revolution was over.

Not Rousseau's love of simplicity but Voltaire's love of luxury finally emerged victorious. The ultimate beneficiaries of the revolution were neither the banqueting court nor the hungry masses, but the bourgeois, who replaced the nobility as the dominant element in the upper classes. The revolution and ensuing wars provided numerous opportunities for bourgeois to cash in through speculation, trade, and manufacture, especially since interest rates and rents continued to rise steadily. After Napoleon took power in 1799 these same people benefited from the Napoleonic policy of "careers open to talent," meaning that bureaucratic and administrative positions were offered to those with ability and education, mainly, that is, to bourgeois. Furthermore, the number of such positions multiplied under the Consulate and Empire. Napoleon also encouraged what he called "the fusion of the classes," meaning the consolidation of new money and old into one ·stable ruling elite. Imperial titles were bestowed upon successful generals, businessmen, and bureaucrats, and all of them were encouraged to intermarry with what remained of the old aristocracy. Thus, the revolutionary period, far from terminating upper-class modes of consumption, only opened up access to a larger group.

What did not change, despite all the changes in political authority from 1789 to 1815, was the social authority of the aristocracy. Even if the bourgeois were reformist or even revolutionary in their politics, like Voltaire they faithfully followed the social traditions and values emanating from the nobility. As a result, courtly standards of consumption survived the destruction of the court. The major difference in consumption patterns during the revolutionary years was that luxury moved out of the private realm of noble households to the public marketplace, a movement already underway before 1789 but greatly accelerated by the revolution itself. In the 1790s, chefs who had worked in aristocratic *hôtels* opened public restaurants; dressmakers and tailors to noble ladies and gentlemen opened shops and advertised their fashions in new journals. The increasing dominance of the marketplace rather than patronage was encouraged by a 1791 law abolishing the corporations. The corporations, which dated from medieval times, had established close contacts with aristocratic patrons and had exercised rigid controls over quantity and quality of production; after their abolition, individual artisans had to establish their own standards and locate their own buyers.

The revolutionary and Napoleonic gains of the bourgeoisie endured even after Napoleon's final fall in 1815, when the European coalition which had conquered him hauled the Bourbon dynasty back to France in its baggage trains. The intransigent aristocrats who returned with the Bourbon king may not have altered their political and social opinions since 1789, but they had certainly changed their mode of life. The ranks of the aristocracy had been catastrophically weakened by execution, exile, expropriation, and the loss of financial and feudal privileges. French nobles after 1815 were far more serious, economical, sober, and cautious than their eighteenth-century counterparts. To Stendhal's disgust, they had adopted the customs of democratic, Protestant Geneva.[12]

In the postwar years emerged a group of *notables* composed of Napoleonic holdovers, revolutionary personnel (no regicides were allowed, however), rich bourgeois, and old nobility, who joined forces to run the government. They had many economic interests in common, which they took care to protect. In 1819, for example, the *notables* secured passage of a new tariff protecting both agriculture and industry, thus further consolidating old wealth with new.

Old and new ideas were not so easily fused. During the 1820s the prerevolutionary aristocracy, still convinced that it alone should control the government, began to claim political privileges and to threaten the basic revolutionary gains of the bourgeoisie—the land settlement, the religious compromise, the principle of careers open to talent. Although the wealthy bourgeois were permeated by aristocratic manners, they had no intention of letting the old nobility run the state. In 1830 they revolted, deposed the Bourbon king, and purged the pre-1789 aristocracy. The Bourbon king went into English exile, to be replaced by King Louis-Philippe, from another branch of the royal family. The old aristocrats for the most part retreated to their *hôtels* in the exclusive Faubourg Saint-Germain to sulk and predict doom, but not to interfere. Finally the town definitively triumphed over the court.

The reign of Louis-Philippe was a sort of bourgeois royalism. He was proclaimed the secular "king of the French people" rather than a divinely ordained "king of France," a compromise between Bourbon legitimism and republicanism typical of the hybrid nature of the regime. In truth, the umbrella-carrying king with a pear-shaped face, who had amassed a fortune before ascending the throne and who hobnobbed with Parisian bankers, served as a figurehead for the rule of wealthy bourgeois. Despite lip service to equality, under Louis-Philippe the hold of the *notables*—bankers, lawyers, industrialists, Napoleonic administrators, academics, and some reforming nobles— was stronger than ever before or since. The hereditary aristocracy had been replaced by an elite open to birth, money, or talent, preferably two of the three, and most preferably a combination that included money.

But this was the 1830s, the eve of the consumer revolution. As the new elite was savoring its triumph over the pre-1789 nobility, below its ranks a far larger group of lower and middle bourgeois was gathering strength. By this time the term *la bourgeoisie* had become obsolete, because it was too simple. Now people were distinguishing the *haute* (high) or *grande* (grand) bourgeoisie, those rich enough to be part of the *notable* group running the state, from the less affluent *moyenne* (middle) or *petite* (little) bourgeoisie—those whose incomes derived from industry, trade, real estate, or government securities, and the propertied shopkeepers, struggling professionals, and better-off urban craftsmen. In the 1830s this less affluent group was not challenging the political power of the *notable* group, thanks to a very high property requirement for voting rights. In the social sphere, however, the lower ranks of the bourgeoisie were asserting their right to live like the upper classes. The specific legal status of nobility was far less important than it had been, but the more general status of "living nobly" was as attractive as ever. The combination of low wages, long hours, and high tariffs enabled French workers to supply a growing domestic market for handmade but relatively inexpensive goods (machinemade goods were even less expensive, but failed to convey the desired prestige) that imitated aristocratic styles from the past. Calicos and cottons were treated to look like silk, while wallpaper with gold floral patterns and chairs upholstered in "Pompadour" style were made for the salons of the middle bourgeoisie. These new consumers adhered faithfully both to traditional decorative styles and to traditional forms of sociability. They gave receptions and attended, if not the opera, at least the opera buffa. They still tried to retire from business as soon as possible. If their way of life was static and unoriginal, it was at least free of trendiness and instability and self-doubt.

Civilization had lost its fighting edge. No longer a bulwark against barbarism, no longer a battle cry against tyranny, it was now a pleasing way of life for the middle classes. Balzac wrote that French civilization of the 1830s was personified by the grocer: "He is civilization in a shop, society in a paper bag. . . . He is the Enlightenment in action, life itself distributed in drawers, in bottles, in sachets, in jars!"[13] The grocer prides himself on his knowledge of literature, which consists of reading Voltaire, and on his good taste in art, which means that in his salon he hangs engravings of Cupid emerging from an eggshell. He covers his furniture with velour and goes to the theatre to cry at melodramas. But, insists Balzac, for all these ridiculous pretensions, with a little imagination the grocer may be recognized for what he is, a truly sublime figure, an indispensable cog in the machinery of modern life.

Balzac on Consumption – Thanks to Balzac's great imagination, the dry bones of historical generalization spring to life in his novels. The bourgeoisie, from its lowest to its highest ranks, forms the collective hero of *La Comédie humaine* ("The Human Comedy"), his series of over ninety novels containing more than two thousand characters. As in his description of the grocer, Balzac could be merciless in deflating bourgeois pretensions, but his mockery was mingled with sympathy and affection. These were, after all, his own people. His grandfather, while of an old and honorable family, was a poor peasant. His father obtained a job as a commissioner for the army, and his sister was married to a debt-ridden noble in an attempt to elevate the family's status. Wedding announcements sent to distant acquaintances were signed "de Balzac," while those to close family friends, who would have ridiculed such aristocratic airs, were signed simply "Balzac." (The marriage, alas, failed miserably.) Honoré kept the *de* and set out to conquer salon society. He made a momentary coup by adopting the habit of carrying a cane, but his lack of polish came out in the way he held the cane, scraping it against the pavement, so that in the end it aroused as much mockery as admiration. His origins were too humble and his waistline too rotund for him to achieve much success in the salons, and he keenly felt the cruelty of those who gracefully but scornfully blocked his way into society. "Those people made me appreciate Rousseau," he confided in a letter to a friend.[14]

Although Balzac's literary genius eventually brought him money and fame, his long sojourn on the borderlines of respectability gave him a rich understanding of how the smallest nuances of behavior and ornament were regarded with utmost seriousness by bourgeois consumers. The way a cravat was tied, how shoes were polished, the type of cigar smoked, not to mention how a cane was held—all these details of style were interpreted as significant markers of social standing.

In *La Comédie humaine* the characters are supremely conscious of such details, both in themselves and in others. In the novel *La Cousine Bette* (1846), to cite one example, the Baroness Hulot, devoted wife of a lecherous husband being reduced to poverty by grasping women, calls upon Josepha Mirah, a well-known singer and former mistress of her husband, to try to obtain a loan. When the courtesan Josepha learns that this grand lady has come to call, her immediate response is to ask one servant to make sure the salon is in order with fresh flowers, and to direct another servant to dress her in her best shoes, a lace gown, and an elaborate hairdo so she would look "crushingly beautiful." The baroness, in turn, when ushered into Josepha's salon, notices at once that it had been redecorated recently:

> This salon . . . was now draped in silks, of a color then called *massaca*, shot with gold. The luxury which great lords of the olden times displayed in the houses of their mistresses, of which so many relics remain to the present day, . . . was here shown to perfection. . . . It was impossible not to envy these beautiful things . . . . Here, the perfection of the unique thing was the surprising charm. . . . To possess things that are not vulgarized by two thousand opulent shopkeepers, who think they show their elegance when they display the costly articles which

they buy for gold, is the sign of true luxury, the luxury of
the modern great lords, the ephemeral stars of the Parisian
firmament. . . . The baroness looked at herself in the mirror, to see if she were out of place in the midst of all this
luxury; but her velvet robe with its point-lace collar had an
air of dignity, and a velvet bonnet of the same color as the
dress became her. [She felt] that she was still regally
imposing.[15]

The women use their possessions to appear "imposing" to
each other. Their sense of identity depends on their sense
of how they impress others with possessions, and in turn
they respond to the impression made by others through
their accumulation of appearances.

Balzac's characters are always looking at each other
and looking in the mirror, trying to size up each other and
themselves by imagery. By showing how his characters
manipulate objects and are manipulated by them, Balzac
insists repeatedly on the "immense significance" (to use
his term) of consumer goods on all levels of society, from
nouveaux riches like Josepha, to decaying remnants of
"great lords of olden times" like the Hulots, down to
"opulent shopkeepers" who pretend to live like lords. All
of them work with the model of luxury associated with the
prerevolutionary aristocracy, but this common theme is
capable of infinite variations. In *La Comédie humaine* these
nuances are weapons people use to battle their way to
higher social status. Far from being agents of enjoyment,
consumer objects are tools of aggression in a wide-open
social war.

There, Balzac felt, beyond the human comedy of pretensions, lay the human tragedy of shattered lives. The
destructive results of this social warfare litter his novels. In
them he shows over and over how modern capitalist society corrupts bourgeois virtues—probity, duty, love of
family, generosity, simplicity, stoicism—by encouraging
these people to desire far beyond their means, to strive far
beyond their abilities, to lose all sense of proportion in a
ceaseless struggle to do a little better. "Just a little more,"

the universal wish, is the universal curse. All are tempted but few are rewarded. The joys sought by bourgeois are artificial ones that would never be missed, but, once incited, keep driving them on to more desires and more consumption, which does not satisfy but only renews desire. As more and more people entered the ranks of the bourgeoisie, the definition of bourgeois status was becoming ever less precise. As a result, the quest for status was becoming open-ended. The limits that used to govern bourgeois life grew weaker as its goals became indistinct. Instead of their traditional traits of economy and restraint, bourgeois increasingly displayed the pride, jealousy, and ambition of the court, all emotions that caused great personal misery. Even misery, however, is ground under in modern social warfare: "Civilization, like the car of Juggernaut, is hardly slowed down by a heart less easy to break than the others that lie in its course; this also is broken, and Civilization continues on her course triumphant."[16]

Unlike Rousseau, Balzac does not reject all civilization, only the Voltairean ideal of it which the novelist calls "civilized egoism."[17] Man is neither good nor evil by nature: if the social order Voltaire upholds only encourages corrupting self-interest, the right kind of social order can improve man, if not perfect him. Such a social order is based on shared traditions and clear principles which encourage looking beyond self-interest to the general good. In a structured, ordered society, limits are set for people, so they have a chance to be at peace with themselves. Religious faith is one element of genuine civilization (Balzac himself was received into the Church shortly before his death), and another indispensable foundation is a strong government. The constant changes of regime in France meant that no government had any real authority, for they all lacked legitimacy and permanence. Balzac particularly scorned Louis-Philippe for his dubious claim to the throne and for the cynical, shabby careerism of the bourgeois who found it convenient to have him there, like the haberdasher Rivert in *La Cousine Bette,* who enthuses:

I adore Louis-Philippe. He is my god, for he is the splendid
and worthy representative of the class on which he based
his dynasty, and I'll never forget what he did for haber-
dashers by restoring the uniforms of the National Guard.[18]

Balzac concluded that only a Bourbon restoration
could bring strong, principled government back to France.
In truth, legitimism was a desperate and unworkable remedy for the nation's political weakness. The practical
chances of a Bourbon restoration were almost nil in the
1830s and 1840s, when there was no attractive pretender
and little popular support, and none at all from the upper
classes, except for a few disgruntled and impotent pre-
1789 aristocrats who were themselves, as Balzac knew,
rotten with intrigues and snobbery. When a change of
regime did come in 1848, the outcome was not a Bourbon
king but the Second Republic. Balzac declared that a
strong republic might be acceptable and even submitted
his name for election to its assembly. As a contemporary
commented, however, Balzac really wanted a republic
ruled by royalists.[19] The Second Republic turned out to be
neither royalist nor strong. By 1851, when it succumbed to
a coup by Louis Napoleon, nephew of the great Napoleon,
Balzac had already died, at the early age of fifty-one.

In some respects the imperial court of Louis Napoleon
restored the glitter of prerevolutionary court life. The
beautiful and vivacious Empress Eugénie sponsored *fêtes,*
dances, and plays; the emperor loved to hunt and watch
military spectacles. But, like the emperor himself, the
courtiers were parvenus united not by noble birth but by
success in attaining power and money. Foreign names
were nearly as common as French ones in this collection of
adventurers assembled around the nephew of the greatest
adventurer of them all. Alexandre Dumas *fils* dubbed
them the *demi-monde,* the half-world or shady underworld,
a far different society from the sunlit world of *le mondain.*
These were not so much aristocrats as rich bourgeois
playing at being aristocrats. Louis Napoleon is aptly remembered for sponsoring the rebuilding of Paris, for the

city rather than the court had come to stand at the apex of social life. But in 1871 Paris fell after France was defeated by Prussia. Louis Napoleon's Second Empire also collapsed and was replaced by the Third Republic. This government managed to last until 1945, largely due to the fact that instead of a strong government it provided only a loose framework for the dominance of the lower and middle bourgeoisie in alliance with the peasantry. Balzac's hopes were in vain. Not only the king, not only the court, but also an ordered, hierarchical social structure were gone forever.

Concluding Remarks: The Fate of the Court – The authority that disappeared was social as well as political. As pseudo-monarchs came and went, as the remnants of the old aristocracy milled aimlessly about the Faubourg Saint-Germain, French society lost a clearly defined group at its summit to establish a model of consumption, just as that group had lost one supreme individual to direct its taste. The social terrain was leveling out. Instead of looking upward to imitate a prestigious group, people were more inclined to look at each other. Idolatry diminished; rivalry increased. Consciousness of differences among these near-equals became greater, although the differences themselves were less than in the past.[20]

The external forms of courtly taste long outlasted the social order in which they originated. In the 1880s deeply carved wooden buffets resembling those at Chambord in the age of Francis I could be seen in the dining rooms of shopkeepers, and in their salons were Louis XV chairs upholstered in patterns like those used at Versailles. Since the social context in which these familiar forms appeared was completely different from that of the court, it was only a matter of time before the forms too began to evolve. The past could not assert its authority indefinitely. There were to develop new models of consumption and new sources of prestige that reflected more faithfully the dynamic of modern life.

But before turning to the new environments of consumption, the old ones deserve one last look. The châteaux of Chambord and Chenonceaux, the palaces of Versailles, the Trianons, and even the "little hamlet" were ransacked during the revolution (Marly was completely destroyed) and their furnishings were dispersed. These empty shells of past grandeur eventually became wards of the French state, which in time expended great efforts to fill them again with appropriate ornamentation. The châteaux and palaces are now museums; the contemporary visitor can tour these buildings, once again decked out with ornate and costly merchandise, relics of a way of life that now seems incomprehensibly frivolous, wasteful, unjust, and above all, irrelevant. Once the cradles of consumption, these buildings have become tombs of a past which few mourn.

Courtly life is dead, but the life of the consumer is more vigorous than ever, and therein lies the contemporary significance of the châteaux. The lords and ladies who lived there were the first people in modern society to experiment with discretionary consumption, to become familiar both with its intellectual and sensual pleasures and with its consequences of envy, vanity, and *ennui*. Today those pleasures and feelings are available to many more people. Frivolity, waste, and inequity in consumption have changed in character but are still social facts. As a consumer class the court has not vanished but has vastly expanded, so that its limits include most people in wealthy societies.[21] Seen from this perspective, the consumer revolution becomes far more than a rise in economic statistics or in available goods. It is more like the Copernican revolution, the overthrow of one world-picture by another: the replacement of a cramped, heliocentric world of consumption, by a vast, centerless universe.

3 The Dream World of Mass Consumption

The School of Trocadéro – The arrival of the twentieth century was celebrated in Paris by a universal exposition spread over 550 acres and visited by 50 million people from around the world. The 1900 exposition was the climax of a series of similar events that began with the Crystal Palace exposition in London in 1851 and continued to be held at regular intervals during the second half of the century (in 1855, 1867, 1878, and 1889) in Paris, the undisputed if unofficial capital of European civilization. The purpose of all expositions was, in the popular phrase of the time, to teach a "lesson of things." "Things" meant, for the most part, the recent products of scientific knowledge and technical innovation that were revolutionizing daily life; the "lesson" was the social benefit of this unprecedented material and intellectual progress. The 1855 exposition featured a Palace of Industry filled with tools, machinery, and sequential exhibits of products in various stages of manufacture. The 1867 fair had an even more elaborately organized Palace of Industry (including the first displays of aluminum and of petroleum distillation), and a History of Labor exhibit showing tools from all eras. At the 1878 exposition the wonders of scientific discovery, especially electricity and photography, were stressed. In 1889, at the exposition commemorating the outbreak of the French Revolution, the "lesson of things" was taught on a grand scale. The two focal points of the 1889 fair were the Gallery of Machines, a long hall with a vault nearly 400 feet across where sightseers could gaze from a suspended walkway at a sea of spinning wheels, clanking hammers, and whirring gears, and the Eiffel Tower, a monument at once scientific, technological, and aesthetic, the architecture of which was derived from that of iron railroad bridges; at its summit was an assortment of apparatus for meteorological, aeronautical, and communications research.

Over the decades, the dominant tone of these expositions altered. The emphasis gradually changed from instructing the visitor in the wonders of modern science and technology to entertaining him. In 1889, for all their serious didactic intent, the Eiffel Tower and Gallery of Machines were popular above all because they provided such thrilling vistas. More and more, consumer merchandise rather than productive tools was displayed. The Crystal Palace exposition had been so innocent of commercial purpose that no selling prices were posted there, but at the Paris exposition in 1855 began the tradition of placing price tags on all objects, as well as of charging admission.[1] From then on the emphasis on selling, prizes, and advertising grew until one booster of the 1900 exposition enthused:

> Expositions secure for the manufacturer, for the businessman, the most striking publicity. In one day they bring before his machine, his display, his shop windows, more people than he would see in a lifetime in his factory or store. They seek out clients in all parts of the world, bring them at a set time, so that everything is ready to receive them and seduce them. That is why the number of exhibitors increases steadily.[2]

At the 1900 exposition the sensual pleasures of consumption clearly triumphed over the abstract intellectual enjoyment of contemplating the progress of knowledge. This emphasis was evident the moment a visitor entered the grounds through the Monumental Gateway, which, according to one bemused contemporary, consisted of "two pale-blue, pierced minarets and polychrome statues surmounted by oriflammes and adorned with cabochons," terminating in "an immense flamboyant arch" above which, perched on a golden ball, "stood the flying figure of a siren in a tight skirt, the symbolic ship of the City of Paris on her head, throwing back an evening coat of imitation ermine—La Parisienne."[3] Whatever this chic madonna represented, it was certainly not science nor technology. Inside this gateway the sprawling exposition had no orderly arrangement or focal points such as previous ones had possessed. Machines were scattered throughout the grounds next to their products, an indication that tools of production now seemed hopelessly boring apart from the things they made. The vault of the Gallery of Machines had been cut up—desecrated like a "secularized temple," complained one admirer of the 1889 version[4]—and overrun by a display of food products:

> [Instead of] a universal workshop . . . a festival hall has invaded the center of the structure. The extremities are abandoned to the rustic charms of agriculture and to the fattening joys of eating. No more sharp whistles, trembling, clacking transmission belts; nothing being released except champagne corks.[5]

Despite this confusion or, rather, because of it, thoughtful observers sensed that the 1900 exposition was particularly prophetic, that it was a microcosm of emerging France, a scale model of future Paris, that something rich and strange was happening there which broke decisively with the past and prefigured twentieth-century society. In 1889 and even more in 1900, the expositions attracted a host of journalists of a philosophical bent who provided not only descriptions of the various exhibits but also reflections on their significance. For the most part their sense of the exposition's prophetic value remained poorly articulated. While convinced that the fair revealed the shape of things to come, they were unsure of the contours and were vaguely apprehensive without knowing quite why. One exception was Maurice Talmeyr (1850–1933), a journalist who reported regularly on the 1900 exposition in a Catholic periodical. No less apprehensive than many of his colleagues, he was unusual in being able to explain why he found the fair so disturbing. He summarized his conclusions in his article "L'École du Trocadéro" ("The School of Trocadéro"), published in November, 1900, just as the exposition was drawing to a close, in the *Revue des deux mondes,* the most prestigious biweekly in France at that time.[6]

The Trocadéro was the section of the exposition on the Right Bank of the Seine, directly across the river from the Eiffel Tower, where all the colonial exhibits were gathered. It was in this "school," Talmeyr contended, that the true lesson of the exposition could be discerned. Exhibits of exotic places were not a new feature. As far back as 1867 expositions had included reproductions of an Egyptian temple and a Moroccan tent, and in 1889 one of the most popular attractions had been the notorious Rue du Caire ("Street of Cairo") where dark-eyed belly dancers performed seductive dances before patrons in "Oriental" cafés. In 1900, when imperial adventurism was at its height, the number of colonial exhibits expanded accordingly to become, in Talmeyr's words, a gaudy and incoherent jumble of "Hindu temples, savage huts, pagodas, souks, Algerian alleys, Chinese, Japanese, Sudanese, Senegalese, Siamese, Cambodian quarters . . . a bazaar of climates, architectural styles, smells, colors, cuisine, music." Reproductions of the most disparate places were heaped together to "settle down together, as a Lap and a Moroccan, a Malgache and a Peruvian go to bed in the same sleeping car . . . the universe in a garden!"

Even more disconcerting were the discontinuities and illogicalities found in the details of particular exhibits.

Talmeyr notes, for example, that the Indian exhibit featured a carefully contrived pantomine acted out by a group of stuffed animals: an elephant with uplifted trunk trumpeted a speech to some hens between his feet, while next to him a wild boar browsed near a serpent coiled and ready to strike. In the same neighborhood a couple of stuffed jaguars were shown feeding their young, while a rose ibis, "evidently surprised," surveyed the whole tableau while standing on one foot. The wildlife of an entire subcontinent was condensed into one scene, an absurdity which was nonetheless, Talmeyr confesses, highly entertaining. "But," he asks, "the 'lesson'? The lesson they are giving us?" It is by no means the lesson the exhibit intends to teach, for we learn nothing about the realities of India. Instead, we learn

> that all trickery is childish. They don't want to show us anything serious, and we have nothing to ask that's serious. But isn't this precisely the vice of all these exoticisms of the exposition? They offer themselves as serious in not being so, and when they cannot be so.

Talmeyr finds the same vice of inherent and pervasive trickery in the rest of the Indian exhibit, which consisted of stacks of merchandise—rugs, cotton balls, plates, sacks of rice, fabrics, jams—all of which reminded him of a "sort of Louvre or Bon Marché of Tyre or Baghdad." (The Louvre and the Bon Marché were two of the largest department stores in Paris.) The spectacle of India as a land of overflowing treasure chests was as enticing and exciting a vision of the exotic as any child could imagine. But that vision hides what is "serious and adult" about India, the reality of India as a subjugated English colony:

> The notion of such an India, of an India-warehouse, so magnificent and so partially true as it may be, is true only partially, so partially as to be false, and all these overflowing rooms . . . speak to me only of an incomplete and truncated India, that of the cashiers. And the other? That of the famine? For this land of enormous and sumptuous

trade is equally that of a frightening local degeneracy, of a horrifying indigenous misery. A whole phantom-race dies there and suffers in famine. India is not only a warehouse, it is a cemetery.

For the moment, Talmeyr does not dwell on this somber analysis but continues to cite amusing examples of the "nullity, buffoonery, gross alteration, or absolute falsity" that abound at the Trocadéro. At an exhibit representing Andalusian Spain at the time of the Moors he attends a sort of circus where camels replace the usual horses—"Camel exercises, camel cavalcades, trained camels that kneel, camels that bow, camels that dance"— while spectators are sold lemonade and beer by hawkers in a room lined with rugs for sale, their prices prominently marked. For two cents the public may also view licentious scenes through a stereoscope. "Perhaps, after this spectacle, there still remains something for us to learn about the Moors of Andalusia," Talmeyr comments sarcastically, so he tells how he went down a staircase to a small courtyard, "deliciously archaic," full of pretty and curious items, complete with vaults, columns, an old well, armaments, and so forth:

> We are here, it seems, in the most legendary Spain, and this time there is indeed a well-done reproduction of great fidelity and delicacy. I feel, in these old walls, in this broken well, in these small columns which are crumbling, in a coat of arms that is obliterated, five centuries of mystery and sunshine. . . . Then I look, I observe more closely, and I notice, above the door, in the patina of the stone, the tracing of Gothic letters. . . . I approach, and what is it I make out?
> Simply: *Menier Chocolate . . .*

Talmeyr concludes that behind the "ornamental delirium" of the Trocadéro, behind its seemingly mad disorder, behind its silly and serious deceptions alike, lies a strictly logical and consistent ordering principle: the submission of truth, of coherence, of taste, of all other considerations to the ends of business. He sees through the false lesson of this school of the absurd to the genuine lesson:

> An exposition must, above all, be an exposition, which is to say a certain type of didactic banking whose first goal is to attract, to hold, and to attract and to hold by the exclusive means of the bank. . . . A framework is provided for [the exhibitor of exoticism], and he will confine himself within it. Obligations of price, of economy, of placement, of health are imposed on him, and he submits to them. And the quest for success, for attraction, for show, for excitement, for everything that amuses, for all that diverts, will necessarily be his guideline. Truth, history, common sense, will be arranged afterward as best they can. So . . . why, in English India, do the panther, wild boar, partridge, elephant, monkey, ibis, and serpent present themselves all in a family and form this touching commune? Because this fable gathers them together, and what matters, above all, is to gather them together. And why is starving India incarnated in well-coiffed, well-nourished, well-clothed Indians? Because famine is not and never can be an exposition attraction. . . . And why does Andalusia—in the time of the Moors—recommend Menier Chocolate to us? Because the authentic Moors and the authentic Andalusia do not, according to all appearances, sufficiently allow for advertisements, and an exposition is not going, never has gone, and never will go without advertisements.

The Significance of the Exposition—The exposition of 1900 provides a scale model of the consumer revolution. The cultural changes working gradually and diffusely throughout society were there made visible in a concrete and concentrated way. One change was the sheer emphasis on merchandising. Even more striking and disturbing, at least to observers like Talmeyr, was the change in how this merchandising was accomplished—by appealing to the fantasies of the consumer. The conjuction of banking and dreaming, of sales pitch and seduction, of publicity and pleasure, is far more unsettling than when each element is taken separately. As Talmeyr appreciates, the conjunction is inherently deceptive. Fantasy which openly presents itself as such keeps its integrity and may claim to point to truth beyond everyday experience, what the poet Keats called the "truth of the imagination." At the Trocadéro, on the contrary, reveries were passed off as reality, thereby losing their independent status to become the alluring handmaidens of commerce. When they assume concrete form and masquerade as objective fact, dreams lose their liberating possibilities as alternatives to daylight reality. What is involved here is not a casual level of fantasy, a kind of mild and transient wishful thinking, but a far more thoroughgoing substitution of subjective images for external reality. Talmeyr stresses the inevitable corruption that results when business exploits dreams. To him all advertising is false advertising. Blatant lies and subtle ones, lies of omission and of commission, lies in detail and in the ensemble, the exhibits claiming to represent the "real Java" or the "real China" or the real anything are not real at all. People are duped. Seeking a pleasurable escape from the workaday world, they find it in a deceptive dream world which is no dream at all but a sales pitch in disguise.

The 1900 exposition incarnates this new and decisive conjunction between imaginative desires and material ones, between dreams and commerce, between events of collective consciousness and of economic fact. It is obvious how economic goods satisfy physical needs such as those for food and shelter; less evident, but of overwhelming significance in understanding modern society, is how merchandise can fill needs of the imagination. The expression "the dream world of the consumer" refers to this non-material dimension. From earliest history we find indications that the human mind has transcended concerns of physical survival to imagine a finer, richer, more satisfying life. Through most of history, however, only a very few people ever thought of trying to approximate such dreams in daily life. Instead, art and religion provided ways to express these desires. But in the late nine-

teenth century, commodities that provided an approximation of these age-old longings began to be widely available. Consumer goods, rather than other facets of culture,
became focal points for desire. The seemingly contrary
activities of hard-headed accounting and dreamy-eyed
fantasizing merged as business appealed to consumers by
inviting them into a fabulous world of pleasure, comfort,
and amusement. This was not at all the future that a
conservative nationalist like Talmeyr wished; it was not
the vision of a workers' society that socialists wanted; nor
did it conform to traditional bourgeois virtues of sobriety
and rationality. But welcome or not, the "lesson of things"
taught by the make-believe city of the 1900 exposition was
that a dream world of the consumer was emerging in real
cities outside its gates.

Exoticism in Department Stores – One obvious confirma-
tion of this lesson was the emergence of department stores
(in French *grands magasins*, "big" or "great" stores) in
Paris. The emergence of these stores in late nineteenth-
century France depended on the same growth of prosperity and transformation of merchandising techniques that
lay behind the international expositions. Talmeyr was on
the mark when he observed that the Indian exhibit at the
Trocadéro reminded him of an Oriental Louvre or Bon
Marché. The Bon Marché was the first department store,
opening in Paris in 1852, the year after the Crystal Palace
exposition, and the Louvre appeared just three years later.
The objective advantages of somewhat lower prices and
larger selection which these stores offered over traditional
retail outlets were not the only reasons for their success.
Even more significant factors were their practices of marking each item with a fixed price and of encouraging
customers to inspect merchandise even if they did not
make a purchase. Until then very different customs had
prevailed in retail establishments. Prices had generally
been subject to negotiation, and the buyer, once haggling
began, was more or less obligated to buy.

The department store introduced an entirely new set of social interactions to shopping. In exchange for the freedom to browse, meaning the liberty to indulge in dreams without being obligated to buy in fact, the buyer gave up the freedom to participate actively in establishing prices and instead had to accept the price set by the seller.[7] Active verbal interchange between customer and retailer was replaced by the passive, mute response of consumer to things—a striking example of how "the civilizing process" tames aggressions and feelings toward people while encouraging desires and feelings directed toward things. Department stores were organized to inflame these material desires and feelings. Even if the consumer was free not to buy at that time, techniques of merchandising pushed him to want to buy *sometime*. As environments of mass consumption, department stores were, and still are, places where consumers are an audience to be entertained by commodities, where selling is mingled with amusement, where arousal of free-floating desire is as important as immediate purchase of particular items. Other examples of such environments are expositions, trade fairs, amusement parks, and (to cite more contemporary examples) shopping malls and large new airports or even subway stations. The numbed hypnosis induced by these places is a form of sociability as typical of modern mass consumption as the sociability of the salon was typical of prerevolutionary upper-class consumption.

The new social psychology created by environments of mass consumption is a major theme of *Au Bonheur des Dames*. In creating his fictional store Zola did not rely on imagination alone; he filled research notebooks with observations of contemporary department stores before writing his novel. Zola's fictional creation in turn influenced the design of actual stores. He invited his friend, architect Frantz Jourdain, to draw an imaginary plan for Au Bonheur des Dames, and not many years later Jourdain began to collaborate on an ambitious renovation and building program for La Samaritaine, a large department store in the heart of Paris. By 1907, when most of the program was completed, the store closely resembled Zola's descriptions of Au Bonheur des Dames. Ernest Cognacq, founder of La Samaritaine, was an energetic entrepreneur who probably served as a model for Octave Mouret, the imaginative and innovative owner of Au Bonheur des Dames.

In loving detail Zola describes how Mouret employed exotic décor to encourage shoppers to buy his wares. One section of the novel portrays the reaction of the public to a rug exhibit on the day of a big sale:

> [T]he vestibule [was] changed into an Oriental salon. From the doorway it was a marvel, a surprise that ravished them all. Mouret . . . had just bought in the Near East, in excellent condition, a collection of old and new carpets, those rare carpets which till then only specialty merchants had sold at very high prices, and he was going to flood the market, he gave them away at cut rates, extracting from them a splendid décor which would attract to the store the most elegant clientele. From the middle of Place Gaillon could be seen this Oriental salon made only of rugs and curtains. From the ceiling were suspended rugs from Smyrna with complicated patterns that stood out from the red background. Then, from the four sides, curtains were hung: curtains of Karamanie and Syria, zebra-striped in green, yellow, and vermilion; curtains from Diarbekir, more common, rough to the touch, like shepherds' tunics; and still more rugs, which could serve as wall hangings, strange flowerings of peonies and palms, fantasy released in a garden of dreams.[8]

Customers kept drifting into the store, attracted by this décor so similar to that of the Trocadéro, "the décor of a harem," in Zola's words. By afternoon the building was overflowing with a crush of excited, eager shoppers. At the end of the day some of them met in the Oriental salon so they could depart together; they were so enchanted by the rug display that they could talk of nothing else:

They were leaving, but it was in the midst of a babbling crisis of admiration. Mme. Guibal herself was ecstatic:
"Oh! delicious! . . ."
"Isn't it just like a harem? And not expensive!"
"The Smyrnan ones, ah! the Smyrnan ones! What tones, what finesse!"
"And this one from Kurdistan, look! a Delacroix!"[9]

It was the most profitable day in the history of Au Bonheur des Dames.

The department store dominates the novel. The virtuous but pallid Denise, Octave Mouret, the crudely drawn entrepreneur who tries unsuccessfully to seduce Denise, and the female shoppers whom Mouret does seduce commercially, are all subordinate to the store, which seems to overwhelm them and control their destinies. It does this through means essentially the same as those employed at the Trocadéro exhibits. The counters of the department store present a disconnected assortment of "exhibits," a sort of "universe in a garden" of merchandise. The sheer variety, the assault of dissociated stimuli, is one cause of the numbed fascination of the customers. Furthermore, the décor of the department store repeats the stylistic themes characteristic of the Trocadéro: syncretism, anachronism, illogicality, flamboyance, childishness. In both cases the décor represents an attempt to express visions of distant places in concrete terms. It is a style which may without undue flippancy be called the chaotic-exotic. But within one exhibit not chaos but repetition is often employed to numb the spectator even further. When rugs are placed on the ceiling, walls, and floor of the vestibule, when the same item is repeated over and over with minor variations—just as the Andalusian exhibit at the Trocadéro had camels here, camels there, camels everywhere—the sheer accumulation becomes awesome in a way that no single item could be. The same effect is achieved when Mouret fills an entire hall with an ocean of umbrellas, top to bottom, along columns and balustrades and staircases; the umbrellas shed their banality and instead become "large Venetian lanterns, illuminated for some colossal festival," an achievement that makes one shopper exclaim, "It's a fairyland!"[10]

Mouret's most stunning coup, however, is his creation of his own exposition, an "exposition of white," to celebrate the opening of a new building. The description of this event forms the final chapter of *Au Bonheur des Dames*, where it becomes a climactic hymn of praise to modern commerce. Mouret constructs a dreamland architecture of "white columns . . . white pyramids . . . white castles" made from white handkerchiefs, "a whole city of white bricks . . . standing out in a mirage against an Oriental sky, heated to whiteness."[11] In this display, exotic fantasies merge with oceanic ones, and dreams of distant places fade into dreams of bathing in passive bliss, surrounded on all sides by comfort, a fantasy of a return to the womb, which has become a womb of merchandise.

The "Aesthetic" of Exoticism – To return to a question already posed: this may be impressive, but is it civilization? Is it even art? Like the displays of Versailles—the silver furniture of the palace, its frenzies of gilt, its acres of mirrors and entire rooms swirling with marble, stucco, and frescoes—department-store displays also are designed to impress the spectator. The difference is in the nature of the audience and the motivation behind the display. At Versailles the audience was the restricted one of the court. The courtiers were impressed mainly by the costliness of the décor, costliness due to the fineness of the materials and to the artistic skill used to work them. These qualities, no matter what motivated them, can be incorporated in objects which have enduring value as decorative art. In the department store, on the other hand, the audience is a large and anonymous public. The stylistic traits of repetition, variety, and exoticism used to seduce it into buying usually have little enduring aesthetic value. The motivation behind the décor is to lure people into the store in the first place and then to imbue the store's merchandise with glamor, romance, and, therefore, consumer appeal. There is no aesthetic connection between this décor and the objects it enhances, objects that generally lack any artistic merit.

To criticize the chaotic-exotic style as "bad taste," a frequent condemnation even around the turn of the century, misses the point. As a quality of aesthetic judgment, taste does not apply to transient décor whose purpose is "to attract and to hold" the spectator's attention. Why the reliance on fake mahogany, fake bronze, fake marble? Because the purpose of the materials is not to express their own character but to convey a sense of the lavish and foreign. Why the hodgepodge of visual themes? Because the purpose is not to express internal consistency but to bring together anything that expresses distance from the ordinary. Exotic décor is therefore impervious to objections of taste. It is not ladylike but highly seductive. In this aesthetic demi-monde, exotic décor exists as an intermediate form of life between art and commerce. It resembles art, it has recognizable themes and stylistic traits, its commercial purpose is wrapped in elaborate visual trappings; yet it does not participate in traditional artistic goals of creating beauty, harmony, and spiritual significance. This hybrid form is an illusion of art, a "so-called artistic element"[12] posing as the genuine article.

Zola, for one, was taken in. He praises Mouret as an aesthetic genius as well as a financial one, for in Zola's mind the two types of genius are indistinguishable. He lauds the exposition of white, the Oriental salon, and the sea of open umbrellas as artistic successes, because they attract so many customers. His judgment reflects a deep-seated confusion of commercial and aesthetic values. Talmeyr, on the other hand, clearly distinguishes the type of decoration used by modern business for its own ends from traditional forms of art. According to Talmeyr, in over fifty years universal expositions had not produced any truly artistic constructions at all, but only a "type of frightful plastered and clumsy heaviness, twisting or declamatory, of all those domes, balconies, pediments, columns."[13] True architecture involves the construction of monuments, while expositions require only *décors*, "stage sets" or "scenery." "Why . . . insist on transferring to that which is ephemeral in intention, to that which is *décor* by nature, the principles and procedures of that which is durable and permanent in essence, *monument* by raison d'être?" Exposition buildings are intended to "make . . . in their fashion a weighty and proud show," the same goal that inspires posters advertising "a new shoe polish or a new brand of champagne in a manner vaguely derived from that of Raphael." The goal is to convey an "industrial image," not an artistic one, and the search for magnitude or lavishness will never bridge the gulf in intention:

> You can imagine the [industrial] image as enormous, as ambitious as you wish, it could be stupefying, it will be no less always and necessarily inept. You can even imagine the façade, the frieze, or the columns pushed to the furthest limits of richness, they will be no less equally stupid.

Talmeyr concludes with the suggestion that décor might be able to invent an authentic style if it renounced the attempt to imitate art and instead realized its own nature. He notes that the only modern edifice of the 1900 exposition which he is tempted to praise is the Monumental Gateway surmounted by "La Parisienne." Talmeyr admits that the gateway is heavy, clumsy, bizarre, and gaudy, and that "La Parisienne" is reminiscent of a peasant girl in a cape. Nonetheless, he remarks, they possess

> a unique merit, that nothing like them has been seen anywhere, *that they resemble nothing*! They are absurd? . . . This is also true! But their quality is precisely to be absurd, in an order of ideas where it is logical to be so, and where the only true absurdity, as a result, is to wish to be reasonable.

In environments of mass consumption, the logic of art gives way to the logic of fantasy.

Distant Visions – For all its innovation in stylistic absurdity, the exotic-chaotic decorative style was traditional in its technology. Its only technical novelty involved the use of increasingly convincing imitation materials to construct "all those domes, balconies, pediments, columns." Nineteenth-century technology developed far more effective ways of creating an illusion of voyage to far-off places, techniques that were dynamic and cinematic rather than static and decorative. They proved so exhilarating and popular that, while occasionally used to publicize products, they more often became products themselves, offered as amusement attractions. At the 1900 exposition twenty-one of the thirty-three major attractions involved a dynamic illusion of voyage. This group of exhibits, like the colonial ones clustered at the Trocadéro, furnished a "lesson of things" in the form of a scale model of a dream world of the consumer.

As Maurice Talmeyr enunciated the lesson of "the school of Trocadéro," so another journalist, Michel Corday (Louis-Léonard Pollet, 1869–1937) assessed the significance of the exhibits providing "Visions Lointaines" ("Distant Visions," or "Views of Faraway Places"). This is the title Corday gave to an article on cinematic exhibits— one of a series he wrote on the exposition—published in the *Revue de Paris*.[14] Corday was well able to appreciate these exhibits from both a technical and a cultural perspective, for he had been educated as an engineer and served with distinction in the army before deciding, at the age of twenty-six, to devote himself to letters. The imprint of Corday's technical training is manifest when he begins by classifying the twenty-one "distant visions" exhibits into five categories, according to the increasing sophistication of the techniques used to convey the illusion of travel: "ensembles in relief," panoramas in which the spectator moves, those in which the panorama itself moves, those in which both move, and moving photographs. One of the more primitive exhibits, an example of the second category, was the World Tour: the tourist walked along the length of an enormous circular canvas representing "without solution of continuity, Spain, Athens, Constantinople, Suez, India, China, and Japan," as natives danced or charmed serpents or served tea before the painted picture of their homeland. The visitor was supposed to have the illusion of touring the world as he strolled by, although Corday hardly found it convincing to have "the Acropolis next-door neighbor to the Golden Horn and the Suez Canal almost bathing the Hindu forests"—the chaotic-exotic style, the universe in a garden, only on canvas! On a somewhat more ingenious level, the Trans-Siberian Panorama placed the spectator in a real railroad car that moved eighty meters from the Russian to the Chinese exhibit while a canvas was unrolled outside the window giving the impression of a journey across Siberia. Three separate machines operated at three different speeds, and their relative motion gave a faithful impression of gazing out a train window. A slight rocking motion was originally planned for the car, but the sponsoring railway company vetoed the idea because it advertised that its trains did not rock.

Corday was even more intrigued by an attraction where not canvases but photographs moved:

> This is Cinéorama, the application—it is surprising that it did not appear sooner—of cinematography to the panorama. This ingenious apparatus . . . is placed in the center of the spectacle to be reproduced. . . . [T]he projector is composed of ten cameras which work in unison and divide the horizon into ten sections, like ten slices of cake.

The Cinéorama could convey the impression of ascending from the earth in a balloon, by a series of panoramic photographs showing things below growing smaller and smaller. To make the illusion even more persuasive, spectators stood in the basket of a balloon to watch the show. Finally, Corday describes some exhibits appealing to many senses at the same time. The Maréorama reproduced a sea voyage from France to Constantinople, complete with canvas panorama, the smell of salt air, a gentle swaying motion (unlike trains, boats were expected to rock), and phonograph music "which takes on the color of the country at which the ship is calling: melancholy at departure, it . . . becomes Arabic in Africa, and ends up Turkish after having been Venetian."

Even sailing to Byzantium was not enough: the surface of the earth was too small to contain human imagination armed with such gadgetry. Corday marvels that new devices allow the masses to realize the "extraordinary voyages" of Jules Verne, to travel not only where few have ventured but also where none have. The Cinéoramatic balloon trip was only the first step in flight from earth-bound reality. At another exhibit a diorama took the tourist far beneath the earth to dramatize its formation by showing vast subterranean and prehistoric landscapes strikingly lit by electricity. In the Optical Palace photographic plates were pieced together to give the impression of viewing the moon from a distance of only four kilometers. Then, according to Corday,

> the diorama makes its appearance; at first prudent, it reproduces with exactitude the lunar landscape: then, fantastically, it paints an imaginary voyage to a star; finally, leaping across centuries as easily as space, it narrates the genesis of the earth in twenty tableaux.

So convincing was this illusion that the spectator was hardly aware of crossing the line between reality and fantasy, of moving from a painstaking reproduction of the moon's surface to a wholly imaginary simulation of a journey beyond the galaxy. Real and fantastic voyages, present and future and prehistoric ones, earthbound and cosmic ones became indistinguishable when all were presented as triumphs of technical ingenuity.

Corday was considerably younger and further to the left politically than Talmeyr, and because of his democratic sentiments he saw another aspect of these exhibits besides their obvious profitability. He took seriously the educational purpose, which Talmeyr rejected as a sham. Corday lauded "the sum of ingenuity, of research and invention, spent there to amuse the masses usefully, to enrich them with new visions in all directions of the universe." Between 1889 and 1900 the masses rapidly developed "curiosity about new horizons, a confused desire to widen a little, if only in appearance, the framework of life." Because modern technology makes it possible to satisfy the curiosity of those who could never afford to travel in reality, these exhibits are part of a "great current of democratization that offers to the masses the precious joys until now reserved for a few." Even if far from perfected, technological stratagems such as these constitute "an extraordinary movement of vulgarization, an enormous scientific toy placed in the hands of the masses."

While expressing forcefully his belief in the educational and democratic benefits of the "distant visions" exhibits, Corday fails to question the reliability of what they teach. He is clearly an intelligent and thoughtful observer, but his interest in gadgetry tends to make him neglect the deeper question of veracity. In his mind the matter of truthfulness becomes transformed to a matter of mechanical ingenuity. This is how Corday invites his reader to tour the exposition with him: "Let us go to attend a veritable concourse of evocations, a sort of agreeable race where each one exerts himself to press closer to the Truth." In this context "Truth" means a mechanically faithful rendering of external sensations, the sights, smells, and sounds of travel or of a place. Corday is so intrigued by the cleverness of the means that he never stops to ask, as Talmeyr does, whether the mechanical illusion is faithful to the total social reality or only to selected external appearances. Talmeyr contends that education cannot be made into amusement without being falsified, while Corday sees no such inevitability. The façades of the Trocadéro, which Talmeyr finds so eloquently expressive of a fundamental mendacity, are dismissed by Corday as lacking in technical sophistication and therefore in crowd appeal: "Certainly, these façades speak to the eyes, teach them about distant architectural styles, but do not really constitute attractions, which is to say efforts combined for an illusion." In contrast, the "distant visions" do attract and hold the crowd precisely because the illusion they create is so convincing.

As Zola confuses aesthetic and commercial standards in evaluating department-store displays, so Corday confuses technical and commercial standards in judging the success of the "distant visions" exhibits. The extent of that confusion is evident at the end of Corday's article, when he marvels at the intoxication the exhibits can induce: "Thanks to them, one can live a long time in a few hours; travel across vast distances in a few steps; they are like liquors sparkling to the eyes, pleasing to the palate, which concentrate power and life in a small volume." This drug-induced dreaming, this magical escape from ordinary constraints—what harm can there be in this confusion of reality and fantasy so long as it provides the masses with a taste of "power and life"? Some of the dangers are suggested in the concluding paragraph, which immediately follows the one just quoted. Corday proposes that

> without injuring the interests involved, without trans-gressing on past contracts, the doors of these attractions might be generally opened to the people. For a few months, for two hundred days, from all points of the continent, trains are going to converge on just one point: Paris. They are like so many miniature societies in motion, which money brutally and frankly divides into three classes. Well, one has to wish that this harsh hierarchy might disappear at the doorway of the Exposition: that those who suffer from it might find in this promised land a short and charming respite from life.

Has Corday himself become unable to distinguish reality from dream? The real world of real train trips was one of first, second, and third classes, corresponding to high, middle, and low incomes. The same business world that ran these trains had invested large amounts of capital in the exposition to advertise their services by operating imaginary train rides at a profit.[15] But Corday seems to imagine that because the voyages at the exposition are illusory, the whole event might become an illusion, a "promised land" of dreams set apart from waking reality. In his muddle he hopes the exposition will not only market fantasies but also become a fantasy. Corday unwittingly testifies to the danger of the intoxication he praises when his delight in a dream world blinds him to its origins in a real social world of classes, profits, and capital.

Cinematic Voyages – The motion picture is the commercial and technological successor to the "distant visions" exhibits. Between the close of the 1900 exposition and the outbreak of World War I, films became a popular attraction in urban France. In 1907 there were two cinemas in Paris; six years later there were one hundred and sixty, and by 1914 cinema receipts in France were 16 million francs a year.[16] Large, well-financed organizations were established to prepare the décors, costumes, and special effects, to devise the script and hire actors, to shoot the film and edit it, to publicize and distribute the product.

"It is a new, and important, and very modern branch of business," wrote Louis Haugmard in 1913. "This development, extraordinary in its rapidity and extent, this swarming, this 'invasion' of cinematography is a fact which deserves to attract the attention of the casual observer who likes to meditate on things." Haugmard was such an observer. Like Corday, like many other young men in literary circles around the turn of the century, he published a considerable body of creative and critical writings without achieving lasting fame—such is the richness of French letters in that era. Haugmard's report on the movies, titled "L' 'Esthétique' du cinématographie" ("The 'Aesthetic' of Cinematography"), appeared in *Le Correspondant*, the Catholic journal in which Talmeyr had reported on the 1900 exposition thirteen years earlier.[17] In that interval the marketing of dreams in cinematic form had been transformed from a temporary fairground curiosity into a decisive and established fact of urban life, a phenomenon, to quote Haugmard, "as immense as it is disquieting."

The jumbled chaos of the exposition had been transferred to the silver screen. Haugmard begins his article by remarking upon the way all forms of entertainment—fantastic, sentimental, comic, dramatic, scientific, historical, moralizing—are shown one after the other in the movie house, so that a Western is juxtaposed with a drawing-room comedy, a social documentary with a travelogue, a comic chase sequence with the fall of Troy. "[There is] nothing that cannot be used . . . for the confection of a film." Distinctions of significance and even of realism are obliterated when all levels of experience are reduced to the same level of technically ingenious entertainment. Haugmard further suggests that this cinematic syncretism is a result of the need to appeal to a large public with varying tastes. "In fact, the public of cinematographic spectacles is not coherent. Many 'milieux' are represented there, and all sorts of minds." Because the mass audience is incoherent rather than homogeneous, film programs are also incoherent, for they include something for everyone, just as newspapers and tourist attractions do.

In defining the cinema as a phenomenon of "the people, in the largest meaning of this term," Haugmard agrees with Corday that modern technology widens the horizons of the masses. Not only does film take people to far-off places, "reproduced in their photographic truth, luminous and trembling"; it also allows them to enter hitherto inaccessible reaches of society through "elegant and worldly dramas which introduce them to milieux where they cannot otherwise penetrate." Whether the distance is geographic or social, film allows the pleasures of mobility.

Haugmard is, however, inclined to side with Talmeyr

in condemning these imaginary excursions as childish escapism. A film advertisement promises "an hour of intense emotion": who could resist this appeal, Haugmard asks? People crave concentrated doses of intense emotion (what Corday called "liquors . . . which concentrate power and life") to get away from "their sorry and monotonous existence, from which they love to escape." Haugmard notes that moviegoers much prefer fantasies to portrayals of ordinary life:

> "The masses" are like a grown-up child who demands a picture album to leaf through in order to forget his miseries . . . [T]he "cinema," which is a "circus" for adults, offers to the popular imagination and sensibility, deprived and fatigued, the "beau voyage."

People want to evade reality, not to learn about it. Certainly the technical dexterity of the medium permits convincing reproductions of visual appearances, "in their photographic truth, luminous and trembling," but "photographic truth" is not truth. Film can give "the exact reproduction of natural reality" while still being

> a factor of artifice and of falsification. . . . If it is the realm of fraud, of counterfeit, of trickery, how will a naïve public know how to make the indispensable distinctions and the necessary selection, under pain of inevitable misunderstandings and multiple errors?

Just because of its photographic realism, film offers a nearly irresistible temptation not only to inculcate political propaganda but also "to vulgarize, which is to say, to deform" the noblest novels, plays, and poems; "'to romanticize' or falsify" history by giving a partial view; and, on current subjects, "to nourish vanities and launch imitations, for the image excites naïve souls."

Because film speaks in the language of imagery, it is at once emotionally exciting and intellectually deceptive. The rapid succession of "realistic" images captivates the imagination of the viewer without engaging his mind. As an example, Haugmard describes the way a robbery is portrayed on the screen in a series of scenes of violence, beginning with the hold-up of a delivery van,

> even down to the mark of the bullet on the wheel; then the judge is shown . . . interrogating the policemen. Imagine the influence on children's minds of the burglary scenes and the ingenious methods used to throw the pursuers off the track. The prefect of police in Berlin thought it appropriate to forbid children under fifteen to enter movie theatres.

Movies excite because they communicate through powerful, concrete, realistic images. They lie because they communicate *only* through images:

> Why does an evening at the movies, however crammed with the most diverse films, despite everything leave in the mind an impression of emptiness, of nothingness? . . . Hardly is the spectacle over and it is forgotten.
>
> It is because only facts are photographed. All the rest is sacrificed, all that which is intellectual and interior life, and in the human order, only intelligence and soul really count! This exclusive capacity to reproduce only the fact entails its consequences. Action, only action, which is rapid and brutal. From this the suppression, almost absolute, of all psychology. Cinematography is a notation by image, as arithmetic and algebra are notations by figures and letters; now, it is convenient to limit as much as possible in the statement or the exposition all that which is not the sign itself. It is the triumph of simplification.

These remarks apply most directly to the silent films of that era, but even when the image is accompanied by a soundtrack its dominance is maintained. The cinema and its descendant, television, remain positivistic mediums, excluding all that is not fact, visually speaking. By excluding so much, by passing off simplification as totality, they are, to borrow Talmeyr's description of the Indian exhibit, true only partially, and so partially as to be false. Haugmard points out that movie actors become " 'types,' " which is to say that their immediately recognizable personal images come to convey a constellation of values and feelings, down to the child actor who incarnates " 'Baby.' " In the same way, the images of the exotic—the colorful rug, the belly dancer, the domed palace—are decorative "types" that incarnate exciting feelings of adventure, romance, and luxury but have little to do with Oriental reality. The language of imagery is also the language of the dream world of the consumer.

Haugmard's final condemnation of the language of imagery is that it goes in one direction only, from screen to spectator. The moviegoer has no need to make a response to be communicated to others, for in the theatre "everything takes place in the domain of silence." The screen does all the work for the viewer, who needs to put forth only the most minimal intellectual effort. "The mental tension required is feeble; fatigue, if there be fatigue at the end of the spectacle, will be purely nervous and wholly passive." Because all the details of the film are explained by a program or narrator, "mental work is already accomplished in advance to suppress the active effort of the spectators." The passive solitude of the moviegoer therefore resembles the behavior of department-store shoppers, who also submit to the reign of imagery with a strange combination of intellectual and physical passivity and emotional hyperactivity. In both cases shared social experience is replaced by uniformity of experience based on response to potent images. In the moviehouse the characteristic sociability of environments of mass consumption is taken to its limit in ordered rows of silent, hypnotized spectators.

Haugmard finds the implications of this behavior so distressing that he evaluates it not in his own words but in the words of an imaginary "man of taste, of a skepticism sometimes morose, sometimes indulgent." In an indulgent mood, the "man of taste" muses that the movies provide tolerable and even delightful illusions, views of lovely landscapes, of strange lands, even of fairylands, for cinematography can realize any dream. What good are Hoffmann, Andersen, and creators of fantasy, what good are poets who invent, when cinematography is there to record scientifically, for the incredulous masses, the wildest phantasmagorias of ancestral myths?

But in the actual world (and here the "man of taste" turns morose) life will become distorted when the behavior induced by the movies becomes habitual. When movies provide the miracle of "an unlimited posthumous life, there will be no more written archives, only films, catalogued and classified, and the 'pressings' of public life, the 'preserves' of the past, often not exempt from falsification." Not only will our view of the past be altered, but action in the present will alter with an eye to how it will look on film. "Alas! in the future, notorious personalities will instinctively 'pose' for cinematographic popularity, and historical events will tend to be concocted for its sake." Already film is becoming, if not exactly the "religion of the masses," then (borrowing the title of a well-known contemporary book)[18] "the irreligion of the future":

> Through it the charmed masses will learn not to think anymore, to resist all desire to reason and to construct, which will atrophy little by little; they will know only how to open their large and empty eyes, only to look, look, look. . . . Will cinematography comprise, perhaps, the elegant solution to the social question, if the modern cry is formulated: "Bread and cinemas"? . . .
>
> And we shall progressively draw near to those menacing days when universal illusion in universal mummery will reign.

Haugmard's meditation beautifully illustrates a type of culture criticism that deserves to be rehabilitated, a type that originates in aesthetic thought but extends to far more encompassing social and moral issues. When Haugmard places "aesthetic" in quotations in his title, he registers his awareness that the term is only approximate, that no pristinely aesthetic response is possible, that, as in the case of exposition décor, appraisal of the visual phenomenon must take into account the commercial motivation behind it. Haugmard experiments with a variety of vocabularies—aesthetic, moral, sociological, psychological—in attempting to deal with a cultural phenomenon "as immense as it is disquieting," too immense, certainly, to be reduced to any one terminology. In this respect he is an experimentalist, like such other French *moralistes* of his day as Talmeyr and Corday. They are trying to devise a language appropriate for events at once significant and unbounded by traditional disciplinary categories. Like the experiences they treat, their vocabulary is hybrid and innovative: new forms of consumption demand new modes of criticism.

The Electrical Fairyland—By now it is becoming clear how momentous were the effects of nineteenth-century technological progress in altering the social universe of consumption. Besides being responsible for an increase in productivity which made possible a rise in real income; besides creating many new products and lowering the prices of traditional ones; besides all this, technology made possible the material realization of fantasies which had hitherto existed only in the realm of imagination. More than any other technological innovation of the late nineteenth century, even more than the development of cinematography, the advent of electrical power invested everyday life with fabulous qualities. The importance of an electrical power grid in transforming and diversifying production is obvious, as is its eventual effect in putting a whole new range of goods on the market. What is less appreciated, but what amounts to a cultural revolution, is the way electricity created a fairyland environment, the sense of being, not in a distant place, but in a make-believe place where obedient genies leap to their master's command, where miracles of speed and motion are wrought by the slightest gesture, where a landscape of glowing pleasure domes and twinkling lights stretches into infinity.

Above all, the advent of large-scale city lighting by electrical power nurtured a collective sense of life in a dream world. In the 1890s nocturnal lighting in urban areas was by no means novel, since gas had been used for this purpose for decades; however, gas illumination was pale and flickering compared to the powerful incandescent and arc lights which began to brighten the night sky in that decade. The expositions provided a preview of the transformation of nighttime Paris from somber semidarkness to a celestial landscape. At the 1878 exposition an electric light at a café near but not actually on the fairgrounds caused a sensation. In 1889 a nightly show of illuminated fountains entranced crowds with a spectacle of falling rainbows, cascading jewels, and flaming liquids, while spotlights placed on the top of the Eiffel Tower swept the darkening sky as the lights of the city were being turned on. At the 1900 exposition electrical lighting was used for the first time on a massive scale, to keep the fair open well into the night. Furthermore, the special lighting effects were stunning. In one of his articles for the *Revue de Paris*, Corday describes the nightly performance:

> A simple touch of the finger on a lever, and a wire as thick as a pencil throws upon the Monumental Gateway . . . the brilliance of three thousand incandescent lights which, under uncut gems of colored glass, become the sparkling soul of enormous jewels.
>
> Another touch of the finger: the banks of the Seine and the bridges are lighted with fires whose reflection prolongs the splendor. . . . The façade of the Palace of Electricity is embraced, a stained-glass window of light, where all these diverse splendors are assembled in apotheosis.[19]

Like the technological marvels already mentioned, this one was at once exploited for commercial purposes. As early as 1873 the writer Villiers de l'Isle-Adam (1838–1889) predicted in a short story, "L'Affichage céleste" (which might be loosely translated as "The Heavenly Billboard"), that the "seeming miracles" of electrical lights could be used to generate "an absolute Publicity" when advertising messages were projected upward to shine among the stars:

> Wouldn't it be something to surprise the Great Bear himself if, suddenly, between his sublime paws, this disturbing message were to appear: *Are corsets necessary, yes or no?* . . . What emotion concerning dessert liqueurs . . . if one were to perceive, in the south of Regulus, this heart of the Lion, on the very tip of the ear of corn of the Virgin, an Angel holding a flask in hand, while from his mouth comes a small paper on which could be read these words: *My, it's good!*[20]

Thanks to this wonderful invention, concluded Villiers, the "sterile spaces" of heaven could be converted "into truly and fruitfully instructive spectacles. . . . It is not a question here of feelings. Business is business. . . . Heaven will finally make something of itself and acquire an intrinsic value." As with so many other writers of that era, Villiers's admiration of technological wonders is tempered by the ironic consideration of the banal commercial ends to which the marvelous means were directed. Unlike the wonders of nature, the wonders of technology could not give rise to unambiguous enthusiasm or unmixed awe, for they were obviously manipulated to arouse consumers' enthusiasm and awe.

The prophetic value of Villiers's story lies less in his descriptions of the physical appearance of the nocturnal sky with its stars obscured by neon lights, than in his forebodings of the moral consequences when commerce seizes all visions, even heavenly ones, to hawk its wares. Villiers's prophecies were borne out by the rapid application of electrical lighting to advertising. As he foresaw, electricity was used to spell out trade names, slogans, and movie titles. Even without being shaped into words, the unrelenting glare of the lights elevated ordinary merchandise to the level of the marvelous. Department-store windows were illuminated with spotlights bounced off mirrors. At the 1900 exposition, wax figurines modeling the latest fashions were displayed in glass cages under brilliant lights, a sight which attracted hordes of female spectators.

When electrical lighting was used to publicize another technical novelty, the automobile, the conjunction attracted mammoth crowds of both sexes. Beginning in 1898, an annual Salon de l'Automobile was held in Paris to introduce the latest models to the public. It was one of the first trade shows; the French were pioneers in advertising the automobile as well as in developing the product itself. This innovation in merchandising—like the universal expositions the Salon de l'Automobile resembles so closely—claimed the educational function of acquainting the public with recent technological advances, a goal, however, which was strictly subordinate to that of attracting present and future customers. The opening of the 1904 Salon de l'Automobile was attended by 40,000 people (compared to 10,000 who went to the opening of the annual painting salon), and 30,000 came each day for the first week. Each afternoon during the Salon de l'Automobile, the Champs-Élysées was thronged with crowds making their way to the show, which was held in the Grand Palais, an imposing building constructed for the 1900 universal exposition. During the Salon the glass and steel domes of the Grand Palais were illuminated at dusk with 200,000 lights; the top of the building glowed in the gathering darkness like a stupendous lantern. People were enchanted: "a radiant jewel," they raved, "a colossal industrial fairyland," "a fairytale spectacle."[21]

Inside, lights transformed the automobiles themselves into glittering objects of fantasy:

> You must come at nightfall. Coming out into the world from the entrance to the Métro, you stand stupefied by so much noise, movement, and light. A rotating spotlight, with its quadruple blue ray, sweeps the sky and dazzles you; two hundred automobiles in battle formation look at you with their large fiery eyes. . . . Inside, the spectacle is

of a rare and undeniable beauty. The large nave has become a prodigious temple of Fire; each of its iron arches is outlined with orange flames; its cupola is carpeted with white flames, with those fixed and as it were solid flames of incandescent lamps: fire is made matter, and they have built from it. The air is charged with a golden haze, which the moving rays of the projectors cross with their iridescent pencils. . . .[22]

Again this is an aesthetic of the exaggerated and showy, of simple but powerful imagery repeated to overwhelm the viewer (what could be more repetitious than two hundred thousand lights?). As with exotic décor, the purpose behind such a display is to win attention and to raise merchandise above the level of the everyday by associating it with exciting imagery.

Unlike images of far-off places, however, a fairyland cannot be accused of falsity because it never pretends to be a real place. Or can it? Electric lighting covers up unpleasant sights which might be revealed in the cold light of day. The illumination of the Grand Palais disguised the building itself. In the words of one visitor:

> The Grand Palais itself is almost beautiful because you hardly see it anymore: the confused scrap-iron and copper-work . . . [is] lost in the shadow; the luminous scallop decorations and chandeliers and . . . allegories, drowned in the irradiation. . . . The roof itself, that monstrous skin of a leviathan washed up there on the bank of the river, borrows a sort of beauty from the light which emanates from it.[23]

Through the obscuring glare the same visitor noted that the poles supporting the light fixtures were ridiculously ornamented with nautical motifs and garlands which were coming unstuffed. Others who viewed the décor of the Salon de l'Automobile were appalled when in the daylight they saw booths with doorways plastered to resemble those of Persian mosques, Gothic churches, or Egyptian temples, other booths constructed like bamboo huts hung with Japanese lanterns, and still others rigged with ship's masts complete with ropes, sails, and flags. The visitor quoted above, horrified by this "so-called artistic element" of the Salon, said that the exhibits showed "an incoherent heap of the most laughable imaginings" which the French should be thoroughly ashamed to display to the rest of the world, except that the displays of foreigners were equally ridiculous.[24] But all that junk miraculously disappeared when the lights came on.

Through fantasy, business provides alternatives to itself. If the world of work is unimaginative and dull, then exoticism allows an escape to a dream world. If exotic décor is heavy, unconvincing, and shabby, then another level of deception is furnished by a nightly fairyland spectacle that waves away the exotic with the magic wand of electricity. Robert de La Sizeranne, art critic for the *Revue des deux mondes,* compared the Salons de l'Automobile to fairytale princesses fought over by "perverse and benevolent powers" so that they were "frightfully ugly all day long [and] at night [became] beauties adorned with dazzling jewels." According to La Sizeranne, this diurnal schizophrenia was being repeated all over Paris. In the day the city displayed "superfluous, ignoble, lamentable ornaments," while at nightfall "these trifling or irritating profiles are melted in a conflagration of apotheosis. . . . Everything takes on another appearance," the ugly details are lost, and diamonds, rubies, and sapphires spill over the city.[25] Instead of correcting its mistakes, the city buries them under another level of technology. In this respect the whole city is assuming the character of an environment of mass consumption. In the day as well as at night, the illusions of these environments divert attention to merchandise of all kinds and away from other things, like colonialism, class structure, and visual disasters.

How much of the history of consumption is revealed in comparing Mme. de Rambouillet's salon of witty conversation and candlelight with the twentieth-century Salon de l'Automobile, a cacophony of crowds, cars, glass, steel, noise, and light!

Dreams of Love and Wealth – It is neither necessary nor possible to catalog all the dreams exploited by modern business. Although their range is as boundless as that of the human imagination, the concepts already discussed should apply to them also, in a general way. One fantasy, however, is so powerful and pervasive that it deserves special mention—the desire for sexual pleasure. If dreams of distant places are materialized in exotic imagery and fairyland ones in electric-light displays, erotic dreams are incarnated in the female image. Once again the expositions provided a prophecy of the commercial exploitation of imagery. The belly dancers of the Rue du Caire at the 1889 fair and the glass-caged wax mannequins at the 1900 exposition attracted large crowds. Both female images had a compelling effect, but the dancer and mannequin were enticing in different ways to different audiences. Men gathered to see the sinuous, half-naked entertainer perform in the shadows of a cabaret, while women were held spellbound by the motionless, elegantly clothed models poised under electric lights. The charm of the dancer is closely related to the appeal of the exotic, for both invite liberation from ordinary conventions and attainment of a more romantic, exciting existence. The appeal of the wax mannequin, on the contrary, is that of a fairytale princess, who is coldly beautiful and proudly remote. The images imply a startling contrast between male and female fantasies, between what men want women to be like and what women want to be like. Can these contrary images be reconciled, in a woman at once exotic and ethereal, at once sensual and remote, at once harem slave and princess?

"La Parisienne" suggests that they can be. This penultimate female, the symbol of the 1900 exposition, was perched atop the Monumental Gateway, an icon both sexy and remote, goddess and slut, and she resembles the women who were portrayed on advertising posters all

over Paris in that era when these posters became a significant art form. Indeed, the triumph of French poster art,
according to Georges d'Avenel (of whom more will be said
shortly), is its mating of contradictory female images in its
ceaseless repetition of "the representation of a female
being with teasing features, half fairy princess and half
'streetwalker.' " The preferred model of the Chéret
brothers, masters of poster art, is "this Parisienne, of a
desirable height, with a hieratic smile, pagan goddess
intoxicated with her own apotheosis." This "illusory
type" always wears the same expression whether she is
shown on horseback, at the beach, smoking, writing to
advertise an ink or carrying a lamp to publicize mineral oil,
always "lending the charm of her petite person to all the
offerings of business."[26]

If this creation is not exactly a triumph of art, it is
surely a triumph of décor. This "type" (which also appeared in all the movie houses) appeals to the fantasies of
both sexes at the same time. Just as cinema programs
include something for everyone, business wants to deploy
images that appeal to as many consumers as possible. The
aim of mass publicity is to make the dream world as
uniform as possible in order to entice as many people as
possible. The creation of a hybrid streetwalker-princess is
one way to achieve this goal.

Another is to reduce fantasies to their lowest common
denominator. This is why the idea of wealth is of such
importance in the symbiosis of commerce and dream.
Desire for wealth is infinitely malleable. People have diverse ideas about how they would indulge themselves if
they were rich, but their daydreams depend on the basic
fantasy of possession of great wealth. With wealth other
dreams can come true. In appealing to this fantasy, commerce can achieve a feat of reductionism and secure the
broadest possible audience.

Environments of mass consumption are places where
consumers can indulge temporarily in the fantasy of
wealth. These environments are Versailles open to all, at

least during business hours. Without having to buy, the department-store shopper can handle and try on merchandise. For the relatively low price of admission, the exposition tourist can enjoy palaces and dancing girls, gaze on luxurious goods, travel in style, and otherwise taste pleasures normally reserved for the fortunate few. In the "picture palace," the moviegoer can be transported to high society to mingle with the rich. At the Salon de l'Automobile young couples can lounge in the crushed velvet seats of luxury vehicles before taking the Métro back home to cramped and drab apartments.[27] Perhaps the consumer revolution intensified the pain of envy by bringing within the realm of possibility the acquisition of a degree of wealth that had formerly been considered out of reach. This point is stressed by Balzac, chronicler of that pain. But the consumer revolution also brought an anodyne in the form of environments of mass consumption, where envy is transformed into pleasure by producing a temporary but highly intense satisfaction of the dream of wealth.

The satisfaction of this dream on a less intense but more lasting basis was another long-term accomplishment of the consumer revolution. The outpouring of new commodities in the late nineteenth century created a world where a consumer could possess images of wealth without actually having a large income. This magic was wrought, in the first place, through the alchemy of scientific and technological advances that permitted hitherto expensive articles to be made much more cheaply or to be imitated convincingly and inexpensively.

The other major advance making possible a widespread illusion of wealth was the vast expansion of credit. As we have seen, courtiers had customarily bought their luxuries with borrowed money; at the other end of the social scale, the poor had long purchased food on credit. During the consumer revolution the habit of borrowing permeated the ranks of the bourgeoisie, and credit buying began to be used for a wide range of consumer goods. Credit became a branch of big business. French retailers of food, drink, and pharmaceuticals had long offered credit (and had traditionally been expensive in consequence), but they did so on a personal, unsystematic, unwritten basis. During the consumer revolution borrowing was transformed into a large-scale, impersonal, rationalized system of installment purchase which made possible the acquisition of goods without ready cash—indeed a fantasy come true.

Installment plans were "developed into a national institution" in France by Georges Dufayel (1855–1916), beginning in the 1870s. His clients generally paid 20 percent of the standard purchase price for household goods at over 400 stores accepting Dufayel's tokens, and repaid the rest in small weekly installments. Dufayel received 18 percent commission on his sales. By the turn of the century the Dufayel firm had served over three million customers and had branches in every large French town. In Paris alone 3,000 clerks were employed to handle the orders and another 800 went out each day to collect repayments.[28]

These figures, however, do not fully convey the significance of credit purchase in allowing an ordinary wage-earner to enjoy a convincing illusion of wealth. The power of that illusion is expressed more vividly in the magnificent store, costing $10,000,000, that Dufayel built in the Rue de Clignancourt just after the turn of the century. "On entering Dufayel's store by the principal door," remarked one admiring observer, "it seems as though you are entering a palace rather than a shop." The entrance porch was richly ornamented with carvings and statues representing themes like "Credit" and "Publicity" and surmounted by a dome 180 feet high. Inside the building were 200 statues, 180 paintings, pillars, decorative panels, bronze allegorical figures holding candelabras, painted ceramics and glass, and grand staircases, as well as a theatre seating 3000 that was decorated with silk curtains, white-and-gold foliage wreaths, and immense mirrors. But Dufayel's establishment was more than a reproduction of a palace of the *ancien régime:* it also incorporated the most up-to-date attractions of consumer society. If there was a traditional cut-glass chandelier inside the dome, on the outside, at the very top, was a revolving light of ten million candlepower (almost as powerful as the search-light on top of the Eiffel Tower) visible for twelve miles— "which makes an excellent advertisement at night." If the theatre was "an object of astonishment and admiration to all visitors," who attended monthly musical performances there, the far plainer Cinematograph Hall in the basement was far more popular. There 1,500 people paid admission to attend each of four hour-long performances every day. "The cinematograph attracts many people to the store, and is an ingenious and profitable method of advertising." Dufayel's genius was to transform the traditional décor of an aristocratic palace into a modern, democratic environment of mass consumption.[29] The décor of the building faithfully symbolized its merchandise: to sell credit was to sell the illusion of princely wealth to the masses.

Dufayel's firm was so successful that rival credit companies were established, and department stores, beginning with the Samaritaine in 1913, began to organize their own credit companies.[30] The proliferation of credit, together with the proliferation of inexpensive imitation goods, permitted (in a phrase then popular) "the democratization of luxury." As the word *democratization* suggests, the dream of wealth, more than any other dream yet mentioned, has a social dimension, and it is therefore worthy of special attention.

Georges d'Avenel on the Democratization of Luxury –
Georges d'Avenel (1855–1939) was the most perceptive French analyst of the democratization of luxury. Around the turn of the century, he published a lively series of articles for the *Revue des deux mondes*, collectively titled "Le Mécanisme de la vie moderne" ("The Mechanism of Modern Life"), which appeared from 1894 to 1905 and which, simultaneously published in book form, went through numerous editions.[31] The title of the series is intriguing.

The word *mechanism*, traditionally associated with means of production, was applied by d'Avenel to means of consumption. In each of his articles he discusses one aspect of modern consumption: institutions like department stores and supermarkets; the manufacture (but this is not emphasized) and retailing (this *is* emphasized) of items like paper, silk, porcelain, clothing, and alcoholic beverages; systems of credit, advertising, and insurance; methods of transportation such as steamships, buses, and the Métro; entertainments such as the racetrack and theater; and domestic consumption in the form of lighting, heating, and home decoration. All these things and more are subsumed under d'Avenel's exceptionally broad understanding of what mass consumption encompasses. The principal value of his commentary lies in his multiplicity of perspectives. He defines the phenomenon as an area for general social inquiry. In the words of one admirer, d'Avenel wields "statistics like an engineer, caprices like a caricaturist, motives like a sociologist, and recollections like an historian."[32]

The historical perspective, the ingrained habit of viewing contemporary events in the light of history, enables d'Avenel to assess his own times with exceptional lucidity. He wrote some well-received traditional historical studies of the aristocracy and Church in seventeenth-century France. In the course of this research, however, he became convinced that the doings of eminent political and ecclesiastical figures bore little relevance to the lives of ordinary people. "The public life of a people is a very small thing in comparison to its private life."[33] No doubt this conclusion reflected d'Avenel's disdain for contemporary public life. The Third Republic of his day was sullied by the adventures of Boulanger and the sordid Panama scandal, and d'Avenel's contempt for its political shabbiness was by no means unique or unjustified. A wealthy aristocrat with the title of viscount, he was not predisposed to favor Third Republic politics, although he was sincerely liberal in religion and social outlook.

   Instead of retreating to the anti-Semitic and legitimist fanaticism of many of his social peers in the Faubourg Saint-Germain, d'Avenel used his criticism of contemporary society to enrich his historical work. Turning off the well-trodden path of public history, he ventured into a realm of private history few had explored—the history of slow changes in material life, in food, clothing, furnishings, lodgings, and lighting, to name only a few examples. The bedrock of his research was a statistical compilation of private incomes and expenditures over seven centuries. Gathering these data involved staggering labor: d'Avenel claimed he examined as many as 75,000 prices as part of his research. He was convinced, however, that household budgets were the key to penetrating lost worlds of private history. From these budgets he concluded that material life had changed radically, that it had been "transformed from top to bottom"[34] over the centuries, and that this transformation had progressed independent of political or legal events, even so-called revolutionary ones. But statistics were only the means to his ultimate goal, which was "to penetrate into the intimacy of humble homes of yesteryear, to scrutinize the relations formerly established between rich and poor, finally, to discover, buried beneath the heap of dead statistics, a thousand secret emotions of our fathers."[35] The dry figures of prices and incomes provided the key to the mental life of the past: "the history of figures becomes the history of men."[36] Spending patterns had never been based on a logical and sober assessment of material well-being; instead, spending was motivated primarily by mental pleasures ranging from the thrill of success in doubling one's income to the "vaporous reveries of inebriation." D'Avenel concluded that "for the poor as for the rich, this question of income and expenses is above all a *matter of imagination.*"[37]

   If his dissatisfaction with contemporary society enriched d'Avenel's historical outlook, his research into the consumption patterns of the past made him an astute observer of the consumer society evolving around him and, above all, of the imaginative pleasures it afforded. In "The Mechanism of Modern Life" he demonstrates over and over how ordinary citizens of his own day could enjoy the illusion of wealth; the backdrop, stated or implied, is the preceding seven centuries, when striking differences in appearance and possessions erected a "brutal barrier" between peasants and courtiers. The consumer revolution had toppled that barrier. In his article on porcelain, for example, d'Avenel describes how the rich used to eat off porcelain and the poor off clay or wood; now Frenchmen from millionaire to peasant eat out of the same dish, as it were. The industrial changes that made possible large-scale production of tableware also revolutionized interior decoration, so that the working classes could afford factory-made rugs and wallpapers that offered some appearance of wealth in the place of the reality. The illusion of riches could be enjoyed in dress, especially in "the democratization of the 'silk dress,' that ancient symbol of opulence, thus procuring the illusion of similarity in clothing—a great comfort for the feminine half of the human race."[38] Although mass-produced silks selling for a franc and a half a meter in department stores were less beautiful than fine Lyonnais ones costing six hundred francs a meter, "they make more people happy." Technological advances had also transformed the feather industry: cheap and persuasive facsimiles of the rarest varieties, or even of totally imaginary ones, could be purchased by any shopgirl. Rabbit pelts could be turned into exotic furs like "Mongolian chinchilla." Artificial flowers with brilliant colors, flexible rubber stems, and papyrus corollas were available to all. The pleasures of novelty could also be enjoyed by everyone. The privilege of following changes in clothing fashions had spread to both men and women, people whose grandparents had probably purchased only a few new outfits in their lives.[39]

D'Avenel wholeheartedly welcomes the mass of cheap imitations flooding the marketplace. Instead of living with constant frustration, the humble could now enjoy the pleasures of being rich:

> Each time [industries] extend their reach, the life of a great number of individuals gains a new satisfaction; they allow the pale and illusory but sweet reflection of opulence to penetrate even to the humble. These vulgarizations are the work of our century: they honor it greatly.[40]

To those who protested the banality of the pleasure derived from these vulgarizations, d'Avenel responds:

> The character of the new luxury is to be banal. Let us not complain too much, if you please: before, there was nothing banal but misery. Let us not fall into this childish but nevertheless common contradiction which consists of welcoming the development of industry while deploring the results of industrialism.[41]

And to those who complained that the democratization of luxury meant the proliferation of "bad taste," d'Avenel suggests that the cause of decline in workmanship is not only technological—the replacement of handwork by machinery—but also social and psychological—the desire to have consumer goods resembling those of the rich. The shopgirl prefers a shoddy, mass-produced silk to a sturdy, handsome cotton because silk, originally valued for its intrinsic beauty, is now valued by the masses for conveying an aura of moneyed glamor. The illusion, and not the fabric, is the source of the consumer's pleasure. D'Avenel defends this subjective satisfaction. When a manufacturer admits to him that the lovely tints of mass-produced silks do not last long, d'Avenel remarks:

> I am not pleading here the cause of the "shoddy"; it doesn't need a lawyer, and if it needed a poet the dyers could say: "Qu'importe le flacon pourvu qu'on ait l'ivresse? . . . " ["What does it matter what's in the bottle as long as it gets you drunk?"][42]

D'Avenel's defense of the joys of cheap imitations stands in refreshing contrast to the frequent condescending dismissals of them by those who can afford better. On the other hand, he is condescending in another way. His very defense of these goods implies the acceptance of a social system where significant inequalities in income endure despite the growing equality in merchandise. Indeed, d'Avenel not only accepts this system but praises the democratization of luxury for strengthening it. In modern society, technology makes possible an "equalization of enjoyments" without a corresponding "equalization of incomes."[43] From his statistical research d'Avenel knew that incomes had in fact become less equal during the nineteenth century: he himself estimated that bourgeois had multiplied their real income by three or four times, the very rich by six to eight times, and the masses by only two times. But he contends that the rich man's increase in fortune has little real meaning, that his additional income buys only "artificial" luxuries, in the form of rarities, rather than genuine comforts. "Leveling consists of this: that the common people have acquired more real well-being, more useful luxury than the wealthy."[44] Mechanical invention diminished meaningful class differences by overturning the traditional relationship between the utility of an object and its monetary value. "There is more difference between a peasant lighted by a resin candle and the lord lighted by wax tapers than between a worker lighted by oil and a bourgeois lighted by electricity."[45] The bicycle is another example: it is much more useful to the poor than the automobile is to the bourgeois, and the Paris Métro would soon give all urban workers the dream come true of a vehicle always at their service. According to d'Avenel, socialist "egalophiles" are not only futile, since improvement in living standards proceeds regardless of political events, but are also unnecessary. "What does inequality in money matter, when it no longer gives rise to inequality in actual enjoyments?"[46]

Critical Remarks—Does it matter? D'Avenel correctly stresses the radical differences between modern levels of consumption and those of preceding centuries. His historical research gives him a clear-eyed recognition of what industrialization means to the vast majority, in practical terms. Many other social critics who contrast past and present regard only differences in production methods. They portray a former utopia of small shops, craftsmanship, and good will, and a present hell of grinding factories, industrial strife, and degrading labor. D'Avenel looks instead at the level of consumption each productive system is capable of supporting. The contrast he draws is between the physical and psychological miseries of ill-fed, ill-clothed, and ill-lodged masses and the far more comfortable and uniform conditions of contemporary life. But his emphasis on higher consumer standards leads him to underestimate the costs of the physically taxing and psychologically unrewarding labor that is often involved in producing modern goods. D'Avenel could argue that working conditions are no worse than before and that they are more than compensated for by the new pleasures of consumption. These responses deserve consideration by anyone proposing an impossible marriage of past production and present consumption. Still, gains in consumption should not be used as an excuse for the persistence of bad working conditions. Improvement of those conditions does not necessarily entail a return to primitive consumer levels. D'Avenel himself cannot be accused of having used this excuse directly, and to fault him for slighting production is to blame him for not covering a topic he never intended to discuss at length. The point is that his arguments could readily be turned into evasions of or excuses for the failings of modern production methods, or even into a defense of consumerism as an opiate to lull workers into forgetfulness of their dissatisfactions.

D'Avenel was aware that many wage-earners remained unhappy despite the leveling of enjoyments. In his article on alcoholic beverages in "The Mechanism of Modern Life," he notes that an enormous number of workers did not use their high wages to gather a nest-egg or to enjoy a more comfortable life, but only to fill their goblets and empty their heads with drink like some "fetishist Negro" of the Sudan. Why would the most cultivated, proud workers in the world behave in this manner, drinking not in jolly festivity but rapidly, silently, grimly?

> You would have to understand their interior life, probably better than they understand it. . . . Only in drink are promises never eluded. . . . The more his reason takes flight and his head strays, the alcoholic, in stupefying himself, loses himself and, however crude be his dream, he dreams![47]

"Qu'importe le flacon pourvu qu'on ait l'ivresse. . . . " In describing the inebriated worker, d'Avenel comes disconcertingly close to describing the dream world of the consumer, whose pleasures he has defended so vigorously. Is there any great difference between solitary drinking and solitary moviegoing, between "stupefying" oneself with a bottle or with a department store, exposition, or Salon de l'Automobile? Does not Corday describe the "distant visions" exhibits as draughts of highly distilled liquor which give the masses a taste of power and life? Perhaps d'Avenel is right in claiming that the worker himself does not know why he craves dreams, but clearly something is desired which is not found in the leveling of enjoyments. Why this flight, by whatever method, from reality to illusion—from sobriety to drunkenness, from reason to stupor, from waking to dream?

One possibility frequently mentioned in twentieth-century analyses of mass culture is that the pleasures of consumption fail to compensate for the dreary work the drinker has to do all day long. Another possibility, raised by d'Avenel's own writings, is that the illusion of equality is not so convincing as he suggests. His social theory assumes that a shoddy silk dress or a "Mongolian chinchilla" gives the same sense of wealth as a handmade silk dress from Lyon or a mink coat. D'Avenel understands the objective differences in quality, but he assumes that the masses won't notice or won't care. Still, if the rich seek the unique and genuine, the work of art rather than the mass-produced, why shouldn't ordinary people want them too? If the rich take pride in having an educated "good taste" that appreciates the difference between a cheap imitation and an expensive original, why shouldn't that education be available to all? Even without a high degree of education, people are aware of the desirability of unique or rare items. In the "Mechanism" series d'Avenel often reminds his readers that wealth consists of the ability to possess, not beautiful or comfortable things, but rare ones. However, he adds, an object cannot be rare and also be possessed by the masses. No matter how desirable the item, no matter what its former associations with wealth, as soon as it becomes cheap enough to find a mass market it loses its rarity and therefore its desirability. D'Avenel notes that department stores tend to accelerate the dissipation of the illusion of wealth. These stores offer objects for mass consumption whose great attraction has been the difficulty of obtaining them because of their costliness (for example, Mouret offered Oriental rugs at cut rates). The results are good business and disillusioned shoppers. The pleasure of the illusion of wealth disappears into the distance as the mass market keeps encroaching, transforming the rare into the commonplace. When everyone can afford an imitation or cheap Oriental rug, then people want a handmade tapestry. The genuine continues to signify wealth, and common people continue to suffer from the vision of unattainable merchandise. There can be no authentic democratization of luxury because by definition luxury is a form of consumption limited to a few. Modern society has instead introduced the proliferation of superfluity.

D'Avenel fails to distinguish luxury from superfluity, and so his theory of the leveling of enjoyments attempts to base social harmony on deception rather than reality. Dreams may be solitary, but reality is inescapably collective. D'Avenel's conviction that change in private life is far more consequential than change in public life leads him to ignore the public consequences that follow from even the most seemingly private acts of consumption. In part the consequences are psychological. When a shopgirl buys a silk dress to fulfill a personal fantasy, she steps out onto the street and discovers that thousands of other women have had the same dream and bought the same type of dress. For all of them the illusion of wealth is shattered. On a more objective level, too, the pleasures of possession may be destroyed when many dream the same dream. As d'Avenel himself concedes, some goods cannot be democratized without losing their inherent charm:

> [It] would doubtless be more pleasant for each Parisian to own the Bois de Boulogne all by himself, or with a small number of friends, rather than share its enjoyment on holidays with 500,000 other proprietors. But it is precisely the glory of Progress to have created this congestion in making accessible to all an outing which used to be very remote.[48]

A "glory," perhaps, but the judgment would be more convincing if d'Avenel himself had to spend his holidays in this congested park. In an imaginary exposition voyage, many people can pretend to visit an unspoiled, uncrowded place; the actual Bois de Boulogne loses its charm because it is invaded by masses of other pleasure-seekers.

The basic weakness of d'Avenel's social theory lies deeper than this, however: it is his assumption that as consumers people seek enjoyment above all. As d'Avenel himself admits:

> If the mass of citizens does not appear to appreciate the . . . new enjoyments with which the nineteenth century has endowed it, it is because the "money question" is not a question of enjoyment, but one of equality; a matter of self-respect and not at all one of pleasure. "To have money," isn't it basically "to have more money than others," and how can it be arranged so that each Frenchman has more money than the others?[49]

With this admission collapses the theory of social harmony through the leveling of enjoyments. Differences in income are objective and measurable; intangible, subjective similarities in enjoyment may be claimed but cannot be demonstrated. People are more aware of tangible class differences than of illusory similarities, more aware of their disadvantages compared with wealthier contemporaries than of their advantages over their ancestors. An obvious conclusion is that people should have real equality in income and seek whatever illusions they crave on their own. But d'Avenel immediately jumps to the conclusion that people will not rest satisfied with equality but will demand superiority of income. The moment he approaches the issue of equalizing incomes rather than consumer pleasures, equalizing realities rather than dreams, he evades the issue in the despairing observation that people will never be happy anyway. It would be more accurate to say that people will remain dissatisfied with equality in consumer goods when so many other differences remain. D'Avenel looks too much at the objects people own and not enough at the flesh-and-blood owners—at the differences in their mortality, education, health, manners, taste, social contacts, leisure, and social and political power. These human distinctions remain despite a democratization of goods.

Concluding Remarks – D'Avenel is the historian of the material side of "the civilizing process" whereby consumer enjoyments originally limited to a small courtly circle gradually spread among a mass public. His contribution in defining and describing this process endures despite the inadequacies of his social theory. Its inadequacy did not keep it from being shared by moderate liberals who also approved of this democratization and even wanted it extended, while at the same time opposing more radical policies of equalization. Other social critics openly lamented the end of elitism in consumption (as we shall see in the next chapter), and still others argued that democratization had not gone nearly far enough, that the mass of consumers needed to acquire far more political and economic power (Chapters V and VII). Nevertheless, all these turn-of-the-century thinkers—moderate, elitist, and democratic alike—agreed that the historical evolution traced by d'Avenel raises fundamental and portentous issues for the future.

Surely it is instructive that in confronting those issues so decent a man as d'Avenel enthusiastically endorsed the idea of equalizing enjoyments rather than money, for, at the bottom, he was approving a vast delusion whereby human inequalities are masked by material appearances. The appeal of the theory only demonstrates how seductive are all the illusions of the dream world of consumption. By imperceptible degrees the charming and seemingly innocent fantasies of Mongolian chinchilla and Moorish courtyards lead to far more serious social deceits.

It is just because the transition is so gradual and easy, Talmeyr warns, that the deception of mass consumption must be resisted from the outset. That is the final lesson he extracts from the school of Trocadéro: truthfulness demands constant effort, and, in particular, effort to use the imagination more rather than less. If people only stare at the Indian bazaar and buy its rugs and fabrics unquestioningly, the realities of colonialism will remain forever buried beneath a mountain of merchandise. Talmeyr's imagination is too active to stop at the barrier of décor. He sees beyond what is displayed to what is not displayed, envisioning the emaciated Indians who are omitted and, furthermore, seeing why they are omitted. Talmeyr contends that laziness is responsible for the successful exploitation of dreams by commerce. The Trocadéro is a commercial success because everyone wants to see distant places but no one wants to go to the trouble of traveling:

> We don't go to the mountain but the mountain comes to us! Only, is it the real Japan, the real New World, and the genuine Honolulu which come? Isn't it a suspect Japan, a contraband New World, a Honolulu from a menu? . . .

> Bah! We don't look too closely, and our whole concern
> has become to avoid any effort above all.[50]

This widespread passivity, both physical and mental, is responsible for other distressing social trends. People love to believe that there is a short cut, an easy way out, and they want to be deceived because it is a way to avoid confronting real problems:

> Neither the voyage difficult to make, nor the language difficult to speak, nor the marriage difficult to endure, we want no more of that, and the same psychology is at the basis of the law on divorce, the decrees which suppress participles, and that which authorizes the opening of a Malaysian section at the exposition. The first tells us, "To be married, you don't need to be." The second: "To write French, you don't need to know it." And the third: "To go to Malaysia, you don't need to go there." Easy methods! But are we really sure of swimming in the ocean by putting a box of salt in our bathtub, and of returning from China, India, or the Sudan by returning from the Trocadéro?[51]

Are we so sure social justice can be achieved by the mass distribution of inexpensive Oriental rugs and silk dresses? An easy method! But truth is not found by dreaming. Time-consuming, unceasing effort is needed to replace confusion with lucidity, simplification with complexity, and deception with reality.

4   The Dandies and Elitist Consumption

The Proliferation of Lifestyles – In *The Theory of the Leisure Class* (1899) American economist Thorstein Veblen introduces the concept of "conspicuous consumption" to describe a way of life where wasteful and ostentatious items like "carpets and tapestries, silver table service, waiter's services, silk hats, starched linen, and many items of jewelry and dress" are regarded as necessities.[1] Conspicuous consumption is the style of consumption first cultivated by courtiers and then adopted by wealthy bourgeois. Veblen calls these groups "the leisure class," and he describes its consumer habits with relentless irony.

The greater irony is that his analysis was becoming obsolete at the moment he enunciated it. The international exposition of 1900, under construction as Veblen's book was being printed, revealed a much more raucous type of conspicuous consumption that appealed to a class which consumed "wastefully" but which was not leisured. At the international exposition and Salon de l'Automobile, at department stores and trade shows, at other environments of mass consumption overflowing with light, noise, and merchandise, a type of consumption was revealed that was alien to the genteel type Veblen had in mind.[2]

The advent of the new model of mass consumption did

not mean the disappearance of the older bourgeois consumption (although it originated in aristocratic circles, in the late nineteenth century this model was most typical of the upper bourgeoisie). The two not only coexisted but to some degree interpenetrated, as, for example, in the hybrid décor of Dufayel's store. At the extremes of the social spectrum the differences between bourgeois and mass consumption might be quite evident—the difference, for example, between the consumer habits of a wealthy, well-established lawyer and his wife who entertained regularly in their tastefully furnished salon, and those of a young clerk and his wife who tried out the plush seats of a luxury vehicle at the Salon d'Automobile and then took the Métro back to their cheap apartment. Between these two extremes there was, as Balzac showed, a subtly variegated social spectrum where the ranks of the bourgeoisie merged into those of the working classes. Here no point can be found marking a definitive break between "bourgeois" and "mass" consumption. These terms are ideal types, not precise descriptions of the habits of individuals or even of well-defined groups.

Furthermore, no matter what their differences, the motivation behind the traditional genteel forms of luxury and the newer varieties typical of mass consumption is similar: in both cases the consumer tries to realize fantasies through merchandise. Bourgeois consumption is also a dream world. In prerevolutionary days the bourgeois dream had been to rise to the ranks of the aristocracy. If that fantasy did not materialize in actual ennoblement, a bourgeois could buy an approximation of it by outfitting his house with a salon like that of an aristocratic *hôtel,* by collecting furniture resembling that of Versailles, by purchasing a sinecure so that he could at least "live nobly." Although d'Avenel praises the democratization of luxury as the glory of the nineteenth century, aspiring bourgeois had been imitating the luxury of the nobility in earlier centuries. In the 1800s, to be sure, the specific goal of ennoblement became less compelling, but the cultivation of genteel consumption continued to express dreams of social status, respectability, and security.

If the use of commodities to create a dream world was not a late nineteenth-century innovation, what *was* new in that era was the great increase in the varieties of dreams appealed to by commerce. The concept of luxury expanded vastly. The traditional bourgeois fantasies had been derived from the specific habits of a specific superior class, and certainly the new masses of consumers adopted some of these artistocratic fantasies (d'Avenel remarks on the potent appeal of the silk dress and fur coat to the shopgirl who wanted to pretend she was a countess). But in mass consumption, along with the aristocratic image of luxury were many other images ranging from South Sea islands to fairytale kingdoms to Oriental harems. The bourgeois dream of leisure meant a life moving from salon to salon, from fashionable watering place to watering place. In the dream world of mass consumption, leisure might just as well mean a lazy tropical sunset viewed from an isolated, palmy beach. The bourgeois concept of wealth was firmly tied to the idea of living in a château or *hôtel*, but for the mass consumer wealth could mean the treasures of an Arabian caliph or an Indian rajah. Not so much the use of merchandise to fulfill fantasies but the content and variety of the fantasies themselves are what distinguish bourgeois from mass consumption. The proliferation of consumers in the late nineteenth century brought with it a proliferation of images of luxury and leisure. The dream world of mass consumption is eclectic and complex. Compared to the bourgeois vision it is primitive and childish, perhaps, but it is also undeniably richer in imagination.

Once the authority of a homogeneous bourgeois style of consumption was questioned, once the notion of experimentation triumphed over obedience to established models, in short, once the possibility of other styles had been raised, they multiplied rapidly. There was no obvious stopping point. The last two decades of the nineteenth century were particularly rich in experiments on the part of consumers who, for whatever reasons, were not satisfied with either a bourgeois salon or a Salon de l'Automobile. The methodology of ideal types is necessary to describe the major alternatives that emerged from this period of experimentation, for it would be impossible to describe a representative sampling from the overflowing store of innovations.

With the aid of ideal types, however, two distinct consumer styles may be seen emerging in the 1880s and the 1890s: an elitist type and a democratic one. For all their differences in detail, many, if not most, of the experiments in consumer models of those decades fall into one or the other of these categories. Both the elitist and the democratic consumers rebelled against the shortcomings of mass and bourgeois styles of consumption, but in seeking an alternative they moved in opposite directions. Elitist consumers considered themselves a new type of aristocracy, one not of birth but of spirit—superior individuals who would forge a personal mode of consumption far above the banalities of the everyday. Democratic consumers sought to make consumption more equal and participatory. They wanted to rescue everyday consumption from banality by raising it to the level of a political and social statement.

Taken together, these four ideal types of consumer behavior—bourgeois, mass, elitist, and democratic—form an interlocking system which still characterizes modern society. This is why the late nineteenth century is such a crucial era in the development of modern consumer society. It was then that cultural homogeneity in consumption was superseded by a distinctive grouping of interdependent lifestyles. This crystallization would not have occurred so rapidly had not each consumer style been developing gradually and unobtrusively in the preceding decades. Indeed, the sources of bourgeois consumption date back to prerevolutionary courtly life, and the "democratized luxury" of mass consumption was present in

Balzac's day, although its pace was greatly accelerated in the last quarter of the nineteenth century.

The origins of the elitist style of consumption (the subject of this chapter) go back to the Napoleonic era, when Beau Brummell and other dandies responded to what they considered to be the encroachments of bourgeois and even mass vulgarity by reasserting traditional aristocratic virtues of daring, élan, and poise. These last courtiers, the dandies, were rebelling against the future, and yet in redefining aristocracy they became social prophets. The residual aspects of dandyism are mingled with the emergent ones; their revival of a dying social world became the creation of a new dream world of the elitist consumer.[3]

The Origins of Dandyism – Although dandyism eventually found its spiritual home in France, its origins were in England. Beau Brummell (George Bryan Brummell, 1778–1840) the incarnation of early dandyism, came from a highly respectable English family and mingled with titled society first at Eton and Oxford and then in the army, where he obtained a commission in an elegantly idle regiment commanded by the Prince of Wales (the future George IV). Brummell was not a noble himself, however. Far from hiding the fact, he tended to represent his family origins as meaner than they actually were. He was bent on defining himself as a new kind of aristocrat, one whose influence did not spring from the usual bases of hereditary name and wealth. Neither did Brummell pretend to serve the crown through military or political service, the traditional justification for aristocratic privileges. He neglected his army duties as much as possible and in 1798 he resigned to take a house in London. There Brummell set about attaining the only kind of power that mattered to him, a purely subjective influence over society, in the sense that Regency England understood the term—as the restricted circle of the wealthy and titled who entertained, intermarried, and gossiped with each other, who assumed that outside the precincts of their houses, clubs, and places of entertainment existed only the grossest social vulgarity.

Beau Brummell was well equipped for success in this quest for social domination. Tall, slender, and attractive, he made his appearance all the more appealing by his careful toilette (he was one of the first advocates of thorough personal cleanliness) and his dress. The nickname "Beau" was due to his clothing, not his personal beauty. Brummell rejected the ostentatious clothes that had long prevailed in courtly circles—plush velvets and gold threads, ermine trimmings, golden slippers, and so forth—and adopted a mode of dress far less conspicuous but just as indicative of superior wealth and taste. The elements were simple: his standard daytime dress was a blue wool coat with lightly boned lapels and brass buttons, a buff waistcoat and pantaloons, and black, nearly knee-high boots. If the costume seemed democratic, almost Rousseauian, in its simplicity, that austerity was deceptive. The time and expense it involved could be appreciated by the wearer's social peers. Only two links of Brummell's watchchain were visible, but they were made of gold. The cut of the coat and pantaloons, close-fitting without being tight, could be achieved only by the best tailors. Even the bottoms of the shoes were immaculately polished. Finally, in order to achieve "the supreme knot" for his white linen cravat, Brummell and his servants went through yards and yards of linen, discarding each unsuccessful attempt, until a knot with just the right degree of casual perfection was tied. Brummell invented the fashion ideal of understated elegance.

Brummell's manners came out of the same mold. His etiquette was impeccable, but, as in his dress, the dandy did the conventional unconventionally well. Within, but only just within, the rules of politeness, he affirmed his superiority by his mastery of the art of the "put-down," the "wisecrack," "one-upmanship" (one sign of Brummell's modernity is the appropriateness of contemporary slang in describing his behavior). When a nobleman with pretensions to elegance asked Brummell's opinion of a new coat, the dandy shrugged, "Do you call that *thing* a coat?"—a response especially devastating because it was made in the presence of a third gentleman. Brummell also asserted his superiority in taste by reminding people that he could not tolerate situations readily endured by ordinary mortals:

> Brummell once explained a cold caught in a country inn with the complaint that he had been put into a room "with a damp stranger." He protested that certain foods were too coarse for his palate: asked if he never tasted vegetables, "Madam," he answered, "I once ate a pea."[4]

Everyone had similar stories about Brummell; these anecdotes were the talk of the town. If people were shocked and amused, rather than angered, by his wit, one reason is that Brummell expressed his contempt for the common herd in a curiously dispassionate way. His verbal thrusts against vulgarity were not made in the heat of emotion but with calculated poise. He possessed an unshakable *sangfroid* (literally, "cold blood"); he was (here again slang imposes itself), above all, "cool." His feelings were always concealed behind an impenetrable reserve. Just as his aggressions were never expressed openly and directly but only through the medium of polished insouciance, so was he never known to express affection for anyone of either sex, maintaining a self-centered indifference. Any lapse into emotional display would have been as gross a social error as a spot on his linen cravat. In Brummell the civilizing process reaches an end point of complete emotional repression coupled with an extraordinary emphasis on material exhibition.

Brummell became a celebrity, a trend-setter, a phenomenon—one of the first persons to whom these terms describing a distinctively modern elite of exemplary consumers may be applied. In London society to receive a greeting or even a nod from him was a privilege, and admission to his toilette a coveted one. If Brummell owed money to a tradesman, in many cases both parties considered the debt paid if the dandy acknowledged the creditor in the street. Brummell set the rules for society: who was in and who was out, how to chat, how to blend snuff, how to dress. To disseminate these rules there sprung up a literary industry of elegant journals, fashionable novels, verses, lampoons, and sketches.

This insatiable appetite for publicity about the dandy and his circle, this adulation and deference and imitation, tell us as much about the society of the time as they do about Beau Brummell's unique gifts. His mastery would not have been possible unless a group of people were ready to be subjected, willing to be hypnotized, and eager to look, look, look at his seductive image. Even before the advent of modern mass advertising, Brummell demonstrates the appeal of publicity for an exemplary lifestyle, as opposed to publicity for specific products. This publicity was immensely flattering to the dandy, but the flattery went both ways. Brummell's audience could take pride in its own ability to appreciate the nuances of his dress and wit. The sense of social superiority assumed by the dandy extended to his admirers. This reassurance was particularly welcome to them at a time when the traditional political and economic sources of aristocratic authority were being undermined. In this situation of transition and uncertainty, Beau Brummell suggested a new concept of leadership, a purely social type of authority enjoyed by trend-setters, obtainable simply through conviction of one's own superiority in taste rather than being dependent upon title, land, or office. Through this conviction alone Brummell established himself as the new "first gentleman of the kingdom." He was a social authority above the prince himself, who obediently adopted the dandy's style of dress even though it was less than flattering to the rotund royal figure.

A break between the social king and the political one was inevitable. When the prince was made regent in 1811 due to the insanity of his father, George III, a number of old and compromising attachments had to be cast off; among them was Brummell. The dandy took this loss of royal support with his usual audacity and hinted that he, rather than the regent, had initiated the break. One day Brummell and a friend met the regent and one of his companions strolling in the street. When the regent stopped to chat with Brummell's friend but ignored the dandy, Brummell turned to the regent's companion and casually inquired, "Who's your fat friend?" Not the loss of George IV's support but debt finally ended Brummell's social dictatorship: the one thing the dandy could not afford to lose in his lonely preeminence was money. In 1816 Brummell fled to Calais to escape his creditors, who would no longer be placated by a nod in the street.

His fourteen years of exile in Calais were tolerable (he was something of a tourist attraction), but after moving to Caen in 1830, again just one jump ahead of his creditors, Brummell's melancholy decline began. After losing his post as English consul in Caen in 1832, he lived off intermittent charity and at one point was imprisoned for debt. After a series of strokes he deteriorated into a drooling, filthy, repulsive, and forgotten old man. All Brummell retained of his dandyism was his emotional isolation. When it came time for him to die in 1840, a charity case in a sanatorium near Caen, he turned his face to the wall so that the nun attending him would not see this supremely private moment.

Dandyism as a Spiritual Ideal–By the time of Brummell's death, the spirit of dandyism was flourishing vigorously not only in London but also in Paris. Political and social turmoil, internal upheavals, and foreign wars had all delayed the introduction of dandyism to France, but the worst of these distractions came to an end after the revolution of 1830. By the time that event installed Louis-Philippe on the throne, the French aristocratic elite had lost its political predominance and was uncertain of its social role in the face of the newly dominant middle classes. The king and some aristocrats adapted to the situation by assuming a bourgeois style of life, but others preferred instead to adopt an uncompromising and unapologetic espousal of waste, idleness, and lavish spending—virtues both of the traditional aristocracy and of the dandy. In a society where bourgeois loudly proclaimed the virtues of thrift, utility, and work, the dandy rejected all these values as vulgar and sordid, and, increasingly, as irrelevant besides. In fifteen days of reckless spending, that golden creature the Comte d'Orsay (1801–1852) conquered London society and thus by deed rather than by word disproved bourgeois homilies on the advantages of financial restraint.

D'Orsay was widely regarded as a worthy successor to Brummell, and his gentler manners made him considerably better liked. Many dandies of the 1830s, however, especially in France, moved in less rarified social strata. Sons of the bourgeoisie were by no means immune to disgust at bourgeois ways; indeed, their revulsion often had a bitterness born of proximity. In particular, those with artistic and intellectual inclinations found in dandyism an expression of a sense of creative superiority, whether or not that feeling of superiority was justified. What emerged was a cross between dandyism and Bohemianism—*la bohème dorée* ("the gilded Bohemian world")—where distinction in dress and manners was cultivated along with literary or artistic distinction. The young Balzac, as a hybrid journalist-socialite with a cane in one hand and a pen in the other, so to speak, is a good example. The merger of dandyism with the rich intellectual and artistic life in France enriched both and transformed dandyism from a social ideal to a spiritual one, or, more precisely, extracted a spiritual significance from the dandy's slavish attention to nuances of style.

Balzac was one of the first to describe the ideal behind the supposed frivolities of dandyism, probably because he himself found the pose so attractive. In the 1830s he published a series of articles in various society reviews elaborating his conviction that small details of fashion reveal the innermost principles of modern thought. The assumption that such details carry a weight of significance, that they convey not just a lesson of things but "a metaphysic of things,"[5] was in Balzac's opinion a new and distinctive characteristic of bourgeois society. Traditional class divisions and barriers were rapidly eroding, and social rank had become unclear rather than self-evident; delicate nuances of dress and behavior assumed unprecedented importance, simply because these distinctions were the only ones left. Gross and obvious differences in manners between nobleman and peasant were gone. In their place, in bourgeois culture, was an array of much finer, much more meticulously observed distinctions. With this analysis of the social significance of "elegant life," as he termed it, Balzac touches upon a basic contradiction in dandyism. The dandy adopts manners and costumes intended to repudiate everything bourgeois, but the very care he devotes to them is typically bourgeois. To reject one lifestyle in favor of another supposedly superior, more refined one is still to acknowledge the dominance of lifestyle in a system of social values.

French writers after Balzac who theorized about dandyism tended to ignore the ambiguities he discerned and simply praised the dandy for his spiritual superiority. The elevation of dandyism to a metaphysical level was above all due to Jules Barbey d'Aureyvilly (1808–1889), then a dandy journalist much like the young Balzac. In his book *Du dandysme et de Georges Brummell* (1845), the "pivotal work upon which the history of the dandy tradition turns,"[6] Barbey portrayed Brummell as the incarnation of dandyism, "the thing itself,"[7] a man whose very existence revealed a spiritual grandeur dwarfing the dull uniformity and mediocrity of bourgeois society. Brummell defined dandyism in a word as "Anti-Vulgarity."[8] Barbey's vision exalted the dandy from a nineteenth-century version of Voltaire's *mondain* into a modern saint, a "holy man" who "carries within himself something superior to the visible world."[9]

After Barbey, the resemblance of the dandy to the old courtly elite became less and less important. What mattered more was the way the dandy embodied a new elite, a spiritual aristocracy, composed of all those who considered themselves elevated in spirit above the ordinary run of mankind, no matter what their birth or fortune. "Civilization" no longer belonged to a social class but found its refuge in the private soul of the superior individual. This redefinition of aristocracy culminated in the life and work of the poet Charles Baudelaire. Unlike Balzac and Barbey, both of whom adopted the aristocratic particle *de* when they assumed the dress of the dandy, Baudelaire derided aristocrats as a class. They were the barbarians of modern times, he sneered—only the dandy was truly civilized. A taste for toilette and material elegance was only the outward sign of the dandy's inner grace: "These things are for the perfect Dandy only a symbol of the aristocratic superiority of his spirit."[10] But Baudelaire also stressed the price that had to be paid for such superiority. Far from being a hedonist, the dandy is suffering stress. Through unceasing effort he conceals behind an imperturbable countenance the gnawing pain of inner despair— *ennui*. This stoicism is the necessary response in a troubled, transitory epoch when a few gifted individuals, without a class, without work, without hope for society,

> but rich in native force, can conceive of the project of establishing a new type of aristocracy, . . . based on the most precious and indestructible faculties, and on celestial gifts which work and money cannot confer. Dandyism is the last burst of heroism in times of decadence; . . . a setting sun . . . without heat and full of melancholy.[11]

Although extravagant and paradoxical, these ideas were influential in creating the late nineteenth-century mystique of dandyism. Their influence should not be overrated, however. Many elegants never read Barbey, and many who dressed like dandies were unaware of Baudelaire's theory that their garments were only symbols of a spiritual aristocracy. Brummell himself, for that matter, would have been bemused by such notions. The superiority he sought was a much more practical variety, and, after reading the later French metaphysicians of dandyism, it is something of a relief to return to Brummell's down-to-earth candor about his aims. When a noblewoman inquired why he had not devoted his talents to a higher purpose, Brummell replied that "he knew human nature well, and that he had adopted the only course which could place him in a prominent light, and would enable him to separate himself from the society of the ordinary herd of men, whom he held in considerable contempt."[12]

The Democratization of Dandyism – As the theory of dandyism was evolving, so was its practice, but the two moved in contradictory directions. Of all the paradoxes of dandyism, none is more striking than the way the loftiest theories of spiritual superiority all depended on the vulgar act of shopping. Perhaps material elegance was (in Baudelaire's words) "only a symbol of the aristocratic superiority of [the dandy's] spirit," but still the material symbol had to be present for the inner superiority to be manifest. Baudelaire himself explained, "The dandy is not simply a dreamer, and his fantasy must be materialized in exterior signs. This is expensive."[13] That fatal word "expensive" is the canker at the core of the ideal. A creative genius could materialize his superiority in works of art, a religious genius in works of charity, but the only signs of the dandy's superiority were the elements of what we would now call lifestyle: dress, furnishings, possessions, and personal habits. In consequence, the dandy ideal was not only dragged down to the level of materiality—an unavoidable fall for any human ideal, since human life is corporeal as well as spiritual—but it was dragged down more specifically, and less necessarily, to the level of the marketplace. The dandy expressed himself as a consumer; dandyism was inherently tainted by commercialism.

Early dandies like Brummell removed themselves from the impurity of the marketplace by ordering everything custom-made and, even more importantly, by devising graceful ways of living beyond their incomes. Like prerevolutionary French courtiers, Beau Brummell manipulated royal prestige to obtain favors from tradesmen. This system worked well until the regent's favor was withdrawn. Then Brummell became more than ever a heavy gambler, since betting offered a way to obtain money quickly and nobly, which is to say, in a way undefiled by toil. These methods did not work forever for Brummell, but they worked well for nearly twenty years. The Comte d'Orsay devised an even longer-lasting method of living beyond his means. He sponged off the largesse of his English patrons, Lord and Lady Blessington, and when the lord died he obligingly left d'Orsay a generous legacy, thereby depriving his own children. When debts accumulated anyway, Lady Blessington feverishly wrote fashionable novels to support d'Orsay in the style to which he was accustomed. Brummell and d'Orsay both managed to enjoy that magical, indefinite credit which Baudelaire concluded was necessary for a dandy: how else could he obtain money for material elegance without stooping to a bourgeois preoccupation with earning money? Many later dandies were less clever than Brummell or d'Orsay in living beyond their means. They may have been equally convinced of their inner spiritual superiority, but their objective financial standing was decidedly inferior. Baudelaire himself is an example. After a brief flush period in the 1840s, when he spent his father's legacy in style, the poet had to attend to his dandy's toilette in a tiny dark apartment where his half-crazed mistress lay mumbling on an unmade bed. The only society to admire the results of his solicitude were the inebriated habitués of sleazy cafés.

For all its theoretical claims to spiritual grandeur, genuine dandyism was an expensive material luxury. Like other luxuries, however, this one was democratized in the later nineteenth century. The exterior trappings of the dandy could be marketed without regard to the ideal they incarnated quite as readily as aristocratic trappings could be purchased by a bourgeois without a title. In both cases the merchandise might not be the same thing as the natural distinction, but it provided a desirable approxima-tion. The genuine dandy ordered all his goods custom-made, but that did not stop manufacturers from mass-pro-ducing an array of department-store items intended to convey an aura of dandyism. Even Baudelaire sniffed at "these imitators from the petty bourgeoisie, these bargain hunters and employees who come out to strut in ready-to-wear clothes set off with cheap tinsel."[14] The pose that originated as a protest against bourgeois mediocrity and uniformity could be transformed into an offering of mass consumption.

Along with this transformation occurred another which had the same result of emphasizing the "exterior signs" of dandyism rather than its inner spirit. The dandy's audience was changing. As the century pro-gressed, so did the dissolution of the exclusive, funda-mentally courtly society where Brummell's wit and behav-ior could be observed at close range, where everyone adhered to a well-understood code of conduct and could appreciate his variations on the code. Even by the heyday of the Comte d'Orsay in the 1830s and 1840s, the decrease in homogeneity was discernible. Not only did the Comte move in both London and Paris society, but he cultivated acquaintances from a much greater variety of circles—artistic, literary, journalistic, political, scholarly, and theat-rical—than Brummell did. Furthermore, even then there were signs that dandyism might appeal to an anonymous mass public. D'Orsay notably attracted the excitement and admiration of the lower classes when he appeared in pub-lic on horseback or in his carriage, and he did not discour-age this attention. The dandy's audience changed from a highly select one to a more eclectic, less discerning, even anonymous, one. He had fewer opportunities to display his wit and manners, and when he did there was less common understanding of standards of politeness. As a result, what was democratized in dandyism was its material show far more than its intangible attributes of imperturbability, audacity, and wit. Barbey and Baudelaire might proclaim that the intellectual qualities of the dandy were far more significant than his physical appearance, but in practice just the opposite was true. The importance of appearance in defining a dandy only increased.

Indeed, the dandy's appearance became ever more striking in order to impress a more varied and distant public. Brummell could restrict himself to conventional dress done unconventionally well because his society was so alert to conventions. D'Orsay was considerably more theatrical in his style. He tended to favor the kind of ostentation Brummell had eschewed—velvets and silks, perfumed gloves, diamond jewelry, and hats with sweeping curves or extravagant height. D'Orsay's gold watch-chain was looped through a buttonhole of his waistcoat so that it seemed to curve for yards across his chest. Once d'Orsay borrowed a sailor's cloak to toss over his shoulders for warmth, and within weeks the style had become a fad in fashionable society. Other dandies too tried to find a readily identifiable stylistic "signature." Balzac carried a large cane gaudily studded with turquoises, and Baudelaire always dressed in black, an eye-catching if lugubrious outfit supposedly symbolic of an age in mourning. (Brummell would have been appalled to know that an ugly color like black would become standard male evening dress later in the century. At a dinner party he asked a fellow guest, who was attired in a black jacket and white waistcoat, why he dressed like a penguin.) By the 1880s and 1890s, would-be dandies became even more wildly unconventional in dress in order to assert their distinction from the commonplace. Robert de Montesquiou (1855–1921), the consummate French aesthete of that era, sometimes wore a white velvet suit with violets at the neck instead of a cravat. Montesquiou also favored a naïve symbolism in clothes, wearing, for example, a grey suit on a rainy day. Even when he gave up his more exotic costumes and took to wearing a conservative, beautifully draped dark grey suit, he still wore a pastel cravat.

The truth is that the reduction of dandyism to an array of material externalities left dandies with little room to maneuver. To proclaim one's individuality and distinction through attire constitutes a very limited means of displaying creativity. Oscar Wilde, Montesquiou's British counterpart (more or less) and acquaintance, lamented, "I find an ever-growing difficulty in expressing my originality through my choice of waistcoats and cravats."[15] One escape from this difficulty was to put an ever greater emphasis on individuality and distinction in other possessions, especially household furnishings. For Beau Brummell, interior decoration was not an especially important form of consumption. His London house was tastefully furnished but small. Although he entertained there with elegant dinners, much of his social life was spent in exclusive clubs like White's and Brooke's, in the drawing rooms of others, at racetracks, theatres, and opera houses. The Comte d'Orsay, on the contrary, was a passionate collector of objets d'art (Brummell had a fine collection of snuffboxes, but that was the extent of his collecting) and decorator of houses in both Paris and London.

By the late nineteenth century dandies displayed an even more marked preference for collecting and decorating, with increasingly bizarre results. The writer dandies Jules (1830–1870) and Edmond (1822–1896) de Goncourt acquired from an aunt the habit of prowling through Parisian antique shops, and in 1868 they bought a house in Auteuil which they crammed with their finds. Edmond de Goncourt is perhaps the first heir to dandyism who considered the décor of his house significant enough to write an entire book on the subject (*La Maison d'un artiste*, 1881). He and his brother loathed the furnishings of their own time and instead displayed objects from the past (e.g., the eighteenth century) or from exotic places (e.g., Japan). With the usual ambivalence of dandies in such matters, they took pride simultaneously in the elevation of their taste above the ordinary and in their role as trend-setters. Shortly before Jules died, he told his brother that they would be remembered for three things, the first being their invention of the realistic novel:

> Now, through our writings, our talking about it, through our purchases . . . who imposed the taste for eighteenth-century art and literature? Who would dare say that we weren't the ones? That's item two.
>
> Finally, the description of a Paris salon full of bits of Japanese art, published in our first novel . . . and the acquisition of bronzes and lacquers during those years . . . and the pages given over to things Japanese in [other books we wrote] . . . don't all these make of us the first propagators of this art . . . one which . . . is in the process of revolutionizing Western culture? That makes three.[16]

The home of the Goncourt brothers was more than a display case for their collections: it was a place where they could create a society of their choice. A dandy like Brummell entered a preexisting society, one whose composition and hierarchy was taken for granted. By the time of the Goncourt brothers, the dandy more often formed his own private circle, which was chosen with great rigor. The Goncourt brothers were as fastidious in their choice of society as in their choice of furnishings, and they were as fanatic about barring vulgar people from their residence as they were about excluding vulgar objects. This retreat to a domestic haven is another striking instance of the basic identity of values between dandy and bourgeois which Balzac noted in the 1830s. Not only were the smallest details of furnishing scrutinized by the Goncourts as clues to character (if admitted to a salon done in nineteenth-century style, they immediately concluded that the host or hostess was not worth knowing), but also they made their own residence into a fortress against a threatening and hostile world.

This tendency of dandies to make their homes into private retreats from ever-threatening forces of mediocrity and uniformity became more and more prevalent in the 1880s and 1890s. Again Robert de Montesquiou represents a sort of terminal case. A fanatic interior decorator and collector, his house in Neuilly was (in the words of Marcel Proust, a visitor there in 1893) "crammed with a hodge-podge of incongruous objects, old family portraits, Empire furniture, Japanese kakemonos and etchings by Whistler." One room was decorated like a snow scene, complete with a polar-bear rug, sleigh, and mica hoar frost. Even more astounding was the bathroom, designed by the glassmaker Émile Gallé, where Montesquiou's favorite flower, the hortensia (hydrangea), appeared in every conceivable material and art form, and where a glass cupboard displayed row upon row of pastel cravats.[17]

Montesquiou was as proud of his poetry as of his distinctive lifestyle, and although most of his verses did not merit his high opinion of them, he did justly describe himself in one memorable line: "I am the sovereign of the transitory." It could well serve as an epigram, or perhaps an epitaph, for the ideal of dandyism. That ideal equated personal distinction with distinction in style of consumption and sought a firm sense of identity through transitory possessions. The eccentricities of dress and decoration affected by Montesquiou are the logical result of this ideal as it adjusted to the new realities of mass consumption.

Montesquiou and his like are often labeled as part of the late nineteenth-century decadent or aesthetic movement. Accordingly, they are regarded as a sort of cultural curiosity, for this movement often expressed itself in spectacularly disordered lives or in lurid and sensational works of art, or they are dismissed as irrelevant to the truly important cultural changes taking place in that era.[18] Both views miss the real significance of late nineteenth-century decadence, which represents a desperate if confused attempt on the part of those who "can conceive of the project of establishing a new type of aristocracy" to carry

out that project after the consumer revolution had democratized luxury and offered a dream world of consumption
to the masses.

Under such conditions, when anyone could play at
aristocracy, how was it possible to identify the genuine
variety? To debate whether or not the aesthetes are true
dandies is unimportant beside this question. Clearly, late-
nineteenth-century decadents are heirs to the dandy tradition, and just as clearly someone like Montesquiou is a
very different kind of dandy from Beau Brummell. What
changed was the social context within which an individual
convinced of his own superiority had to move. Dandyism
originated as a revolt against the dominance of bourgeois
culture, but by the end of the century it also had to resist
mass culture. Our amusement and astonishment at some
of the poses of decadents or aesthetes should not blind us
to the realization that they confronted a serious dilemma
of modern society: how to secure a sense of individuality
in the face of mass merchandising.

In this confrontation, Montesquiou has a symbolic
importance that goes beyond his own accomplishments
(however they may be rated) as a poet, collector, and
clotheshorse. As the friend and loyal patron of many
gifted artists and writers—among them the Goncourt
brothers, the poet Stephen Mallarmé, the writer Joris-
Karl Huysmans, Barbey d'Aureyvilly, and the painter
James McNeill Whistler—Montesquiou became transformed in the art of others into the incarnation of latter-
day dandyism, "the thing itself," as Brummell had been
at the beginning of the tradition. Marcel Proust immortalized and to some extent revenged himself upon Montesquiou by transforming him into the tragic Baron de
Charlus in *À la recherche du temps perdu*. Mallarmé was
similarly fascinated by Montesquiou, especially when the
count befriended the poet's dying young son with a
typically outlandish gift of a cockatoo. When Mallarmé
described the extraordinary count to his friend Huysmans, Huysmans plied Mallarmé for more information

and eventually visited Montesquiou himself in order to gather material for a projected novel.

That is how Montesquiou became des Esseintes, the most memorable consumer in French literature, the hero of Huysmans' *À Rebours* ("Against the Grain," 1884), the book that became the "breviary of the Decadents."[19] Its immense popularity, or notoriety, indicates that it struck a responsive emotional chord in many readers of the time. *À Rebours* is a work of fiction which even more than the biography of an actual dandy illuminates the pleasures and perils of elitist consumption; it portrays a lonely and agonized attempt to salvage the elitist ideal in an age of mass consumption. *À Rebours* deserves scrutiny for its prophetic insight into the fate of the elitist consumer.

The Flight to Fontenay – Des Esseintes is the scion of an ancient noble line. After enduring a bleak youth in an unloving family and a strict Jesuit school, he is able and quite willing to afford himself the pleasures of women, wine, and revelry. In fact, he becomes a conventional dandy, indulging in the usual excesses of dress and décor, but he is soon worn out by the demands of the role and the tedium of having to interact with the general run of coarse humanity. He retires to a house at Fontenay, near Paris, "a hermitage combined with modern comfort, an ark on dry land and nicely warmed, whither he could fly for refuge from the incessant deluge of human folly."[20] Des Esseintes decorates the house with exquisite taste— even a bedroom outwardly resembling an austere monastic cell is outfitted with the finest materials—and fills it with his favorite books, liqueurs (stored in a cabinet built like an organ on which he composes symphonies of taste), and paintings (mostly macabre).

At the outset des Esseintes amuses himself with all these things and simultaneously begins to meditate on his boyhood, his past love affairs, his religious training, and other experiences. As memories and thoughts accumulate, he feels increasingly tense and distracted in his solitude. He tries to calm his nerves by ordering a truck-load of flowers so exotic they seem artificial; by immersing himself in harmonies of perfumes; by planning a trip to London from which he turns back at the last moment, preferring to travel in imagination instead; and by reading religious literature. All these stratagems fail to halt his nervous deterioration into hallucinations, delusions, coughing, fever, and vomiting. His *ennui* worsens until finally his doctor is summoned. The physician orders des Esseintes to leave the hermetic existence of Fontenay and "to return to Paris and take part again in the common life of men."[21]

Only fear of an agonizing death impels des Esseintes to follow these orders. As he sits listening to the movers packing his belongings, he ponders the world he must reenter. He knows no compatible person with whom to socialize; the religious faith he craves is always aborted by doubts arising from logic and common sense; the bourgeoisie is triumphantly disgusting, the old aristocracy a rotten corpse; and even the consoling arguments of Schopenhauerian pessimism are powerless to comfort him:

> Des Esseintes dropped into a chair, in despair. "In two days more I shall be in Paris," he exclaimed; "well, all is over; like a flowing tide, the waves of human mediocrity rise to the heavens and they will engulf my last refuge; I am opening the sluice-gates myself, in spite of myself. Ah; but my courage fails me, and my heart is sick within me!—Lord, take pity on the Christian who doubts, on the skeptic who would believe, on the galley-slave of life who puts out to sea alone, in the darkness of night, beneath a firmament illumined no longer by the consoling beacon-fires of the ancient hope."[22]

As with any novel of merit, a plot outline does not begin to do justice to the richness of the work. In it comedy and irony are mingled in a texture of immense pathos which reaches its climax in the final paragraph, quoted above. What Huysmans' book conveys most powerfully are not events, of which the novel is largely bare, but the visions of des Esseintes's dream house at Fontenay and of the hero's anguished inability either to stay or to leave. If des Esseintes is a consumer, he is an heroic one. For all his perversities and eccentricities, in the final scene where he abandons Fontenay he is a profoundly moving figure. With courage and determination he has single-handedly tried to resist an unauthentic market and to create his own ideal of consumption. As a tragic hero he fails; he goes down struggling against his fate, fully aware of the defeat of his ideal but still defiant.

Des Esseintes is also, at the end, utterly isolated. Huysmans originally titled the novel *Seul* ("Alone"), for trying to live "against the grain" is a lonely endeavor. Solitude had always been a fundamental condition of the dandy, who communicated indirectly through objects rather than directly through emotional expression. Des Esseintes finds even this limited communication intolerable. He so loathes the "half-closed lids and . . . magisterial air" of respectable bourgeois, the "meagre brains of . . . tradesmen," and, most of all, the boastfulness of the "new types of self-made men" that the very sight of these monstrous creatures fills him with horror.[23] So he takes dandyism one last step, to Fontenay, where he can interact only with objects and can dispense with human contact altogether. There, in the universe of matter, unlike that of humanity, he can be king. Des Esseintes is both dandy and audience, both host and guest in this most exclusive of salons. With him, elitism turns into solipsism.

The Indictment of Modern Consumption – Des Esseintes is driven to this extremity by his conviction that in modern society the individual is inevitably contaminated by a form of consumerism that would be ridiculous were it not so vile. While the dandy tradition as a whole scorns the bourgeois style of life, never is the indictment so savagely expressed as in *À Rebours*. Des Esseintes blasts the bourgeois as crude, pushy show-offs, devoid of genuine taste or manners, capable only of a false pride based on ownership of status items such as diamonds, Oriental rugs, or fancy reception rooms. The only pleasure they derive from possession, aside from a shallow and transitory amusement at trivial follies, is the purely exterior pleasure of owning an indication of high social standing. But status is never secure and amusement does not last, so the bourgeois are caught up in a ludicrous scramble for goods they cannot afford.

Des Esseintes muses on this futile and pathetic consumerism in his splendid isolation at Fontenay. He recalls his friend d'Argunande, whom he sadistically urged to marry after learning that this friend's fiancée wanted to move into a chic new Parisian apartment house with a circular floor plan. The newlyweds ordered an entire suite of round furniture to be made for their new home, although they could ill afford the expense. The wife found herself short of money for clothes and prevailed upon her husband to move to a cheaper apartment built in the ordinary fashion. There the round furniture would not touch the walls and the shoddily made drawers began to warp, but there was no money to replace or repair them. The couple quarreled ever more bitterly over these petty irritations, while the maid took advantage of their distraction to raid the cashbox. The marriage soon broke up, to des Esseintes's immense satisfaction.

After recalling this parable of bourgeois woe, des Esseintes begins to think of other examples of the human misery caused by uncontrolled material desires, this time among the popular classes. He realizes that the bourgeois style of consumption is spreading rapidly through the masses like a loathsome infection. The trains running from Paris to Fontenay are hauling hordes of Sunday tourists; Oriental rugs are being sold at discount prices to any tradesman willing to buy them; even luxuries like jewels and flowers, at least the cheaper varieties, are being purchased by the common herd. In short, the masses are being seduced by a relentless desire to consume which will lead them to the same vexations and woe now afflicting the bourgeoisie.

In this connection des Esseintes recalls another anecdote. One day he happened upon a sixteen-year-old street urchin, Auguste Langlois, whom he took to a brothel to let Auguste have his choice of the women. There des Esseintes explained to the madam:

> I am simply trying to train a murderer. Now just follow my argument. This boy is virgin and has reached the age when the blood begins to boil; he might, of course, run after the girls of his neighborhood, and still remain an honest lad while enjoying his bit of amusement; in fact, have his little share of the monotonous happiness open to the poor. But by bringing him here and plunging him into a luxury of which he had never even suspected the existence, I shall make him acquire the habit of pleasures which his means forbid his enjoying; . . . well, at the end of three months, I shall stop the little allowance I am going to pay you in advance for the kindness you show him. Then he will take to thieving to pay for his visits here . . .
>
> If worst comes to worst, he will, I hope, one fine day kill a gentleman who turns up at just the wrong moment as [Langlois] is breaking open his office; then my object will be attained, for I shall have contributed, so far as I could, to creating a scoundrel, one more enemy for the odious society that wrings so heavy a ransom from us all.[24]

In recalling this episode, des Esseintes is annoyed that he has never read in the newspapers that Langlois had gotten into trouble with the police. "It would be a thousand pities," he muses,

> for, by acting in this way, I had really been putting into practice the parable of lay instruction, the allegory of popular education, which, instead of definitely and mercifully putting out the wretched creatures' eyes, tries its hardest to force them wide open that they may see all about them other lots unearned by any merit but more benign, pleasures keener and more brightly gilded, and therefore more desirable and harder to come by.
>
> . . . The more we endeavour to polish the intelligence and refine the nervous system of the poor and unfortu-

nate, the more we shall be developing the seeds of moral
suffering and social hatred.[25]

Huysmans here denounces the very democratization
of luxury which d'Avenel praises as the glory of the
nineteenth century. Despite certain reservations, d'Avenel anticipates that the spread of material enjoyments will
lead to more personal happiness and social harmony—
exactly the opposite conclusion from des Esseintes's grim
prophecy that the phenomenon will cultivate "moral suffering and social hatred."

The difference in tone is as significant as their difference in opinion. While d'Avenel gracefully reflects upon
moral issues in the voice of an historian and social observer, Huysmans, through the voice of des Esseintes,
thunders like an Old Testament prophet. This contrast in
mood is most evident in their consideration of the exploitation of Catholicism in peddling merchandise to the
masses. D'Avenel tells how a small-town merchant in
Normandy made a fortune selling Benedictine liqueur
after his well-publicized but dubiously authentic "discovery" of a medieval recipe in a monastery there. The
shopkeeper subsequently used the monastic name to en-
dow the product with religious and historical associations.
D'Avenel recounts all this chicanery with great flair and an
air of detached amusement. Des Esseintes is not amused
by this kind of exploitation. On the contrary, he is out-
raged that the Church, which in the past had cultivated art
and beauty for their own sakes, is being invaded by the
market like all the rest of society. In his opinion the
Benedictine bottle is a lie because its dark green form, so
medieval and liturgical in appearance, deceitfully dis-
guises a liqueur "startlingly modern and feminine." Mon-
asteries have since turned to producing chocolates and
medicines as well, while at the Mass itself magnificent
plainsongs have been discarded for modern, pretentious
works borrowed from Italian operas, "due partly to greed
for offerings, partly to a supposed attraction the music

exercised on the faithful." The sanctuary itself has become another place of amusement to attract consumers, a place where women can parade their fine clothes and quiver with emotion at hearing opera tunes.[26] Because des Esseintes had hoped that the Church would be an outpost against the rage to consume which devours modern society, his awareness that this last bulwark has fallen is bitter and despairing. The spreading flood of mediocrity that drowns quality in a tide of mass-produced goods is lapping at the very communion rails: shameless dealers now manufacture communion hosts from cheap potato flour rather than from fine wheat flour. No wonder faith is tottering, des Esseintes mutters, when one constantly faces the prospect of being duped, even at the communion table. Nothing is sacred anymore. Commerce has profaned everything. This meditation comes just before des Esseintes's final tortured prayer to a God whose existence he doubts as he is submerged under the foul flood rising to the dark and silent heavens.

Devising an Alternative – As an indictment of the duplicity, greed, folly, and shamelessness of modern consumption, *À Rebours* is without equal in imaginative literature. That fact alone accounts for much of its popularity. The book powerfully articulates the disgust for both the bourgeoisie and the masses prevalent in French literary circles, imbued as they were with the dandy tradition. But the novel is far more than a negative indictment. It also portrays des Esseintes's attempt to create an authentic style of consumption uncontaminated by the marketplace. This aspect of the novel must also have contributed to its popularity both in France and abroad, for a considerable number of readers were so smitten by des Esseintes's fictional lifestyle that they tried to copy it.

The starting point of des Esseintes's experiment in lifestyle is his complete isolation from the mass market. There can be no compromise with the flood of mass consumption, no dabbling a toe in its waters; the only choice is to seek shelter in an "ark," like Fontenay, which rides on the waters while the wicked are drowned. Des Esseintes's withdrawal is so radical that he tries to cut himself off from nature as well as from human society. Since consumption is both an organic and a social act, serving both physical survival and social status, to find liberation des Esseintes tries to eliminate the demands of the body as well as those of society, even though he cannot totally deny his organic needs. In particular, he keeps his meals as simple as possible, and even experiments with enemas to avoid eating altogether. At the same time he allows himself the wildest extravagances when it comes to satisfying spiritual and intellectual needs. His life at Fontenay is thus a curious blend of the ascetic and the luxurious. Des Esseintes minimizes consumption that satisfies desires of the body and of social status in order to attain more freedom in consumption that satisfies his cravings for the ideal. His ambivalence is so extreme as to be pathological: des Esseintes at once loves and hates to consume.

Having reduced what he considers base needs to the minimum, des Esseintes proceeds to surround himself with objects that serve what he considers higher needs. He chooses each item at Fontenay with great care so that it will respond to his memories, whims, and fantasies. Instead of collecting things to impress others, he collects them to stimulate his personal vision. Ultimately it is the vision, not the item, that counts. Des Esseintes meditates at length on the nature of the active interaction of object and imagination which for him makes possible the vision of the ideal. His most extended meditation on this mysterious interaction comes when he is sitting in his dining room, which he has constructed to resemble a ship's cabin, complete with beamed ceiling, portholes, bulkheads, plank floors, steamship schedules on the walls, nautical instruments and charts on the tables, chairs and anchors heaped in a corner, even a tarry odor throughout. Between the wall of this cabin and the original wall of the house he has placed a huge aquarium filled with schools of mechanical fish which "swim" behind the portholes. Des Esseintes delights in the thought that with the help of this meticulously constructed environment, his mind has been freed from sordid reality to rise to a realm of perfect self-sufficiency:

> The whole secret is to know how to set about it, to be able to concentrate the mind on a single point, to attain a sufficient degree of self-abstraction to produce the necessary hallucination and so to substitute the vision of the reality for the reality itself.
>
> To tell the truth, artifice was in des Esseintes's philosophy the distinctive mark of human genius.[27]

Since the glimpse of the ideal is far more significant than the material means by which that glimpse is attained, des Esseintes remains quite unattached to specific possessions. When his exotic flowers wilt and his jewel-encrusted tortoise dies, he feels no regret for the investment they represent. They have served their purpose in stimulating his imagination, and he discards them just as he redecorates a room or throws out a book that no longer produces "the necessary hallucination." He does not value things for their durability but consumes them the way others consume drugs or alcohol. In fact, des Esseintes admits,

> he had resorted to opium and hashish in order to see visions, but the only result had been to bring on vomiting and intense nervous disturbances; he had been obliged to give up their use and without the help of these coarse excitants to ask his brain of itself alone to bear him far away from everyday life into the region of dreams.[28]

This peculiar ascetic demonstrates a sort of perverse Puritan self-reliance. He insists on realizing his fantasies through imagination alone rather than relying on "coarse excitants" that require no active participation on his part.

Des Esseintes's mode of consumption, exotic and extreme though it may be, suggests an ethical alternative to that of the masses and the bourgeoisie. He interacts imaginatively with things rather than surrounding himself passively with them; he selects each item to respond to his personal spiritual needs rather than those of social status or physical maintenance; he remains unattached to particular objects instead of allowing himself to become weighted down by them. Above all, des Esseintes rises above crabbed notions of thrift and utility to put matter at the service of an ideal, or, to put it another way, he rejects trivial notions of utility for a much grander definition of it. He values things for the purpose they serve, to be sure, but he always bears in mind that the purpose should involve spiritual vision rather than petty amusements, creature comforts, or social status.

The Deception of the Alternative – But is des Esseintes's style as a consumer a genuine alternative or only a fraudulent one? Despite his desperate attempts to exclude the values of the marketplace from Fontenay, they remain potent, acting like invisible magnetic poles casting a field of force over his life, relentlessly pulling and distorting all his feelings and choices. The emotional energy he expends in resisting the market is testimony to its power. Des Esseintes's very attempts to resist modern consumption, heroic as they may be, are themselves shaped by it. This is not to conclude that the decadents merely imitated bourgeois or popular patterns on a more exotic level.[29] Des Esseintes's repudiation of those patterns is genuine, and so is his effort to forge an alternative. But when mass consumption is a phenomenon so pervasive that his own experiment is necessarily shaped to a great extent in opposition to it, the result is a relationship in which opposition and imitation, scorn and mimicry of the thing scorned, are all entangled.

The complexity of this relationship is evident when des Esseintes decides on furnishings for Fontenay. Along with the positive criterion of stimulation of his imagination, however, functions a negative one—the refusal to accept any object that has become a popular item of consumption. It is the second standard which ultimately takes precedence over the first. Des Esseintes may admire the "sacerdotal character" of the amethyst, but he refuses to own one because it is "spoiled by its frequent use to ornament the red ears and bulbous hands of butchers' wives who are eager to bedeck themselves with genuine and heavy jewels at a modest cost."[30] Even worse, des Esseintes has to become a closet admirer of Rembrandt, surveying his collection of that painter's works only on the sly, now that the artist has become so popular:

> Just as the finest air in the world is vulgarized beyond all endurance once the public has taken to humming it and the street organs to playing it, so the work of art that has appealed to sham connoisseurs, that is admired by the uncritical, that is not content to rouse the enthusiasm of only a chosen few, becomes for this very reason, in the eyes of the elect, a thing polluted, commonplace, almost repulsive.
>
> This diffusion of appreciation among the common herd was in fact one of the sorest trials of his life; unaccountable triumphs had for ever spoiled his enjoyment of pictures and books he had once held dear.[31]

In the final analysis, des Esseintes himself is unable to evaluate objects independently of their market value. In a reverse way his mode of consumption is just as dependent on the mass market, just as devoid of individual integrity, as that of the butchers' wives. As soon as an item becomes available to the "common herd," he rejects it, irrespective of its intrinsic merits. Such is the secret bondage of the supposedly independent snob. The market des Esseintes has tried to flee invades even his hermitage at Fontenay, forcing him to reject amethysts and Rembrandts and a host of other objects.

The frightening possibility is that the "diffusion of appreciation" that des Esseintes laments and d'Avenel lauds has made a genuinely independent assessment impossible. Every object, from jewelry to painting, has a marketplace evaluation. Whether one buys from a herd instinct to own what is popular or from an elitist instinct to own what is unique and rare, the choice is still dictated by market value rather than by personal assessment, or, rather, personal assessment is so entangled with market assessment that the consumer can never be entirely sure whether he genuinely wants something as an individual or whether he wants the status (whether elitist or conformist) that it confers. The debasement of objects is not physical, for the paintings of Rembrandt remain unscathed in a material sense, just as a melody is made up of the same written notes whether it is played by a symphony orchestra or whistled in the streets. The debasement is a spiritual one on the part of the consumer, who can no longer be sure of his own good faith. Someone like des Esseintes can no longer admire certain paintings or melodies without feeling himself classed with boors who admire these things only to show an appearance of culture.

The concept of class, traditionally associated with a person's relationship to the means of production, invades the realm of consumption in *À Rebours*. Des Esseintes's world is rigidly class-structured, but he classifies people by what they consume rather than by what they produce. He frantically resists being declassed from one of the "chosen few" to one of the "common herd," and he is convinced that this would happen were he to handle objects of popular consumption. His sensitivity in this regard is so extreme that it could be called a taboo. For him the mass market endows its objects with a power to defile that borders on the magical. Huysmans' work of fiction confirms d'Avenel's sociological analysis that in modern times the wealthy are engaged in a "furious search for the 'unique'" because

> Extreme superiority of income no longer gives either "comforts" or even "beauties" but only rarities. It does not give the most beautiful things, but only the most expensive . . . Modern luxury has "rarity" for its objective, *because it cannot have any others*.[32]

No one, no matter how rich, is above the mass market. The market restricts the rich to purchasing what is non-reproduction, non-imitation, un-common, or un-usual. Just as objects can no longer be judged according to intrinsic value independent of symbolic market qualities, money no longer has an inherent connection with usefulness, comfort, or beauty.

For the elite this situation presents practical problems as well as philosophical ones. Des Esseintes, for example, can hardly keep ahead of the ever-encroaching mass market, which keeps turning rarities into commonplaces as consumers ransack the world for new status symbols. First amethysts became popular, then diamonds, and while des Esseintes can still permit himself to collect sapphires, they may well be the next gem to become fashionable. When Rembrandt achieves a disgusting popularity, des Esseintes begins to collect avant-garde painters like Odilon Redon, but the day will soon arrive when the bourgeoisie begins to snap up avant-garde works! Des Esseintes has to retreat from one luxury item to another in the face of the ever-advancing forces of commerce. The elitist consumer never finds a resting place, never attains an equilibrium, but must keep buying and discarding, picking up and dropping items, perpetually on the move to keep one jump ahead of the common herd. He therefore shares the fate of the mass consumer, who, as d'Avenel pointed out, finds that illusions of wealth are always disappearing as once-unusual objects are sold in every department store and therefore lose their capacity to convey the aura of wealth. Both types of consumers are always on the run, because for both the image of self is closely tied to possessions.

It is in such ways that *À Rebours* illuminates as well as condemns modern consumption. Fontenay's relation to modern society is like that of the expositions: it is a distorting mirror which throws back images at once recognizable and strange, with certain angles and contours exaggerated. In fact, des Esseintes constructs a sort of private exposition at Fontenay. Dreams of the Middle

Ages, of monastic life, of exotic voyages, of erotic pleasures—such fantasies make up the "exhibits" of his
home, which he tours in solitude in order to fend off
sordid reality. Des Esseintes would not mingle with the
crowd in the Rue du Caire, but he indulges in similar
exotic and erotic dreams by gazing at a favorite painting of
Salome, and his underwater dining room serves the same
purpose as the Maréorama described by Corday. Des
Esseintes is indeed as fascinated by gadgetry as the exposition crowds: he tinkers not only with mechanical fish but
also with a "liqueur organ" and perfume devices.

Both the fictional Fontenay and the actual expositions
force us to redefine modern economic life, so often described by adjectives like "utilitarian," "work-oriented,"
"rationalistic," and "thrifty." These distorting mirrors
suggest that if these terms are true, they are true only so
partially as to be false. French bourgeois, and to an increasingly great extent the popular classes as well, appear
to have pursued a dream world of fantasy and evasion
through consumption. When des Esseintes describes his
aim as substituting "the vision of the reality for the reality
itself" or as transporting himself "far away from everyday
life into the region of dreams," he could be defining with
equal accuracy a significant aspect of mainstream culture,
that aspect called here the dream world of the consumer.
When we look closely at the efforts of Huysmans' fictional
hero to salvage the dandy ideal, we see that the elitist
mode of consumption is by no means wholly separate
from and contrary to the bourgeois and mass modes.

Nevertheless, the model of a mainstream culture and a
minority "counterculture" flowing in opposite directions
has proved appealing to modern thinkers. The model is
often expressed in sweeping theories that describe modern society in terms of an opposition between "bohemian"
and "bourgeois," or, to use sociological jargon, between a
"cultural principle of self-gratification" and an "economic
principle of efficiency."[33] In the first place, as des Esseintes's indictment of mass consumption makes clear, the

prevailing mode of consumption is by no means based on "bourgeois" values of efficiency, thrift, and the like, but, rather, on amusements and status-seeking, which may be termed forms of "self-gratification." In the second place, even when des Esseintes takes extreme measures to create a bohemian culture in opposition to prevailing norms, he finds that genuine independence is unattainable. We are all submerged in the same "flowing tide . . . of human mediocrity."

Similarities of Decadent and Mass Consumption – Des Esseintes is a complex hero precisely because he understands his kinship with what he despises. This awareness of the similarity between his thirst for vision and that of the "common herd" saves him from being a one-dimensional mouthpiece for elitist diatribes against the masses. In one of his "mental excursions,"[34] he recalls how he visited vulgar Left Bank cafés in Paris:

> He realized the meaning of these cafés, saw that they corresponded to the state of mind and imagination of a whole generation; he gathered from them material for a synthesis of the period.
> Indeed, the symptoms were plain and unmistakable; the legalized brothel was disappearing, and each time one of them closed its doors, a beer-tavern opened.
> This diminution of official prostitution, organized for the satisfaction of clandestine amours, was evidently to be accounted for by the incomprehensible illusions men indulge in from the carnal standpoint.
> Monstrous as this might seem, the fact was that the beer-tavern satisfied an ideal.[35]

Despite modern "utilitarian tendencies," des Esseintes concludes, today's youth "reserved, deep down in its heart, an old-fashioned flower of sentiment, a vague, half-decayed ideal of love."[36] Therefore young men would not go into a legal brothel to strike an honest bargain there, but insisted on courting tavern waitresses who were less attractive than most prostitutes and who demanded much time and money before submitting:

> Great God! des Esseintes could not help exclaiming, what simpletons these fools must be who flutter around beer-halls, for, to say nothing of their ridiculous self-deception, they . . . ignore the danger they run from the low-class, highly suspicious quality of the goods supplied, to say nothing of the money spent in drinks, all priced before-hand by the landlady, to forget the time wasted in waiting for the delivery of the commodity.[37]

This may be "ridiculous self-deception," but it still repre-sents a striving toward an ideal of love. In their own way these youths too take a "mental excursion," and the route they choose to achieve a "semblance of victory" in love is no more absurd than that of des Esseintes himself. At one point he recalls how he increased his pleasure in lovemak-ing by taking to bed a ventriloquist who pretended that another of her lovers was shouting furiously outside the bedroom door.[38]

The identity between Fontenay and working-class cafés becomes even plainer when we consider that in both cases pleasurable illusions depend basically upon self-deception, ridiculous or not. Des Esseintes prides himself on achieving his visions through self-deception, or, as he puts it, through a "clever system of adulteration" trans-ferred "into the world of the intellect" so that he may "enjoy false, fictitious pleasures every whit as good as the true."[39] With a little imagination, while in seclusion at Fontenay he can pretend he is on a trip to London or sailing on the high seas, or he can pretend he is in another time and take a mental excursion to antiquity or to the Middle Ages. What is more, des Esseintes recognizes that the delusions he enjoys are part of a much broader social pattern. One November day, he recalls, as he lounged in an apartment at Pantin, enjoying the smell of fresh flowers and the heat of the stove, he imagined he was on the Riviera in the springtime:

"Now seeing that, in these times of ours, there is no single thing really genuine to be found; seeing that the wine we drink and the liberty we acclaim are equally adulterate and derisory; considering how remarkable a dose of credulity it takes to suppose the governing classes to deserve respect and the lower to be worthy either of relief or commiseration, it appears to me," concluded des Esseintes, "neither more absurd nor more insane to demand of my neighbor a sum total of illusion barely equal to that he expends every day in his life for quite idiotic objects, that he may successfully persuade himself that the town of Pantin is an artificial Nice, a factitious Menton."[40]

As des Esseintes's stay at Fontenay lengthens, this mildly amused cynicism darkens into bitter pessimism. By the time he considers how cafés are replacing brothels, he sees the relations between young men and tavern girls as one link in a vast chain of deceit:

Workmen toiled, families cheated one another in the name of trade, all to let themselves be swindled out of money by their sons, who in their turn allowed themselves to be plundered by these women, who were in the last resort drained dry by their fancy lovers.

From end to end of Paris, east to west and north to south, it was one unbroken chain of petty trickeries, a series of organized thefts continually repeated one after another.[41]

Des Esseintes himself is part of the chain. He would no doubt argue that the fantasy of being on the Riviera is worthwhile, not idiotic, and that at least he is out to deceive himself rather than others. Still, his exaltation of deceit in his own life makes it difficult for him legitimately to condemn the deceits of others, or to claim that the pleasures they obtain from self-deception are any more ridiculous than his own. His rage against commercialism is always being frustrated because he clings to the principle of deception for himself but finds it disgusting when practiced on the open market.

This dilemma becomes most painful in his last hours at

Fontenay. Then des Esseintes becomes infuriated when he thinks how the Church has been invaded by commerce, which dilutes the wine of the Eucharist with alcohol and adulterates the hosts with potato flour. The days are gone forever, he mourns,

> when, by the custom of Cluny, three priests or three deacons, fasting, clad in alb and amice, after washing their face and fingers, sorted out the wheat grain by grain, crushed it in a hand-mill, kneaded the dough with cold spring-water and baked it themselves over a clear fire, singing psalms all the while![42]

But mixed with his nostalgia for natural whole-grain goodness is his recognition that the replacement of fine handmade meal by cheap potato flour cannot really interfere with the holy mystery of Communion. Des Esseintes has to mock theologians who suggest that God may refuse to be made flesh in potato meal (the case of rye meal, he notes sarcastically, being in doubt): "how to accept an omnipotence that is hindered by a pinch of potato meal or a drop of alcohol?"[43] The whole concept of the Eucharist relies on mental adulteration, on the substitution of ordinary goods for precious ones in short supply, while the consumer willingly deceives himself into accepting the imitation instead of the genuine article. Far from being the last outpost against the counterfeit, the holiest sacrament of the Church depends on an exalted form of dupery.

By mocking the worried theologians, des Esseintes is acknowledging that the validity of the sacrament depends on the quality of faith in the consumer, not on the quality of the product used to stimulate the divine vision. Yet he remains instinctively disgusted by the commercial deception involved. What can he say when the highest mysteries of faith and the sleaziest business practices seem based on the same principle of duplicity? Des Esseintes is in a bind. He is appalled by the adulterations of the market, yet indulges in his own mental ones; he insists on the finest quality for his possessions, yet if imagination be omnipotent it can transform cheap products as well as rare ones; he indulges in a private unbroken chain of petty trickeries to evade the unbroken chain running through an intolerable society. He cannot effectively use his dream world to criticize another dream world.

The Collapse of the Dream World—À Rebours simultaneously makes a powerful case for the seductiveness of a dream world—the fascination of artifice, the beauty of the imagination, the pleasure of self-deception, the flattering sense of initiation into mysteries, the thrill of questing for an ideal—while providing an even stronger case that the way of illusion is ultimately self-destructive. The dream is lovely, but the dreamer must awaken. The eventual failure of des Esseintes's experiment in consumption involves more than his personal eccentricities or his weak digestive system: failure is inherent in the attempt to satisfy the cravings of the spirit through matter. Just as his self-deceptions reflect a larger pattern of deceit running through society, so does the collapse of his dream world suggest intrinsic weaknesses in the larger universe of fantasy-made-merchandise outside Fontenay. Therefore it is well worth considering the causes of the fall.

At the outset, des Esseintes's dream world appears far more secure than most—because he is rich. All the particular illusions of Fontenay are based on the premise of one grand illusion, that of an unlimited income from unspecified sources which enables des Esseintes to "live aristocratically" (which is to say, in leisure) and to spend lavishly. He can afford sapphires rather than amethysts, exotic plants rather than lowly geraniums, and what is more, he can spurn mass-produced items in order to buy the time of servants, physicians, bookmakers, in fact a whole army of skilled and expensive labor. All des Esseintes's reveries are based on this reverie of limitless wealth or at least the "unlimited credit" which Baudelaire deemed necessary for any genuine dandy. Instead of excoriating common people for their sordid pleasures, des

Esseintes might, rather, praise their imaginative capacity for tailoring dreams from the unpromising fabric of mass-produced goods, restricted budgets, and endless bills. Their dreams seek to evade this cramped reality, but the reality of money does not intrude at Fontenay. There the flow of income is magical in its inexhaustible reliability, and all des Esseintes's other dreams ride on that flood.

But his dream existence collapses anyway, from internal causes rather than external ones. The most obvious source of its disintegration is des Esseintes's own mortality, the deterioration of his health, which eventually causes him to return to Paris by his doctor's orders. He tries to escape the bonds of both society and nature, but those of the latter at least prove inescapable. Des Esseintes's own material being marks the point at which deception halts and reality asserts itself. The jewel-encrusted tortoise and the artificial-looking hothouse plants are obvious parables of his own condition, for these organisms die when nature at last rebels against des Esseintes's attempts to treat life as artifice. In the same way he treats himself as a work of art only to have nature rebel against the outrages he commits against her.

Even if des Esseintes had taken better care of his health, however, his experiment would have failed. The inherent flaw in the dream world is as much psychic as organic. His attempt to slip the bonds of society is no more successful than his attempt to escape the dictates of nature. Gradually the pleasures of privacy mutate into the sufferings of solitude. The society of matter, which des Esseintes substitutes for human society because it can be controlled more perfectly, gradually gets out of control too. Things begin to function independently of his will. Illusion does not stay within its assigned limits but spills over to spread like another foul flood. Memory does not rejuvenate or create, but threatens and destroys. He samples bonbons in order to call up dreamy half-remembered amorous encounters, but instead the sweets "tear the veils from before his eyes and show him the bodily reality, in all its brutal force and urgency."[44] He experiments with perfumes in order to escape a hallucinatory odor of frangipane, but it returns stronger than ever, causing him to faint. He is seized by a morbid craving for a white pasty cheese and onion on bread and begins to hear noises of running water, buzzing wasps, and ringing bells.

When the universe of objects closes in oppressively, Fontenay becomes not a luxurious refuge but a prison or asylum. Having invested objects with great potency, des Esseintes discovers that they can generate terrifying visions as well as enticing ones. When he orders exotic plants to stimulate his imagination, they only induce a frightening nightmare from which he awakens gasping, "Thank God, thank God! it is only a dream."[45] He consumes objects as others consume drugs, and so he risks a "bad trip." In his isolation distinctions among dream, nightmare, and reality become confused, swirling around in his head until their separate identities disappear. By the time des Esseintes realizes that he is returning to Paris, he groans, "Ah! to think that all this is not a dream! to think that I am about to go back into the degraded and slavish mob of the century!"[46]

At this point, he awakens from his dream world, not to daylight reality but (to borrow an expression from Joseph Conrad's *Heart of Darkness*) to a "choice of nightmares."[47] He is roused from a dream-turned-nightmare of animate objects to a reality-nightmare of a loathsome society. In both cases he is utterly alone with the horror. The solitude of dream has been transmuted into the solitude of nightmare. This psychic disintegration testifies that the mind has its imperatives just as the body does, that des Esseintes can no more evade the need for human contact than he can escape the need to eat.

Des Esseintes retreats to Fontenay with the conviction that his mind is so far above that of the common herd that he should not have to tolerate contact with his inferiors. By the end of his sojourn, he has regressed to an animistic universe in which objects overwhelm the senses and reason itself, a state of mind which could be considered primitive rather than superior. Savages and children, those other "barbarians," may be envied for the fertility of their imaginations, but the reverse side of this capacity is that savages live in terror of angry gods and children are susceptible to nightmares. The sinister accompanies the splendid in an animistic universe of unpredictable objects, where both wishes and fears take shape in vivid and vital forms. The most obvious name for this psychic state, in its extreme form, is madness—for what else is madness but living alone with one's illusions, whether terrifying or pleasurable? The blurring of fantasy and reality in the dream world of the consumer often seems too benign to be called insane. But in the fictional case of des Esseintes, the evolution from harmless self-deception to psychic disintegration forces us to admit that madness is indeed the ultimate result of the confusion of dream and reality. It was, after all, Brummell's fate.

In the Marxist tradition, where individual psychology is always considered in relation to social and economic phenomena, the increasingly animistic universe of des Esseintes could be seen as an example of commodity fetishism, the displacement of life from people to objects discussed by Karl Marx in the first chapter of *Capital,* or, "to use the term nearly unanimously adopted in Marxist literature since the writings of Lukács . . . [of] reification."[48] Although it would be a reductionist fallacy to read *À Rebours* only as a novel illustrating the process of reification, it would be even more of a mistake to ignore a concept which links des Esseintes's private hell with the social hell he desperately wants to escape. The concept of reification expands upon but does not contradict other interpretations already mentioned. As a general process, it may be seen as an element of what Elias calls "the civilizing process." Marx's term *commodity fetishism* suggests the primitive element in the mind of a consumer like des Esseintes, who chooses his possessions according to a strict taboo on the ordinary. In its description of how objects take on a life of their own, the concept of reification posits a kind of social, as opposed to purely personal, insanity. The roots of that shared madness lie in the potency and mystery that objects assume once they are placed on the market, qualities which have nothing to do with their authentic function or value. This transfer of vitality is plainly evident in *À Rebours* as des Esseintes becomes progressively unstable and passive while the goods at Fontenay become ever more active and potent. The transfer comes about because des Esseintes replaces relationships with nature or with people by relationships with things—specifically, with market items. In fleeing to Fontenay he has not escaped the grip of the market, for it continues to dictate its values to him. The transfer of value-making from human personality to goods, the transformation of values into qualities of things rather than human choices, is the ultimate fantasy, a "phantasmagoric illusion."[49] The elitist mocks the delusions of the bourgeoisie and popular classes, but in the end he submits to the most engulfing delusion of all.

The Need for Other Alternatives – The experiment in lifestyle portrayed in *À Rebours* may have ended in tragedy, but this fact did not at all deter many contemporary readers from imitating that experiment. Since then, the appeal of elitist consumption has continued to prove more powerful than any warnings about its futility. Mania for personalized objects, individualized collections, or distinctive accessories is familiar today. Although elitist consumers try to keep one step ahead of the mass market, the market itself has incorporated the appeal to elitism. Adjectives like *finesse, quality, grace,* and *style* have become so hackneyed in advertising language that it is hard to believe that these words ever had genuine meaning or that they could have described the behavior of living people rather than static attributes of objects.

The late nineteenth-century literature of decadence explores the dilemmas of the neo-aristocrat in a democratic age, and in particular the neo-aristocrat who tries to assert his superiority through an unusual or even perverse lifestyle. Like dandyism earlier in the nineteenth century, decadence is at once residual and emergent. It depends upon literary conventions, images, and vocabulary inherited from Romantic writers dating back (in France) to the 1830s, and includes themes even from late Roman times. A more thorough analysis of *À Rebours* might demonstrate how it incorporates such literary and cultural traditions in its response to contemporary social changes; here, the emergent aspect of decadence has been stressed.

It was with Baudelaire, a poet concerned above all with developing an idiom and sensibility expressive of modern life, that dandyism began to mutate into decadence. His disciples were equally conscious of their historical role in reworking old language and ideas to express unprecedented experiences. In a famous preface to the first posthumous edition (1868) of Baudelaire's *Fleurs du mal* ("Flowers of Evil," 1857)—a preface which served as the first manifesto of decadence—Théophile Gautier proclaimed that decadence represented the "necessary and inevitable idiom of peoples and civilizations in which factitious life has replaced natural life and developed unknown wants in men."[50] Anatole Baju expressed a similar urge in his manifesto of 1886, which appeared in the first issue of the journal *Le Décadent littéraire et artistique,* which he founded and edited: "[E]verything undergoes an ineluctable transformation. . . . To new needs correspond new ideas. . . . Therefore the necessity of creating unheard-of words to express such a complexity of sentiments and of physiological sensations."[51] This concern with "new needs" and "unknown wants," this conviction of a general transformation to a "factitious life," suggests that in their own way the decadents were responding to the consumer society emerging in those decades. They played the role of social prophets, and while they were often silly and awkward, often trapped by outworn conventions and attitudes, their efforts to deal with the emerging society remain highly relevant.

Of more interest at the time was the question of where things could go after decadence. Decadence posed a problem it could not resolve: the literary tradition which produced *À Rebours* was one of transition, not of culmination. Huysmans demonstrates the futility of an isolated effort to escape the mass market, the impossibility of wholly autonomous consumption cut off from the rest of society, the spurious nature of pride in being above the ordinary run of mankind, the curse of the kind of superiority which expresses itself in an eccentric and finally mad isolation. Although *À Rebours* may show vividly that elitist consumerism does not compensate for the lack of satisfactory social relations, it does not show what can do so. Huysmans is too honest to retract or soften des Esseintes's condemnation of that foul flood of modern commerce which drove him to Fontenay in the first place. The hero is left suspended between nightmares. At the end des Esseintes is reminiscent of the aging, sick Louis XIV, pacing the halls of his splendid palace, stoically facing the ruin of a system of consumption he created so carefully and yet which proved so futile. Outside the walls of each carefully created environment is an entire society so frightening and threatening that incarceration in a self-created silk-lined prison is preferable to venturing outside. Barbey d'Aureyvilly called Brummell "the futile king of a futile world": this same epigram could well be applied to Louis XIV and des Esseintes, the dandy consumer-kings before and after Brummell.

Most people, unable to endure *ennui* with such stoicism, seek a cause, a conviction, which will save them from a sense of futility. In his 1884 review of *À Rebours*, Barbey wrote, "After such a book it only remains for the author to choose between the muzzle of a pistol or the foot of the Cross." He had made a similar remark years before to Baudelaire, who chose a sort of slow suicide through dissipation and drugs. Huysmans finally took the other alternative and converted to Catholicism. Barbey's own youthful dandyism slowly faded along with his political liberalism, and eventually he converted to conservative Catholicism and became a leading apologist for the faith in France.[52]

But are these the only choices? Does the individual determined to rise above the banality of mass merchandising have no alternatives but to go mad, kill himself, or take refuge in religious dogmatism? Just as the literature of decadence prophesied this personal and cultural impasse, so the evolution of French literature afterward suggests other possible resolutions. Those resolutions took some time to emerge, however. At first the school of decadence merged with that of symbolism, which even more explicitly embraced a dream world divorced from ordinary reality. The dream world of the symbolists proved just as tenuous and troubling as that of their decadent predecessors. The symbolist quest for an artistic ideal led to flight either to a fantasy realm (such as that portrayed in Villiers de l'Isle-Adam's *Axël*) or far-off places (represented by Arthur Rimbaud's personal odyssey in the Near East).[53] In both cases the evasion proved self-destructive and futile. What was needed was a fresh response cast in entirely different terms.

The remarkable generation of the 1890s in France finally stormed the dream world of the symbolists with the battle cries of life, reality, and nature. The generation of the 1890s declared that the alternative to dream did not have to be a nightmare of bourgeois materialism or mass hypnosis. Art did not have to create an "artificial paradise" (to use Baudelaire's term) but could find an accord with real life so that "aesthetic and ethic tend to merge in the fecund unity of a superior form of action."[54] The slogan of this generation was the need to construct a "social art." The literary school of *naturisme* was one result of the renovation of cultural life resulting from this quest for a social art. Another was a broad movement to reform the decorative arts, that is, to reform the design of ordinary consumer objects so that they would be useful without being utilitarian, socially expressive without being conformist, practical without being philistine. Consumption was to be detached from dreams but not from ideals. The goal of the decorative arts movement was not only to reform the design of everyday goods but also to reshape the social values represented by consumer objects. The result of this experiment was the definition of yet another style of consumption, one which expressed social consciousness rather than the quirks of individual personality, one which incarnated democratic rather than aristocratic values. All this is the subject of the next chapter.

5   Decorative Arts Reform and Democratic Consumption

The Odyssey of a Generation – In 1890, at the age of eighteen, Camille Mauclair (1872–1945) made his debut in Parisian literary life. His talent, exuberance, and sense of social concern are representative of the exceptional generation of the 1890s in France. The story of his coming of age constitutes at once a personal odyssey and the history of his generation. When Mauclair wrote his memoirs in middle age, he recalled that he "entered [literary life] among the decadents," or, as they would soon be called, the symbolists.[1] J.-K. Huysmans himself wrote complimentary letters to Mauclair in praise of the younger man's first works. Mauclair visited Huysmans several times to thank him and came away feeling that the hero of the decadents was "truly a man to respect."[2] But Mauclair's principal literary idols (and this was true of his generation as a whole) were the symbolist poets Paul Verlaine and Stephen Mallarmé. He did not know Verlaine personally but from a distance worshipped his poetic genius as equal to that of Baudelaire. Mallarmé he knew well, and venerated his supreme moral stature as well as his poetic powers.[3] Mauclair was also a fervent supporter of Wagne-

rian music, impressionist painting, and Rodin's sculp-
tures. For his generation all these enthusiasms coincided.

Furthermore, for Mauclair and many of his contemporaries, these artistic causes were linked to the political
cause of anarchism. In the 1890s both Europe and America
experienced a series of dramatic anarchist "gestures"—
thefts, bombings, and assassinations—that terrified respectable society. Mauclair was not predisposed to favor
anarchism. Before moving to Paris his parents had lived in
Alsace-Lorraine, the part of France which had fallen to
Germany in the Franco-Prussian War of 1870–1871. They
were fiercely patriotic, eager for national revenge, and
solid supporters of the French Third Republic. Their son
was not entirely comfortable with the internationalist
stance of anarchism. But Mauclair rejected some of his
parents' opinions, especially their anti-Semitism, and his
faith in the republican ideal was shaken by the sleazy
opportunism displayed by French politicians in the Bou-
langist episode and Panama scandal of the late 1880s and
early 1890s. In 1892 occurred the event which finally
turned Mauclair into an anarchist. The "honest and unhappy worker" Vaillant, acting on anarchist principles,
threw a bomb into the middle of the French Chamber of
Deputies, slightly injuring two deputies. Although his
gesture was almost harmless, the hapless Vaillant was
guillotined:

> The execution of Vaillant was and remains in my eyes
> a social crime. I wanted to attend. I returned sick with
> anger and disgust, with an unspeakable aversion against
> the death penalty and even more against the men who
> had dared apply it to Vaillant. . . . Such a sanction for a
> crime characterized as political seemed to me the ugly
> vengeance of a bourgeois collectivity which was afraid
> and which hypocritically invoked the necessity of making
> an example.[4]

This anarchist phase marked the extreme point of Mauclair's immersion in the political fantasy world inhabited
by many of his generation—or so he saw it later:

> I imagined an anarchism that was aristocratic and still the
> friend of the people, and I sided with a universal pacifist
> fraternity while still mistrusting internationalism. . . . It
> was a rather pretty pile of absurdities. But I certainly
> believe that no neophyte around me was any less absurd,
> nor any more embarrassed by the way these contradictions
> were heaped pell-mell.[5]

Mauclair found himself defending terrorists who were
considerably more sinister and effective than Vaillant as
"martyrs of individualism." He indiscriminately hated
"deputies, policemen, judges, army officers, all the up-
holders of the social order, as much as philistines," and
clung to a mystical belief in the "red dawn" of anarchist
triumph.[6]

Gradually, however, Mauclair realized that anarchism
was permeated by an "insincere snobbism." He was himself "from a plebian clan, being poor and of lowly birth,"
but many of his anarchist comrades were elegant young
men of literary bent who openly referred to themselves as
"the elite" and who claimed to love the common people
while recoiling from any genuine egalitarianism. They
might have dirty hands, Mauclair noted, but not callused
ones. For such "dilettantes of anarchism" it was "very
chic" to be compromised by receiving a visit from the police, although none of them would risk imprisonment or
even donate a hundred francs to a popular cause. There
were indeed genuine anarchists, poor workers "without
illusions," who were generous and courageous. These
"poor devils, having taken all this seriously," were the
ones who actually ended up in court. Elitist anarchists
usually ended up instead as advocates of the *culte du moi*
("cult of myself") of Maurice Barrès, which Mauclair deni-
grated as "an anarchism of fantasy."[7]

Mauclair began to see that other literary circles were
afflicted by a similar undemocratic snobbism that was out
of touch with social reality. Even the symbolists were not
immune: although they included a wide range of social
types, among them was a not inconsiderable number of

young men of means, cultivated, well-dressed, exuding the easy allure of a wealthy upbringing, fond of talking about Dream and Pure Art and scorning anyone who wrote for money. Even those of lesser fortune adopted this taboo on writing for gain, which kept them impoverished but "pure." Among the symbolists there was a great deal of artistic snobbishness which often led them to adopt ridiculous poses. They had a mania for adding esoteric, mysterious, and superfluous epigraphs to their poems. They used inks, waxes, and papers "of extraordinary nuances" for their works. The very thought of a typewriter was unspeakable. As for the content of symbolist works, the aversion to everyday reality was worthy of des Esseintes himself. One symbolist swore to Mauclair that he would always remain an idealist, aloof from the flat reality of modernism, incapable of writing a banal word like "taxicab" (*fiacre*). When this "pure artist" ended up writing naturalistic novels a few years later, he could only laugh when Mauclair reminded him of his vow. "And well he might," Mauclair commented. "Is he the only one who fooled himself?" Mauclair himself had gone through a "crisis of pure art," but he eventually saw through the pretensions of that pose. Many symbolist hangers-on, he decided, were unable to cast off their self-delusions. They crowded around famous names, circulated among literary cafés and symbolist reviews, and dismissed talented realistic writers like Guy de Maupassant as unworthy in order to divert attention from their own lack of ability:

> I adopted a salubrious disgust for Dream. This was the refrain of the failures. By looking at them [these knights of the fog of Dream] I understood that Dream is the negative of militant, lucid, creative Thought. Dream was their cocaine.[8]

By the mid-1890s Mauclair had concluded that anarchists and symbolists alike lived in a dream world of sterile elitism. But what were the alternatives? There was the literary world of elegant salons, of wealthy bourgeois and chic aristocrats who supported *arriviste* authors willing to write to please this audience. With some self-righteousness, Mauclair insists in his memoirs that this milieu of careerism failed to tempt him—not only, he admits, because noble spirits like Mallarmé imbued him with disdain for a sordidly mercantile mentality, but also because he did not wish to be condemned to years of "hard labor" (he uses the English expression) chasing the fugitive satisfactions of fame. He might crave reality rather than dreams, but the spectacle of careerism only filled him with "profound *ennui*."[9]

One other alternative, however, promised more personal satisfaction and social benefit. He could join the socialists. By the 1890s French socialism had become, for the first time in the nation's history, reasonably united and successful (in 1893 forty-eight socialists were elected to the Chamber of Deputies). Furthermore, socialists explicitly rejected the futile theatricality of "direct action" and the "beau geste" which had seduced anarchists. Yet Mauclair could not bring himself to join a party prone to denunciations of art as an irrelevant bourgeois luxury. He might have a social conscience, but he was also a man of letters, a fervent believer in the necessity and glory of art. He felt a "lively aversion" to "leveling socialism, the 'party of stomachs' . . . which seemed to prepare a world in which dreamers, thinkers, and artists could not breathe." The Marxist definition of reality was far too constricted for him. Marxism made a "fearful cult of *fact* and *utility*" and focused only on the physical needs of man as if he had no spiritual needs. As a result, for all their denunciations of the bourgeoisie, socialists "have thought in a bourgeois manner about the subject of artists and ideologies," and just like good bourgeois they long only for "'the useful! Facts, nothing but facts!'"[10]

Mauclair found himself suspended between two schools of thought, each of which divorced art from everyday life, but for entirely different reasons. Decadents, the dandies before them, and symbolists after them all scorned the idols of money, success, and practicality which supposedly dominated bourgeois thinking; they proclaimed their superiority to such petty considerations and dedicated themselves to an aesthetic ideal far above the insect level of money-grubbing. The classic statement of their position was expressed by Théophile Gautier, the critic and writer who was an ardent admirer of Baudelaire: "There is nothing truly beautiful except what is useless; everything useful is ugly, because it is the expression of some need, and those of man are ignoble and disgusting like his poor, infirm nature."[11] This revulsion from ignoble organic needs was the tradition behind des Esseintes's peculiar asceticism, which led him to repress bodily functions like eating at the same time that he spent wildly to surround himself with bejewelled tortoises and rare hot-house flowers.

The irony is that such an attitude was quite acceptable as well to the bourgeois so despised by des Esseintes and his like. These bourgeois, as well as socialists who "thought in a bourgeois manner," also accepted the separation of art from everyday life, not to elevate the purity of art but to elevate the importance of the utilitarian. Art could be accorded lip service (as many bourgeois did) or rejected as a frivolous, class-bound luxury (as many socialists did) so that attention could be directed to the hard facts of economic life. Mauclair came to recognize this hidden affinity linking seeming cultural enemies: "The principles of the bohemian are the principles of the bourgeois upside down, but not opposite."[12]

By 1895, not long after his youthful debut as a writer, Mauclair found himself without a literary or political home. Anarchism was in disarray, due in part to government prosecution but also due to its own indulgence in inept and fantastic romanticism. The ranks of the symbolists were scattered, partly through death and distraction among its adherents, partly because its battle to achieve literary significance had largely been won, and partly because its flights into exoticism and fantasy were becoming more extreme and destructive. Yet for Mauclair literary careerism and socialist utilitarianism were also unthinkable. His lack of orientation was a practical problem as well as a spiritual one. While he certainly did not want to "prostitute" himself as a writer, to use the symbolist expression, on the other hand he had no source of income except his pen. He was running out of money and needed to publish in a review which would pay him a decent price for his work; symbolist journals paid little or nothing.

Mauclair worked up the courage to present himself at the offices of the *Nouvelle revue,* a journal which along with the *Revue des deux mondes* was disdained by the symbolists as the incarnation of stuffy bourgeois respectability. "I took myself there as full of pride as of apprehension, determined to be very courteous but not to sacrifice any of my convictions to that universal philistinism which supposedly began beyond the confines of the symbolist world." Mauclair was cordially received by Mme. Juliette Adam, publisher of the review, and he left "conquered" by her grace, vivacity, and intelligence. Soon after began his long collaboration with the *Nouvelle revue:* it was the first time Mauclair had earned money from his writing. In his autobiography he pays tribute to Mme. Adam, who became a lifelong friend:

> I owed everything to two beings in my life: Mallarmé opened unforgettable horizons for me through the perfection of his spirit and the nobility of his life; Mme. Juliette Adam welcomed me before anyone else, made me understand how one could earn a living with his pen without submitting to or offering lies, and the spectacle of her existence helped me get rid of a series of stupid and malevolent prejudices. . . . For me she mitigated that hour, so painful to the sensibility and naïve pride of a young man, when he had to allow a vocation, dreamed of as chimerically intransigent and pure, to become depoeticized through the necessity of serving also as a profession by which one lives.[13]

Out of this existential crisis emerged Mauclair's enthusiasm for a new understanding of art, a "social art" that would similarly find a middle ground between ethereal reveries and banal utilitarianism, that would reject chimerical dreams without rejecting ideals. This new understanding was the subject of his first article for the *Nouvelle revue,* published in February, 1896, under the title "La Réforme de l'art décoratif" ("The Reform of Decorative Art"). It radiates the buoyancy of its author, who in this reform movement simultaneously found a resolution of his personal, political, and artistic dilemmas. "We are . . . at the hour of an [artistic] harvest. . . . If optimism has a domain, it is in criticism and art." The occasion for this overflow of optimism was the announcement that the French government had agreed to let a group of decorative artists redesign the nation's coinage. Mauclair interpreted this decision as the initial step in an artistic revolution that would beautify ordinary objects of utility, beginning with "the most universal and banal: a coin." The coinage reform testified that the modern age was finally casting off the visual heritage of the past to find its own distinctive style based on contemporary needs. The redesign of objects of everyday use would achieve a marriage of beauty and utility, of art and life, of dream and reality that both symbolists and bourgeois-minded utilitarians had denied. Finally the generation of the 1890s had found its own voice. The arrival of a new wave of decorative artists, Mauclair declared, was just one element in a general upheaval in which his generation was freeing itself from the burden of the past, slowly revealing its own soul through an indistinct "fog" of experimentation, until a new lesson emerged from the epoch:

> We are in a period which is especially attractive, for all the arts correspond with each other. New literature and new music, ornamentation and furnishings, impressionism and symbolism, essays and dramas . . . all that . . . becomes strengthened in harmonious relations, in deep or subtle works, in slow and sure diffusions.[14]

This chapter will tell the story of the decorative arts movement as viewed through Mauclair's evolving relationship with it. He and his fellow reformers usually relied upon the language of art to describe their ideals, for this was their accustomed language. But at the same time they were defining a new style of consumption. The decorative arts (or "applied" or "industrial" arts, as they were also called)[15] are, first and foremost, the arts of the consumer. The basic goal of the reform movement was to improve both art and society through improving the design of ordinary items of consumption—dishes, pots and pans, bed and table linens, clothing and jewelry, furnishings. At the same time that Mauclair and many of his generation were articulating an artistic and social ideal, they were defining a new style of consumption—democratic rather than elitist, yet not of the masses. The tragedy of the movement was that the ideal was so rapidly reduced to the lifestyle.

The Principles of the Decorative Arts Movement–Along with most other partisans of decorative arts reform, Mauclair advocated three fundamental principles for the design of ordinary consumer items: modernity, appropriateness, and democracy. The first principle means that designs should not be copied mindlessly from the past but should be revised to reflect modern habits and sensibilities. Each epoch must disavow the styles of preceding times in order to discover its own spirit. This advice sounds obvious enough until one begins to recall how many households across all of France, from the merely respectable to the grandest, were filled with Louis XVI chairs, Renaissance buffets, or Pompadour divans. This style of decoration, inherited from courtly circles and diffused among the bourgeoisie, is Mauclair's implicit target when he holds aloft the banner of modernity as a principle of design. It is an anti-bourgeois principle, and Mauclair has only scorn for respectable snobs who "give themselves a Louis XVI soul to 'go with' their Louis XVI boudoir."[16] His larger target is the whole consumer mentality that seeks prestige by adopting aristocratic trappings.

The second principle of appropriateness states what should replace prestige as a guide to design, and so it naturally follows the first principle of modernity. Mauclair prefers the term *appropriateness* to *utility*, since the latter word is uncomfortably reminiscent of the concept of *utilitarian*, which he associates with bourgeois or socialist philistinism. The general idea is the same, however. The design of an object should be reduced to the simplest terms dictated by the practical use of the object. Beauty lies not in a superabundance of decorations but in a modified form adapted to modern needs of simplicity and manageability. Beauty and utility are not only compatible but are for the most part identical.

This principle of design is now familiar as *functionalism* (a term that came into usage in France only decades after Mauclair wrote),[17] and its contemporary applications are visible everywhere—in the clean lines of teak tables and bookcases, in the forthright simplicity of unadorned glass goblets, in the shaggy integrity of durable wool rugs. But this very familiarity with the aesthetic results has made us less sensitive to the ethical implications of the functional principle, implications to which Mauclair and his contemporaries, who first enunciated them, were especially alert. As the principle of modernity directly challenges the bourgeois style of consumption, so the principle of appropriateness expresses a revulsion from the ornate, fantastic, exotic-chaotic décor so characteristic of mass consumption. Mauclair despairs of what he calls "the art of the rabble"—vulgar melodramas, cheap novels, insipid color prints—and accuses the bourgeoisie of corrupting popular taste with this junk.[18] His aesthetic disdain for these ugly wares is inseparable from his moral disdain for their social purpose. They are deceptive, for their ordinary use is disguised by attempts to make them appear expensive and impressive by adding a clutter of ornaments or by using materials worked to look like something else. Design should be *honest*. Objects have integrity when they are designed to serve everyday human needs, not when they are designed to serve social pretensions.

In an age when technological progress was making available to the consumer all sorts of parodies of wealth, all sorts of showy but inexpensive ornamentation, the principle of appropriateness rejected this liberation in favor of a return to necessity. It was an aesthetic of exclusion that emphasized the elimination of the ornaments and imitations typical of the democratization of luxury. In the opinion of decorative arts reformers, the liberty afforded by modern technology had been put to such appallingly ugly uses—"Liberty! what crimes have been committed in thy name!" quotes Mauclair[19]—that a voluntary return to the restrictions of physical necessity seemed the only way to salvage beauty in the modern age. That was the aesthetic component of the call for a return to necessity in design. The ethical component was the conviction that the ordinary needs of ordinary people were not to be despised as "ignoble," as Gautier and his disciples had done, but were to be regarded as complex, dignified, even poetic—and entirely human. The basic needs of the consumer were brought out of hiding, so to speak, and accorded a place of honor.

The principle of appropriateness in design is therefore inherently democratic. It confers dignity upon needs common to all rather than to social status open only to a few. If the democratization of luxury means only the proliferation of social pretensions, the "democratization of art"—a slogan adopted by Mauclair and many others—would bring a genuine revitalization of both art and society. Art would once again be put in touch with the life of the people, so that it would again become part of everyday life rather than a luxury for the rich. The debilitating hierarchy that places the fine arts, such as painting and sculpture, above applied arts like weaving and pottery, and artists above artisans, would be ended. At the same time—and here aesthetic theory becomes social theory—the life of the people would be regenerated by being brought into contact with examples of beauty. Surrounded on all sides by such models, the taste of the masses would gradually improve and would cast off the shackles of bourgeois bad taste. Mauclair explains:

> It is in the ornamentation of everyday objects . . . and not in the success of unique and very expensive things that we can usefully seek the diffusion of taste, that we can envision the disappearance of monotony and of ugliness, the artistic education of the public by humble and everyday examples, locks, utensils of constant usage which cost no more when they are made attractive.[20]

This artistic education would also be an education in social morality. The change in taste would gradually disseminate the attitude that dignity is to be found in everyday life, not in the chase of superfluity and social status. According to Mauclair, by "giving examples of taste to the masses," artists would lead them

> little by little to a more delicate and intellectual state of mind, so that the day of the economic revolution would not install in power a mob of brutes whom the bourgeoisie has carefully deprived of all opportunities for improvement.[21]

As these remarks make clear, Mauclair's ideal of democratization in art does not mean that the people themselves will create art. Educator-artists are the ones who will give the people "examples of taste." Furthermore, his reference to a "mob of brutes" betrays considerable fear of these masses who so desperately need to be educated. Mauclair may blame this brutalization on the bourgeoisie, but the fear remains. And so does the condescension. His program for public education through the medium of "humble and everyday examples . . . utensils of constant usage" derives from an assumption that the fine (or speculative) arts cannot be appreciated by the masses:

> It is madness to dream of communicating speculative art to the crowd, which cannot understand it; but there is a way

to establish an intermediary through the application of art
to industry (as the art of the painting or poem cannot do
without compromising itself), in the decorative arts, from
dress to furniture to tableware to wallpaper. . . . Practicality, comfort, cheapness, simplicity, it permits all this which
[speculative] art cannot.[22]

This concept of democracy, along with the principles
of modernity and appropriateness, made up an aesthetic
ideology that had great appeal in the 1890s. To use other
terminology, this program uniting artistic and social reform was a "sociological aesthetic" opposed to the aesthetic of "art for art's sake." Adherents of the latter were
put on the defensive by the emergence of the talented,
socially committed generation of the 1890s.[23]

The aesthetic ideology of the decorative arts movement especially attracted individuals, like Mauclair, who
would not conform to the rigidity of Marxist doctrine. The
ideology was flexible enough to accommodate both Mauclair, who was profoundly and consistently sympathetic to
the left, and someone like Jean Lahor (Henri Cazalis,
1840–1909), who was fiercely nationalistic and anti-
Semitic, irrationalist and anti-egalitarian, having nothing
in common with Mauclair except a friendship with
Mallarmé. In his autobiography Mauclair describes
anarchism as "not a system of social life, but a form of
youthful sensibility,"[24] and the same description might
well apply to the decorative arts movement. It was certainly not a political party or even an artistic school,
although it has often been reduced to an episode in art
history under the rubric of Art Nouveau.

Until the boundaries of the movement are more clearly
defined, the social background of its adherents can only be
guessed. What seems likely is that the decorative arts
movement attracted educated people of democratic sympathies (even Lahor called himself a socialist, although his
politics were certainly far from what is usually understood
by that label) but who felt themselves socially isolated—
"outside of parties,"[25] in Mauclair's words, and even to

some extent outside of social class. Mauclair, for example, felt set apart from common workers by his education, talent, and intellectual profession, but at the same time he did not feel comfortable with the traditional upper classes. For such a person the decorative arts movement suggested a style of life at once artistically superior and politically democratic, incorporating both popular sympathies and distinction from the masses. The basic ambivalence of this attitude is expressed in the concept of democratized art given to the people by an artistic elite. Lahor put the matter more bluntly than Mauclair ever would have when he titled one of his books *L'Art pour le peuple à défaut de l'art par le peuple* ("Art for the People for Want of Art by the People," 1903). Mauclair was much more tactful, but he expressed the same mixture of fear and sympathy with regard to the masses when he talked about giving examples of taste to the crowd.

The spirit of the decorative arts reformers is therefore not so far removed from the elitism of literary dandyism as it might seem at first. This is an elitist democracy, so to speak, and, like dandyism, this aesthetic ideology and the style of life it implied enjoyed an international appeal among a limited but influential public. Finally, again like dandyism, the style of the decorative arts movement could be adapted to the requirements of impoverished elitists as well as wealthier ones, for much of its appeal involved a taboo on the ordinary. Mauclair recounts that Claude Debussy—who in his younger years scraped together a living by teaching music and had to keep moving from one cheap apartment to another—could not abide the ugly fixtures of his quarters, so he saved enough money from his tiny income to commission the sculptor Alexandre Charpentier to design some "modern style" latches which could be moved with him.[26]

The Fate of the Decorative Arts Movement – It is to Mauclair's credit that he became aware of the bad faith of this ambivalent democratic-elitism. He turned into a perceptive critic of decorative arts reform, rather than continuing to boost the cause as Lahor and many others did. In 1906, ten years after his buoyant article in the *Nouvelle revue* heralding a new generation of decorative artists, he published a somber study titled "La Crise des arts décoratifs" ("The Crisis of the Decorative Arts") in the *Revue bleue,* an eclectic weekly. In the early years of the twentieth century, Mauclair was to write a series of articles for the *Revue bleue,* all of which tried to analyze the nature of this "crisis" and its causes. Together they constitute a realistic critique of the dream world of democratic consumption. At first glance, Mauclair admits in his 1906 article, decorative art seems to have realized all the hopes held out for it in the 1890s. "It is fêted at the salons. . . . There is a brilliant décor. But there is nothing behind this décor, and this golden façade poorly conceals the impending decadence of one of the most beautiful virtues of French art."

What is the cause of this triumph of a deceptive décor over genuine art? Mauclair reminds his readers of the "genuine and logical goal" of decorative arts reform, "a modification of ordinary forms by a quest for convenience, for adaptation to new needs."[27] In practice, however, the canon of appropriateness had been reduced to a fad for a handmade, roughhewn "natural" look, a sort of back-to-basics in design. Along with this pretentious simplicity went another fad for adding symbolic messages of a banal sort, much as symbolist poets had indulged in a mania for epigraphs to their poems. Heavy, sturdy buffets were inlaid with dreamy landscapes, and quotations from Baudelaire were inscribed on chunky flowerpots. The result was summarized by Mauclair as a "hygienic and economical art . . . nudity mingled with childish symbolism."[28] No consistent tone emerged:

> From this mania of "playing at industrial art" resulted that strange style that we know, a composite and baroque style, influenced by English art and Belgian art, mixed with illogical fantasy, neither practical nor sumptuous, amalgamating the naïveté of Brittany, Berry, or Picardy [in other

words, the "peasant look"] with pre-Raphaelite aestheti-
cism, the floral symbolism of the School of Nancy and the
spiral ornaments of the ornate letters of the school of
William Morris, zigzags, ellipses, medievalisms, in a pretentious and uncomfortable heap.[29]

All of this may have been new—indeed, the common
factor of this "heap" was a quest for novelty—but it was
not modern in the sense of expressing contemporary
needs. Mauclair found "modern style" items anything but
appropriate and specifically criticized their "lack of adaptation to the proposed end."[30]

Such is the style known as Art Nouveau, a style that
has its lasting glories but has endured as an aesthetic
curiosity rather than as the distinctive and universal idiom
of modern life. Any generalization about Art Nouveau is
suspect, however, since, as Mauclair himself points out,
the style is above all heterogeneous and composite. It
certainly includes examples of spare, rectilinear design
which would now be called "functional," but the French
in particular preferred elaborate organic motifs and an
exaggerated curvilinear style. At the international exposition of 1900 and even more at the exposition of design held
in Turin in 1902, French models were criticized for their
overwrought ornateness in contrast to the relative sobriety
of German, Belgian, and Scottish examples.

Probably the major influence pushing French decorative art in the direction of fantasy and elaboration was that
of Émile Gallé (1846–1904), founder of the School of Nancy
referred to above by Mauclair. If any one man in France
may be compared with William Morris in England, it is
Gallé, and a number of his contemporaries indeed drew
that parallel.[31] Like Morris, Gallé disseminated his ideas as
a creative artist, as a teacher who trained others in his
workshop (best known as a glassmaker, he also built
furniture), and as a theorist of the decorative arts in his
speeches, lectures, review articles, and exhibit notices. A
good introduction to Gallé's theories may be found in the
introduction to the statutes of the School of Nancy. Pub-

lished in 1901, the statutes formalized the existence of the group of Lorraine artists which had long since gathered around Gallé:

> [The goal of the school] is to conserve in modern French objects, as much for objects of simple utility as for those of luxury, the sense of logic in construction, in the rational use of materials, the practical instinct of convenience and comfort, under an ornamentation of elegance, beauty, and intellectuality.[32]

Besides retaining a distinction between "objects of simple utility" and those of "luxury," a distinction which any genuine democratization of art would eliminate, the philosophy of the school distinguishes utilitarian considerations of logic, convenience, and comfort from aesthetic ones of beauty, elegance, and intellectuality. The aesthetic qualities are superimposed upon the first group: if beauty and utility are compatible, they are certainly distinct. In practice, too, Gallé imposed decoration onto useful objects rather than modifying their forms so that utility itself became the basis of beauty. Gallé regarded the vases and chairs he made as carriers for the symbolic expression of emotions, which is what really mattered to him. He inscribed jars with verses from his favorite poets (Baudelaire, Montesquiou, Verlaine) and embellished bureaus with flowers and landscapes—all this decoration being intended, in the words of one of his admirers, to make these everyday objects "evocative of thoughts beyond the appearances they assume."[33] As for practicality, Gallé preferred to work with glass, because it is such a malleable and versatile material, but its fragility is self-evident. His furniture was notorious for its discomfort and lack of mobility. The physical requirements of daily life were not emphasized by Gallé and the School of Nancy, although they did pay lip service to them. They cared most about the spiritual function of useful objects. In Gallé's words, art has "a function of human culture, of awakening minds and souls by the translation of beauties in the world." In particular, he adds, artists have a duty to create objects which will bring beauty to city-dwellers exiled from nature, so that artists serve as "educators, apostles of color, of line, of beauty, missionaries to the interior."[34] The decorative arts movement certainly had a "missionary" impulse entirely missing among the dandies and decadents, but in this conviction of their own spiritual elevation and the superiority of aesthetic ideals these reformers are quite similar to the decadents. It was, after all, Gallé who designed Montesquiou's hortensia-filled bathroom for him.

Mauclair finally decided that this elitist sense of superiority was ultimately responsible for the visual failures of the decorative arts movement. Its disasters of design were the external manifestations of the fundamental ideological failing, its lack of democracy. Designs were not modern or appropriate because they were not arrived at democratically. Genuine artisans had been pushed aside by moneyed amateurs, caught up in the decorative arts fad, who churned out third-rate leather goods or misshapen pottery. Fine artists amused themselves by playing at applied art while continuing to make conventional paintings or statues. Once the decorative arts were allowed in the official salons, "a snobbism in reverse was born: and you saw artists formerly full of arrogance declare themselves, with comic pride, 'worker-painters' and 'worker-sculptors.' "[35]

Even more than among the producers, among the consumers the hollowness of the democratic ideal was evident. The handcrafted tooled leathers, ceramics, furniture, and glass were "reserved for millionaires," notes Mauclair, and even when more ordinary objects like forks were produced "the prices . . . were not exactly democratic!" The same sort of reverse snobbism that impelled artists to call themselves "workers" led wealthy buyers to display rustic furniture and porcelain soup-dishes, all carefully made to have the look of spontaneous popular craftsmanship, although "these 'returns to simplicity' cost

very dearly, and this art had nothing 'social' about it."
Such attempts to imitate simplicity with costly materials
and handiwork, remarks Mauclair, reminded him of des
Esseintes, who used the finest wool to make a carpet
mimicking the flagstones of a monastic cell.[36] Such snobs
play at the illusion of democratic simplicity, so long as it is
an obviously expensive simplicity. This is an inauthentic
asceticism based not on a genuine conviction of the unim-
portance of material things but on an elitist desire to
cultivate the "natural" and "simple" in order to show
one's distance from the false gilt and ornateness offered
on the mass market. Mauclair's disdain for such self-
deception derives no doubt from his experiences with
well-bred youths who played at anarchism in a similar
way.

As for the majority of consumers, they had not been
converted to modern, appropriate designs. Mauclair has
to admit that the vast majority of better-off bourgeois
continued to buy imitations of aristocratic styles. For this
group the craze for Art Nouveau was a brief and transitory
episode, except that some Oriental motifs were added to
the native repertoire. "Modern style" was in general too
different, too extreme; furthermore, it looked cheap, while
these respectable citizens demanded above all that their
possessions look expensive.[37] The lower classes resisted
the new styles for much the same reasons. While trendy
artists and some well-heeled consumers might want to
"play with simplicity as with tin soldiers," the masses
regarded the look of rugged simplicity as the look of
poverty. Instead, Mauclair concludes,

> they love bad taste, false gilt, weepy engravings, . . . all
> that can excite their imaginative vanity and imitate rich
> interiors as they suppose them to be, just as a wine
> decanted into a vintage bottle gives them the impression of
> a *grand cru*.[38]

Common people covet the appearance of wealth, not
washable interiors filled with simple furniture. They crave

the democratization of luxury, not the democratization of art. If forced into the kind of plain dwelling favored by decorative arts reformers, Mauclair sighs, lower-class people would fill it with tacky color prints, Oriental vases won at a fair, and clothes hanging on the line. Some rich people may want to play at being poor, but the poor would rather play at being rich.

This is not to say that Art Nouveau designs had no effect on the middle and lower classes. The style did incorporate an elaborate if naïve symbolism as well as the "natural" look, and the more ornate examples of "modern style" were relatively compatible with popular taste. Furthermore, as new forms of luxury, they assumed an appeal as status objects, along with more traditional models. Before long, mass-manufactured imitations of handmade Art Nouveau items appeared on the market. One of the dogmas of the decorative arts movement had been the need to free design from imitation of past models; the parodies of Art Nouveau, while imitating contemporary designs rather than traditional ones, derived from the same intention of conveying a pleasing illusion of wealth. (One alternate name for Art Nouveau was "Yachting Style," because objects designed in this manner were supposed to remind one of the décor of a luxury yacht.) Mauclair laments that the creations of master artisans quickly fell into

> the last degree of ridicule by the clumsy imitations which bourgeois commerce made of them. Everywhere today you find traces of these pretentious pursuits, . . . objects of false silver, with false catseyes, what-nots in papier-mâché aping the models of Gallé, . . . blotters of embossed leather which are only paper-leather.[39]

Even fashionable furniture manufacturers in the quarter of Paris that had been "the citadel of Louis-Philippe taste," those who had always been an "inexhaustible source" of imitations of eighteenth-century styles, began to add timid touches of Art Nouveau, hesitant twists or dragon-shaped scrolls, while the smallest retailer sold "modern-style" hatpins for twenty cents. "This trash has not spared snobbism the ironic injury of its admiration."[40] Restaurants catering to the upper middle classes as well as department stores serving the masses began to employ Art Nouveau themes in interior decoration.

As commerce adopted the style, it became even less simple and more symbolic, ornate, and outlandish: "noodles and all types of filaments, animal and vegetable, symbolic screens, everything contributed to this carnival."[41] Art Nouveau designers let their imagination wing from the fantastic to the grotesque, from reality to dream or to nightmare. Alphonse Mucha fashioned light fittings using motifs from flowers said to be poisonous, arranging the fatal petals to conceal the electric light bulbs. René Lalique carved flowers from horn and placed them under beetles made of gold whose wing cases were fashioned from enamel or set with precious stones. Although relatively restrained by his botanical training and pride in scientific exactitude, Gallé himself sometimes gave way, using exotic or even macabre motifs such as borders of stag-beetle mingled with poppies, or re-creations of fossil flowers. Dragonflies were a favorite motif. In a feat of technical ingenuity, Gallé produced a vase on which dragonflies seem to be sinking into the glass. Lalique and other designers created a new mythological creature, half-woman, half-dragonfly, which provided a variation on another favorite Art Nouveau emblem, a dreamy, heavy-lidded maiden wrapped in billows of draperies and hair—half streetwalker, half goddess. Everywhere floated strange sea creatures, above all seahorses, for designers seemed hypnotized by the mysteries of submarine life and even created whole rooms to reproduce the sense of being underwater.[42] They would have felt quite at home in des Esseintes's dining room, where mechanical fish could be glimpsed through the "portholes," as des Esseintes would have delighted in the macabre themes of Art Nouveau—if only the masses had not also discovered the delights of perversity.

The fate of the decorative arts movement in France was prefigured by des Esseintes's vow to flee Fontenay for a healthy, invigorating excursion to utilitarian England, only to lose his nerve and end up back with his carpeted flagstones, submarine dining room, and hothouse plants. And just as des Esseintes, for all his sense of superiority over the masses, created nothing other than a private exposition-grounds at Fontenay, so the decorative arts movement, although intending to repudiate the dream world of mass consumption with modernist, functional designs, ended up creating its own exposition (or "carnival," as Mauclair says) of exotic-chaotic, fantastic, erotic, submarine, technically ingenious images. The decorative arts movement began as an alternative to bourgeois, mass, and decadent lifestyles. In the end it interacted with and borrowed from all of them. There is no more striking evidence that the late nineteenth century created a pervasive, interlocking system of consumer lifestyles.

Mauclair's Proposals for Salvaging the Ideal—Thus another dream world of the consumer invaded the supposedly rational and sober precincts of decorative arts reform. Mauclair concluded that this outcome was inevitable because decorative arts reformers had been living in a dream world of their own: "We attribute to the people the psychology we wish it had, not that which it actually has."[43] As a result, advocates of the cause promoted a type of design they felt the people *should* appreciate, but which in reality it did not. Samuel Bing opened his famous shop called Art Nouveau—the name of the style comes from the merchandise he carried—convinced that consumers would be delighted to have these goods made available at reasonable prices. "What an illusion." exclaims Mauclair. "The workers didn't buy. . . . The excellent Bing lovingly prepared models of complete dining rooms for workers; it was pretty, it was rustic, everything was signed. . . . But there were never any buyers."[44]

Mauclair came to realize that the difficulties were mental, not material. Once more he forced himself to shed pleasing illusions and to face the facts of popular consumer mentality. His efforts to do so, to reconcile those facts with his own aesthetic aspirations, led to some of his most thoughtful writings on art and society. His new tone is evident in the opening paragraphs of "Le Besoin d'art du peuple" ("The People's Need for Art"), published in the *Revue bleue* in 1906. He begins not by making assertions but by asking questions. In particular, he questions the reformers' axiom that the people have a right to beauty:

> What is a right of which [the common people] do not feel a need? . . . What is the common people? What sort of beauty is accessible to it? Must it find [beauty] for itself or receive it from the hands of another caste? This is what I would like to know before discerning its need and fixing its right.

Mauclair then vigorously attacks "pseudo-educators" who think they have all the answers and assume that the masses have a need and right to art which they, as artistic superiors, will give them. As a result these "preachers of social art" pursue two erroneous courses, one of which is to embark on programs to disseminate artistic masterpieces to the masses:

> They portray the people as starved for masterpieces, waiting impatiently for the opening of museums and libraries whose gates are unjustly closed to them. It isn't true: they aren't hungry, and our preachers of social art are trying to break down open doors. . . . Why should we lie in the face of the evidence?[45]

Other "pseudo-educators" try to elevate the public by redesigning objects of utility, ignoring the evidence that the people prefer "bad taste, false gilt, weepy engravings" to a "hygienic and economical art." Dream worlds of consumption may rely on fantasy, but popular preference for them is a social fact that cannot be wished away.

Mauclair does not suggest that intellectuals and artists

give up their missionary zeal and accept the bad taste of the public. Their task is to alter the moral and social psychology that is at the root of aesthetic preferences. A need for art will emerge only when preliminary, non-aesthetic needs are first met: "for example, hygiene, neatness, the desire for order around oneself, and self-respect." The character of the individual must first be transformed so that he likes baths and a clean home and dislikes alcohol and swearing. Only then is a "ground for art" prepared. For the ordinary worker, "the work of art begins with himself." The proper task for intellectuals is to stimulate a need for art rather than assuming that the need already exists. "In a word, it involves forming the character of the masses to prepare them for art, and not to anticipate that by putting them in direct contact with art their character will be formed."[46]

Mauclair is repeating what John Ruskin, spiritual god-father of the decorative arts movement in England, had said at least half a century earlier: art is the product of social character. William Morris had repeated that conviction and became a revolutionary socialist because of it. One of the tragedies of the decorative arts movement in both England and France is the rapidity with which the insights of its founders were trivialized or forgotten. For Mauclair to remind his audience of those insights is in itself a contribution. But Mauclair goes further. He asserts that the preliminary moral education of the masses is only the first step in encouraging them to make their own art rather than simply appreciating the art given to them by an elite. Only when ordinary people create their own art can they learn to appreciate anyone else's. Aesthetic taste cannot be instilled in the common man *qua* consumer. Only as a *producer* will he learn to express his aesthetic wants and needs. The people are "made to create art," and "we artists" must renounce trying "to give them a taste for what we invent in thinking that we are giving them pleasure—perhaps they will enjoy only an art that they once more begin to invent for themselves."[47] Only by working actively with materials will people learn to appreciate the qualities of line, materials, adaptation, and harmony that are essential to aesthetic understanding. Mauclair is still convinced that the decorative arts are an intermediary between the common man and the fine arts, but now he sees the artistic education they offer in terms of an active process rather than passive contemplation. The worker learns the "lesson of things" by creating them. No longer do objects somehow teach people; now people teach themselves through labor. Mauclair therefore rejects the tacit division of labor between artist-producers and people-consumers that prevailed in the aesthetic ideology of the 1890s. Having seen the ridiculous failures of artist-producers, he is more inclined to trust ordinary people, who now seem to him like potential artists, not like a "mob of brutes."

Mauclair's faith in the artistic capabilities of the people does not arise from the contemporary facts of workers' homes filled with cheap color prints and false gilt. His faith comes from the evidence of the past. In previous centuries, Mauclair argues, the masses demonstrated an unquenchable need to produce art; indeed, all the achievements of the fine arts were based on their creative energies. Once again the people must be allowed to produce useful objects at home or in small shops. Mauclair is well aware how drastic would be the economic changes necessary to restore domestic production. The trends to reduction of handwork and to the increasing division of labor would have to be stopped and then reversed. Still, it must be done: "Everything being done right now for the artistic education of the people is only bragging, boosterism, or blundering. There will be solid results only through the reform of the industries of art." Because socialists are enamored with modern industrial methods, they offer little hope for bringing about the changes Mauclair advocates. Instead, he invests his hopes in a restoration of the prerevolutionary corporations that provided the institutional framework for the development of memorable deco-

rative styles in the past. The disappearance of the corporations at the time of the French Revolution, not the simulta-
neous advent of political democracy, was responsible for
the subsequent decay of French industrial art. Since 1789
France has continued to produce numerous talented
craftsmen, but they compose "a disbanded army, which
goes nowhere or employs itself where it can." The secret
of the revival of the industrial arts "lies in this tomb" of
the corporative spirit, which must be revived in one form
or another.[48]

But it is notoriously difficult to raise the dead. As
Mauclair continues to explore the idea of a revival of the
corporations, the obstacles loom ever larger in his mind. He
realizes that the businessmen who currently dominate
industrial art organizations like the Central Union of the
Decorative Arts "voluntarily confuse" the interests of the
applied arts with their own business interests. The creation
of new models requires a large and risky investment, while
"the imitation of old styles means certain sale and easy
execution." After all, "the immense majority of customers"
want such imitations, because they want luxury or the
impression of luxury. The businessmen therefore claim
that they simply give the public what it wants. They do
make a pretense of encouraging new designs by introducing some modern models each season, but these are hasty,
illogical, ludicrous deformations of the projects originally
fashioned by the craftsmen, who are, moreover, badly paid
for their efforts. Because the businessmen are not serious
about encouraging new models, the results are predictable.
The public continues to prefer pseudo-antiques, the
owners declare again that they can sell only imitations, and
everyone concludes that there is no style left in France. A
few connoisseurs scrounge for examples of good modern
workmanship in the back alleys, "but what is their limited
action compared to the imposing capitalism of the big
merchants?" The intelligent artisan, discouraged from proposing new designs, is forced to earn a living by making
imitations, and so is "fatally led to unintelligence."[49]

What can be done to circumvent capitalist resistance? Mauclair cites experiments to gather artisans into societies or unions which would exhibit directly to the public "independently of industry, which edits [their designs], and of commerce, which distributes them." These occupational groups would receive state assistance through the creation of national workshops; new designs would become state property. Still, Mauclair is suspicious of such schemes because he fears both the veto of business interests and the restrictive consequences of government intervention. He continues to advocate a corporative system, whether it be composed of unions, federations, or societies. But he is vague about the program and does not suggest how it could overcome business opposition.[50]

Critical Remarks: The Varieties of Functionalism–Again Mauclair has run into an impasse. He began his relationship with the decorative arts movement by praising the reform of French coinage as the first step in a program to beautify ordinary objects. Now, ten years later, he has to deal with coins not as designs but as embodiments of the monetary power of capitalism. The economic problems are far more intractable than the visual ones. In a sense, his rejection of socialism has come back to haunt him. The very inclusiveness and flexibility of the aesthetic ideology he embraced in preference to socialist dogmatism proved, in time, to have their own liabilities. Because the decorative arts movement lacked solid theoretical underpinnings, because it could appeal to such a wide spectrum of political and social convictions, it easily slipped off its tracks and foundered in intellectual and programmatic confusion. Marxist doctrine at least has the virtue of insisting on the facts of economic interest, but Mauclair faced these facts only belatedly; moreover, once he faced them he could not handle them except through a vague proposal to reestablish corporations in the face of business opposition. Even he had to admit that the prospects for that proposal were dismal, and he was right.

But what other solution was available to him? He had always considered himself a member of an artistic and intellectual elite outside class and party. Even when he came to see through the pretenses of the elite, he was still in the habit of thinking about himself outside of class terms. It was a mental habit typical of his generation. As a result, Mauclair—who had begun by heralding the future, advocating a distinctively modern environment for living—ended by succumbing to a hopeless nostalgia regarding the means for achieving his ideals. His program for home workshops is more than nostalgic; it is almost primitive. One would have to return to extremely distant times, almost to prehistory, to discover a society where everyone makes his own furnishings, pottery, clothing, housing, and so forth. The elimination of the division of labor and of machine production (as opposed to their modification) is only a daydream. The proposal for a restoration of corporations seems only somewhat less anachronistic, depending as it does on an artisanal rather than on an industrial work force. Mauclair seems to think of corporations as groups of honest craftsmen who work independently of the industrial system, somehow reaching the customer without going through the intermediary of a profit-oriented market. But this is just a return to the idea of a producing elite—genuine craftsmen, perhaps, rather than fine artists, but still a creative elite—designing objects for the consuming public, as if a mass market could be served with preindustrial tools. This is the dichotomy of producer-consumer which Mauclair himself had condemned. What he forgets is that people may be producers at leisure as well as at work, and in this sense the democratization of luxury—the luxury of free time—may in fact encourage the democratization of art, if not the marriage of beauty and utility.

Mauclair's dilemma is that he wants both. The aesthetic ideal whereby beauty and utility are merged in functional form is not necessarily compatible with the democratic social ideal. If in good democratic fashion consumers vote with their dollars for the styles they want, Mauclair cannot deny that they frequently vote for the wrong candidates. They choose not a lean, efficient form reminiscent of the workplace, but elaborate, luxurious forms that represent an escape from it. Mauclair wants democratic choice, but he also wants what he considers good design. He is fighting a battle on two fronts: good models must be produced in the first place, and then they must win public support. If the objects never find their way into the average consumer's life, what will have been gained by designing them well? At times Mauclair may blame capitalism for failing to offer consumers attractive modern styles, but at other times he admits that many consumers do seem to prefer ostentatious imitations, that businessmen have a point when they say they give the public what it wants.

Mauclair's most important insight is to see that the task is not to reform the decorative arts but to reform consumer consciousness. Above all, this means changing the social consciousness which makes people want to appear and feel wealthier than they are or to flaunt the wealth they do have. Such attitudes are closely related to a class structure, associated with modern capitalism, in which bourgeois want to live like aristocrats of old and workers want to live like bourgeois. Institutional change is required, but that is not all. The roots of envy go far deeper than a particular economic structure. Social ambitions did not appear only with the advent of capitalism, however much capitalism may further the growth of such ambitions. Although Mauclair identified the transformation of consumer consciousness too closely with cleanliness and neatness, this does not detract from the validity of his general thesis that the necessary transformation lies in the realm of social morality.

But that transformation cannot come about so long as consumer objects are seen as serving only physical functions. The concept of "appropriateness" tends to perpetuate this attitude by emphasizing convenience, washability, and the like. Here Gallé had a point: objects of consumption, or at least some of them, also serve a function of the spirit, a "function of human culture." Gallé's aesthetic idealism led him astray at times, to be sure. It seems more sensible to let a flower vase minister to the spiritual need for beauty and to let an armchair serve the organic need of supporting the body comfortably, instead of turning the armchair into a clumsy carrier of quotations from Baudelaire. Still, Gallé was at least alert to the needs of the imagination, and Mauclair shared this alertness. He had rejected Marxism largely because it focused so narrowly on physical utility as the basis for social and personal life. "Is there really a need to demonstrate that there is a utility of the second degree, an abstract utility?" Mauclair protested. Marxism had to broaden its outlook to recognize moral and spiritual needs as well as material ones, to recognize art as "useful from the eternal point of view, from the viewpoint of secondary utility."[51]

The great appeal of the dream world of mass consumption, the reason the masses preferred it to the rational world of the decorative arts reformers, lies precisely in its appeal to the imagination. The trouble with this dream world is not that it appeals to the imagination—a legitimate function, a legitimate need—but that it does so deceptively and in a way that ultimately serves the needs of the market first. In particular, the dream of wealth is stressed above all others, and the importance of social hierarchy in giving a sense of personal identity and worth is overemphasized. But to hope to eliminate the dream of wealth entirely, to break all relationship between consumer objects and social status—this too is probably an illusion, somewhat akin to the Marxist illusion of a completely classless society.

All societies seem to have included some kind of social differentiation. Man has not just organic and spiritual needs but social needs as well, and consumer objects have traditionally served those social needs along with the other ones. Possession of goods marks off one group from another and provides concrete evidence of the social hierarchy. This was true long before capitalism. In medieval times the knight's sword and priest's censer were objects signifying place in the social order. By the nineteenth century, however, wealth alone—not criteria like faith, courage, learning, or leadership—had to a large extent become the only significant determinant of social prestige. The social value of various consumer objects became tied to their market value. Because wealth is so obviously expressed in a person's ability to consume, objects of consumption no longer related to a social hierarchy externally defined; instead, they became themselves the hierarchy. When objects no longer serve as symbols of the social order but become themselves the concrete determinants of that order, we confront a social (as opposed to an individual) form of reification.

What should be criticized is not the concept of social differentiation, of various levels of prestige and function, but a social hierarchy which has been reduced to the common denominator of money. That reduction is the social cause of many of the visual disasters of the nineteenth century—both the proliferation of cheap ostentation and the degradation of formerly noble objects (for example, as des Esseintes lamented, the manufacture of Communion wafers from potato flour). This confusion in design betrays a confusion about the relative merits of various activities, of various contributions to society. The theory of functionality in design evades this whole problem. It would suppress ornament altogether and eliminate everything except what is needed for physical usage, rather than face the dilemma of determining what is socially appropriate. On the other hand, Gallé's preference for natural motifs also ignores the social implications of consumer items. He was taking refuge in an ethereal realm of classless beauty.[52] What was needed was to explore the middle ground between the fundamental physical needs of human beings and the loftiest needs of the spirit—the social ground where consumers are seen not as isolated individuals, not as animals or as angels, but as people living in society.

The Discovery of Modern Beauty–In his developing awareness of the connection between artistic reform and social consciousness, Mauclair traveled a long way from his youthful enchantment with the symbolists, and even from his early advocacy of decorative arts reform. By 1906, when he was still only in his mid-thirties, he had gained a far more complex understanding of the artistic and social issues which had seemed relatively straightforward to him when he was in his twenties. What he had lost was optimism. By concluding that only fundamental changes in social consciousness and economic institutions could lead to a genuine reform in the design of everyday objects, Mauclair condemned himself to frustration. He knew what needed to be done, but, as an artist and intellectual outside party and class commitment, he was unable to do it.

This was the predicament of many of Mauclair's generation. By 1905–1906 many artists and intellectuals were losing interest in the public issues which had so stirred them in the 1890s. The prevailing mood was to return to the creed that no true artist would possess a political opinion which might detract from the purity of his art. The revival of classicism became a dominant literary movement, and nationalism and traditionalism were the cultural slogans of the day. Mauclair found himself accused of, rather than praised for, a continuing commitment to social art.[53] Even he, in the face of seemingly intractable social and economic problems, to some extent retreated to the realm of pure aesthetics. Perhaps, he suggested, the way to resolve the contradiction between aesthetic ideals and modern social reality is for the artist's role to be defined as that of the discovery of beauty in what others have spontaneously created. In other words, instead of trying to alter social consciousness, the artist would alter his own consciousness. This solution can only be interpreted as a retreat to privacy away from seemingly insoluble public problems, and yet it is a solution with considerably more interest and potential for development than those years' better publicized and more popular retreat to classicism and traditionalism.

Mauclair explains this new alternative in two articles published in the *Revue bleue* during the period when in the same journal he was analyzing the crisis of the decorative arts. The first article, titled "Le Style de la rue moderne" ("The Style of the Modern Street"), appeared in December, 1905, and "Le Nouveau Paris du peuple" ("The New Paris of the People") was published the following month. In these essays Mauclair turns from particular consumer items made for individual use to the undistinguished, unadorned, utilitarian milieu of modern urban life on a collective scale—the new suburbs springing up then to the south and west of Paris. These are working-class quarters, Mauclair cautions, which you might have visited as a child and never cared to revisit, quarters the bourgeoisie thinks of as "obscure and tragic places" where women are hacked into pieces and revolvers are fired in broad daylight. While these suburbs are not so grim in reality, they are certainly not beautiful in the traditional sense of the word. Then, Mauclair suggests, perhaps our understanding of beauty should be altered so that our consciousness will keep pace with our visual impressions:

> The mind clings to prejudices which vision no longer approves. . . . We still condemn things of which the sight seduces us, and if we find beautiful a smoking factory in the late afternoon of an autumn day, we protest, nonetheless, against applying the epithet "beautiful" to this factory, because the verbalism of old classifications possesses us and the idea of greater *character* is not yet equivalent for us to the idea of greater *beauty*. Thus we may judge poorly our own sensations before the new appearance of suburban Paris.[54]

Rather than saying that beauty should be democratized, Mauclair is saying that it *is* being democratized if the artist actively tries to alter his perception of it. "We grieve in saying that our age lacks style, but at this very moment we are in the process of composing one for it. . . . For we must not look on but participate, and our duty is to try to understand." The source of difficulty is that we depend upon the same aesthetic terminology to describe our response to a crooked medieval house and to a new suburban one, although the purposes of the two structures are different. If we see the two side by side, we are struck by a general impression of their incompatibility, of a disharmony and antithesis which make us suffer. We express this suffering by saying that one is beautiful and the other ugly. As a result, "we always have a tendency to consider ourselves intruders in the life we have made for ourselves."[55]

In the new suburbs there is no such painful contrast. The modern structures replace nothing of interest (unlike the so-called improvements of Montmartre, which Mauclair deplores), and so we are able to look at them in and of themselves and to perceive their own distinct beauty. This is first of all the beauty of utility in the obvious sense of cleanliness and comfort—an aesthetic of hygiene, open space, air and light and trees, far preferable as a place to live than narrow passages heaped with trash. "They have not substituted something utilitarian and ugly for something inconvenient and pretty, but simply something clean for something filthy."[56] The picturesque is only one form of beauty, that of detail, and the beauty of the suburbs is to be found not in particular objects or ornaments, not even in particular buildings, but in the overall impression of harmony found in the general silhouette and mutual relations of volumes. The geometrical alignment of the houses and streets, so often dismissed as sterile monotony, has a horizontal rigidity that corresponds to the vertical geometry of the tall buildings. The rectilinear design originates in modern needs—the need for long, regular streets to carry increased traffic, the need for taller structures to accommodate more people in less space—and this utility becomes a "linear harmony" quite unlike the accidental and capricious harmony of old cities.[57] There is a grandeur to these vistas, especially in the spectacle of energy presented by the factory-filled plain of Saint-Denis "with its thousands of smokestacks, its smelting fires, its innumerable beacons, its interlaced highways where from all sides spreads the beautiful mother-of-pearl smoke which the twilight embraces." When night falls, the beauty of the suburbs reaches its height. Electrical lighting creates a magical scene, making lighted houses and factories look like great motionless ships afloat on a black ocean.[58]

Mauclair is groping to apprehend a new kind of social art that will truly unite beauty and utility and the ordinary needs of ordinary people without condescension. Yet what is most striking about Mauclair's apprehension is not what he sees, but his distance from what he sees. He is very much an outsider, an "intruder," as he contemplates the smoking factories and the working-class apartments and streets. He gazes at the distant vista of the cityscape in much the same way that other self-conscious modern observers have admired the rural landscape—not as a familiar, practical, working place, but as an abstract object of aesthetic contemplation. This vision, which regards places of production primarily as a source of aesthetic stimulation, as an example of "style," is the vision of a consumer: the aesthetic distance between the onlooker and the distant scenery reflects the social distance between production and consumption which has become pervasive since the industrial revolution.[59] And it is really this social distance—the distance that makes bourgeois avoid working-class quarters as obscure, tragic, and dangerous places—that makes us feel we are "intruders in the life we have made for ourselves."

Mauclair is vaguely aware of this, for his contemplation is troubled by doubts and hesitations. Perhaps, he suggests, the "style of the modern street" is not really a form of beauty, but an aesthetic of power. That is why this new style may be appreciated more fully in New York than in Paris, for "it is by the relationships of volumes that the series of houses of New York have taken on an aspect of grandiose Assyrian barbarism which, especially at night, with the magic of the lights, invites the visitor to an unforgettable spectacle from the Brooklyn Bridge."[60] Is this beauty at all, or is it another environment of mass consumption, an "unforgettable spectacle" which overwhelms the passive, distanced spectator and saturates him with a display of force? Is this a style appropriate to the modern age, or one appropriate to "Assyrian barbarism"?

This suspicion of neo-barbarism forces Mauclair to reconsider his own admiration for the magnificent spectacles of modern urban, industrial society. He becomes a critical admirer; he does not cease to be impressed by these spectacles, but he realizes that they appeal to primitive instincts which are not really aesthetic in character. In another *Revue bleue* article, written somewhat before "The Style of the Modern Street" and "The New Paris of the People," Mauclair had already mused that the appeal of iron architecture—the basic modern architecture of suburban housing developments, factories, and bridges—was "barbarous, in the true sense of the word." Nowhere is this primitive character more evident than in the great iron beams of the Eiffel Tower, the central icon of the 1889 exposition, which at once seems very new and very familiar:

> Structures such as the Eiffel Tower seem familiar because they remind us of the caprices of barbarous kings, of Babylonian festivities. . . . In its frank and brutal novelty [the tower] retains a prehistoric aspect. Its armatures rise up from the ground . . . like skeletons of monsters, and in looking at them we return to the confused stupor of our childhood before the bones of whales in the museum. It is something primitive, unfinished, and huge which repulses us, disturbs us, and attracts us.

The scale of iron structures takes us back to days when primitive peoples

> had to resolve terrible problems with imperfect knowledge and clumsy tools, and they nonetheless wanted to build large. The enormity of the construction was the first sign by which despots wanted to demonstrate their power.[61]

Two years after writing these remarks, Mauclair visited the 1907 Salon de l'Automobile. In an article on its "Décoration lumineuse" ("Luminous Decoration") he analyzes further the barbaric character of environments of mass consumption whose aesthetic appeal depends on the size and volume of their structures, their unearthly lighting, their vast silhouettes and grand vistas. He feels compelled to pay tribute to the "extraordinary spectacle" at the Grand Palais that entrances the crowd: "There is [at the Salon de l'Automobile] a sort of eruption of forces which creates a special lyricism." But he also feels that that lyricism is permeated by a disturbing quality:

> Just as autolocomotion is based on intermittent and disciplined explosion, it seems that the beauty of this place is that of a disciplined fire. Something is borrowed from the sinister to make something splendid.
>
> Each day at sunset a campfire lights up in the middle of the Champs-Élysées; the power of the fire fascinates creatures, and irresistibly the feeling of a return to primitive times imposes itself.[62]

Louis Haugmard had wondered if the cinema, another spectacle "as immense as it is disquieting," was a modern equivalent of ancient bread and circuses. At the Salon de l'Automobile Mauclair too feels that "the dominant sensation conveyed by this colossal industrial fairyland is that of the unexpected return of ultra-modernism to barbarian pageantry."[63]

The social imperative behind aesthetic primitivism, Mauclair concludes, is the obsession to display power. The luminous decoration of the Grand Palais "is powerful, if not exactly beautiful." In its affirmation of power over beauty, the Salon de l'Automobile becomes a "symbolic affirmation of a spiritual current" evident throughout Paris. The same current is seen when "war chariots, called automobiles" run down pedestrians more and more frequently; when the brilliance of electrical lighting chases away nighttime shadows "as the spotlight of a battleship searches the nocturnal waves to find the enemy"; when the night sky is blasted by advertisements for toothpaste, liqueurs, and egg noodles (Mauclair cites the prophecy of Villiers de l'Isle-Adam); when entire houses and shop windows are lit by a "fixed, impartial glare." There seems no end to these displays of power. The violence of commerce, which keeps multiplying its advertisements and automobiles and displays, imposes itself more and more:

> It cannot be affirmed that the spectacle offered by the Salon de l'Automobile presents the maximum of luminous industrialized force. Obviously they will go further in brutal power. The newspapers tell us with complaisant admiration that there are two hundred thousand Paz and Silva lamps there. The automobile industry triumphs: it will require four hundred, six hundred thousand lamps in two years. It will ignite [Paris] from the Louvre to the Étoile, from the Invalides to Montmartre, if it wishes.[64]

While the lighting at the Salon de l'Automobile may be ultra-modern in its technology, its atavistic purpose is to impress the masses with a display of "brutal power." It constitutes a throwback to times when (in Mauclair's most disturbing analogy) "Nero lighted his gardens with Christians smeared with pitch, luminous decoration far too symbolic, sinister, and nauseating." But we are not far removed from reviving such barbaric horrors, he warns: "Modern warfare, with the mine, the shell, and the bomb, knows how to invest death with a wholly Neronian sadism."[65]

When the artist discerns modern beauty in industrial suburbs, in New York at night, in the Eiffel Tower, in the glare of the Salon de l'Automobile, is he liberating his consciousness or is he bowing in neo-primitivistic awe before "industrialized force"? Simply to raise the question removes any possibility of wholehearted aesthetic admiration for environments of mass consumption. The artist must, at best, be suspicious of his own enthusiasm. The concept of an aesthetic of the primitive is no more limited to matters of art than is Haugmard's "aesthetic" of the cinema. Both Mauclair and Haugmard try to show that the artistically sterile is also socially pernicious. Both critics are painfully conscious of the commercial motives behind displays designed to stun the spectator into a passive, confused stupor so that he is only able "to look, look, look." The neo-barbaric is an aesthetic that seeks to overwhelm through magnitude, whether in the size of a building or vista, the number of lights, or the elaboration of ornamentation. No matter how large the dimensions, the result is one-dimensional. It is not that magnitude is incompatible with beauty, for the history of art presents many examples of their coexistence, and Mauclair himself praises the "nude and severe beauty" of certain outsized primitive structures,[66] but in itself "the search for maximum effect has never been the criterion of an art."[67]

The aesthetic of the primitive is therefore a political concept as much as an artistic one. Sheer disproportion of scale reveals in an immediately visible way the disproportion of power between ruling "despots" and ordinary people. This is true of the monuments built by barbarous kings, by Roman emperors, and also by Renaissance princes whose Loire châteaux rose in splendor above peasant hovels. Then, Mauclair asks, who are the contemporary equivalents, the modern despots eager to demonstrate their power through a search for maximum effect? It is "the force of industrialized illumination," he asserts, that displays its "brutal power" by lighting up the Grand Palais, that manufactures cars and bombs, that assaults city-dwellers with a continual glare of advertising. The violence of commerce provokes regression to a state of savage awe similar to a childlike belief in fairy tales.[68]

These are evasive answers. Not human beings but the

abstractions *industrialized force* and *commerce* are claimed as the rulers of modern society. Mauclair's rejection of Marxist rigidity has its price; he loses also the clarification a Marxist analysis would bring to his question, "Who are the contemporary despots?" But this failure should not detract from the importance of his concept of aesthetic neo-barbarism as a means to understanding the hypnotic appeal of dream worlds of the consumer. Barbarism, childhood, and dreams all arouse cruder and stronger emotions than those of waking civilized adulthood. They are at once fascinating and disturbing experiences, as des Esseintes found when his isolation at Fontenay ended in regression to those cruder, stronger emotions. The sinister and splendid dream world of the consumer may be ultramodern in its techniques, but it conveys a fundamentally primitive experience.

The End of a Generation – By the time Mauclair wrote these articles on the discovery of modern beauty, he was again isolated. He was no more comfortable with socialists and anarchists than he had been ten years before, and in addition he was to an unprecedented degree alienated from other artists and intellectuals. In the 1890's the artistic community had formed a sort of extended family for him, compensating for his political isolation, but by 1905 or so Mauclair had become disillusioned with the snobbish elitism of artists who played at decorative arts reform. In addition, he found that commitment to a genuine social art was being deserted for a return to literary classicism and political nationalism of a traditional sort. He became convinced that he was observing a watershed in French intellectual life—the supplanting of the ideals of the generation of the 1890s, his generation, by alien concerns. He was further convinced that the crisis of the decorative arts could only be understood in terms of this general collapse of concern for social issues which had inspired his contemporaries to such exciting and fruitful experiments in art and life.

In a 1905 article in the *Revue des revues* Mauclair combines an intensely personal testimony with a general description of this cultural transformation. His tone is elegiac as he recalls the 1890s with deep nostalgia and pays tribute to its memory:

> I made my literary debut in 1890. I was eighteen years old. I realize today by comparison that I became involved with "intellectuals" (the word is as good as any) at a very interesting moment in modern history, at a moment of paroxysm. . . . We mixed with public life by leaving behind theories of art for art's sake and dandyism. . . . I loved [my generation] infinitely, because it was active and frank, because its purposes, its excesses, even its ridiculous ideas (we had them, and how!) were born from a great desire for inquiry, for moral liberty, for new formulas. . . . Yes, it was an exciting decade, that of 1890 to 1900. What interesting personalities were revealed and developed in it! What ardent changes of tack, what desires and plans, what ideas taken up, rejected, and taken up again, what a surprising need for general transformation, what a curious movement of artists toward social life. We saw many things die and we wanted to create many others. It was the moment when the war generation [referring to the Franco-Prussian War] was surpassed by a new one which firmly intended to free itself from the fearful hesitations, from the depression of its predecessor, and we fell upon all prejudices, we had a great desire to renew everything, to re-create forms, expressions, frameworks, to prepare the future. . . . My generation was a rich storehouse of ideas, intentions, hypotheses.[69]

In contrast, the intellectuals of 1905, in spite of their formidable literary virtuosity, seem to Mauclair profoundly and willfully ignorant of everything going on in society at large. His loyalty to the ideals of the 1890s makes him feel like a cultural anachronism, although he is only in his mid-thirties: "The generations come so quickly and the 'transmutation of values' is so rapid in the overheated alembic of contemporary life."[70] When the transience of the marketplace invades cultural life, the result can be extraordinarily painful in personal life. Individuals do not shed one set of ideals for a more up-to-date set as easily as they acquire new material possessions. Mauclair refuses to concede that the ideals which formed his intellectual personality are just another fad, now outdated. He insists that the concepts of cosmopolitanism, knowledgeability, and, especially, artistic involvement in public life have a permanent validity, that they represent not just relative change but absolute progress. He refuses to bid farewell to his generation. Like that other stoic hero, des Esseintes, Mauclair confronts the rising tide of modern life with a certain nobility, but he too finds himself utterly alone and retreats to a personal code of honor in the face of alien values. When even fellow artists and intellectuals have deserted him, with whom can he communicate except the dead?

> I lived this period of which I speak so intensely and so quickly that, although having joined with men older than myself by some years, I soon came to think of myself as of the same age: the battles shared, the setbacks accepted, the bad times and the good put us abreast. And I knew some rare and beautiful beings who have died, and who carry away perhaps the finest memories of friendship that I will ever have been given on earth . . . every conscience, every soul among the survivors seems to me, I must confess, of a crystal less pure: and with [those departed] I live at least as much as with contemporaries, and often find myself less alone.[71]

In 1909 Mauclair published one last look at the decorative arts in the *Revue bleue*. The article makes depressing reading. Once again he chews over the course of the experiment which began with Bing's store and ended in "a moral and material bankruptcy." Merchants still use the same excuses for making imitations rather than innovative designs; artists who make promising experiments are patronized only by a small elite of connoisseurs and work in isolation; "the public does not at all feel the need of a social art and is still indifferent to it all";[72] the ridiculous hierarchy that places the fine arts above the industrial ones remains unaltered.

Mauclair still advocates reestablishment of corporations, but at the end of this article he revives an old proposal, when he mentions plans then under discussion to hold "an exposition of social art to try to give a lesson of things." He no longer hopes that an exposition will teach the general public very much, but he does think artists may learn from it as "a serious examination of the themes of the future." Even for this restricted purpose, however, Mauclair foresees great difficulties from officials, bureaucrats, and merchants. Because of special interests, each of which would lobby for an arrangement drawing attention to itself, only an artistic dictator could organize the exposition properly:

> It would require the authority of an artist, of an organizer, of an economist, of a lofty spirit imbued with the philosophy of art, with knowledge of all industrial and artistic techniques, and, finally, endowed with an indomitable character, to organize such a demonstration, to retain all its meaning, and to extract the true lesson from it. Should such a man be found, he would, moreover, require an enormous social power to resist the coalition of jealousies, routines, greed, and vain incompetence. His intervention would be equivalent to reforming the teaching methods of the state schools, disarming the bureaucracy, conquering the egoism of the merchants, returning to art criticism its dignity and scope—now paralyzed by paid advertising—to galvanize the ignorant, lazy, or frivolous public. Do we still have such giants for this type of labor? It would require nothing less than a Colbert![73]

Mauclair's exasperation with the obstacles he has observed for fifteen years reaches the point of despair. His yearning for a Colbert is both futile and melancholy. Jean Baptiste Colbert (1619–1683), the ruthless dictator of French economic life under Louis XIV—organizer of vast public works, friend of the corporations, creator of royal manufactures and new industries—still was not able to

bring prosperity to France or to reform the wholly inadequate fiscal system of the nation; his tireless labors as an
administrator did nothing to correct the fundamental social and political weaknesses of the Old Regime. The story
goes that he died of a broken heart after he heard Louis
XIV speak disparagingly of Versailles, whose construction
Colbert had supervised.

If the high hopes roused by Colbert's projects were
unfulfilled, it is also true that the buoyant expectations of
the 1890s were disappointed. If Mauclair's sense of futility
is especially sad because his youthful enthusiasm was
wholehearted and generous, it was far from unique
among his generation. Other advocates of decorative arts
reform arrived at a similar impasse. Mauclair's response—
to remain loyal to the need for reform while acknowledging its extreme difficulties, if not its impossibility—occu-
pies a middle ground between two other possible reactions: to retreat, as many did, to nationalism or classicism,
or to press for reforms on an even larger, Colbertian scale.
Jean Lahor, for example, instead of questioning the aesthetic ideology of the 1890s as Mauclair did, extended that
ideology from domestic objects to workers' houses to "art
in the street" and, finally, to the whole environment, rural
and urban. His methods also remained the same and only
grew in scale—getting publicity through books, articles,
and speeches, starting an organization and enlisting both
government and private support, and then using that organization to sponsor projects such as the collection of
models of design, establishment of regional museums,
sale of cheap reproductions of artistic masterpieces, and to
hold more conferences and increase the membership. All
this activity culminated in the city-garden movement,
which had as its goal the unification of city and country in
a planned environment.[74]

In all this effort Lahor seems to have been prey not to
despair but to evasion. With the temperament of a doer, not
a thinker, he was too busy with propaganda and organization to reflect on their ultimate efficacy. All the same, his

evolution toward advocacy of an ever larger scope of design constitutes a tacit admission that consumer taste is not to be reformed on an individual level: a general social solution that treats consumption as a collective phenomenon is required. The increase in scale does not alter the assumption that society may be improved by surrounding people with the right things, that is, with things designed by an artistic elite for the benefit of the people. Indeed, when this assumption is extended to environmental design it becomes more authoritarian than ever. Individuals may have some choice in purchasing particular objects but they often have no choice about their surroundings.

Like the decorative arts movement of the 1890s, the city-garden movement of the first decade of the twentieth century appealed to many parts of the political spectrum. The first city-garden built in France was commissioned in 1904 by the Company of the Mines of Dorgues as housing for its workers,[75] but those who claimed socialist ideals found the idea of large-scale design as enticing as company management did. There is a remarkable congruence between the town built by the Dorgues firm and the ideal factory town described by Émile Zola in his novel *Travail* ("Labor," 1901). The planned community has none of the frenzied greed of the department store Zola described in *Au Bonheur des Dames*, but it also has none of the liberty. One of the sadder characters in *Travail* is Lange, a potter of anarchist politics, whose work is naïve but lovely, a "happy development of the taste of the people," combining beauty and utility in the design of ordinary items. When the utopian city-garden is finally established, the small shop of this independent artisan is replaced by an immense factory that churns out tiles, bricks, crockery, and other decorations to adorn workers' houses. Lange refuses to give up his craftsmanship. Since he is no longer needed to make domestic furnishings, he creates useless little figurines.[76] Zola admires Lange, but he feels that such artisans must inevitably give way to the forces of technical progress. When a whole city can be furnished tastefully by factory production, its inhabitants must surely be happy in their clean, attractive surroundings. The magnitude of scale made possible by modern technology has Zola so dazzled that he never inquires about consumers' tastes and wishes, about consumer consciousness. In a world of planned environments, Lange—and Mauclair, who also refuses to go along with the latest trends—is an anachronism.

Concluding Remarks—Anyone who participated in the outpouring of social causes and political enthusiasms of the American 1960s cannot fail to be moved by Mauclair's tribute to the generation of the 1890s in France, so similar in its youthful buoyancy and concern for the larger community. Anyone who has endured the sorry decline of that buoyancy and concern in the 1970s can appreciate the frustration and isolation Mauclair felt in the early years of the twentieth century. In the American sixties, the aesthetic of Design Research (as with Art Nouveau, the name of the retail outlet identified the style) provided a visual correlative for the social consciousness of the decade. This style appealed to consumers who were relatively well-educated and affluent, who were concerned about the poverty-stricken and powerless but who were clearly not a part of these groups. For such people to adopt the contemporary version of the bourgeois lifestyle—wall-to-wall carpeting, floral draperies, and armchairs in velveteen upholstery flanked by ornate plated floorlamps—was just as unthinkable as it had been in Mauclair's day. For them, as for the group of the 1890s that felt above class or party, the functional aesthetic provided a way of dressing down tastefully. DR items too were returns to simplicity, honesty, and utility, but relatively expensive versions which would never be confused with the simple and honest utility of Third World poverty. This was, in fact, liberal chic rather than the more extreme and hypocritical forms of radical chic that Tom Wolfe decried, just as Mauclair had decried the radical chic of 1890s anarchists.

By 1909 Mauclair had concluded that the decorative arts movement had ended in "a moral and material bankruptcy." In 1979 Design Research succumbed to material bankruptcy in the form of foreclosing banks. Its moral bankruptcy had come earlier, in its promotion of High Tech, the industrial look in home furnishings—clearly an attempt to find a new look which would ring up new sales, and a genuine example of radical chic in its exploitation of the factory look for those who would never work in a factory. The democratic lifestyle is by no means defunct, however; its message has only lost its clarity through excessive diffusion. Just as Art Nouveau designs were translated into mass-produced hatpins selling for twenty sous, Design Research models were imitated in cheaper versions by better-managed companies. The democratization of its version of luxury was indeed one important reason for DR's demise. The type of person originally attracted to the DR merchandise found himself drowned in the democratic tide.

What alternatives are left? We can surrender to the neo-primitivism of throbbing neon signs, Golden Arches, and Babylonian shopping centers, claiming to "learn from Las Vegas," that is, to discover non-traditional beauty in a world hostile to its traditional forms.[77] Or we can increase the scale of design, building or at least planning habitats, machines for living, model cities under geodesic domes, futuristic cities in the desert—now that the earlier ideal of "garden cities" has been degraded into the modern suburb. And then there is always the possibility of retreating from social concerns to personal concerns. We could trade the political decade of the 1960s for the "Me Decade" of the 1970s (again the expression is Tom Wolfe's), and cultivate a lifestyle of the distinctive, the tailormade, the personalized.

At the moment the elitist style of consumption may seem to have triumphed, but the appeal of the democratic mode is not dead. Undoubtedly, these two alternative modes of consumption will continue to alternate in dominance for some time to come. The reason is that each of these ideals—one of privileged individualism, the other of egalitarian uniformity—has merits that compensate for the shortcomings of the other. Georges Palante, a contemporary of Mauclair and an intriguing and neglected social thinker, described the relationship between them as one of "antinomy." In his book *Les Antinomies entre l'individu et la société* ("The Antinomies between the Individual and Society," 1913) Palante includes a chapter on "Economic Antinomy" in which he identifies two major theories of consumption, the "aristocratic and individualistic" and the "democratic and egalitarian." The first one, he points out, has the virtue of liberty in admitting "the greatest variety of enjoyments, the greatest diversity of life." Its flaw is its injustice:

> The aristocratic and individualistic theory is that of the partisans of luxury. Luxury represents exception, privilege in economics; the refinement of needs and tastes. . . . The aristocratic individualist admits that since society has no other goal than to produce superior men, it is natural and legitimate that an army of slaves and workers sacrifice its life and its ideal of democratic well-being to the comfort and luxury of the privileged.

Socialists and others who support the "democratic and egalitarian" ideal would forbid egotistical luxuries and ensure that no one is privileged as a consumer—a fairer solution, but one that sacrifices diversity to an enforced unity. Palante, who like Mauclair loves individual self-expression as well as social justice, cannot choose between the two and feels that society in general is equally unable to choose:

> There is today a strong tendency to the equalization of the conditions of existence, to the interdiction of luxury in consumption. But on the other hand there is also among men a great diversity of tastes and of appreciations. Each individual has or can have his opinion of comfort, his particular ideal of well-being. This can be a source of

division between individuals, families, classes, and social sub-classes. In fact, luxury consumption is maintained or even increased. The rich buy autos and the defenders of capitalism console egalitarian democrats by persuading them that the time will come when automobiles will be within the reach of all purses. Thus is continued and perpetuated, without being resolved, the conflict between the desire for privileged and individualized consumption (luxury) and the democratic tendency to make equality prevail in consumption.[78]

Since Palante's day society has indeed kept wavering between these two alternatives to bourgeois and mass consumption. They both express a higher ideal but are locked in an antinomy wherein the demands of personal liberty confront those of social justice. To borrow from the Marxist vocabulary, their relationship is a dialectical one and society is caught in their contradiction. Is it possible to imagine a synthesis of the aristocratic and the democratic ideals in consumption? Palante makes a suggestive remark: "Throughout the vicissitudes of this conflict, one given nonetheless remains constant: a measure of impersonal evaluation which gives to luxury itself, in our civilization, a character of banality and anonymity."[79] The common denominator in the aristocratic and the democratic theories, Palante adds, is that of supply and demand. The antinomy is only apparent. Both theories reduce the moral and economic dilemmas of the consumer to a choice of lifestyles, to an arrangement of impersonal objects found on the marketplace which operates according to supply and demand. They are not alternatives to mass and bourgeois consumption but are part of the same moral universe, where appearances and images are accepted as reality, where merchandise with its "character of banality and anonymity" is taken as a significant indication of vital human character. That moral universe, as Balzac pointed out as early as the 1830s, is one in which minute details of dress, furnishings, and manners are assumed to be "unspeakably significant." Merchandise is seen, or rather heard, as making a statement. Spoken language is replaced by the language of lifestyle, by a silent, "unspeakably" portentous communication through things.

To return to the historical examples of the late nineteenth century—so valuable in discerning the origins of the modern obsession with lifestyle—we see that aristocratic decadents and democratic decorative arts reformers both attributed tremendous power to *things*. For them objects not only revealed and expressed human beings but actively shaped personalities and destinies. In the words of one socialist partisan of decorative arts reform, there is "a morality of the created thing (*une morale de la chose créée*) which attests to that of the creator and which afterward reacts back on him."[80] This belief that consumer objects both express and mold the individual, that they carry a profound moral burden, is just as typical of des Esseintes, who for that very reason is acutely sensitive to the merchandise around him, even to the point of insanity. So perhaps it should be no surprise that Huysmans, the creator of des Esseintes, was one of the earliest and most perceptive critics of the decorative arts movement, which shared this faith in, and dread of, the power of objects. In 1886, when Mauclair was still a *lycée* student, Huysmans correctly predicted the fate of decorative arts reform. He wrote a short article in the *Revue indépendante*, a favorite journal of the decadents and symbolists, to protest proposals then being aired to establish a museum of the decorative arts:

> The objects which will compose it will be for the most part apocryphal, parliamentary recommendations forcibly trying to impose on us a heap of lard; furthermore, the ignominious trash of the imitations launched forth by commerce will soil forever the truly artistic models which a beneficent fate will perhaps permit to slip into the pile of antique sham.
>
> It will be like the antique coppers whose deplorable imitations fill the storerooms of the Bon Marché and the

Louvre; it will be Japanese art for export, printing on faïence and cloth, pasteboard manufacture of Cordovan leathers on papier-mâché, it will be cheap luxury. . . .

. . . I know you don't have to buy them, but you have to see them because they fill up entire boulevards and streets! . . . You have to submit to [this horror] because the eye . . . wanders all the same toward it and lingers there; there is in it a forced, morbid impulsion, the attraction of the horrible, the morbid appetite for the monstrous, the unnatural craving for the ugly![81]

Huysmans concluded that the building destined for such a museum should be consigned to purifying flames, for "then, perhaps, people would realize that Fire is the essential artist of our times."

Huysmans not only predicted the visible details of the decorative arts fad, he also foresaw that decorative arts reform would never provide a viable alternative to the choice of nightmares facing des Esseintes. Huysmans' perception was largely due to the fact that in des Esseintes he had already analyzed a species of decorative arts reformer who surrounds himself with artistically designed objects as protection against the vile proliferation of bourgeois and mass commerce. The fate of des Esseintes gives prophetic insight into the fate of other reformers, even if they were democratic rather than individualistic in inspiration. À Rebours, it will be recalled, presents a concrete example of the process of reification. The hero's vitality is slowly eroded while the objects around him become progressively more animated and finally act independently of his will. In this confusion of priorities that accords more significance to the collection of things than to the evolution of life, in this inherent reification, both des Esseintes and decorative arts reformers mimic the bourgeois and mass consumption they attempt to evade. They may accumulate objects that are, according to their standards, beautiful and spiritual rather than ugly and banal, but still these are objects understood as potent and active agents. Des Esseintes, bourgeois or mass consumers, and decorative arts reformers have this in common: they rely on objects to create a material refuge, an illusory universe preferable to a less attractive or even hostile social reality. They *all* seek dream worlds of the consumer.

When things are invested with such importance, they become vital, in the way that objects at Fontenay came alive to torment des Esseintes. On a seemingly benign level, decorative arts partisans habitually referred to consumer items as "companions" of man,[82] or, in Gallé's version, as "brothers."[83] To them, useful objects were living beings invited into the home, where they established an intimate relationship with the owner. But Mauclair, for one, was aware of the unsettling implications of this supposed camaraderie between people and possessions. In an essay written at about the same time as those analyzing the crisis of the decorative arts, Mauclair discusses painters of still life, *nature morte* (literally, "dead nature"). Mauclair rejects the French terminology in favor of the German *Stilleben*, comparable to the English "still life" or the French *la vie en silence*. Objects do have a life, he contends, wordless and mysterious, and a consciousness with a uniquely fantastic quality:

> There takes place with objects what takes place with domestic animals: a constant exchange with man, and a subtle community of "feelings," certainly indefinable, as far as objects are concerned, but we would be illogical indeed if we were to conclude the inexistence of what we can't define directly. . . . Usage develops the physiognomy of an object; contact with its possessor puts into it resources of expressiveness. . . . Not only do time and its patina act on an object as on a living being and reinforce its significance, but also an object is sedate or laughable, comfortable or ill at ease, according to where it is placed, like a being. . . . There are relations of affection or of antipathy between an object and its owner, and, in some way, a whole restrained imitation of our relations with beings that move. . . .
>
> . . . Not only have we admitted that the object accumulates feelings scattered around it, but we can, more-

over, be led to think that, by a sort of countershock, it might restore these sensibilities *not always in the order foreseen by us* [italics his]. It thus would have a second life, personal and independent of our control, and here we enter into the "fantasy" of which I spoke. . . .

    . . . I think that objects have their special life, that subtle relationships are established among them when they are juxtaposed in the same atmosphere for a long time, that they learn to esteem themselves, to know themselves, to fear themselves, to understand themselves. We have assembled them with a certain taste to create a harmony—and I don't speak only of luxury items, for even a kitchen is harmonious by the arrangement of the utensils. There are here relationships of forms, color, proportions: would I be mad to conclude that these relationships constitute a life analogous to that which governs by reciprocities the elements of a crowd?

Would this be madness? or does this rather frightening description of reification only hint at the insanity that invaded Fontenay? Mauclair ends his essay by urging contemporary artists to pay more attention to past masters of still life (like Chardin) because

contemporary art is preoccupied with expressing silence, with speaking "the language of flowers and of mute things," with introducing into painting a whole order of presciences, allusions, creations . . . the age of symbolism latent in everything, the suggestion of appearances, with going, in a word, to search for life and reality beyond that which we see, behind the shell of appearances, in the full region of the subconscious.[84]

The element linking the decorative arts and the fine arts is their attribution of life to objects, their common "revelation," as Mauclair puts it, "of the *permanent* life of the *inert*" (italics his). In both the decorative and the fine arts this tendency may have the benefit of imbuing ordinary consumer objects with significance and dignity, but it runs the risk of ending in a surreal universe that is a jumble of concrete but absurd objects, of materiality gone mad, a universe of matter which has become opaque to the ideal.

Instead of upholding the value of art as he intends to do, Mauclair only restricts that value when he puts so much weight on the visual arts (whether decorative or fine), on things, as opposed to other aesthetic forms. He forgets how much non-visual forms of art can do toward creating bonds of social sympathy, which in the end must be given priority over any mysterious sympathy between man and object. Literature is one example. In a 1912 article one decorative arts reformer concluded that the imminent failure of the cause could be avoided only if novelists began to portray artisans as heroes. The resources of language could convey the intelligence and character of artisans and describe the lovely things they make. Since the public prefers showy Oriental styles to simple modern ones, laments this writer, the novelist could arouse public sympathy and interest and direct it to shop windows displaying new designs, where the masses would see for themselves the vast superiority of these designs over the vulgar objects now in their houses.[85] Here is the aesthetic ideology of the decorative arts turned upside down: now a fine art, literature, is called upon to be an intermediary between the public and the decorative arts, to arouse the sympathy and understanding which are not being communicated by unmediated objects.

Literature is not, however, the only non-visual art that can be called upon to educate the masses. In 1902 Mauclair himself, always a lover of music and especially of Wagner, predicted that music would be "the future cult, . . . the grand communion of feeling for the masses in the future, because it exalts all dreams and touches the soul without preliminary precautions." He went on to praise the "essential utility of this art from the social point of view, that is to say as the global emotion of souls."[86]

This rediscovery of the social value of high art corrects the patronizing assumption that ordinary people will respond only to things affecting their most immediate needs, that they are incapable of being reached by what Mauclair had called "speculative" art. The emphasis on the assimilation of art to ordinary objects is condescending in its assumption that arts are basically crafts and that, with a little training, anyone can become an artist. It is not necessary to return to an extreme version of "art for art's sake" in order to maintain that the roots of the arts go deeper than satisfaction of physical needs; music, dance, drama, language, and other arts have emotional and intellectual sources unrelated to consumer needs. Only an inadequate understanding of artistic motivation assumes that one must appeal to people's practical interests as consumers—or as producers—to arouse a love for art. Consequently, failure to form an alliance between art and economic life hardly means the death of beauty. Human beings retain a capacity to create and respond to the arts on an entirely different level. If they did not, if the survival of art depended on its infusion into economic activities, the future of art would be bleak indeed. Art survives because people like to create it and appreciate it, because it has origins not only in economic and social structures but also in pleasures outside the logical adaptation of means to ends.

When Mauclair tried to marry art and life, he reduced art to lifestyle. By foregoing "speculative" art as too demanding for ordinary people, he downgraded the one crucial enterprise that could express criticism of a culture where objects were assuming a dominant role in self-definition and social consciousness. As Mauclair learned with some pain, to adopt a new lifestyle, no matter how simple, honest, or democratic, is to remain locked within the system of lifestyles. Des Esseintes learned the same lesson, and also with pain. His concept of art was no less a variety of consumerism, although aristocratic rather than democratic. Both Huysmans' fictional hero and Mauclair in real life tended to define themselves and other people according to the objects they possessed. Both ended up balked and frustrated, and were too honest and lucid not to realize that their identification of art with lifestyle had led to the impasse.

And yet that identification is precisely what makes them social prophets. The four lifestyles which have been described here, each of which accords a misplaced authority to appearances, have become dialects of a common moral language in modern society, or, rather—for lack of a coherent and genuine one—a pseudo-moral code. Lifestyles have also become a social language because people tend to seek a sense of community based on similarity in consumer habits; again, this is a false community which does not replace the genuine ones uprooted by industrial capitalism. In these moral and social capacities, lifestyles have come to serve as guides in making choices, in setting limits, in providing traditions, in establishing reference points for individual behavior. The tragedy is that these guides and limits and points of reference are not based on ideals of personal or social good but on structures of power and money embodied in consumer objects. Furthermore, the language is by no means a coherent one. Many details of consumer behavior, far from being "unspeakably significant," may be largely irrelevant in assessing the person who assumes them.

Is it possible to move beyond this pervasive system of judgment by appearances, to devise a genuine alternative to the system rather than deceptive alternatives within it? The question was already being raised in turn-of-the-century France. To answer it, however, means moving from the level of design to that of thought, undertaking a critical evaluation of the consumer revolution rather than further experimentation in styles of consumption, analyzing the sources of consumer consciousness rather than proliferating its nuances. This task of criticism was going on in France at the same time as the experiments in lifestyle just described. Students of social psychology, economics, and moral and political philosophy took up the problems posed by, but left unresolved by, the decadents and decorative arts reformers. It is to these thinkers that we shall now turn.

Part Two

The Development
of Critical Thought
about Consumption

*Wise consumption is a far more difficult art
than wise production.*

John Ruskin, *Unto This Last*

6 From Luxury to Solidarity: The Quest for a *Morale* of the Consumer

The Revival of the Debate about Luxury – "And no one puts new wine into old wineskins; if he does the new wine will burst the skins and it will be spilled, and the skins will be destroyed" (Luke 5:37). Yet often in thinking about social change, new wine—the flow of revolutionary historical events—is poured into the skins of outdated categories. The unprecedented changes caused by the consumer revolution were contained by traditional concepts. Eventually these concepts burst apart, but they served until new ones were fashioned. We have already seen how the venerable concept of decadence was called upon in a late nineteenth-century protest against mass and bourgeois consumption. However, the category most frequently used to criticize the implications of the consumer revolution was that of luxury.

Warnings about the malevolent effects of luxury can be traced back to the Church Fathers, to imperial and republican Rome, to classic and Homeric Greece, even to iron-age civilizations mentioned in the Old Testament. When Voltaire, Rousseau, and other eighteenth-century *philosophes* engaged in their debate about the ethics of luxury (see

Chapter II) they were reviving an ancient concept that carried enormous spiritual authority in Western civilization. The Enlightenment debate constituted an attempt to modernize the idea of luxury by recasting the terms of the argument, from its alleged effects on the individual soul to its alleged effects on society or, to use the term preferred at the time, on civilization. Voltaire took the position that since ideas about virtue were only relative, warnings about the evils of luxury were woefully outdated. A morality originating in an age of universal poverty was inappropriate for an age of growing wealth. Even Rousseau based his opposition to luxury not on an appeal to ancient authorities but, rather, on reason, social utility, and the general welfare.

Thus even in the eighteenth century the notion of luxury was being stretched to hold new historical facts, especially the accumulating prosperity of the bourgeoisie. How much more would the concept be stretched by the late nineteenth century! In the intervening period occurred a whole series of events which vastly altered consumer habits. The dandies initiated an extreme and distinctively modern form of aristocratic consumption—a sort of parody of the refined and eminently civilized luxury praised by Voltaire. Decorative arts reformers introduced another modern style of consumption that reflected nostalgia for natural and uncomplicated values—a sort of parody of Rousseau's simple life. Above all, the rise of mass consumption introduced an entirely new social category of consumers whose tastes, needs, and wishes spilled out of traditional bourgeois forms. Luxury was being democratized, and civilization was dissolving into a collection of lifestyles. By the late nineteenth century the need to reconsider and redefine both categories had become imperative.

In the United States and many other European countries, this sort of intellectual task would be accomplished in a diffuse and disorganized way, through journals, conferences, lectures, and other such forums. In France, however, a specific institution is designated by the state to investigate such issues, and this is the Académie des Sciences Morales et Politiques in the Institut de France. In France the dominant role of the central government in directing cultural and intellectual life took hold under the Old Regime and survived the French Revolution. Under the late monarchs various academies were recognized for specific purposes. For example, the Académie Française was created in 1635 to oversee the purification of the French language, and the Académie des Sciences was formed in 1666 to encourage scientific and technical knowledge (its formation was one of Colbert's projects). In addition, there were flourishing provincial academies, including the one at Dijon which sponsored the prize Rousseau won with the essay that launched his career. In 1795 the revolutionary governing body decided to replace these academies, which had already been suppressed and some of whose members had been guillotined, by a central institution that would uphold republican rather than royalist values.

This is the Institut de France. By the time the Institut reached its final form under the reign of Louis-Philippe, it was composed of five academies, each with its own jurisdiction and its own funds and secretaries, as well as access to a general fund and common library: the Académie Française; an academy devoted to ancient history and literature; the Académie des Sciences; an academy devoted to fine arts; and the Académie des Sciences Morales et Politiques. This last body was responsible for investigating questions of morality, philosophy, public law, politics, economics, and general history. Its jurisdiction looked forward to what are now called the social sciences, but looked back as well to traditional concepts like that of luxury. Its thirty members, originally chosen by the government and thereafter by existing members, received an annual allowance, and there were also forty unpaid "correspondents" from foreign countries. Admission to one of these academies was the ultimate honor that could be accorded French scholars. Some of them devoted their entire careers to a pursuit of the right to wear the green robes of membership and to attend meetings of the Institut in its domed baroque building, fronting the Seine, in the heart of Paris. Although the forty members of the Académie Française were called "the immortals," in fact most of them, as well as members of the other academies, proved to have very mortal reputations. Indeed, most have been condemned to historical oblivion and many of the French thinkers whose reputations have proved most durable were never elected (for example, Rousseau, Balzac, and Zola). Membership in the Institut was less a recognition of genius than of accomplishment according to the rather restricted standards of upper-class bourgeois culture, of which the Institut de France is the creature par excellence.

Henri Baudrillart (1821–1892) was a good example of the membership of the Académie des Sciences Morales et Politiques: sound, respectable, plodding, and now largely forgotten. But it is to his credit that Baudrillart directed the attention of his fellow academicians to the subject of luxury. While teaching political economy at the Collège de France in the 1860s, Baudrillart was dismayed by the spectacle of unrestrained luxury during the Second Empire—both the public variety, consisting of the rebuilding of Paris with magnificent buildings and squares, and the private kind centered in the court of Louis Napoleon. Consequently, he began to investigate the history of luxury. The resulting opus magnum, his *L'Histoire du luxe privé et public depuis l'antiquité jusqu'à nos jours* ("The History of Private and Public Luxury from Antiquity to Modern Times") was finally published, in four thick volumes, between 1878 and 1880. In this work Baudrillart's goal as an economic historian was to describe the types of luxury through the ages. As a moralist, his purpose was to outline a new ethic of luxury "appropriate to our customs and to our time." It was becoming obvious that democracy was no bar to excessive forms of consumption which had hitherto been associated with monarchies and aristocracies. "What," Baudrillart asked "does luxury have to do . . . with the working classes?"

> It is natural to wonder if we attribute only ideas of sumptuousness and elegance to this expression [luxury]. But . . . it should be extended to cover undesirable superfluity in all its forms. . . . There is neither harshness nor paradox in maintaining that the popular classes also must curtail something. . . . The need for enjoyments, hitherto restricted to the superior classes, for whom religion reserved its teachings delivered from high in the pulpit,—this need for enjoyments, by spreading more and more widely, has created a new congregation for new preachers . . . whose task is to convey the same truths in the name of science and reason.[1]

Baudrillart argued for a moderate position between "rigorists" who wished to abolish luxury altogether and "apologists" who defended it in all its forms.

Despite the apparent reasonableness of this position, in 1881 Baudrillart's tome was attacked as overly permissive in an article in the *Revue des deux mondes* by Émile de Laveleye (1822–1892), a Belgian economist and correspondent of the Institut de France. De Laveleye plainly declared himself a "rigorist" and condemned luxury on moral, economic, and political grounds. His article was expanded into a book published in 1886 under the straightforward title *Le Luxe* ("Luxury").[2] De Laveleye's book was in turn reviewed by Baudrillart at a session of the Académie des Sciences Morales et Politiques held on July 30, 1888. Considering the sharpness of de Laveleye's criticism, Baudrillart's response was generous. He conceded that it was preferable to lean toward severity rather than indulgence in this matter, and he wondered mildly if luxury deserved the "complete and uniform anathema" de Laveleye accorded it.

Other members of the Académie, some of whom were writing on related subjects, entered the discussion. At the session held the following week (August 6), the leading

orthodox French economist of the day, Paul Leroy-Beaulieu (1843–1912), presented a vigorous rebuttal to de Laveleye in the form of a long prepared statement that began:

> The principal use man makes of his increase in productive
> power is the augmentation of his consumption and of his
> enjoyments, notably his consumption of luxury. The more
> a society is civilized, the more is luxury widely distributed
> among all levels of the population.[3]

This paper inspired a general discussion of the morality of
luxury at that session of the Académie and at the following
one (August 13). One of the participants speaking out
against luxury at these sessions was Paul Leroy-Beaulieu's
brother, the political scientist Anatole Leroy-Beaulieu
(1842–1912). The Académie debate subsided, but discussion in print continued for some years. Paul Leroy-Beaulieu, for example, developed the ideas in his Académie
paper into a much more thorough discussion of luxury
published in the *Revue des deux mondes* in 1894 and expanded again two years later in his massive five-volume
Traité théorique et pratique d'économie politique ("Theoretical
and Practical Treatise of Political Economy").[4] Various
correspondents of the Institut, as well as non-members,
took up the subject.[5]

The debate was considerably milder than the eighteenth-century one that had pitted Voltaire against Rousseau, largely because none of the participants had the
intellectual and personal vitality of those two *philosophes.*
These debaters were not part of the effervescent generation of the 1890s, although the debate continued into that
decade, for de Laveleye and Baudrillart were old men by
then (they both died in 1892) and the Leroy-Beaulieu
brothers were middle-aged. The interest of the discussion
lies in the fact that it shows the response of this older,
established group—the upper-bourgeois heirs of aristocratic luxury—to the introduction of new democratized
forms of luxury. Rather than tracing all the twists and
turns of the discussion as it wound through the 1880s and

1890s, we shall examine the views of one spokesman defending luxury—Paul Leroy-Beaulieu—and one attacking it—Anatole Leroy-Beaulieu—for their arguments are fairly representative.

The fact that the two disputants were brothers born only a year apart adds human interest to the debate, and has symbolic significance as well. Anatole and Paul Leroy-Beaulieu were upper-bourgeois intellectuals. They shared the advantages of an excellent education in Paris followed by foreign study (Anatole traveled extensively in Russia, while Paul studied in Bonn and Berlin). They both became professors at the École Libre des Sciences Politiques (Anatole eventually became the director), and they were both active on the conservative side in Third Republic politics (Anatole served as a counselor-general, and Paul stood unsuccessfully as a center-right candidate for the municipal council of Paris and for the Chamber of Deputies). The fact that they were members of the Institut indicates that they had both earned the highest respect of their peers.

Yet on the subject of luxury they worked from different premises and arrived at opposite conclusions, while retaining a tone of mutual respect toward each other's position. Their respectful disagreement indicates a severe split in the mentality of the social class from which they both emerged. This ambivalence was already noticeable in the eighteenth century, when Voltaire and Rousseau enunciated opposing ethics of luxury, but that was a disagreement between a well-established intellectual and a quirky outsider; in the late nineteenth century the debate had come to divide the innermost *conscience* of the upper bourgeoisie.

The French Tradition in Economic Thought – Paul Leroy-Beaulieu has been praised by contemporaries and later commentators as the most able and interesting of the "Paris group" of economists who then dominated French economic thought. Paul Leroy-Beaulieu's ideas on luxury have to be understood in this intellectual context. The

Paris group was so called because from that city it controlled the prestigious *Journal des économistes* and most other economic publications, professional societies, the teaching of economics at the Collège de France and other institutions, and, above all, the Académie des Sciences Morales et Politiques in the Institut de France. According to Joseph Schumpeter (in his *History of Economic Analysis*) these "ultras of laissez-faire" had control of the profession "to such an extent that their political or scientific adversaries began to suffer from a persecution complex."

For leftist economists this complex was justified, for the Paris group used its dominant position mainly to refute socialist doctrines. True to the tradition of economic liberalism, they were uniformly free-traders and monometallists, firm believers in the sanctity of private property, and equally firm opponents of all state regulation. "But," Schumpeter adds,

> what matters to us is the fact that their analysis was, in its methodology, as reactionary as their politics. All of them were simply unconcerned with the scientific aspects of our field. J. B. Say [Jean-Baptiste Say, 1767–1832] and Bastiat [Frédéric Bastiat, 1801–1850], plus a vague theory of marginal utility, satisfied their scientific appetite.[6]

In other words, the Paris group was generally unimpressed by the Austrian school of economists, consisting of Carl Menger (1840–1921) and two generations of his students, who were then renovating economic thought by contending that the value of a market item does not depend on its production costs, as Adam Smith and his disciples had claimed, but on its utility to the consumer. The law of marginal utility associated with the Austrian school relates market value to an object's capacity to satisfy the desires of the consumer in a concrete, direct, and personal way. The Austrians believed that economics could be an exact science, untainted by moralism and historical relativism, and so they tried to discover objective laws which would describe and predict the subjective decisions of the consumer. However, they were not especially interested in expressing their theories in mathematical terms, and in fact Menger insisted that relative utilities could not be measured quantitatively and that the numbers he assigned them on his table of marginal utility were only approximations.

Other economists enamored of the Austrian theories did go on to express them in quantitative terms. Methods were devised to graph a curve of decreasing satisfaction as a consumer obtains more of an item, until the point of satiety is reached. This quantification of economic thought is another critical element in the late nineteenth-century reconstruction of the discipline. As a result, the concept of marginal utility was expanded into the more general theory of market equilibrium expressed in mathematical equations.

From all these developments French economists remained aloof: this is what Schumpeter means by their lack of scientific appetite. On the other hand, Schumpeter admits, the Paris economists were in close contact with business and politics, so their work displays "an atmosphere of realism and wisdom that compensates in part for their insufficiency of scientific inspiration." It is clear, however, that for him this advantage does not at all make up for their lack of objectivity and detachment.

The Paris group would have protested mightily against Schumpeter's assessment. They were convinced of their own objectivity. Like the Austrians, they upheld the orthodoxy that economics should be an exact science, a description of certain objective phenomena separate from moral or practical advice. In practice, however, they were moralistic economists. At a time when German- and English-speaking economists were attempting to represent the complexities of consumer behavior by precise laws and mathematical formulae, their French counterparts remained unabashedly, some would say hopelessly, impure in handling the same theme, or, for that matter, in handling almost any economic theme. The very titles of some typical works indicate their bent. Paul Leroy-Beaulieu's first book (first published as an essay winning a prize from the Académie des Sciences Morales et Politiques) was titled *L'Influence de l'état moral et intellectuel des populations ouvrières sur le taux des salaires* ("The Influence of the Moral and Intellectual State of the Working Populations on Wage Rates," 1867). Other members of the Paris group published studies on *La Morale économique* ("Economic Morality," 1888), *La Morale de la concurrence* ("The Morality of Competition," 1896), and *Les Rapports de la morale et de l'économie politique* ("The Relationships of Morality and Political Economy," 1860).[7]

The sources of this moralizing tendency lie deep in the national tradition of economic thought. The basic doctrine of the eighteenth-century Physiocrats (see Chapter 2, p. 41) was an essentially ethical distinction between the sterile and deceptive wealth of gold or silver and the productive and honest wealth of agriculture. Bastiat, the disciple of Say (both of whom are mentioned by Schumpeter for their influence on French economic thought), preached free trade and other economic doctrines in an impassioned, even religious, manner that drew the fire of "scientific" economists, one of whom criticized Bastiat's "pathological excitation" as "sinister and declamatory" and added:

> From the first pages of his work, Bastiat's belief in God is visible and in the last chapters . . . where he talks about *Social Mover, Evil, Perfectibility,* we are no longer dealing with an economist. It is Saint John of Patmos who speaks.[8]

This moralistic tone has condemned Bastiat, the Physiocrats, and the Paris group alike to relative obscurity. As the mainstream of economic thought has cut ever deeper channels of objectivity, scientific purity, and mathematical sophistication, the French have by contrast seemed to be splashing around in intellectual backwaters. Schumpeter is correct in saying that by prevailing standards their methodology is reactionary and unscientific. Undoubtedly their approach is out of fashion. The important question is whether French economic thought is therefore worthless. No claim can be made that Paul Leroy-Beaulieu has the stature of Carl Menger, for example, but what can be claimed is that the French economic tradition deserves reassessment because of the type of question it poses. If French economists were not overwhelmingly successful at answering those questions, it may not mean they were inept. On the contrary, Paul Leroy-Beaulieu and others have considerable mental agility. However, the kinds of issues they raise are inherently more complex because in them economic considerations are mingled with ethical and social ones. The distinctive contribution of French economists is in handling the points where economic, ethical, and political issues join and knot. Their concept of economics is inclusive, whereas that of the Austrian and mathematical schools tends to be exclusive.

The difference is particularly obvious in the way the French school handled the economics of consumption. The Austrian school may have given a new emphasis to consumption over production, but the law of marginal utility and the mathematical curve of consumer satisfaction depend on a dated, crude model of *homo œconomicus,* a cardboard creature whose only motivation is rational self-interest, who acts only to maximize pleasure and to minimize pain. Furthermore, the Austrians and their more mathematically inclined disciples tried to simplify their discussion of consumption by leaving out political judgments—they claimed that their analysis was impartial regarding class interests—as well as ethical judgments—they defined *utility* as the property of satisfying the consumer's desire without venturing any evaluation of the morality of that desire.

The French, on the other hand, resisted these simplifications. When they took up the matter of consumption, they focused on luxury, a topic which has moral and political dimensions as well as economic ones. As Baudrillart himself acknowledges: "There are few subjects which touch both moral and economic considerations so closely. In [the subject of luxury] they appear, whatever one may say, closely, solidly united."[9] Baudrillart particularly stresses the importance of addressing the conflict between economic and moral responsibilities which seemed inherent in modern industrial development. As early as the 1840s Bastiat suggested that industrial crises of overproduction and unemployment should be allayed not by protective tariffs but by an expansion of domestic consumption which would absorb the increases in production made possible by mechanization. This call for a proliferation of wants worried Baudrillart, Paul Leroy-Beaulieu, and other Paris group economists. How could the modern economic imperative to multiply needs be reconciled with the moral tradition inherited from Christian and non-Christian antiquity, which counseled self-discipline and restraint of desire? Baudrillart poses the dilemma in these terms:

> What are we to think of such a conflict, which seems to place modern societies between two terrible alternatives, those of renouncing morality or of renouncing progress? Between the theory of the indefinite development of needs and that of moderation in desires, is there an incompatibility? Must civilization come to a halt in order not to perish?[10]

Most modern economists would reject such questions as "unscientific," as Schumpeter did. But this does not mean the questions are insignificant, only that they lie outside the restrictive boundaries contemporary economists have drawn around their discipline. The conflict between the call to spend, to buy, to consume, which echoes every day throughout modern consumer society, and the quieter but persistent call to restrain self-indulgence, to seek spiritual rather than material blessings—this conflict still tears apart the *conscience*. Paul Leroy-Beaulieu tried to reconcile these conflicting calls, and if in doing so he sounds more like an Enlightenment *philosophe* than a twentieth-century economist, perhaps that is to his credit.

Paul Leroy-Beaulieu on Luxury – In fact, Paul Leroy-Beaulieu often sounds like Voltaire reborn. One of his main arguments in favor of luxury is the Voltairean one that desire to consume more than other people do stimulates enterprise throughout society, thereby benefiting everyone. That is why even seemingly useless luxuries like the expensive cars and diamonds that captains of industry buy for their wives have a beneficial purpose, for

> it is often to procure these goods, for his wife or his daughters, and, for himself, the luster that reflects from them, that certain men have labored, invented, confronted risks, created industries useful to the entire world.[11]

Private greed therefore results in public good in the form of abstract progress: this is Voltaire, and through him de Mandeville, brought up to date.

Like these eighteenth-century *philosophes*, Paul Leroy-Beaulieu also fears that without the goads of material desires and envies, the natural laziness of mankind would triumph and civilization would slide back (in Leroy-Beaulieu's words) "into the intellectual somnolence and material privations of primitive ages." So much for Rousseau's vision of a golden age! Leroy-Beaulieu fears that contemporaries who prefer increased leisure time to more possessions may be encouraging a "relaxation of the intimate springs" of human activity which would lead to a "state of economic stagnation."[12] He particularly worries that material equality will have similar results. Only when people see that others have more than they do are they stimulated to work harder and longer. "The question of luxury is only one side of a wider question, that of the inequality of conditions."[13] Luxuries are those goods that only a privileged few enjoy. They are "that part of the superfluous which goes beyond what the generality of the inhabitants of a country at a specified time consider as essential not only to the needs of existence but even to the decency and agreeableness of life."[14] A luxury item is something most people in a given society think you can do without, for the simple reason that most people have to do without it. "Each class considers as luxury the objects which its financial situation does not permit it to possess and which the superior class, on the contrary, has the means to use."[15] Far from being capable of democratization, luxury is defined by its restriction to an elite.

On the other hand, Paul Leroy-Beaulieu contends that the consumption of superfluities is found at all levels of society and in all historical epochs. All luxuries are superfluities, but not all superfluities are luxuries, which is to say, they are not all expensive. The distinction is important. Ordinary people do without luxuries because they must, but no one goes without superfluities. To be human is to consume above the level of survival. Paul Leroy-Beaulieu rejects Bastiat's proposal that survival needs (e.g., food) developed first among mankind and superfluous needs (e.g., adornment) only later. The instinct for superfluity, argues Leroy-Beaulieu, is innate and demanded expression since the beginning of civilization. Any attempt to classify needs by their degree of superfluity is bound to be arbitrary. The only reasonable way to classify types of consumption is by their object—food, clothing, entertainment, education, and so forth—leaving aside the question of superfluity as a false and misleading category.

While needs originate in the unvarying demands of man's physical and psychological nature, they are "indefinitely extensible and variable in their forms or their objects." Needs become ever more varied and animate through the combined operations of imitation, habit, and heredity. The development of consumer habits goes far beyond the physical requirements of man to express "the aspirations of his intellectual and moral nature, notably the thirst for the ideal." As an example of how biological needs can evolve into expressions of spirituality, Paul

Leroy-Beaulieu cites the need for ornamentation (*parure*) "which appears precisely the most frivolous . . . [but which] is the most universal and permanent." This need is found even among the poorest tribes. Originating with the human body, it is extended to a person's dependents and then to everything belonging to him—lodgings, tombs, domestic animals, furniture—and finally "constitutes . . . the category of the ideal at least as much as that of vanity."[16]

This tribute to the spiritual possibilities of superfluous needs is one of Paul Leroy-Beaulieu's finer moments. In language of which Huysmans might approve, he lifts consumption from the level of animal survival to that of human expression in its broadest sense. But the economist certainly does not intend to approve all forms of super-fluity, especially the perverse kind cultivated by Huysmans' hero des Esseintes. As a moralist, Paul Leroy-Beaulieu (like his mentor Baudrillart before him) walks an intellectual tightrope. If on one side they approve of luxury in opposition to rigorists like de Laveleye, on the other side they cannot accept the degenerate practices of the decadents or the trivial amusements of the masses.

Leroy-Beaulieu achieves a balance by distinguishing two general categories of luxury, "healthy, intelligent" ones and "unhealthy, extravagant" ones.[17] In order to describe the two categories he appeals to historical experience. There are different types of luxury corresponding to different historical epochs: the primitive luxury characteristic of patriarchal societies through the Middle Ages (an unhealthy and extravagant type); decadent luxury, as in the declining Roman Empire or in the contemporary Orient (also unhealthy and extravagant); and modern luxury, found among prosperous peoples today (the healthy and intelligent type).

As simplifying and generalizing concepts applied to historical data, these models are ideal types, to use the term Max Weber would introduce about a decade later. By introducing them Paul Leroy-Beaulieu goes beyond a repetition of Voltaire's ideas; like many other nineteenth-century thinkers, he turns to historical evolution rather than to abstract reason for his evidence.

Primitive luxury is characterized by the presence of a large number of servants, by desire for ostentation, and by sheer quantity of goods consumed. This is the tradition of luxury inherited by the Renaissance courts in Europe, and while it has disappeared in the contemporary West it still exists in some parts of the world such as Russia. (Paul Leroy-Beaulieu cites some examples of primitive luxury gathered by his brother Anatole during the latter's travels there.) Decadent luxury, instead of serving normal physical or intellectual needs, "consists only in the search for very costly pleasures and objects, only because they are costly, in systematic wastefulness, in the unique satisfaction of extreme vanity." This "grotesque, . . . criminal, . . . degrading, harmful, inavowable" luxury is not widespread in modern times, for society as a whole is not in decadence. However, Leroy-Beaulieu warns that there have appeared "in the past several years, in certain social circles, those who make a profession of dilettantism and of the decadent spirit," such as certain aristocrats or the degenerate sons of rich bourgeois. He does not see the emergent side of decadence, but only its residual or, in his opinion, its atavistic aspect.

Leroy-Beaulieu describes these two kinds of luxury in order to demonstrate how radically different is the modern variety. This last type is characterized by a search for comfort rather than for magnificence, so that modern luxury is much less ostentatious than that of the past. Instead of being displayed in public, luxury has gone indoors, so to speak, to be revealed in the privacy of the home in the company of a few friends. Modern luxury is, above all, domesticated luxury. Dwellings have been transformed from rude shelters into homes that are "neat, agreeable, diversified, animated by a number of interesting objects." Contemporary luxury is productive economically because it stimulates manufacture instead of wasting human and natural resources. Instead of tending to sheer sumptuousness and quantity in a limited number of items, modern luxury prefers diversity and elegance. Furthermore, it consists not of transient objects and experiences but of durable items of which the consumption is slow rather than rapid, such as jewels, furniture, works of art, parks, and tapestries, all of which are lovingly cared for according to the principle of *entretien* ("upkeep"). All these are what Paul Leroy-Beaulieu calls "the capital of enjoyment."

Finally, today's luxury is not confined to a small elite but "embraces and penetrates all of life; it reaches, in different degrees, all classes of people." Echoing d'Avenel, Paul Leroy-Beaulieu credits new materials and techniques with making "the difference between the lives of men of diverse classes . . . much less in the real enjoyments they can procure than in the value they possess." Technological progress enables even workers to have clothes and furniture which "for untutored eyes, for myopic eyes, and even for the actual utility of things, [give] an approximation tending to equality."[18] In all these differences between primitive or decadent and modern luxury—public vs. private, ostentatious vs. comfortable, elitist vs. democratic, unproductive vs. productive, quantity vs. quality, transience vs. durability—the modern type is vastly superior.

Paul Leroy-Beaulieu then spells out the political implications, as he sees them, of his historical models. If modern luxury is both economically and morally far superior to the old forms, the lesson is that moral improvement comes about not through ethical exhortations or government actions but through the slow and natural development of customs. Further improvement in the morality of consumption will come about as social life continues to evolve naturally without interference from the state or other institutions. Paul Leroy-Beaulieu is especially opposed to sumptuary laws as a method of improving public morality in matters of luxury. Not only would they be an unwarranted invasion of personal liberty but they would also be futile, for "insofar as the nature of most men has not been transformed by philosophy or religion, it would be, from the economic point of view, a fundamental error to try to suppress luxury."[19] Of course, he adds, private individuals should be encouraged to direct public opinion against harmful excesses. Basically, however, the consumer should be left free to make his own choices. The gradual enlightenment of public opinion on matters of morality should be left to the civilizing influence of religion and philosophy.

Thus Paul Leroy-Beaulieu reaches the political conclusions which, as a stout nineteenth-century liberal, he was aiming for all along: in consumption, as in production, laissez-faire should reign. But to arrive at this conclusion he has to drop his useful distinction between luxury and superfluity. According to his formal definition, it will be recalled, luxuries are necessarily limited to a few, being "that part of the superfluous" that most people in a certain society and historical period consider inessential. But in praising modern luxury, Leroy-Beaulieu describes it as something that "reaches . . . all classes of people." At one point he does correct himself by saying that the democratization of luxury in modern times means that ordinary people may enjoy luxuries "in the sense of superfluities,"[20] but this only confuses terms that should be kept distinct. It would be more precise for him to say that superfluity has been increasingly democratized—for it has always been democratized to some extent, according to his historical survey—while luxury, defined as a type of consumption available only to a few, has survived and been moderated.

This confusion of terminology arises from a more fundamental confusion about the subject of social inequality, which Paul Leroy-Beaulieu rightly points out as the broader question raised by the question of luxury. To some extent he favors the modern trend toward equality. It is the source of his optimistic faith in laissez-faire, for it means that social injustice can be remedied without socialism and that inequalities can be eliminated effortlessly through natural evolution rather than requiring legal action. At the same time he maintains that inequality among consumers is desirable. Only inequality inspires everyone to produce more and thus to further the progress of civilization.

Inequality brings progress, equality brings social harmony: which is preferable? Paul Leroy-Beaulieu's cautious praise of modern luxury for its "approximation which tends to equality" indicates his awareness of this predicament. Directly after that statement he adds, "Thus the reign of machines prepares the era not of a complete equality, certainly, which would be a misfortune, but of a sort of uniformity of enjoyment and of comfort among men."[21] His muddled language reflects the confusion in his thinking. If democratic luxury makes people feel they share a "uniformity of enjoyment and of comfort," they will have no motivation to work and will sink back into primitive torpor, according to his assumptions. But if democratic luxury is not a convincing facsimile of the real thing, it will not bring social peace. In short, like Georges d'Avenel, Paul Leroy-Beaulieu prefers a specious equality in goods to a genuine equality in people. He is willing to accept "an approximation tending to equality" which he hopes will suffice "for untutored eyes, for myopic eyes," instead of asking why everyone should not enjoy equally the pleasures of educated, clear vision.

This basic reification—seeing equality in terms of facsimile objects rather than in terms of life—is especially disappointing because in other ways Paul Leroy-Beaulieu suggests a psychology of consumption considerably richer and fuller than that of a rational, self-interested *homo œconomicus*. The reason for his advance in psychological understanding is mainly his reliance on historical perspective, in contrast to the eighteenth-century tendency, so persistent in economic thought, to posit an atemporal model of human motivations. One strong point of his historical theory of luxury is his appreciation that as the availability of material goods changes over time, so do people themselves change in their perception of needs. A nineteenth-century person classifies as necessities many goods which used to be considered luxuries. Furthermore, Leroy-Beaulieu uses historical evidence to demonstrate to rigorists like de Laveleye how universal and potentially liberating is the human taste for superfluity. But his convincing arguments for superfluity are unfortunately tied to far less convincing arguments that luxury (in the sense of superfluity reserved for a few) is necessary for the prosperity of civilization as a whole. This latter thesis constitutes a rejection of nineteenth-century historical thought, reverting to an eighteenth-century rationalism (or pseudo-rationalism) of the sort that claims that all links in the Great Chain of Being must be filled for the good of the universe, thereby justifying evil by the argument that individual suffering is somehow necessary to the abstract whole.

If Paul Leroy-Beaulieu is inconsistent in his use of the terms *luxury* and *superfluity*, in his evolution of the relative virtues of inequality and equality, and in relying alternately upon historicism and rationalism, it is because his ideas are being pulled out of shape by a preconceived notion of the right kind of luxury. What he calls modern luxury is really the luxury not so much of an age but of a class—the upper bourgeoisie, to which he belongs. The type of luxury displayed at the expositions or in movie houses was equally modern, but it is not at all the type he would encourage. Instead, he begins with an ideal of bourgeois or genteel luxury (salons in substantial homes, books and pianos, good art and good wines, travel and conversation) and then proceeds to justify this style of consumption as an ultimate ideal. The ideal is by no means indefensible or wrong-headed, but it is not arrived at by an honestly independent inquiry. The result is ethical as well as intellectual confusion. For example, Paul Leroy-Beaulieu condemns luxury that "prefers material superfluities to . . . intellectual pleasures"[22]—good bourgeois advice, but advice which contradicts his own theory that "material superfluities" stimulate moral progress and that material and moral needs are interchangeable parts of the evolution of civilization. He suggests no goal of civilization more exalted than the bourgeois luxury of his own time. In formulating an ethic of luxury, Paul Leroy-Beaulieu retreats to the conventions of his class rather than using thought to formulate an independent moral code. He turns to his culture to correct the deficiencies of his theory, when as an economist-*moraliste* he should apply thought to correct the deficiencies of contemporary culture.

But it would be a mistake to denounce Paul Leroy-Beaulieu for trying to be an economist-*moraliste* in the first place. In fact, to criticize him for making moral ideas subservient to class interests is to draw upon the insights of another nineteenth-century economist-*moraliste*, Karl Marx, who for all his claims of scientific objectivity is also highly moralistic as an economic thinker. In 1919 one of Marx's Russian disciples, Nikolai Bukharin, wrote *The Economic Theory of the Leisure Class* to analyze the sociological roots of the Austrian school's critique of Marx. Bukharin concluded that the theory of marginal utility glorified the psychology of the consumer and justified the interests of a *rentier* class which does not have to labor and fears any change in its privileged position as a nonproductive, consuming class. While this analysis may not be entirely applicable to the Austrian economists, it does seem appropriate to the defense of luxury enunciated by Paris group economists. That theory, as exemplified in the writings of Paul Leroy-Beaulieu, may have merits, but its fatal weakness is that it is class-bound.[23]

The Role of the Church in France—Paul Leroy-Beaulieu's defense of luxury springs from his faith in the doctrines of nineteenth-century economic liberalism. He is well aware that his ethical position contradicts the teaching of another, far older faith, the religious faith adhered to, at least nominally, by the majority of Frenchmen. The position of the Catholic Church is that proliferation of material possessions hinders spiritual development. Paul Leroy-Beaulieu's way of handling this conflict is to acknowledge the beauty and inspiration of the Christian gospel while asserting that most people will not be able to live up to its lofty standards. Just as he opposes sumptuary laws on the grounds that "the nature of most men has not been transformed by philosophy or religion," Paul Leroy-Beaulieu appeals to historical experience in order to warn against indulging in excessive hope for humanity. Jesus, the apostles—and Buddha, he adds—are "fortifying examples" which should encourage us to moderate "unbridled desire for wealth" and which demonstrate "that mediocrity or even poverty can be allied with contentment." But there is no possibility that an entire society will be composed of people like Jesus or Buddha, "for the overwhelming judgment of the human race has proclaimed Jesus and Buddha as God, which is to say, super-human."[24]

This is the voice of resigned realism. Paul Leroy-Beaulieu does not mock or attack the Church as Voltaire did so fiercely; he simply dismisses it as irrelevant, while paying his respects to its ideals. He can afford to adopt this relatively mild tone in part because the Catholic Church in France was far less powerful in his day than it was in Voltaire's. Under the French monarchs Church and State had formed a united authority; under the Third Republic, the two were locked in an unceasing battle for power, with control of the school system and tolerance of religious orders as the major battlegrounds. The Enlightenment *philosophes* had wanted to banish forever what they considered to be religious superstition and to nurture instead a vaguely benevolent deism. They did not succeed. The Catholic Church survived the Revolution, and the ideals of the *philosophes* were degraded into a materialistic, agnostic, and militantly anticlerical positivism. By the late nineteenth century the two faiths were bitter rivals. On the one side were fanatic anticlericals, most of them Freemasons, who suspected Jesuit conspiracies everywhere and celebrated "so-called Good Friday" by attending banquets where they defied the Church by gorging themselves on sausages. On the Catholic side were zealots just as implacable, ones who subscribed to Louis Veuillot's anti-Semitic, antidemocratic newspaper *L'Univers*, who clamored for the Church to be granted complete and unrestricted control of public education, who were utterly opposed to the Third Republic, and who celebrated Lent by going on mammoth pilgrimages sponsored by the Assumptionist Fathers (who made available special discounts on railway rates).

This noisy and vindictive political struggle, which tended to drown out voices of moderation, was not the whole story of religious life in France, however. In the early 1890s Pope Leo XIII recommended a policy of *Ralliement*, advising French Catholics to "rally" around the republic, to accept its institutions and defend the interests of the Church by participating in political life. The hope of the Vatican was that Catholic politicians would merge with moderate republicans to form a large and united conservative party rather than stagnating in intransigent monarchism. The policy was by no means a striking success. Radical republicans were profoundly suspicious that the Vatican was playing a trick, and most monarchist Catholics openly resisted any accommodation to a secularist, anticlerical republic. Still, the conservative center did show signs of strengthening as the Vatican had hoped. The power of monarchists declined in the Chamber of Deputies as Catholics increasingly gave their votes to moderate republicans. These moderate deputies in turn developed greater sympathy for Catholic and conservative ideas as monarchist defectors joined their ranks. Even more important than these political changes were the social ones. While the aristocracy had been Catholic since the Revolution, the upper bourgeoisie had largely fallen away from the Church. Now the latter began to return to the faith, in part because it began to see the growing atheistic socialism as a greater danger than declining monarchist Catholicism.[25]

One such upper bourgeois was Anatole Leroy-Beaulieu. Without the moral guidance of the Catholic Church, he feared, democracy would prefer power to liberty and would end up with either a repressive socialist regime or with a Caesarist military dictatorship. To survive, democracy should ally with the papacy, as Leo XIII had proposed in his encyclical *Rerum novarum* (1891). These convictions of Anatole Leroy-Beaulieu, although encouraged by the papal initiatives of the early 1890s (he was an enthusiastic supporter of the *Ralliement*), had originated earlier in his admiration for the Catholic thinker and social scientist Frédéric Le Play (1806–1883). Just as the views of Paul Leroy-Beaulieu have to be understood with reference to the traditions of French economic thought, those of his brother must be viewed in the context of the Le Playist tradition.

All the time that Church and State had been engaging in their virulent political struggles, on a far quieter and more productive level the Catholic Church in France had been producing a wide variety of ideas on social and economic issues. In the intellectual sphere the Church was not the monolith that its enemies claimed. There were Catholic liberals who advocated economic liberalism from a Catholic perspective, as well as a motley collection of Social Catholics and Christian Democrats all sympathetic to workers' organizations.[26] The former group resembles non-Catholic liberals, and the latter is reminiscent of socialist or quasi-socialist groups outside the Church, but the Le Playists addressed social and economic issues in a way that has no obvious secular parallel. In this originality lies the interest of the Le Playists, and it also explains historians' tendency to ignore them. Their program, which centers around religion, family, and management (*patronat*) as the foundations of social order, seems alien today and, in the opinion of many, reactionary as well. Yet some Le Playists objected to having the school classified as Catholic at all, on the grounds that its doctrines were inspired not by Christian revelation but by scientific objectivity. Le Play's remarkable role in organizing the international exposition of 1867 reveals an enthusiasm for modern science and technology that can hardly be called reactionary. All this is quite bewildering and, as a result, Le Playism is usually summed up as an unlikely mixture of religion and social engineering. But the school has more coherence than this, more complexity than is suggested by the slogans of family and *patronat,* and, on the subject of consumption, considerably more relevance and importance than have usually been attributed to it. If Anatole Leroy-Beaulieu is a perceptive critic of modern consumption, it is largely because he viewed the problem from the perspective of Le Play.

Le Play was a pioneer in social research, and the basis of his research technique was the family case study designed to gather information on the family's consumption patterns. The detailed questionnaire used by the Le Playists included spaces for incomes and expenditures of all types, not only monetary ones down to the last centime, but also less tangible ones such as recreation, education, and even virtues and vices. The family monograph which resulted from analysis of this questionnaire recounted the family's history and also assembled all its activities in the form of an annual budget of which the itemized categories were labeled in advance. "Le Play takes family budgets as the criterion of his observational method, . . . that is to say, a pure criterion of the consumer."[27] Like any technique, this one can be taken to extremes and can easily be made to appear ridiculous. At times Le Play, engineer and graduate of the École Polytechnique, seemed to think that human facts could be mined like coal. Yet even today social researchers are trying to devise ways to quantify nonmaterial income and expenses in order to devise a genuine "social accounting" procedure, although usually on behalf

of a corporation rather than families.[28] Far from being absurd, the concept of a social accounting that includes intangible contributions and liabilities is more realistic than a
strictly monetary chart of debits and credits.

Furthermore, Le Play did not stop with collecting data
on consumption, but tried to apply them—as did the
historian Georges d'Avenel, who worked with the same
kind of information from families in the past—to reveal
the passions and essential concerns of life. Le Play concluded that family life is the cradle of social morality in
general and of consumer habits in particular. Family life
and consumption can be understood only in terms of each
other: for Le Play the concept of needs is familial and, by
extension, social, rather than individual, as economic liberals assumed. He saw that needs understood in this
sense extend beyond those of physical survival to social
needs like education and recreation, and that they extend
in time from generation to generation. (Le Play advocated
liberté testamentaire, the legal right of a person to will at
least half his estate to whomever he chooses, as a means of
strengthening generational ties. French law then required
that estates be divided equally among sons.) To regard the
family as a consumption unit, to see the family rather than
the individual as the basic unit of a healthy society, to
regard consumption in familial and generational terms
together illuminate the dynamics of both family and consumer life in a way that is a good deal more significant
than is suggested by the usual bald reference to Le Play's
being "for the family."

The same sort of criticism can be made of the remark
that Le Play was "for the *patron.*" It would be more
accurate to say that Le Play was opposed to the notion,
upheld by liberals like Paul Leroy-Beaulieu, that civilization advances when each individual seeks his own idea of
happiness. Le Play criticized the assumption that people
know how to make themselves happy. Left to themselves,
he felt, people might tend to seek immediate personal
well-being, but their egotism was often unwise and might

not result in happiness. People need the guidance of authority to correct the shortcomings of unenlightened self-interest. That guidance should originally come from religious faith, especially as expressed in the Decalogue. But a creed is not enough. Authority has to take human and personal form. That is why one foundation of social peace is paternal authority. In addition, other social authorities, unattached to the state but enjoying general respect, dispense peace and guidance according to the paternal model. This is the role Le Play saw for the *patron*. While not opposed to state action on principle, as liberal economists were, Le Play felt that the state had only a subordinate role. He preferred to trust decentralized, local government and the influence of social authorities. The model he had in mind was derived from stable patriarchal, religious communities such as those of eastern Europe, where he had traveled widely.

Le Play is unquestionably sexist, authoritarian, undemocratic, and generally unappealing to an egalitarian and secular age. This does not mean that he and his followers should be dismissed entirely, however. There is nothing inherently absurd or reactionary in the proposition that individuals do not organize their consumption wisely in view of their general happiness, or that actions taken to aggrandize personal well-being may turn out to be (to use the modern term) counterproductive. At the least, this analysis encourages reconsideration of the classical liberal assumption that the consumer is the best judge of his own interests when he is left to act according to his own, supposedly rational, assessment. Furthermore, the suggestion that nongovernmental social authorities may play a crucial role in guiding consumption draws attention to the importance of "role models" in this respect, and also to possible alternatives to legislation as means of fostering restraint. We need to extract what is valid in Le Play's analysis from the inadequacies of his specific remedies, and we should do the same for his follower, Anatole Leroy-Beaulieu.

Anatole Leroy-Beaulieu on "The Reign of Money" – Anatole Leroy-Beaulieu published articles in the Le Playist journal *Réforme sociale*, spoke at organizations instituted by the school, and delivered a eulogy at the funeral of Émile Cheysson, one of Le Play's most important disciples, but he was not a thoroughgoing disciple himself. Anatole Leroy-Beaulieu gave more emphasis than did the Le Playists to the role of the pope as an ultimate social authority, a supreme father, but his sympathies with Le Playism are evident from the general tenor of his thought. Like Le Play himself, he was fascinated by eastern European societies, especially by Russia; his scholarly specialty was the political science of Russia. Also like Le Play, he was convinced that only religion could "lift up [the] soul [of the people] again,"[29] and that the doctrines of liberalism, which were crowding out the doctrines of religion, were deceptive and dangerous. Liberalism would substitute an illusory rational man for the actual one who is passionate, egotistical, and fallen. The French Revolution should be superseded by a spiritual revolution establishing a true reign of justice, a reign not of Reason or other metaphysical entities but of personal "faith, feeling, instinct, and love."[30]

In short, Anatole Leroy-Beaulieu disagreed entirely with his younger brother Paul. In them the ideological debate between liberalism and its critics took flesh and blood as a fraternal quarrel. The week after Paul presented his paper defending inequality and luxury to the Académie des Sciences Morales et Politiques, Anatole made a short statement to the members in which he quoted the Gospels on the evil of excessive wealth ("It would be easier for a camel to pass through the eye of a needle than for a rich man to enter the Kingdom of Heaven") and ironically praised luxury as a virtue because when a rich man throws away his money on luxuries, financial inequality is diminished. Anatole's so-called defense of luxury, remarked one participant in the Académie debate, relied on "arguments diametrically opposed to the fraternal ones."[31] Yet this difference of opinion did not keep Paul Leroy-Beaulieu from repeating, without irony, Anatole's point as a justification for luxury in his *Principes*! The printed evidence of their disagreement suggests that it was eminently civilized, according to conventional standards, even as they debated the definition of civilization.

When Anatole Leroy-Beaulieu published his views on luxury opposed to his brother's, he did not attempt a direct rebuttal but instead responded obliquely in a two-part article titled "Le Règne de l'argent" ("The Reign of Money") published in 1894 in the *Revue des deux mondes*.[32] As the title indicates, the subject is not luxury narrowly defined, but the broader problem of the role of wealth in modern civilization. Despite lip service paid to Christian virtues, contends Anatole Leroy-Beaulieu, in fact the reign of money has replaced that of Christ. A few people still celebrate the virtues of poverty and abstinence, but their attitude is only a form of "dandyism" or of unrealistic nostalgia. In truth there are hardly any genuinely poor people left. Even those who disclaim opulence assume a high level of comfort and well-being which is also expensive. This modern assumption is largely due to the rise of industrial, scientific civilization ("what we call progress"), which has enormously multiplied people's needs. "The boundaries of the necessary have receded." This all echoes Paul Leroy-Beaulieu, but the elder brother regards this recession as false rather than genuine progress, as enslavement rather than triumph. "We are slaves of our needs, prisoners of our arts, of our industry, of our urban life, hence serfs of wealth, subjected to the reign of money." Far from echoing Voltaire, Anatole Leroy-Beaulieu sounds like a latter-day Rousseau: luxury is an evil because it reduces human freedom.

The kind of freedom Anatole Leroy-Beaulieu has in mind, to be sure, is not so much political as spiritual. The decline of religious faith, which is a second cause of the contemporary reign of money, has only restricted man drastically: "Man's horizon has contracted; his view is limited to the earth and to earthly goods; heaven, with its starry depths, which used to beckon the soul, God's heaven has been blocked off from view." These words recall the cry of des Esseintes, alone at sea under dark skies no longer illumined by the beacons of hope. From this perspective, it can be seen that des Esseintes's frantic consumerism has its roots in spiritual despair. According to Anatole Leroy-Beaulieu, when man's vision is limited to the earth, poverty no longer has any meaning. In the past, although religious faith never completely conquered "Mammonism," it did hold greed in check. Once faith has fled, man is left pathetically alone. Money becomes the only idol he can worship. In both Christianity and Judaism the traditional virtue of poverty has been turned into an empty piety.

In 1893, the year before he wrote "The Reign of Money," Anatole Leroy-Beaulieu published a thoughtful and well-received book, *Israël chez les nations; les juifs et l'anti-sémitisme* ("Israel among the Nations; Jews and Anti-Semitism").[33] In "The Reign of Money" he expands upon the theme that modern anti-Semitism is one result of the contemporary idolatry of money. A common argument of anti-Semites, he observes, is that Jews worship only money. At best, this kind of anti-Semitism may represent a revolt of conscience against Mammonism as personified in the Jew, but it is a confused and ultimately mistaken revolt. The reign of money should not be identified with Jews. In the first place, most of them are poor. In the second place, money worship, where it does exist, is not an inborn Semitic trait but has been bred into that culture over the centuries because it has been the only power of the Jew respected by Christians and Moslems. This leads to the third argument against anti-Semitism: it is hypocritical, originating not in a pious aversion to wealth but in a distinctly unchristian envy of those who have more. Christians should search their own hearts for lust for money before they impute Mammonism to Jews.

The passion of envy is also a fundamental reason why

the rise of political democracy has been a third cause of the modern reign of money. The so-called democratization of luxury has only meant the proliferation of jealous greed. Formerly, possession of a fortune was generally accepted as a privilege of caste. Now, everyone wants to get rich. Worldly goods appear to be within the reach of all, so that being left out of the general scramble for wealth seems an injustice. In today's society money is sovereign. Like traditional sovereigns, money has a nobility: the forms of democracy scarcely hide the existence of a new aristocracy based on money. In the case of the old nobility, whose legitimacy was derived from personal distinction, a fortune was regarded only as a secondary accompaniment to that distinction. Now wealth is the primary quality by which the new aristocracy "establishes its titles and affirms its domain." This is why the new aristocracy displays ostentatious luxury:

> Money has to show off. . . . When social distinctions are established almost uniquely on wealth, everyone is led to make a show of what he possesses. Mammon, the new king, loves to give himself over to a spectacle, . . . he does not hesitate to offend others; he needs to amaze his neighbor. And since people everywhere imitate the powerful of their day, the common people are persuaded to copy the kings of money. For them it is a means of extricating themselves from the common herd. . . . from the top to the bottom of society, as it calls itself, down to the slightest bourgeoisie, we see an emulation of luxury, an assault of banal and artificial elegances.

Anatole Leroy-Beaulieu is especially sensitive to the political dangers inherent in this situation. Although the displays of luxury made by the new aristocracy are often shabby or in poor taste, they are still highly irritating to the masses who cannot afford such indulgences. The displays are "an artificial barrier, a partition specifically erected to separate people and to make them more aware of difference of conditions." In order to establish its dominion, money must be displayed, but then the democratic spirit, which provokes money to show itself in the first place, is shocked at its exhibitions. Display of wealth through luxury is now more necessary than ever for the aristocracy and yet is tolerated less.

Of all aristocracies, that of money excites the least respect and the most envy and is therefore highly unstable. Democracy brings at once the reign of money and a jealous revolt against its displays. The inability to live either with or without the tyrant is the reason for France's many revolutions:

> The reign of Mammon is never peaceable for long. The masses rise up against what they call the privileges of the rich, and socialism comes out of Mammonism. But in its revolt against the kings of money, democracy attacks not wealth but the wealthy. It doesn't want to destroy wealth but intends to share it. It is not impelled by the Christian spirit, the spirit of renunciation and sacrifice, joyously detached from the goods of this world. On the contrary, popular socialism is only the trade union of appetites and the formulary of greeds. In the civil wars of the kingdom of Mammon, the satisfied and dissatisfied are, in reality, imbued with the same spirit, one wanting to take, the other wanting to keep. Two egoisms grappling with each other.

Anatole Leroy-Beaulieu has returned to the theme of the democratization of luxury which is so central to an understanding of modern consumer society. He argues that wealth and the luxuries it buys have not really been democratized. The masses are not fooled into mistaking cheap imitations of luxury items for actual possession of wealth. What *has* been democratized is the passion for money and the hope, however remote, of obtaining it. This situation cannot be corrected through institutional change or through suppression of a particular group, either Jews or capitalists. Nor is there substance to the idea that everyone can enjoy both more leisure and more goods, an illusion based on dreams of a miraculous multiplication of wealth reminiscent "of the alchemists who

1. The château of Azay-le-Rideau is set on pile foundations in a bend of the Indre River in the Loire region of France. It was built in the early sixteenth century by Gilles Berthelot, president of the Chamber of Finance and a devoted courtier of Francis I. (In homage to his king, Berthelot had the initials of Queen Claude, wife of Francis I, introduced into designs throughout Azay-le-Rideau.) Berthelot became involved in some unfortunate business affairs and in 1527 had to flee the country, crossing the frontier just in time to escape being hanged. The château was confiscated and is now a museum of Renaissance art. (Photograph by the author.)

2. The Galerie des Machines, 1889 exposition, Paris. The photograph is taken on one of the raised side aisles which made a favorite promenade. In 1889 visitors looked down upon clanking, churning machinery; in 1900, upon a display of food products. (Lantern slide in the Rotch Visual Collection, M.I.T.)

4. The Hall of Mirrors at Versailles as seen from the War Salon at one end of the Hall. During the daytime the mirrors sparkled with the sunlight entering the large windows opposite; at night they reflected the light from gilt candlestands and from three rows of chandeliers. (Lantern slide in the Rotch Visual Collection, M.I.T., from d'Espouy, vol. 1, pl. 26.)

3. The front entrance to Versailles, as it appeared at the end of the reign of Louis XIV. (Lantern slide in the Rotch Visual Collection, M.I.T.)

5. Exterior view of the Grand Palais, built for the 1900 exposition and later used for a wide variety of public events, including the Salons de l'Automobile. The facade of stone, featuring an Ionic colonnade before a mosaic frieze, is architecturally conventional. Far more striking (especially when the Grand Palais is viewed from a distance) and more innovative are the steel and glass domes forming the roof of the main part of the building. (Lantern slide in the Rotch Visual Collection, M.I.T.)

6. Interior view of the Grand Palais taken during the 1900 exposition, when the area under the domes was used for sculpture exhibits. This area was used shortly afterward for automobile exhibits. (Lantern slide in the Rotch Visual Collection, M.I.T.)

7. Pavilion at the 1900 exposition, Paris, representing Andalusia in the time of the Moors. A band of gypsy women had been imported from Seville to add authenticity to this evocation of an exotic time and place. (From Philippe Jullian, *The Triumph of Art Nouveau: Paris Exhibition 1900*, London: Phaidon Press, 1974.)

8. Pavillon de la Mode, 1900 exposition, Paris. The wax figures represent a wedding-gown fitting at an expensive store—an evocation of high society for a mass audience. (From Philippe Jullian, *The Triumph of Art Nouveau: Paris Exhibition 1900*, London: Phaidon Press, 1974.)

9. Statue of La Parisienne, 1900 exposition, Paris. This fifteen-foot-high statue stood at the very top of the Monumental Gateway. It represents an elegant Parisian lady wearing a creation of the famous dressmaker Paquin. In the years immediately following the 1900 exposition, La Parisienne's sculptor, Moreau-Vauthier, specialized in making small full-length bronze figures of actual Parisian ladies of fashion, which were exhibited by these ladies in their salons. Most of these figures too were dressed in Paquin gowns. (From *Architectural Record*, vol. 13, no. 3, March, 1903: 223. Courtesy of *Architectural Record*.)

10. The Monumental Gateway (La Porte Binet) on the Place de la Concorde during the 1900 exposition, Paris. The Gateway consisted of one high entrance arch and two smaller arches, under which were located fifty-six ticket offices. Above the triangle formed by the three arches was a dome, and on top of the dome stood the statue of La Parisienne. The slender pyramid-shaped minarets on either side of the arch were studded with crystal cabochons and were lit at night from inside. The overwrought polychrome decorations of the Gateway seemed the creation of a mad jeweler. (Illustration from *Paris 1900* by Franco Borzi and Ezio Godoli, published by Rizzoli International Publications, New York.)

11. The Maison du Jockey Club, a tailor shop on the Boulevard des
Italiens. The Jockey Club had long been a fashionable haunt of Parisian
dandies, and this shop assumed the name in order to lend prestige to
the business. The façade, an example of the application of Art Nouveau
motifs to commercial establishments, demonstrates the creative use of
electrical lighting by stores: the names and signs are written on glass lit
from behind. (From *Architectural Record*, vol. 26, no. 2, August, 1909:
116. Courtesy of *Architectural Record*.)

12. The dandy Beau Brummell, by Robert Dighton (1805). (From Ellen Moers, *The Dandy: Brummell to Beerbohm*, New York: Viking, 1960.)

13. A dining room designed by Charles Plumet and Tony Selmer-sheim, exhibited at the 1900 exposition, Paris. Note the elaborate decoration and huge, impractical scale of this Art Nouveau suite. (Illustration from *Paris 1900* by Franco Borsi and Ezio Godoli, published by Rizzoli International Publications, New York.)

14. Glass vase by Émile Gallé, mounted in silver by Bonvallet. The inscription reads (in translation): "We shall win, God is leading us. Émile Zola." It refers to Gallé's faith in the innocence of Dreyfus and to Zola's leading role in establishing that innocence. The vase is now in the Musée des Arts Décoratifs, Paris. (From Philippe Jullian, *The Triumph of Art Nouveau: Paris Exhibition 1900*, London: Phaidon Press, 1974.)

15. Façade of La Samaritaine overlooking the Rue du Pont-Neuf. Beginning in the 1890s, this department store—along with many others in Paris—embarked upon a major rebuilding program. The principal architect was Frantz Jourdain, who was inspired in part by Zola's descriptions of the fictional *Au Bonheur des Dames.* This building was innovative not only in visual appearance (an undisguised steel frame filled with polychrome decorations) but also in its elaborate ventilation, heating, drainage, and electrical systems (for example, one electrical switch closed all the window blinds automatically). (Lantern slide in the Rotch Visual Collection, M.I.T.)

16. The Grand Bazar in the Rue de Rennes, designed by Henri Gutton of Nancy and completed in 1906. Like Jourdain's La Samaritaine, which greatly influenced Gutton, this building united an exposed steel structure with wide glazed surfaces framed by black-and-gold panels. (Lantern slide in the Rotch Visual Collection, M.I.T., from a photograph in *L'Architecte*, 1907, pl. 15.)

17. Grands Magasins du Printemps, at the corner of the Rue de Rome and Boulevard Haussmann, Paris. The store had been built by Paul Sédille in 1881, but major renovations were made around 1910 by René Binet, who had designed the Monumental Gateway (La Porte Binet) for the 1900 exposition. This slide is undated but probably shows the department store around 1910 or 1911. (Lantern slide in the Rotch Visual Collection, M.I.T.)

18. The Grand Hall of Binet's addition to Grands Magasins du Printemps, as it appeared in 1911. Instead of hiding the elevators in an inconspicuous place, as previous department-store architects had usually done, Binet made three large elevators prominent decorations of the Grand Hall, which was seven stories high. An admirer of Binet's design explained, "The intensity of life no longer permits the shopper to pass slowly from one level to another by a staircase; the shopper wants to be carried instantaneously from the ground floor to the highest story, without fatigue, with a speed equal to that of his automobile." (Photograph from *L'Architecte*, 1911, pl. 10.)

19. The main entrance to Dufayel's credit establishment, Rue de Clignancourt, Paris, as it appeared in 1902. On either side of the central doorway are seven-foot-high bronze groups representing "Credit" and "Publicity," and over the doorway is an elaborate clock seven feet in diameter. The bas-relief above the clock portrays "Progress Leading on Commerce and Industry." The wrought-iron railing in front (thirteen feet high and a hundred and twenty feet long) could be raised by hand, by electricity, or by hydraulic power. (From *Architectural Record*, vol. 12, no. 4, September, 1902: 432. Courtesy of *Architectural Record*.)

20. Interior view of the dome above the entry porch, Dufayel's credit establishment, Paris. The dome was constructed mainly of iron, steel, and bronze; wood was used as little as possible. The four sculpted figures represent Paris, Lyon, Marseille, and Bordeaux. At the very top, inside the cupola, hung a cut-glass chandelier. At the bottom can be seen the enormous clock on the front of the building as it appeared from the inside. (From *Architectural Record*, vol. 2, no. 4, September, 1902: 436. Courtesy of *Architectural Record*.)

21. Exterior view of the parking garage at 51 rue de Ponthieu, a model of "appropriateness" in design. Its utilitarian façade frankly revealed the use of the building and its construction from reinforced concrete. (Photograph from *L'Architecte*, 1908).

22. Interior balconies of the Bon Marché, a Left Bank department store, in 1876. The architects were Boileau and Eiffel—the latter being the designer of the Eiffel Tower erected for the 1889 exposition. (Lantern slide in the Rotch Visual Collection, M.I.T.)

23. Interior view of a parking garage at 51 rue de Ponthieu, Paris, designed by A. and G. Perret, as it appeared in 1908. By that date there were already numerous parking garages in Paris, especially in the western, wealthier quarters of the city. In this garage elevators raised the automobiles to the desired level, and then a rolling bridge and turntable were used to move them to individual stalls. (Photograph from *L'Architecte*, 1908.)

tried . . . to transmute copper or base metals into gold." Until such a marvelous "philosopher's stone" is found, only a few can enjoy luxuries. The only solution is to renounce the belief that salvation lies in wealth and material civilization. "The sickness is in us, and cannot be cured by exterior remedies." Moral disease requires a moral remedy. The law is a dead thing when the need is to reform the inner person. Only a vital religious faith can root out the softness, the love of comfort, and the vanity and sensuality that afflict us; only faith can reorder priorities and purify the soul so that the reign of money will finally be overthrown.

The Search for a Secular Moral Code – Anatole Leroy-Beaulieu's discussion of the sources and forms of what his brother calls "modern luxury" makes Paul Leroy-Beaulieu's analysis seem superficial by comparison. Perhaps it is fairer to say that the difference really lies in the area of concern. Paul Leroy-Beaulieu's topic is the aggregate whole, the abstract unit called "civilization" whose progress depends on its economic vitality. Anatole Leroy-Beaulieu is concerned with the concrete, flesh-and-spirit individual who feels strong envies and passions and who suffers from the competitive fervor of modern life. The differences in their ethical conclusions follow accordingly. The economist who looks at the overall process concludes that its natural development will resolve conflicts of consumption. The proper ethical response for the individual is to go along with the flow of evolution by which needs and desires multiply in number and complexity. The political scientist, focusing on these conflicts as they rage in the individual breast, concludes that outside help is needed to aid the troubled soul. The only proper ethical response is to resist the "natural" evolution of modern society toward a reign of money. The papacy is one source of help in this resistance, and the state is another: the hope of the *Ralliement* was that these two authorities could work in harmony. Anatole Leroy-

Beaulieu does not specify concrete measures to help the consumer in resolving his inner conflicts, but as a *Rallié* and Le Playist he would be open to creative legislation; his brother's dogmatic laissez-faire liberalism, on the other hand, would never permit such initiatives. Paul Leroy-Beaulieu counsels do-nothing because he is basically defending the way the world is and the way it is going. Beyond this defense he has nowhere to go, intellectually speaking, whereas his brother, as a critic of the prevailing order, is free to maneuver, to suggest new paths, to move to new intellectual positions.

This kind of mobility in thought became increasingly necessary as the 1890s progressed. The faint signs of reconciliation between Church and State which were in the background when Anatole Leroy-Beaulieu wrote his 1894 article faded away. The Dreyfus Affair in the latter part of the decade pitted traditionalist Catholics against republican anticlericals in a bitter and prolonged quarrel. When Dreyfus was finally vindicated of the charge of treason, the anticlericals took advantage of their triumph to dissolve the Assumptionist Fathers and most other religious orders and finally to push through the Law of Separation (1905) removing all state support for the Church—setting it adrift, so to speak, on the seas of modern materialism and indifference. At least this is how separation was seen at the time by the Church. However many long-term advantages separation may have had in reconciling Church and State, its passage marked the nadir of relations between the two. The papal successor to Leo XIII was as intransigent on his side as French anticlericals were on theirs. By the early years of the twentieth century, it was obvious that Paul Leroy-Beaulieu's resigned realism was a more accurate assessment of the chances for a general revival of faith than was his brother's pious hopefulness. Only for individual believers like Anatole Leroy-Beaulieu himself would the Church serve as a social authority encouraging restraint of material desires. For the population at large, the Church would not be able to fill this role, for many people were either indifferent or actively hostile to it.

This situation found the political leaders of France in a predicament. They were quite aware of the dangers to the state from competition for material goods—the dangers of discord, envy, and "spirit of revolt" which Anatole Leroy-Beaulieu had enumerated and which might cause the people to turn to socialism in hopes of sharing the wealth. They were also aware that such passions could not be restrained through legislation alone: popular moral education would be far more effective. The Catholic Church was the institution that had traditionally undertaken popular moral education. In fact, many republican politicians would have been happy to let the Church continue to carry out that task, but they had long since concluded that the Church was unwilling to settle for spiritual authority and would always try to interfere in temporal affairs by nurturing allegiance to ecclesiastical authorities over republican ones. Moreover, the Church would inculcate outdated superstitions along with ethical principles. The dilemma facing the leaders of the Third Republic was how to appropriate the moral authority of religion without fostering the institutional power or the supernatural mythology of the Church. The obvious solution was for the state itself to undertake the moral education of the people. The village schoolteacher, not the priest, would be the person responsible for inculcating precepts of conduct. Those precepts would be explained and defended in humanistic rather than supernatural terms. The ultimate sanction for self-restraint in material desires would be the good of society rather than the fear of God.

The search for a code of morality grounded in secular principles was a central preoccupation in French thought beginning in the 1880s and continuing into the early years of the twentieth century. In that era scholarly journals were flooded with articles on morality and related topics of education and sociology; many books on moral thought were published; and the subject was discussed at numerous academic forums, among them the Académie des Sciences Morales et Politiques. But interest was by no means confined to scholarly circles. "The grand metaphysical questions which it would have seemed would be excluded from worldly preoccupations became the object of passionate discussions in novels, theatrical plays, and even the conversations of the idle."[34] Journals of general circulation such as the *Revue des deux mondes* carried articles on weighty topics like "The Reign of Money." Decorative arts reformers like Camille Mauclair discussed aesthetic concerns as part of a contemporary quest for a new moral code (through "the morality of the created thing," as one of them put it).[35] Economists like Paul Leroy-Beaulieu discussed economic issues from a moral perspective. The decorative arts movement, the debate on luxury, and the quest for a new *morale* all originated in the 1880s and should be seen as part of the same broad intellectual movement.

The practical consequences of this preoccupation with social morality were by no means insignificant. It inspired a reform of criminal law, along with a reconsideration of the traditional moral justification for the punishment of offenders. The institution most affected, of course, was the school system. Secondary education was revised to include special courses in morality for the third and fourth classes "which were recommended to the professors by ministerial instructions."[36] In 1904 the École de Morale charged a number of professors and scholars with the task of teaching the public about recent major systems of morality from which it could choose, including those of Charles Renouvier, Auguste Comte, Friedrich Nietzsche, and even Karl Marx.[37]

By that time, however, both discussion and action were subsiding. The international exposition of 1900 could be regarded as the last large-scale attempt to bring about the moral education of the masses through a "lesson of things." The exposition demonstrated to intellectual and political leaders the fact that despite all their efforts, the masses seemed to be turning into amoral consumers rather than into citizens of sterner fiber. The early years of the twentieth century brought a sense that the search for a moral code was futile. In 1905 one observer commented that over the previous two decades, "despite the *fêtes* to which our country has invited a world astonished by our national activity, despite centenaries, whose celebration is well designed to implant in the popular consciousness the grand ideas which should guide it, still it is legitimate to speak of a crisis of *morale* and of *moralité*."[38]

This movement to define a new code of social morality, even if ultimately frustrated, constitutes an immensely important attempt to come to terms with the implications of the consumer revolution. The key word of the movement is the French term *la morale*, of which the English expressions "morality," "moral code," and "social morality" are all inadequate translations. In English, *morality* and related terms generally refer to the practice of virtue or to a general awareness (as opposed to a rigorously defined concept) of the distinction between right and wrong. Unfortunately, the idea of morality has been trivialized in its connotation to the level of didactic moralizing, the sort of preachiness associated with the Victorians. In the twentieth century the intellectual reaction against that type of moralizing has been so pronounced in the English-speaking world that the whole realm of moral thought has been neglected. As a possible alternative the term *ethics* is not much more satisfactory than *morality*. Traditionally, ethics has signified the branch of philosophy dealing with moral duty or a system of moral principles and as such ethical thought has suffered from the general decline in philosophical speculation in the modern age. Today *ethics* is commonly associated with specialized rules of conduct, sometimes having legal or quasi-legal status, governing the behavior of practitioners of medicine, journalism, politics, and the like; it has become reduced to a narrowly professional frame of reference. Moreover, both morality and ethics tend to be applied only to individual behavior, in the former case to sexual conduct in particular and in the latter case to professional conduct. Both terms therefore lack a social dimension.

The French *la morale* as used in modern times has distinct advantages over the English vocabulary. Since the twelfth century the French have used this word to refer to the science of good and evil, and for nearly as long it has signified the practice of right conduct as well as its theory. In the late nineteenth century *la morale* became invested with a more specialized meaning, implying the whole network of habits and values in a given society and, even more specifically, the scientific study of such a system in a society. *La morale*, used by itself, came to mean the study of social morality, the appraisal of moral ideas and practice in a social context. The definition and clarification of this term by such eminent social thinkers as Émile Durkheim (whose contribution will be discussed in Chapter VIII), as well as by a host of lesser-known figures, provided a most useful category of thought—one less rigorous than ethical philosophy but not degraded to feeble moralizing, one that goes beyond individual *conscience* to collective *conscience*, one that is open to sociological, philosophical, and psychological ideas alike.

As such the term *la morale* represents a great advance over the concept of *le luxe* ("luxury"). It looks forward rather than backward. The problem with the concept of luxury is precisely the enormous weight of the past, the crushing prestige of ancient philosophers and Church Fathers who were responding to radically different material conditions. To describe new conditions as "modern luxury" or "democratized luxury" confused rather than clarified understanding. The implication was always that modern consumption is a variation on an ancient theme rather than something qualitatively different.

As early as 1888, in the course of the Académie debate on luxury, this inherent limitation of the term *luxury* had been recognized. One of the participants, J. G. Courcelle-Seneuil (1813–1893), a member of the Paris group of economists, warned, "I truly believe that if we keep talking about this word *luxury*, undefined and indefinable, we could keep up a discussion that would last for centuries, classifying ourselves as rigorist, permissive, and moderate, without advancing a single step." It was a catch-all word, he continued, encompassing the luxury of the poor as well as that of the rich, although the two should not "be submitted to the same material rule." In addition, most ideas about luxury were inherited from ancient philosophers, who uniformly considered wealth a matter of indifference or scorn, unworthy of attention from an elevated soul. "This is," said Courcelle-Seneuil, " . . . the theory of Plato, of Aristotle, of the Stoics and of Epicurus himself: it is also that of the Cynics and it was adopted by the Church Fathers." Their attitude was understandable in societies where wealth was obtained by slavery, pillage, and other unsavory means, but today the social origins of wealth are far different and on the whole more respectable. Moreover, modern society enjoys a sheer quantity of riches which the ancients could never have imagined.

Courcelle-Seneuil concluded that the precepts of the ancients regarding luxury had little relevance to modern life. Young people may learn them as part of their general classical training (which was heavily emphasized in French secondary education), but if they take these rules seriously they are completely lost when they graduate, seeing "nowhere the contempt for riches with which they have been inculcated." Luxury still remains an important topic for intellectual inquiry, being of moral matters "the most important of all . . . at the present moment, the true social question. It is a question of general conduct of which the solution must be found." It is time, however, to cast aside the intellectual tools of antiquity and "to underpin this part of the social edifice, to repair it with solid materials, attending to all the resources we can find in the knowledge of our time." This task would require going beyond the category of luxury, a crudely moralizing term with no possible scientific content, to pose the larger question: "What use should men make of riches in the diverse conditions in which they find themselves placed?"[39]

This is precisely the kind of question addressed by Anatole Leroy-Beaulieu when he submerged the concept of luxury in the far broader categories of a reign of money and a new aristocracy of consumers. It is also, for the most part, the question addressed by the numerous other thinkers who sought a *morale* for modern France. But this is not to say that in surpassing the topic of luxury these thinkers discarded the intellectual heritage of the past any more than Anatole Leroy-Beaulieu discarded the essential teachings of Christianity. Instead, many of them sifted through the ideas of the past for elements that might still be appropriate for modern life, despite the changes in material conditions described by Courcelle-Seneuil. Just as Anatole Leroy-Beaulieu returned to the Gospels to propose a remedy for the reign of money, other thinkers in search of a secular *morale* detached from Christian revelation returned to the teachings of ancient philosophers for guidance. This was almost an instinctive response among a group of educated men rigorously drilled in the classical heritage. Yet Courcelle-Seneuil was not entirely fair in condemning this reflex. The revival is not pedantic but creative when it involves an effort to extract from ancient philosophies the teachings appropriate for modern times and to interpret them for a contemporary audience.

The Stoic Ethic of Consumption – Of all the ancient philosophies, Stoicism proved the most pertinent to the dilemmas of the modern consumer. In its counsel of detachment from material things, based on a theoretical distinction between the active soul and passive matter, the Stoics directly addressed the question of the proper relationship between a person and his possessions. Furthermore, their distinction between soul and matter led to an ethical code nearly identical with the Christian one, which was based on a religious distinction between spirit and flesh. To turn-of-the-century French intellectuals who were not Christian believers, Stoicism had great appeal, for it supported traditional Christian virtues, such as poverty, discipline of desire, and scorn for carnal pleasures, without recourse to supernatural sanctions. Some of these intellectuals (such as Anatole France) suggested that the Greek Stoics prepared the way for Christianity by their austere monotheism and elevation of spiritual reality over fragile materiality. They implied that Stoicism was an early, pristine form of Christian ethics, untainted by later doctrinal accretions. As such, Stoicism offered a secular ethic of renunciation with which to combat the ethic of material self-interest preached by liberal economists.

By the turn of the century a considerable number of books and articles on Stoicism were being published in France. For our purposes the most stimulating of these are four articles written by Louis Weber from 1905 to 1909 for the *Revue de métaphysique et de morale* collectively titled "La Morale d'Épictète et les besoins présents de l'enseignement moral" ("The Moral Thought of Epictetus and the Present Needs of Moral Education").[40] Although Weber was trained in philosophy and published articles on the subject in learned circles, he was eager to cultivate a nonscholarly audience as well. He reviewed philosophy for the *Mercure de France*, a literary magazine with a wide circulation. He took a special interest in educational reform, and he earned his living as a bureaucrat in the Ministry of Labor. Weber himself stated that his goal was to link new ideas with the traditions of ancient humanism.

His articles on Epictetus do this. In part they expound Stoic ideas, but their author is most of all attracted by Stoic methods of inculcating those ideas in a practical and effective way so that they become vital guides to social conduct. Weber wants to address the problem that seems so intractable—how to "conquer for morality" the young person who sees all around him "a fierce and merciless battle for the conquest of material well-being." Weber appreciates that "the contrast of this spectacle with the tableau of duties outlined in manuals of morality is truly ironic . . . one feels the impotence of phrases and theories." The real crisis in morality involves motivation, not ideas. The essential task is, "in a word, to effect a *conversion.*"

Weber purposely uses a religious term. He respects the practical methods used by the Church to convert individuals to a life of moral behavior. He does lament that the Church has lost the spirit of reasoned inquiry, of unfettered thought and free criticism, which flourished in ancient schools of philosophy. This intellectual tradition lives on in modern philosophy, but philosophy in its turn has lost the habit of organizing sects to inculcate its precepts in a practical way. Religious education is therefore the only contemporary example of a successful *method* of moral education. The Church trains and indoctrinates its students until they "learn to will, and to will according to moral rules or conventions." The training of the will, not that of the mind, is paramount.

Weber argues that this type of training should be detached from supernatural sanctions and reunited with reasoned inquiry. "*Edification,* that is to say, the formation of the personality and the polarization of tendencies in a determined direction, is not at all the exclusive privilege of religious faith." Stoic philosophy also understands moral consciousness as the result of edification. The Stoics equate immorality with ignorance. For them morality is not an inborn trait (as Rousseau mistakenly argues) but a straightforward "matter of instruction . . . The leading idea of Stoic philosophy is that morality is a *technique,* that the distinction between good and evil is an idea which is acquired by degrees."

This view of morality as a learned technique is one area where Stoicism is relevant to contemporary needs: a second is its identification of good with liberty and evil with dependence. As the physical universe is divided between active force and passive matter, so the individual is divided between the inner force of reason, which belongs to him freely and is under his direction, and the external

forces of circumstances (bodily health, material possessions, political and social events) he cannot control. The
individual must see that all external necessities are a
matter of indifference, and that happiness can be found
only in the practice of right reason. In particular, the
philosophical spirit appreciates that happiness can never
be found in material possessions, which are sources of
dependence, "slaves by nature," being subject to loss,
theft, poverty, and other uncontrollable factors. The moral
person who desires something submits his emotions to
reason. He reflects on his desire and asks whether it
relates to something external and enslaving or internal
and liberating. According to this "reflective and voluntary
judgment" he either acts on his desire or rejects it. The
immoral—which is to say, the ignorant—person is
swayed passively by his impressions. He is incapable of
reflecting on his feelings and is confused about the distinction between what he can control and what he cannot. As
a result he becomes a slave to his own desires, which
prove deceptive and disappointing, and loses direction
over his own life.

According to Weber, the Stoic concept of happiness as
liberty makes this philosophy particularly appropriate for
the moral education of youth, who are at a stage of life
where they are trying to develop a sense of autonomy.
Although the contrast between freedom and bondage is
no longer immediately and concretely visible, as it was in
ancient times, the young person today is well aware of
modern slavery when he sees

> the ignorant and brutal masses, who still clearly give the
> impression of enslavement to the crudest instincts. The
> crowds who rush to the racetracks, or who fill the café-
> concerts on Sundays, the café terraces and bars at cocktail
> hour, are they much more sensible to the voice of reason
> than slaves in the time of Epictetus?

Stoicism appeals to the strong sense of pride that makes
young people want to rise above this common level. "Let

us not be at all scandalized in a hypocritical way regarding a moral education which takes as its main support the self-love and naïve ambition of adolescence, for he who wills the end wills the means." The young person gains a sense of personal dignity by deciding, from among the many moral environments of modern society, which ones to reject. "He will acquire feelings of opposition with regard to environments dominated by the preoccupation of material satisfaction, an opposition not at all of hostility but, rather, of a distance at which it is proper to stand from vulgar consciousness." He faces the choice between being one of the herd or becoming a philosopher, and he must consciously renounce the former if he is to become the latter.

Besides the negative example of "the ignorant and brutal masses," a youth must also be offered positive examples. The authority of reason must be personalized in the form of moral heroes whose inner security and mental fortitude he will want to imitate. In ancient times this exemplary role was played by teachers of philosophy. Young men of the Epictetian school were awed by Stoic heroes like Socrates and Diogenes and were "seduced by the prospect of themselves belonging to an intellectual elite constituted of philosophers." Contemporary society too needs chosen men to be "coaches" of moral development. Their absence is keenly felt by young people. The grandsons of 1848 egalitarians have become worshippers of a Nietzschean hyperaristocracy—"The *Superman* is in style"—and while this is an extravagant ideal, its overblown rhetoric indicates a deep longing for moral example. The government may want schoolteachers to instill its official morality, but they are not so well adapted to their mission nor so specialized in function as ancient teachers of philosophy. Modern society needs instead

> chosen men, specially trained, who do not reflect only the ordinary ideals, depreciated because they have fallen into the domain of the mediocre, but who give the example of

moral action superior to the average level. . . . People seem to want a moral elite as they now have, thanks to higher education, an intellectual elite.

This elite should be gathered in non-religious centers of morality so that the Church does not have a monopoly on the institutionalization of moral discipline. Such centers, serving as replacements for the ancient schools of philosophy, would resemble seminaries, ethical societies, or the schools of Protestant sects such as the Quakers in the United States or the Methodists in England.

Weber anticipates the objection that such centers for moral education would be "in a certain sense aristocratic (because such an education could not be given to all)." This is true, he responds, for they would not be frequented by the sons of workers or peasants. However, such a limitation exists for any kind of higher education. There are no theoretical grounds prohibiting a Stoic education for the common people, but, practically, the necessity of daily labor keeps them away. Only those with leisure can participate in the long preparation necessary for the edification of the will. On the other hand, the very wealthy live in an environment detrimental to the development of a spirit of sacrifice and resignation. Somewhere between the extremes of wealth and poverty, somewhere between the temptations of the rich and the "thousand obstacles to a sense of personal dignity" bred by poverty, may be found that rare soil in which morality flowers.

Weber's main contribution was to transform the need for moral "conversion" from a devout hope (as expressed by Anatole Leroy-Beaulieu) into a practical possibility. The first and crucial step is to reject the general notion that knowledge of right behavior is innate. The Stoic and the Christian agree that desire is strong and reason weak in "natural" man. In particular, liberal economists' idea that the consumer intuitively understands his self-interest *qua* consumer must be scrapped. Once this fallacy has been exposed, then the path is cleared for all sorts of experi-

ments in helping the consumer comprehend the relationship between material commodities and personal happiness, and in inculcating habits of reflection so the consumer can act with conscious and reasoned foresight
rather than remaining prey to fleeting and ill-formed
whims. Furthermore, Weber sees that this type of training
is an important part of the general education of youngsters, and that the most potent educational method is that
of example. If not done consciously this teaching will be
done haphazardly. Rather than allowing a haphazard
education by adults who are themselves confused as consumers, it is in the social interest to provide coherent
moral examples for the next generation.

Where Weber must be criticized is in his particular
plan for youthful moral education. Its overwhelming
weakness is that, as Weber himself confesses, it is limited
to young bourgeois males. With this admission Weber
reveals that the Stoic education of the will is really very
unlike the religious indoctrination he claims as his inspiration. The moral education of Christianity is universal
because it is based on a belief in the equality of all before
God. The moral education of a neo-Stoic ethical culture is
parochial, being based on a narrow appeal to the sons of
bourgeois neither too rich nor too poor to receive its
message. Weber may be correct in believing that pride and
independence are effective motivations for self-restraint
among such youths. But how many are left out!—the rich,
the poor, the middle-aged and elderly, as well as children
(for them Le Play would emphasize the schooling of
family life), and especially women, whose supposedly
insatiable craving for material things, according to so
many nineteenth-century novels, could drag down a Stoic
father or husband to financial ruin. Above all, how would
an elitist Stoic education ever encourage self-restraint
among the masses who crowd to café-concerts and racetracks in an age of democratized luxury? It might be
argued that the neo-Stoic elite would set an example, but
how could this be done on a basis of scorn? For example to

be effective, there must be some basis in common humanity, some acknowledgment of similarity. In Christian moral teaching the example of Jesus is effective because He is a
suffering savior, human as well as divine—a point that
Paul Leroy-Beaulieu ignores when he argues that Jesus
should not be taken too seriously as a model for humanity
because He is "super-human." A race of ascetic supermen
who regard suffering as a matter of indifference could
offer no guidance to humanity at large.

The Ascetic Tradition and Modern Consumption – The
larger issue which should be addressed here is whether
the ascetic tradition offers any form of guidance to humanity living after the consumer revolution. As was pointed
out in the Académie debates, that tradition originated in
times of acute material scarcity. As Voltaire had said more
succinctly in "Le Mondain," "Was it virtue? It was pure
ignorance." Accordingly, Voltaire in the eighteenth century, and Baudrillart and Paul Leroy-Beaulieu in the nineteenth as well, rejected asceticism as an anachronistic relic
that should be replaced by a more enlightened, up-to-date
view of moderate luxury as a virtue.

The kind of luxury they had in mind, it must be
emphasized, was a particular type derived from aristocratic forms and assumed by wealthy bourgeois like Voltaire and Paul Leroy-Beaulieu themselves. In Voltaire's
age this was the only kind of luxury that existed, so his
defense of it could be uncomplicated. By the late nineteenth century, however, democratized luxury had appeared—a model not at all genteel but raucous, ill-bred,
exotic and erotic, primitive and hypnotizing—and its presence meant that any defense of luxury was more uncertain
and ambiguous. How could luxury be defended as a
general concept without opening the way to approval of
its peculiarly modern forms? The spectacle of mass consumption furnishes a sort of distorting mirror for the
theory of the evolution of needs; it is a spectacle of
evolution gone awry, and it thereby exposes the inadequa-

cies of a theory of endless development of needs unrelated to any final goal. The shoddy, banal consumption of the crowd reflects the habits of wealthier classes, who may be more "refined" in their choice of goods but who also lack any concept of a final goal of consumption. Baudrillart, who initiated the late-nineteenth-century debate on luxury when he published his *Histoire du luxe*, recognized this relationship. At the end of his massive work, when he turned to confront "the characteristics and tendencies of the luxury of our times," he admitted that the tendency of the poor to waste money on unhealthy luxury constituted a perverted imitation of the rich:

> The people are we ourselves. The people express our skepticism by a brutal atheism, our studied refinements by enjoyments that are within their reach, our love of luxury by passion for superfluity harmful to body and soul. If [the people] put materialism and its joys above all else, it is because others more highly placed have taught them to do so.[41]

Nowhere is this uneasy conscience behind the late-nineteenth-century defense of luxury more evident than in response to international expositions, those spectacles of mass luxury. For supporters of the ascetic tradition there was no ambivalence, for they condemned the expositions along with all other modern forms of luxury. (Anatole Leroy-Beaulieu expressed his opinion of the 1889 exposition in a letter from an imaginary Siberian visitor. "It is the masterpiece of the ancient Enemy, disguised as an angel of light in order to deceive man all the more . . . . God is absent, God has not been invited." The imaginary visitor flees to the new Tower of Babel, the Eiffel Tower, where he views the voluptuous exposition—"It smiled at me and tempted me"—and finally spits down on "the siren.")[42] Proponents of luxury found the expositions something of an embarrassment. Baudrillart devoted a long section of the last volume of his *Histoire du luxe* to recent expositions, admitting that "it is notorious . . . that these great exhibitions, above all devoted to striking and charming the eyes of the general public, appeal to all that glitters and seduces" rather than to anything of genuine use. He can see why some would disapprove of this spectacle:

> They fear, not without reason, that for every philosopher who, in the presence of these dazzling marvels, exclaims: "Here are so many things I can do without," thousands of spectators will say softly: "There are so many things I would love to have!" They fear that the poor person will be excited to envy the rich by these exhibitions, which display so many objects that are beyond his reach.

Yet Baudrillart cannot wholly side with such "moralists and religious people" without undercutting his whole theory that the development of luxury benefits society, since expositions are unquestionably "one of the most powerful means for the diffusion and propagation of luxury that has existed in the course of history." He can only argue that reason will overcome envy, that expositions as symbols of civilization's progress will inspire abstract admiration rather than personal resentment:

> The poor person will be struck . . . by the enormous quantity of useful products put at his service every year under more accessible conditions. The man who possesses only a small income will convince himself that the majority of these luxury objects have their inferior analogies that are within his reach. All finally will understand that the expositions do nothing which is not done every day by civilization which, in raising the human condition, also multiplies the causes of temptation.[43]

This multiplication of temptation is precisely why Anatole Leroy-Beaulieu condemns both expositions *and* the whole civilization so vehemently. By contrast, Baudrillart's tone is defensive and uncomfortable. So is Paul Leroy-Beaulieu's when he argues that consumers' desires can be moderated by reason, that they will understand that inequality is necessary to the progress of civilization.

Like society in general, the defenders of luxury are caught in a conflict between aristocratic and democratic ideals of consumption. They praise luxury as the elegant bloom of civilization, the refined and gracious flower available to the few who can appreciate it—and yet they recognize that everybody wants to be among the few. In the never-never-land of the expositions, the conflict is resolved temporarily. There alchemy works, there the philosopher's stone is found that enables everyone to be an aristocrat with commodities and leisure at his disposal. The question of opportunity magically disappears, and the gnawing pain of envy is transmuted into the joy of dreaming. But in the waking world self-denial is still necessary, at least for the masses, and self-indulgence is possible only for a few. The general rise in consumption levels means that the content of the categories of asceticism and luxury has changed, but they are still meaningful categories of moral behavior.

This conviction of the enduring relevance of asceticism unites late nineteenth-century advocates of austerity. In other respects, however, they are a motley group of mavericks. Anatole Leroy-Beaulieu and Louis Weber enunciate the Christian and the philosophical traditions respectively, but ascetic ideals are also expressed in less familiar terms. Des Esseintes is an ascetic of decadence: consider his strange self-discipline, his thirst for spiritual ideals and scorn for purely physical maintenance, his quest for salvation, his disdain for the consuming masses, and his fear that generalized envy will lead to homicide rather than to "progress." Camille Mauclair is an aesthetic ascetic, so to speak. Decorative arts reform was part of the late-nineteenth-century debate about luxury because the reformers wanted to combat a false identification of art with luxury. They argued that objects are truly beautiful only when designed without extravagant, dishonest—luxurious—ornamentation extraneous to physical function. Functionalism is austerity in aesthetics. Aesthetic and moral thought converge in a common concern for honesty and restraint, for genuine needs as opposed to spurious ones, for the elimination of the unnecessary so that life can be liberated to express its inner simplicity and harmony. In a reaction against the complications and confusions arising from a flood of consumer goods, moralists and artists alike yearned for the beauty of necessity.

Even the moralist-historian Georges d'Avenel, for all his praise of banal "vulgarizations" as the glory of the nineteenth century, for all his appreciation of the imaginative pleasures provided by shoddy mass-produced silks, even he in the end has to be numbered among the believers in austerity. While the nineteenth century has brought mines, telegraphs, sewers, political systems, and pleasures of all sorts, d'Avenel concludes, it has not brought "resignation and the ideal, which is to say, peace and hope. Do the smoke of locomotives and tobacco contain more than the smoke of incense?" Not consumer pleasures but only religious faith can cure the sickness of the century:

> If one piled up a hundred times more enjoyments, humanity would be the prey of a terrible *ennui,* an *ennui* that one feels in looking at cities which no steeple, no dome, no tower surmounts—all things of first necessity, although perfectly useless in themselves. Workers, peasants, all may become "bourgeois" in the sense we give this word today, . . . and will despair at being in this world, having lost the certainty of finding a better one upon leaving it. Then the people will vomit up the lay religions, laboriously fed to them; they will cry to have a soul and for someone to give them a God.[44]

The tone of condescension that runs through d'Avenel's defense of cheap, mass-produced goods echoes in his conclusion that "the people" will eventually cry out for a God. Unlike Anatole Leroy-Beaulieu, d'Avenel does not advocate religious faith because he is himself convinced of its validity; he only says that faith is necessary for "the people."

This condescension, this opposition of "the people" vs. oneself, is worth remarking because it is so persistent, indeed dominant, among all these advocates of austerity. Des Esseintes's style of consumption permitting him to possess only rare and unique items derives from his overwhelming need to demonstrate that his soul is also rare and unique, far above the level of the loathsome masses. The style of consumption typical of the decorative arts movement, while it embraces simplicity rather than perversity, shares this taboo on the commonplace. Even more blatantly, Louis Weber apeals to proud elitism as a motivation for youth to adopt Stoic austerity. The aristocracy of money, to borrow Anatole Leroy-Beaulieu's expression, calls forth its opposite in an aristocracy of renunciation. Both elites are intent on marking their distinction from the crowd, while the crowd is left with "a thousand obstacles to the sense of personal dignity," with no leisure or motivation to develop an ascetic morality. The proud renunciation of those better-off is not likely to speak to them, while the message that *will* be communicated is that their values and activities are disdained, that their souls are lost to Mammon with no promise of eternal salvation. The modern slaves are left to crowd into café-concerts, bars, and expositions, to dream their dreams in stupefied awe, while "superior individuals" extol the virtues of austerity. Those who renounce the sin of greed seem to succumb to the sin of pride.

But this sense of superiority, of isolation from the contamination of the crowd, is illusory. The mass consumer and modern elitist ascetic are mirror images of each other. To oppose mass consumption so consistently acknowledges its potency just as much as to participate in it does. Furthermore, the liberty and individuality which Paul Leroy-Beaulieu extols in defending luxury are the same values ascetics like des Esseintes and Louis Weber regard so highly. Finally, voluntarily doing without can be just another status symbol in a society of consumers. In the modern age, asceticism is easily warped into the status of another lifestyle—a new aristocracy of simplicity.

This peculiarly contemporary version of asceticism

does not bring the calm self-assurance that the traditional type promised. Instead, it is accompanied by feelings of unease and apprehension. The pride of the ascetic is a troubled pride. Even those who despise the crowd cannot evade its presence; in his isolation des Esseintes is still not out of the reach of the encroaching mass market, just as patrons of the decorative arts cannot shake off pursuit by cheap imitations. "I know you don't have to buy them" (as Huysmans remarks of decorative arts objects) "but you have to see them because they fill up entire boulevards and streets!"—as do the crowds the neo-Stoic cannot help seeing in the cafés, the streets, the boulevards.

This inescapable spectacle of mass consumption not only offends the taste of the neo-ascetic (says Huysmans, "the eye . . . wanders all the same toward [this horror] and lingers there [in an] unnatural craving for the ugly!"). The spectacle is also frightening. When may the unrest and envy of the masses explode to shatter the proud isolation of superior individuals? Mauclair fears that a socialist revolution may install a "mob of brutes" in power; des Esseintes condemns society for training criminals like Auguste Langlois; and Anatole Leroy-Beaulieu predicts that the masses would "rise up against what they call the privileges of the rich." The apprehensions of the neo-ascetics are expressed as a general pessimism about the future that is in sharp contrast to the optimism of a liberal like Paul Leroy-Beaulieu. They are Malthusians of consumption, for they believe that proliferation of needs will always outrun the proliferation of resources to satisfy needs. Like conventional Malthusians, their predictions cast a threatening shadow over the nineteenth-century belief in progress. In both cases the underlying fear is that material resources can never expand fast enough to keep up with the consequences of human desire. This is why Georges d'Avenel, for example, is apprehensive of the future despite all the progress that has been made in democratizing luxury:

In measure as individuals mingle and conditions improve, the poor person has more resources, enlightenment, and desires, but his desires perpetually surpass his resources. Even when we shall have endowed the most disinherited among us with abundant food, comfortable clothes, an agreeable dwelling, and much leisure, all this in exchange for a little work, do you believe he will think himself happy? Oh no! And what therefore is happiness? Alas! it is precisely satisfaction with what we are, with what we have; it is resignation. This resignation is the opposite of progress; and the opposite of resignation—ambition, effort—is progress itself . . . . Ardor for improvement, which is profitable for the collectivity, is in some way destructive of the happiness of the individual, because it encourages him never to be satisfied. In this regard civilization, which gives so many real enjoyments, does not give moral happiness; perhaps it is even contrary to this, because it incites more appetites than it can satisfy, and imaginary sorrows are no less painful.[45]

This somber view of an inescapable and irresolvable conflict in society, a sort of permanent sickness at its core, is also held by Louis Weber. In 1913 Weber published *Le Rythme du progrès, étude sociologique* ("The Rhythm of Progress, A Sociological Study"), after many years of thinking about the relationship between moral and material progress. Weber concludes that civilization is governed by a "law of two states" which "simply express[es] this fact, that the human intelligence seems to have progressed . . . by alternating phases of technical activity and of ideological [or reflective] activity."[46] As a result, there is inevitable incompatibility between the ideas and modes of thought emerging from technical intelligence and those emerging from reflective intelligence. There will always be a time lag between the two faculties, for one develops as the other stagnates. The nineteenth century, for example, has seen prodigious technical activity while moral reflection has languished. This tragic but inescapable imbalance is the result of the inborn dichotomy of the human intellect whereby mankind cannot deal with things and ideas at the same time.

Now we can begin to appreciate the profound emotional sources of the asceticism of this disparate collection of late-nineteenth-century thinkers. It provided a moral code that could serve as a personal refuge in a hostile society, a society which made them depressed and sometimes desperate. Religious faith provides personal but not social salvation. The same is true of the quiet, philosophical heroism Mauclair and Weber adopted after they discarded their more ambitious programs for social reform. Stoic philosophy in particular may be seen as a holding action for individuals, a personal barricade against confusion in an age that is incapable of evolving a generally accepted moral code. Stoicism served this purpose as an ethical refuge during the waning days of the Roman Empire, and it could serve the same purpose in the latter days of western Europe's industrial and colonial empire. As Louis Weber points out, for the Stoics the concept of moral progress is purely individual. The Stoic does not blame his vices on his society, nor does he assume that the morality of the individual (at least of the superior individual) depends on general progress in customs and institutions. This view, Weber cautions, is very different from the modern one, which sees individual perfection in terms of general progress toward greater social, legal, or economic solutions. Since Weber does not hold out much hope for general moral progress in his age, he addresses himself to the few enlightened persons willing to undertake their own moral development. The modern ascetic is above all lonely. He has built a barricade, but he mans it alone.

From Individualism to Solidarity–Weber's variety of asceticism may not transcend an isolated individualism, but along with Anatole Leroy-Beaulieu's Christian version it does break out of the moral universe of lifestyle. The asceticism of des Esseintes and of decorative arts reformers, as we have seen, tends to degenerate into another version of consumerism. In both cases the im-

pulse toward austerity submits to a reification that identifies spiritual superiority with supposedly superior possessions. In contrast to this sterile dandyism, both Stoicism
and Christianity, by returning to the antique sources of
asceticism, stress the duality of soul vs. things, of spirit vs.
flesh. They directly challenge the domination of material
values by renouncing them in favor of non-material ones;
their primary emphasis is upon the personal and to some
degree the political liberty that can be attained only
through refusing submission to material things.

Surely the point is still valid. The less one consumes,
the more one gains in money, in mental energy, and,
above all, in time, which is otherwise committed not only
to acquiring possessions but also to their upkeep. Still,
even those who in good faith decide to live simply in order
to maximize their liberty cannot entirely evade being
judged on the basis of lifestyle. To survive physically,
some possessions are necessary, and an ascetic lifestyle,
no matter how plain and unadorned, is still a lifestyle. To
affirm the superiority of non-material values, the ascetic
must do more than live in a Spartan manner. He may not
be able to avoid judgment on the basis of lifestyle, but he
can go beyond it. He can demonstrate that for him material simplicity is a means to an end. Through what he does
and says with his relative liberty, not through how he lives
in material terms, the modern ascetic can communicate a
message that is not phrased in the language of lifestyle.
This type of austerity goes beyond a negative indictment
of the masses, beyond the varieties of consumerism, to a
positive statement of other values.

But *what* other values? For ancient ascetics, as well as
for modern ones like Anatole Leroy-Beaulieu and Louis
Weber, those values concern the contemplation of eternal
truth—the contemplation of God, for the Christian, or of
reason, for the philosopher. In this tradition the dichotomy between commodities and spirit is parallel to that
between the temporal and the eternal, between the deceptive and the true, between action and thought. This un-

derstanding of value is wholly out of favor in the modern world. Since ancient times the scale of values has completely reversed; now the active life, not the contemplative life, is given priority.[47]

There is, however, no necessary reason why the liberation afforded by austerity has to be devoted to contemplative values, as Max Weber discovers in his classic study *The Protestant Ethic and the Spirit of Capitalism* (1904–1905). He shows how the ascetic spirit could be made to serve the capitalist accumulation of material goods rather than the contemplation of the immaterial. It is true that what Weber calls "asceticism" might be better termed "self-restraint" or "self-scrutiny," since the mentality he describes admits a highly comfortable, if not lavish, style of life. Weber's point nonetheless stands: the habit of limiting desire can be dissociated from contemplation and can be attached to different values. The inherent contradiction of the "Protestant ethic," of course, is that restraint in consumption on the part of capitalists only leads to the accumulation of more and more resources which have to be consumed by *somebody* in order to maintain economic stability. The relative asceticism of the producers has to be balanced by the hedonism of the consuming masses. If we are to advocate a more generalized austerity, if we are to find an asceticism that can be shared by the masses, some other value than that of material production must be served.

The supreme question of modern asceticism is what values could and should be liberated by a decreased emphasis on material consumption? It is in responding to this query that the turn-of-the-century French search for a *morale* is so suggestive. As we have seen, all sorts of alternatives were presented, from neo-Kantianism to neo-Stoicism. But by far the most important alternative, the one that attracted the most attention then and remains of the most enduring interest, is the *morale* of solidarism (or solidarity).

Although these terms now tend to be associated with

socialist comrades singing "Solidarity Forever," the French concept of solidarity in that period was, if anything, regarded as a bulwark against socialism. To a certain extent, solidarism was a political doctrine competing with the other "isms" of the French Third Republic—not just socialism but also radicalism and opportunism—but it would be a mistake to analyze it primarily in political terms.[48] Solidarism was less a principle for governing the state than a basis for a moral education above politics that would nonetheless complement and strengthen the political order. It would function as a sort of social engineering, a "social technology," to use a popular phrase of the day, on the assumption that (as another popular phrase put it) "the social question is basically a moral question."[49] Admittedly, the line between solidarism as a political doctrine and solidarism as a moral code to complement political life is a fine one, and in practice it was of course impossible for the French government to sponsor a doctrine independent of politics. In fact, solidarism became a sort of quasi-official philosophy of the Third Republic. But the ideal is persistent. A century later, Americans are being warned that their nation's political and economic problems cannot be solved until they reform themselves spiritually. In particular, we are told that the "social questions" of inflation and energy are basically "moral questions" requiring self-restraint and self-discipline. The need for a moral code to supplement the political order is still vital, and the significance of solidarism lies in its role as an experiment in realizing this ideal.

The basic concept of solidarity is the definition of morality as a commitment to the "social whole." Its justification is the observation that an individual involuntarily incurs obligations to the social whole simply by living in society. The citizen is the passive recipient of social benefits: he is, in fact, first and foremost a consumer. "Before being a producer, he begins by being a consumer of material products as well as of moral, artistic, and intellectual ones, products accumulated over the centuries by toil, by suffering, by the genius or the labor of generations past."[50] And, like any good consumer, this citizen lives in perpetual debt. He consumes more of this social capital than he can ever produce, and this involuntarily acquired debt is the basis of his moral obligation to society. Solidarism answers the question of value in this way: the highest value is the development of the human community, and the individual should contribute his talents and labors to the service of collective life.

In turn-of-the-century France these ideas were typically expressed in legalistic language, but the great advantage of solidarism over competing *morales* was that it could also be justified by appeal to the facts of history and especially of science. The solidarity of the human species could be explained as an inevitable result of biological evolution, which always tends to the greater interdependence of living creatures. The facts of history could be cited to confirm this scientific theory. To an age enamored of biological and historical explanations, this *morale* seemed intellectually up-to-date and objectively valid in a way that raised it above the relativity of other philosophical systems, such as Stoicism, which were competing for favor. The moderns triumphed over the ancients.

Another reason for the widespread acceptance of solidarist thought was that it approached moral questions, and specifically the morality of consumption, from a collective point of view. Nearly all the thinkers discussed up to this point, whether they advocate luxury or asceticism, view consumption in individualistic terms. As in so many other respects, des Esseintes serves as a prototype, if not as a parody, of the modern consumer, for his choices, pleasures, and pains all take place in solitude. An economic liberal like Paul Leroy-Beaulieu thinks of the consumer as an isolated person motivated by self-interest; his Catholic brother, as a sinner who must seek personal salvation through faith; a philosopher like Louis Weber, as an individual whose moral fibre needs to be strengthened so that he will shun the café crowd; and even decorative arts reformers usually think in terms of improving the taste of individuals through better design of products for personal use, like jewelry or furniture. In all cases the emphasis is on the liberty of the autonomous consumer to govern his own habits, to choose indulgence or renunciation. If there is a social dimension to this concept of consumption it is that of competition, whereby the individual uses products to mark his distinction from the masses, his superiority of wealth, of self-discipline, or of artistic taste.

But all this emphasis on personal liberty can charm us into thinking that the consumer enjoys more liberty than he in fact does. When a consumer decides to buy something, he does so because he has a mental image of how his life might be improved if he, and he alone, owned that object. At the same time thousands and even millions of other consumers may be forming the same mental image and arriving at the same decision. The collective reality which results is entirely different from the image that motivated the purchase. In the first place, when many people decide to buy an object, it loses its luxury status and hence some of its desirability. Second, the massing together of personal decisions may have serious objective results. An obvious example is the automobile—the difference between the image of comfort and speed aroused by the sight of the cars at the early Salons de l'Automobile, and the reality of foul air and traffic jams only a few years later when many people owned cars. The consumer's dream is solitary, but reality is collective. The freedom of the individual consumer is necessarily curtailed by the effects of other people's consumption. Although the consumer may be sovereign in his own little sphere of choice, he is powerless in the much larger sphere of mass consumption. He has individual but not collective liberty.[51]

In contrast to the misleadingly individualistic view of consumption which dominated discussion of the subject then, and does still to a certain extent, Norbert Elias reminds us that "the civilizing process" in both its material and non-material aspects is inherently a shared experience and can no more be lifted out of the social context than out of the historical context.[52] To be sure, we have seen hints of how consumption might be treated in a social context. The economists debating luxury distinguished "public luxury" (meaning state-supported projects) from "private luxury," and agreed that the two types were entirely different in character. The social dimension of the Christian gospel lies in its recognition of the basic equality of sinful human beings before God, and Anatole Leroy-Beaulieu interprets this to mean that the sin of "Mammonism" involves us all, rich and poor, Christian and Jew, conservative and socialist.

Another type of collective consumption may be seen at the expositions, automobile shows, department stores, and other environments of mass consumption, but these are mainly negative examples, which demonstrate that the multiplication of personal experiences is not the same as the sharing of them. Contemporary descriptions of these environments of mass consumption emphasize the isolation and mental passivity of the visitors, despite their physical proximity. They all receive the same experience but do not pass it on to each other or modify each other's experience. Instead, they are locked in private reveries. This kind of mass consumption is the extension of individualism in consumption, not its antithesis. To look forward rather than backward, the social experience of environments of mass consumption can be defined in the terminology of Émile Durkheim, who characterized "mechanical solidarity" as a "social solidarity that comes from a certain number of states of *conscience* which are common to all the members of the same society." This solidarity of likeness is born when the "collective *conscience* completely envelops our whole [individual] *conscience*," when "our individuality is nil . . . . The individual *conscience* . . . is a simple dependent upon the collective type and follows all of its movements as the possessed object follows those of its owner." The preferable alternative, according to Durkheim, is an "organic solidarity" whereby individuals are distinctive because "each one has a sphere of action which is peculiar to him, so that personality is born and social bonds strengthened at the same time."[53]

It is the possibility of an "organic solidarity" in consumption that will be explored now. By viewing consumption as a social phenomenon, we can break out of the narrow confines of the debate between hedonism and asceticism, since neither the ethic of personal self-interest nor that of personal self-denial addresses the collective dimension of the problem. The *morale* of solidarity does, in two major ways. In the first place, solidarism is based in evolutionary theory, and more specifically in the idea that a new biological reality is created when many similar organisms interact. When applied to consumer society, this biological emphasis suggests that consumption must be understood as creating a new organic environment which in turn reacts back on individual consumers. Indeed, the appreciation of the ecological implications of intensive consumption—an appreciation that has increased dramatically in the last decade or so—may be seen as an extension of the principle of solidarity to the relationship between human and non-human nature.

In this study, however, the emphasis will be on solidarist ideas which address the moral, subjective consequences of collective consumption rather than physical, environmental ones. Solidarism suggests new possibilities for the regulation of consumption through social but nongovernmental restraints. It shuns the two alternatives of purely individual regulation (that is, religious or philosophical conversion) and of wholly legislative ones, and proposes instead that social consciousness can be transformed at least in part through the phenomenon of shared consumption itself. Society can encourage consumption: why cannot it also work to limit consumption? The possibility of establishing a new kind of social authority, at once a product of the consumer revolution and the source of its regulation, is the theme which will now be examined in the works of Charles Gide, Émile Durkheim, and Gabriel Tarde. When modern consumer society was seen in terms of the *morale* of solidarity rather than those of luxury, modern consciousness began to ponder the implications of the consumer revolution in terms of the future rather than of the past. New wine was being put into fresh wineskins.

7 Charles Gide and the Emergence of Consumer Activism

The Making of an Unconventional Economist – Charles Gide (1847–1932) was raised in the south of France near Nîmes and came to Paris as a young man to study economics. He later recalled that in his courses the word "liberty" tolled repeatedly like a bell whose plangency could work miracles. In other words, Gide was thoroughly inculcated in the dogmas of the Paris group economists. He himself taught the prevailing orthodoxies when he became a professor at the University of Bordeaux in 1874. But from his earliest years of teaching Gide was uncomfortable with the doctrines of laissez-faire and self-help. They seemed to preclude social improvement, and to justify a complacent acceptance of the status quo. Accordingly, they failed to satisfy his restless and visionary spirit.

When Gide moved back to his native region in 1880 as a professor at the University of Montpellier, his doubts had deepened. His early articles in the orthodox *Journal des économistes* gained him some notoriety among the Paris group for his unconventionality, especially when in 1883 he published an article sympathetic to the American agrarian reformer Henry George. The following year brought

Gide's definitive break with classical political economy. In 1884 he published the first edition of his *Principes d'économie politique* ("Principles of Political Economy"), a best-selling text that was widely read and translated, thanks to the author's clear and pleasing prose style. But it "made a scandal among the classical economists," in Gide's own words, because of its "quite heretical doctrines on landed property, on the regime of the wage-earning class, on competition, on the bankruptcy of laissez-faire, on the role of the State."[1] Most scandalous of all, the book gave socialist theories as much attention as liberal ones and even treated them with some sympathy. This catholicism could only shock economists like Paul Leroy-Beaulieu who mentioned socialism only to condemn or ridicule it.

Yet Gide was by no means ready to accept socialism in place of liberalism. He agreed with socialists in criticizing the liberal acceptance of the status quo, for he too desired an economic order more just than the prevailing one. But Gide was so little of a revolutionary that he was repelled by doctrines of violent expropriation, as well as by socialism's extreme egalitarianism. He considered the school of Le Play as an alternative approach to economics, for he admired its historical method and careful observation of social facts. However, its traditionalist emphasis on authority, and especially on the authority of the Catholic Church, was unacceptable to Gide, who was Protestant. Like Camille Mauclair, Gide rejected the prevailing ideologies and found himself isolated—an ardent soul seeking a cause which would enable him to unite fervently held ideals of justice and liberty.

All this time, however, the makings of a new departure were slowly coalescing in Gide's mind. The first book of political economy he ever read was Bastiat's *Harmonies*, which "enraptured" him by its "enchanting tableau of an economic world where . . . everything conspires to serve the general welfare, and where egoism itself is only an instrument that serves the final end."[2] Although rejecting the optimistic assumption that individual interest and the general interest necessarily coincide, Gide retained the vision of social harmony, as well as Bastiat's admonition that economics should be treated from the point of view of the consumer. Next he read the works of Swiss and Austrian economists, and more than any other important French economist Gide became their disciple. In his opinion they put a human face on economics by basing value and utility on the concrete needs of the individual rather than on abstractions like property or even labor. Gide also read extensively in the works of John Stuart Mill, whom he felt had anticipated the Austrian economists in many ways. Finally, Gide developed a "filial veneration" for the early French utopian socialist Charles Fourier. He later claimed that Fourier's work persuaded him to decide on a career in economics (Gide had first planned to study law like his older brother Paul, an eminent jurist), and he praised Fourier as the most imaginative thinker of the nineteenth century except for Edgar Allan Poe.[3]

All this reading provided hints and suggestions: what united them and allowed Gide to discover a new economics encompassing both justice and liberty was the concept of solidarity. The idea was in the air, or, to use Gide's own metaphor, as the twentieth century approached its reverberations grew ever louder while those of "liberty" became ever fainter.[4] Still, Gide did adopt the term long before it was generally discussed, and he was the first to apply it to economic thought. In the centennial year of 1889, at a conference in Geneva held in late March, Gide announced the formation of a new economic school of solidarity, as opposed to the school of liberty (the Paris group), that of authority (the Le Playists), and that of equality (socialists). His speech expressed his profound excitement at having found a way out of an impasse both personal and intellectual. Like Mauclair and many other literary figures of the day, Gide issued a manifesto to declare his rejection of past traditions and to proclaim a new departure. In his concluding remarks he proclaimed:

You [Swiss] have in your mountains a wind you call the *föhn:* it is, if I am not mistaken, a mild wind that blows from the south in this season and which announces springtime; it provokes the melting of the snows and makes the glaciers and snowbanks stream down the slopes of the mountains in a thousand sources of dancing waters which descend, singing, toward the valley, toward the lowlands, as if they were joyful at feeling themselves delivered from their prison of ice and being able finally to do something useful and good in this world, were it only to quench the thirst of a blade of grass or to turn the mill wheel or to give some bread to man. Now this is the *föhn* which blows at this moment in the domain of economics, in those inaccessible regions where science has been enthroned far above poor men, at the height of the eternal snows. It is this new breeze which makes old doctrines melt, like the old snow, and carries them away in a torrent and makes them descend at last from the heights down to the lowlands, to the very low lands, to serve for something good, to penetrate even into ordinary life.[5]

Gide's eloquence as a speaker was immensely inspiring. Nearly everyone who came in contact with him referred to him sooner or later as an "apostle" or a "preacher." Although he rejected the doctrines of the Paris group, he kept its moralism. His moral fervor was in fact uniquely intense because it was derived from profound religious conviction. French Protestants were a highly self-conscious religious minority. Gide's mother and father both came from families which had produced many Protestant pastors, and Gide himself practiced his faith devoutly. He often spoke to Protestant groups in pastoral tones and helped organize L'Association Protestante pour l'Étude des Questions Sociales ("The Protestant Association for the Study of Social Questions"), as well as other religious and charitable groups. Sometimes Gide's acquaintances were surprised to hear him make a spontaneous and thoughtful commentary on the Bible, with which he was profoundly familiar.

For the most part, however, Gide's piety, as well as his

capacity for patience and charm, were hidden beneath a highly intimidating glacial reserve. When he did speak, it was often with a brutal frankness or sarcasm, that only increased the terror he inspired. Gide was scrupulously truthful but seemed unable to combine tact with his honesty. Although his social awkwardness was largely due to timidity, nervousness, and deafness, this did not ease the humiliation suffered by his targets. Gide's distance from others was painfully personal as well as social. The elder of his two sons was killed in World War I. Because of "an absolute dissidence in our social ideas," to quote Gide himself, he was unofficially separated from his wife during the last decades of his life. (She was from a Swiss patrician family and considered his social ideas dangerously radical.) She resided at the family estate near Nîmes, while Gide lived alone in Paris for most of the year. He could usually be found in his silent apartment, where he worked late into the night at a desk next to a fireplace.[6]

The paradox of Gide's personality is that this apostle of solidarity found it so difficult to express love or to draw close to other people. After standing in mute solitude among ten people in a salon, he would deliver a vivifying speech on brotherhood to an enormous audience in a lecture hall. His illustrious nephew André (son of Paul Gide) summarized the contradictions of his uncle's character in an obituary article for the *Nouvelle revue française*:

> [Charles Gide was] capable, it is true, of the most faithful attachments, but always a little *in abstracto* and remaining as unpenetrating as impenetrable, except in the realm of idea . . . . I cannot imagine a human being who more commanded admiration and who more discouraged sympathy . . . . Always steady and consistent and faithful to himself, he could not understand others except through thought, or understand from others anything but thoughts. Nevertheless, deeply capable of the most sublime and lively emotions, but of a general order; he could not have been less concerned with the particular and with what differentiates . . . . He lived among entities. Even

love and friendship had to be depersonalized to find access to his heart, which never beat so strongly as for the collective.[7]

No *föhn* ever delivered Gide from his own prison of ice. He remained in frigid isolation, aloof from the prominent economists of his day, from friends, from his family. His yearning to break out of that prison, "to be able finally to do something useful and good in this world," all that congealed emotion was channeled into the ideal of solidarity. Let us now examine more thoroughly the social ideas which to some extent compensated Charles Gide for his unsociable life.

Solidarity and Economics: Power to the Consumer – Moral concerns, no matter how passionately felt, have to be justified by objective criteria—this is Gide's conviction and that of many other *moralistes* of his day. The principle of solidarity is supremely convincing to him because it is not just another moral theory but "a fact, a fact of capital importance in the natural sciences, because it characterizes life."[8] The ideal of liberty has no foundation in science, which can accept only determinism in its sphere; nor does science support equality, since, according to Darwin, natural inequalities are the basis of selection and progress; and as for "fraternity, this outdated word no longer has any credit" among "serious men" who believe only in personal interest. But the scientific reality of solidarity is demonstrated every day in every living creature. Life itself is made possible by the solidarity of diverse functions, and death is only the rupture of that solidarity. Moreover, the facts of history agree with the facts of nature. The evolution of human needs over the centuries has made people more dependent on each other, and the technological and medical discoveries of the nineteenth century have greatly accelerated interdependence.

There is another reason why Gide is convinced of the validity of the concept:

> Finally, the school of solidarity has grown from yet another tributary coming from an entirely opposite source, by which I mean Christian philosophy and theology . . . . The dogma which forms the basis of Christian doctrine is the knowledge that all men . . . are condemned to carry eternally the penalty of the original sin of a single man, the first man, but that they can all escape from this condemnation by appropriating the merits of another unique man, the Man-God, dead on the Cross—this double dogma of the fall and redemption, this great and tragic explanation of the origins and destinies of the human species, is obviously nothing but the theory of solidarity itself taken to its highest power.[9]

Besides this accordance with Christian doctrine, the general spirit of solidarity fills the New Testament, which proclaims that we are all parts of the same body in Christ. For this reason "social Protestantism"—and Gide denies that Protestantism is an individualistic religion—welcomes the idea of solidarity with enthusiasm, "has immediately claimed it as her own and even complains that it was stolen from her in the first place."[10] For Gide this "striking coincidence"[11] between the teachings of the Gospel and those of evolution makes possible an economics that is ethical as well as objective. In the debate about luxury the moral lessons of science and religion seem contradictory, but solidarity allows their reconciliation. As solidarity became an increasingly popular slogan, Gide took pains to emphasize its spiritual dimension. In particular he rejected the "organic" solidarity popularized by Durkheim and other sociologists—a solidarity achieved through the division of labor so that each person depends on the specialized work of others to satisfy his own needs. This, declares Gide, is an unconscious, fatalistic, and therefore immoral form of solidarity, that "of the blind and paralyzed."[12] In contrast he emphasizes conscious moral intent. It might be true that the gradual development of a cooperative spirit among mankind is inevitable because biological life necessarily moves in that direction, but human beings still have an obligation to encourage the growth of solidarity, the essence of human progress. Gide's idea of solidarity is compatible with his religious faith because both are active and participatory rather than contemplative. Gide is intent on seeing solidarity realized in practical terms so that it will not remain locked in theoretical ice.

That is why Gide identified solidarism with the establishment of cooperative associations. In 1889 he noted that the new school of economics he was founding could be called either the "cooperative school" or the "solidarist school": "Solidarism, cooperativism, it's all the same thing."[13] The idea of cooperative associations was by no means new with Gide. In early French socialism the call for producers' cooperatives had been standard, and in the later 1800s numerous credit and mutual aid (insurance) companies were being formed. Gide's approach is unique because he insists that *consumer* cooperatives should be the preeminent and ultimately the only form of association.

"The Reign of the Consumer" is the title of Gide's best-known speech, which he delivered in Lausanne in January, 1893, to a group enrolled in a university course on cooperation.[14] It remains the most concise and forceful statement of Gide's central themes: the consumer has been unjustly subjected to the producer and must assert his supremacy through establishment of consumer cooperatives. Gide begins with an impassioned defense against accusations that activities of consumption are inherently sensual, parasitical, and amoral. "If consumption is ignoble," he proclaims, "life is also, for consumption is life, and to develop the powers of consumption is to develop in the same proportion the powers of life." This is not life in the sense of biological maintenance but life in the sense of accomplishment and communion:

> To consume is not only to eat a good dinner,—for those who like to treat themselves alone are very rare!—it is to invite some friends, it is to offer flowers or candy on New Year's Day, it is to let others enjoy the pleasures of good

company along with oneself . . . . It should not be forgotten that even under its most vulgar and animal form of eating, consumption has perhaps a more sociable character than production, and the proof is that people have never found a better means of fraternizing than eating together at the same table—and even the most august symbol of communion is an act of consumption, a table with bread and wine, the Lord's Supper.

For too long, Gide complains, captains of industry or workers alone have been lauded as modern heroes: in truth the consumer is the hero of economic life.

Gide then turns to criticize economists like Bastiat and his liberal heirs who pay lip service to the theory that consumption is the true end of political economy. On a practical level, the only power they are willing to grant the consumer is the negative one of refusal to buy—a paltry right indeed. They pretend the reign of the consumer is an accomplished fact, when it is only a distant ideal:

> In fact, it is not true that the economic world is organized in view of consumption; on the contrary, it is uniquely organized in view of production, or, if you prefer, it is organized in view of profits and not of needs. In fact, each time any enterprise whatsoever is established in the world, he who establishes it is never preoccupied with knowing if it responds to a social need (although he would perhaps say so in his prospectus) but only if it will reap profits, if it will make money for him.

Liberals like Bastiat falsely flatter the consumer by claiming that the consumer is the best judge of his own interests. Because "the whole art of industry is . . . to bring forth the need" rather than to serve genuine needs, society has been inundated with advertising. Buried beneath this flood, consumers have become corrupted by cravings for unneccessary objects. They long for a prodigious variety of absinthes and aperitifs only because "manufacturers and retailers have covered the walls with juxtaposed posters repeating a hundred times: *Byrrh! Byrrh! Byrrh!* or

Kling! Kling! Kling! until the consumer is hypnotized." For similar reasons, each year fashion announces that last year's clothes are hopelessly out of style, and industry then thoughtfully provides new ones out of fabrics which "instead of lasting for generations as did those of our forefathers, last only a season." The consumer follows along because he is half-mesmerized into acting by instinct, although "no one today believes in the infallibility of instinct, even among animals." His choices betray laughable ignorance in satisfying his physical needs—he can no longer recognize decent wine or meat—and downright stupidity or perversion in buying entertainment or reading material. As small commerce rapidly and inevitably becomes extinct, the consumer is increasingly at the mercy of the "commercial feudalism" of huge department stores that exploit their personnel, waste money on interior decoration, and encourage unnecessary purchases "to the point of making it a genuine form of madness called *kleptomania.*" The mass of unorganized consumers serves only as an outlet for producers (who *are* organized into powerful unions) "as the role of bottles is to receive the wine poured into them."

The consumer is as ignorant of his responsibilities as of his rights. He looks only for low prices without considering whether they are made possible by the murderous exploitation of workers. Nor does he consider his duties toward domestic animals, so often mistreated, or toward wild animals, sacrificed to satisfy whims of fashion, or toward "inanimate nature, forests, plants, natural resources, pillaged by modern industry." Unless the consumer awakens to his responsibilities to the environment, the great hillside vineyards of France will disappear in the face of competition from cheap lowland wines. The forests, which act as watersheds and bird sanctuaries, will be cut down unless coal is burned in place of wood. "How stupid and depredatory is the present function of the consumer!" exclaims Gide, "and how efficacious and beneficial it could be for the world if it were put to good use!"

The purpose of consumer cooperatives is to allow the consumer to reign in practice as well as in theory, to enable him to assume both his rights and his duties. Cooperatives will for the first time give form and consciousness to a hitherto amorphous, passive "herd of sheep." On the most basic level, cooperatives will restore the consumer's right to good merchandise at low prices. Moreover, they will act in a moral and educational role as well as an economic one. By educating the consumer, the cooperative will be an instrument of social justice and moral transformation. This education will be in part material, teaching, for example, that good bread is not pasty and white; in part economic, by expounding the role of capital, the dangers of credit, and the details of running a business; and, above all, moral, by arousing awareness of responsibilities to society and nature. The cooperative can inquire into the origin of products and give preference to those made by unionized workers or by producers' associations. It can insist on decent wages and working conditions for the producers, since intermediaries can no longer hide unpleasant facts of production from buyers. Cooperatives can also forbid altogether the sale of dangerous, stupid, or immoral products, such as alcoholic beverages, pornographic literature, or feathers from rare birds. The experience of cooperation would show a moral alternative to egoism and competition, by "reacting against the individualism that desiccates us" without going to the other extreme, leveling through coercion. Above all, cooperation would instill honesty by teaching members "to banish lies in the form of advertisements and fraud in the form of falsified commodities, . . . to acquire the sense of commercial honor."

Gide's vision of consumer cooperatives goes even further, disclosing a glimpse of a classless society of lasting harmony. For now, he predicts, associations of production, credit, and insurance will exist along with consumer cooperatives, but these other associations will gradually wither away as the role of consumer cooperatives continues to expand. Credit and insurance associations apply only to certain people on certain occasions; producers' associations represent the interests only of that group; but the activity of consumer cooperatives will penetrate the daily life of everyone and, even more significantly, will represent the general interest rather than special interests. In economic life the consumer cooperative is the equivalent of universal suffrage in political life, "for everyone is a consumer just as everyone is a citizen." That is why the consumer cooperative is the germ of a classless society. In time this institution will assume responsibilities of credit and insurance and even of production, as it begins to manufacture its own bread, wine, and industrial goods in its own factories and farms. When this happens the antagonism between producer and consumer will disappear in a Hegelian synthesis: the two will merge into one higher being.

Then a *pax romana* will settle over mankind. Instead of the present conflict of interests, consumer-workers will share an interest in procuring the most goods at the least expense. This is also to the benefit of all humanity. The reign of the consumer will completely reorient economic thought and practice. Gide ended his speech on "The Reign of the Consumer" with the ringing tones of prophecy: "The nineteenth century has been the century of the producers; let us hope that the twentieth century will be that of the consumers. May their kingdom come!"

The Consumer Cooperative Movement – With Charles Gide the consumer revolution attains self-consciousness. The economic changes comprising the consumer revolution had been proceeding steadily but mutely during the previous three or four decades. What is new with Gide is an alert and articulate consciousness of those changes, and the resolution to alter social and political forms in response to them. Other thinkers mentioned so far have shared that awareness to some degree, but their response was ambivalent and muted. Gide is lucid, positive, and unambiguous in proclaiming "the reign of the consumer." For him that reign is not a problem but an opportunity, for he views its implications in collective, or solidarist, terms. The opportunity he sees is to go beyond the false liberty of individualism—the liberty of each person to decide what and how much to consume—to what Gide considers the genuine liberty of association. From his point of view the debate over luxury should be translated from the level of personal choice to the level of collective responsibility. (Gide followed the debate in the Institut de France and contributed to it in later editions of his *Principles d'économie politique*, but his views were too radical to allow him to be considered for membership in the Institut.) Gide emphasized that luxury should not be thought of as discrete items purchased by individuals, but should be viewed in the context of the overall level of consumption in the community. The consumer should be aware of how much collective wealth or labor is represented by luxury products when present social wealth is inadequate to fulfill the basic needs of many:

> It appears as a very categorical duty not to divert towards the satisfaction of a superfluous need a large part of the energy and wealth available for the necessities of existence. It is a question of proportion. Bad luxury or prodigality consists in a disproportion between the quantity of social labor consumed and the degree of individual satisfaction obtained.[15]

By emphasizing that luxury is a collective phenomenon, Gide is also stressing that the ethics of luxury should be considered in human rather than material terms. So often the morality of luxury is reduced to an evaluation of this or that item—a form of reification that regards certain things as immoral rather than the truly immoral degradation of humanity. Gide understands that the ethical issue of luxury is fundamentally one of the amount and type of labor extracted from human beings. Once again reminding rather than inventing, Gide is reiterating the moral view of

John Ruskin, who pointed out to the rich that the luxury they enjoy "does not cost money only. It costs degradation." Ruskin went on: "Not to make unnecessary demands upon others—this is the first lesson of Christian—or human—economy . . . . This law forbids no luxury which men are *not* degraded in providing."[16] Ruskin and Gide, who share a staunch social Protestantism, insist on viewing both luxury and economics in general as collective rather than individualistic, human rather than material.

Just because Gide insisted on economics as a collective, human phenomenon, he could not remain a theoretician. Part of his quarrel with Paris group economists stemmed from their rigid separation of economic science from economic art, and of theory from practice. Gide felt that the demarcation was unrealistic, since ideas and action necessarily interpenetrate. He also felt it was uncharitable. For economics to diagnose problems and then to refuse treatment earned it a reputation as a dismal science, as a science without a heart—or, rather, without a brain, in Gide's opinion. Accordingly, his involvement with cooperation was practical as well as intellectual.

In 1885, when Gide was still formulating his own approach to economic theory, he heard about some Protestant cooperators in Nîmes, his home town. Gide wrote to one of them, Édouard de Boyve, to offer his services. The timing was fortuitous for both. De Boyve had just returned from the first general congress of consumer cooperatives in France. At this meeting in Paris, about one-third of the three-hundred-odd consumer cooperatives then scattered around the country had agreed to establish a national federation, officially called the Union Coopérative des Sociétés Françaises de Consommation ("Cooperative Union of French Societies of Consumption") and unofficially called the School of Nîmes because of the leadership of the Nîmois cooperators.

Gide was the first economist of repute to show any interest in the new federation. De Boyve immediately asked him to edit a new journal which would serve as the official organ of the School of Nîmes. Gide gave it the name *Émancipation* and the motto "Ni révoltés ni satisfaits" ("Neither rebellious nor satisfied"). The following year Gide delivered the opening speech at the second national congress. On that occasion his address on "The Prophecies of Fourier," which outlined the moral and social as well as the economic goals of cooperation, was received with tumultuous, almost ecstatic applause. Three years later, in 1889, Gide again addressed the annual congress, which was held in the Palace of the Trocadéro during the centennial exposition. By that time he was clearly established as the prime spokesman of the consumer cooperative movement in France.

The societies belonging to the School of Nîmes usually began as food cooperatives, especially for staple foods like bread and wine. Many of them later extended their services to items such as furniture and clothing. The cooperatives sold at prevailing retail prices—unlike many retailers then, they did not offer credit—and returned some of the surplus to individual members. The rest of the surplus was used to support programs of education and production, either by setting up factories or by supporting separate producers' cooperatives with capital and purchases. The purpose of the refund was to attract members; the purpose of the collectively held benefits was to encourage the ultimate goal of organizing production. No matter how much a member purchased from the cooperative, he had only one vote, for the aim was to run the organization like a small republic. The School of Nîmes adhered strictly to a position of political neutrality. Since consumers were supposed to represent the general interest, the cooperatives stayed aloof from the program of any political party, religious group, or social class.

This moderate program continued to attract new societies. The total number of consumer cooperatives grew to about eight hundred by 1889 and double that by 1900. To be sure, societies adhering to the national union continued to be a distinct minority. Although the number of adhering societies approximately tripled from 1886 to 1893, in this latter year there were still only about one hundred and fifty societies belonging to the national federation, out of approximately one thousand consumer cooperatives in France.[17]

In attaining this modest success, the School of Nîmes had to overcome hostility on three sides. One source of opposition—which may not have deterred the common man but which did discourage other leaders of Gide's caliber—came from the Paris group of economists, led by Paul Leroy-Beaulieu. The establishment of cooperatives was not inherently contrary to economic orthodoxy. Liberal economists accepted the concept of free association for mutual aid among workers. Consumer cooperatives could be regarded as a praiseworthy if not very significant effort which might tend to calm revolutionary or socialist passions. These cooperatives could also be defended by orthodox economists for encouraging savings in the form of the annual refund, and for providing healthy competition for traditional retailers.

From the beginning, however, elements of the School of Nîmes program disturbed the orthodox. Although the School renounced revolutionary collectivism and dogmas of class struggle, it retained a popular and even quasi-socialist character. Its ideals of replacing competition with cooperation, of emancipating the working class, and of eliminating intermediaries between producer and consumer were also suspect. The definitive break came when Gide concluded his address to the 1886 congress with the declaration that the distant goal of the consumer cooperative movement was "the emancipation of the working class through the transformation of the wage-earning system."[18] With this pronouncement the School of Nîmes openly shed all associations with bourgeois conservatism and thus forsook the role seen for it by liberal economists. Paul Leroy-Beaulieu was shocked to hear such words from another professor. In *L'Économiste français,* the journal he edited, he scolded that "Wage-earning is the form of contract par excellence. Its suppression appears neither practicable nor desirable to us. There are certain fixed positions from which humanity will not stray."[19] Leroy-Beaulieu further declared that doctrines of solidarity, cooperation, and mutual aid could never have anything in common with the laws of political economy.

Gide was not deterred in the least. When in 1889 he again addressed the congress, he proposed that consumer cooperatives should take control first of commercial establishments, then of industry, and finally of agriculture. It was the centenary of the outbreak of the French Revolution, and a revolutionary tone pervaded Gide's speech. "What is the consumer?" he asked his enraptured listeners (paraphrasing l'Abbé Sièyes's famous query of a hundred years earlier, "What is the bourgeoisie?"). And Gide thundered Sièyes's response: "Nothing. What should he be? Everything." Paul Leroy-Beaulieu first reacted with scorn, comparing cooperation with a frog who wanted to make himself as large as a cow. Then he retreated to stony silence. Thereafter the *Journal des économistes* and *L'Économiste français* suppressed even any chance reference to the School of Nîmes or to Gide in their pages. After 1889 the rupture between consumer cooperation and the Paris group was complete and permanent.

A second group which initially regarded the School of Nîmes with mixed sympathy and suspicion were Catholic cooperators, especially Le Playists. Although Le Play himself never advocated cooperation, many of his disciples did—but their concept of cooperation differed from that of the School of Nîmes. Gide wanted the societies to be run like democratic republics, while the Le Playists envisaged them as a means to allow *patrons* to exercise stewardship. In the words of one Le Playist, "[The cooperative society] should furnish to classes privileged with regard to fortune and education one of the best ways of exercising the duty of patronage incumbent upon them."[20] Underlying this difference in social perspective was the difference in religion. Gide compared the Protestant preference for consumer cooperatives with the Catholic preference for corporations uniting *patrons* and workers in the same trade. The word *corporation* "holds no terror for us," he remarked, since the idea of uniting poor and rich in the same organization was always laudable. But the corporation as envisaged by Catholics had "a character a little too aristocratic, implying a state of dependence of the working classes which renders it always a little suspect in our eyes."[21]

This was a mild reproof, for Gide was eager to win any support he could and he hoped to forge an alliance with interested Catholics. At first the signs looked favorable. M. Fougerousse, editor of the Le Playist journal *Réforme sociale*, was so sympathetic that he was named secretary-general of the national federation and took an active part in the early congresses. However, he was unhappy with the emphasis placed on the eventual goal of transforming the wage system by taking over ownership of the means of production. Fougerousse argued that it was foolish for societies to devote some of their benefits to such far-fetched schemes when they could instead invest in benefits of self-evident value such as pensions, insurance, or housing. The more radical societies in the School of Nîmes in turn chafed at Fougerousse's conservatism. In 1889 the most radical group, the cooperatives of the Paris area, refused to vote for Fougerousse as secretary-general, and he had to quit the post. Later he became involved in a sorry lawsuit against cooperators from Nîmes who had published a pamphlet he considered defamatory. This rupture too was complete and lasting, much to the regret of Gide and other leaders who considered Fougerousse a man of enlightened and sincere convictions who could have aided the School of Nîmes even while disagreeing with some of its aims.

A third hostile group was composed of socialists. However, instead of a tentative accord followed by schism, socialists and Nîmois cooperators began in discord and ended in reconciliation. The "reign of the consumer" eventually turned into what Gide liked to call the "socialism of the consumer." This transformation was by no means inevitable. The cooperative movement of the 1880s could have moved in any number of different directions. Eventually it moved to the left rather than to the right: why?

Socialism and Cooperation–Early French socialists—Gide's hero Fourier, Saint-Simon, Louis Blanc, and others—had been enthusiastic supporters of many types of cooperation. But the new breed of European socialist that emerged in the 1870s and especially the 1880s was heavily influenced by Marxism, which condemned such associations as feeble bourgeois reformism benefiting a few privileged people and distracting workers from the socialist revolution. While the doctrinal rigidity of these tough-minded Marxist socialists had the virtues of moral vigor and intellectual clarity, it was at the price of discarding many promising suggestions advanced by earlier utopian socialists. Their rigidity also alienated many intellectuals like Gide (and Camille Mauclair) who were sympathetic to the broad socialist ideals of equality and justice. Gide commented ruefully that cooperation was too socialist for the liberals, too liberal for the Catholics, and too bourgeois for the socialists.[22]

The feeling of incompatibility was mutual. Socialists were wary of the School of Nîmes because its leaders were bourgeois, unconventional ones to be sure, but still bourgeois, and Protestant ones at that, "which is to say," Gide explained, "of a religion which is reputed to be ultra-individualist, even capitalist." Gide responded that Protestantism should be "social" rather than "ultra-individualist," and as for being bourgeois, "I have never personally denied my origins. There is no more justification for blushing at being bourgeois than to be proud of it, and besides modern socialism owes almost everything it is to the bourgeois."[23]

The most fundamental and serious source of discord

was that socialists believed in the primacy of the producer and Nîmois cooperators in the primacy of the consumer. According to socialists, value comes from labor, and economic wealth therefore belongs to the producer. According to cooperators, value is determined by final utility, the satisfaction of the consumer's desires. Furthermore, the socialist concept of class struggle was at odds with the cooperators' claim that the consumer stands above class interests.

These theoretical disputes led to significant practical differences. As Gide was the first to admit, a union of producers would make demands—for higher salaries, shorter hours, or decreased production to prevent unemployment—diametrically opposed to the interest of consumers in obtaining low prices and abundant products. In particular, strikes set producers and consumers in opposition. From the consumer's point of view strikes are an evil, although Gide was willing to accept them in some cases for the higher purpose of getting rid of the wage-earning system. He trusted that in time the need for strikes would disappear. If cooperators were suspicious about how unions might use their collective power, socialists were equally uneasy about the potential power of consumer cooperatives. Some socialists argued that when a person lowers his cost of living by obtaining goods more cheaply through a cooperative, he is also lowering his wages as a producer.

Despite all their objections, socialists realized that consumer cooperatives could be highly attractive to workers, and so they helped to organize some. Certain Parisian consumer cooperatives under the influence of Jules Guesde, the leading Marxist in France at that time, were among the liveliest in the nation. All but a few of them boycotted the School of Nîmes and denied its right to the title of a national union of consumer cooperatives. The Parisian societies that did join were the ones instrumental in removing the Le Playist Fougerousse from the leadership. The majority of French socialist-cooperators decided to establish their own federation rather than join one of what they considered questionable character. Therefore in 1895 socialists established their own national organization, the Bourse des Coopératives Socialistes ("Exchange of Socialist Cooperatives").

In a number of ways the cooperatives of the Bourse differed from those adhering to the School of Nîmes. The socialist ones usually admitted only workers, or at least wage-earners, rather than being open to all comers. Also, while in principle socialists condemned as capitalistic and egoistic any distribution of refunds to individuals, in practice they distributed a large part of the benefits to individual members in order to attract others. Any surplus was devoted mainly to insurance or pension schemes or to free medical services.

Finally, the Bourse cooperatives were openly socialist rather than claiming political neutrality, which they denounced as an evasive charade. This issue of neutrality was the most hotly debated one in the long and bitter invectives between the two federations. Gide was convinced that a neutral political stance was absolutely necessary—first, as a matter of tactics in attracting members, and second, as a matter of principle in demonstrating that the consumer represents the truly general, truly human interest. Doctrinal differences were exacerbated by the rather more mundane fear of the leaders of each federation that a merger would eliminate their influence.

The consequences of the rivalry were, Gide lamented, "deplorable."[24] Foreign cooperators called the French movement the least impressive in Europe. Many cooperatives decided not to join either federation rather than take sides in the quarrel. Each of the federations finally rallied only three or four hundred societies out of the three thousand or so that existed in France by 1910.

The beginning of a détente was in large measure due to the influence of leftists from Belgium, where cooperators and socialists had worked together smoothly for some time. Although Belgian cooperators did not agree entirely with the program of the School of Nîmes, they attended the 1889 congress in large numbers and adhered, with only a few reservations, to the program formulated there. In subsequent years, reconciliation was also advanced by the arrival of younger socialists who, unlike Guesde, had been influenced by early French utopian socialists as well as by Marxism—Eugène Fournière, Benoît Malon, and, above all, Jean Jaurès. Their efforts were aided by continued appeals from foreign socialists, especially the Belgians, that French socialists accept the Nîmois program as sufficiently advanced. The advent of a new generation of cooperators sympathetic to socialism also helped the cause.

On Christmas Day in 1912 the two federations finally merged into the Fédération Nationale des Sociétés Françaises de Consommation ("National Federation of French Societies of Consumption"). The Bourse and the Cooperative Union were both dissolved. The new National Federation was organized on the basis of a manifesto which made numerous references to collectivism and concluded by calling the new organization an "organ of the emancipation of workers." This phrase disturbed Gide, who wanted consumer cooperatives to recognize workers only insofar as they are also consumers, but he was satisfied that the manifesto did not mention either the class struggle or adhesion to a socialist party. Instead, the manifesto declared that while the principles of cooperation were in accord with those of international socialism, the cooperative movement was autonomous. Distribution of benefits was left to individual societies. The only cooperatives excluded from membership were "capitalist and *patronal*" ones with specifically anti-democratic rules. On both the right and the left the more extreme cooperatives refused to join, but their loss was more than compensated for by new adhesions; so the new federation began with about a thousand member societies.

The alliance between cooperation and socialism endured and strengthened. By the end of World War I, the

National Federation had nearly twice as many member societies as at its inception in 1912. In 1921 Gide and over one hundred and fifty other professors signed a manifesto elaborating a program for the "socialism of consumers." In the same year Gide assumed a Chair in Cooperation established for him by the National Federation at the Collège de France. This was the pinnacle of his academic career. About the same time the National Federation established close ties with the C.G.T. [Confédération Générale du Travail], the largest trade union in France.

When Gide wrote a brief history of the School of Nîmes in 1926, he noted that of thirty-six members of the Central Council of the National Federation at that time, only three were of the first generation of the School. He felt that the future of cooperation was in good hands with the new generation. "The School of Nîmes only wanted to be one of the modest tributaries whose destiny is to swell a little the grand current of universal cooperation and to lose itself in it joyfully."[25]

Widening Circles of Influence – Charles Gide was nearly eighty when he wrote those words, but they had a spirit of youthful enthusiasm. In marked contrast to so many of the thinkers already mentioned, he never despaired of the cause of his youth, never abandoned his dreams, never retired to a more remote philosophical or religious perspective. Gide's manifesto of 1921 is as buoyant as that of 1889. His generation did not die away but passed on its vitality to the succeeding one.

This unusual consistency is in part due to the rigidity of Gide's personality, but in part also to the considerable practical success of the cooperative movement. While it hardly brought about a classless society of universal harmony, it did accomplish enough to encourage Gide. In this respect the fortunes of the consumer cooperative movement form an intriguing parallel to the movement to reform the decorative arts and that to institute a new social morality. All of them were at once intellectual and institutional initiatives, seeking to renovate both thought and social practice. All three originated in the 1880s and reached a climax around the turn of the century. After that came the parting of the ways. By 1905 or so the decorative arts movement had largely degenerated into commercialism and trendiness. Educational reform and corporatism had foundered, while the *Ralliement* had been aborted by the Dreyfus Affair and the final separation of Church and State. The consumer cooperative movement was also at a low point, but unlike the others it recovered and not only survived the First World War but came out of it more exuberant than ever.

In the short run consumer cooperation achieved this relative success just because it was willing to "lose itself . . . joyfully" in the grander current of socialism. In the long run, however, it has not been the socialist current that has carried along consumer cooperatives, but the rising tide of consumer organization in a more general sense. While the formation of consumer cooperatives in France has stagnated since the 1930s, other forms of consumer activism have proliferated. Gide's call for a "reign of the consumer" seems to be finding realization not so much in cooperatives, not so much in traditional socialism, as in an amorphous and complex variety of consumer groups—everything from local *ad hoc* groups to government bureaucracies to national investigative bodies. All of these initiatives would have been welcomed by Gide, who himself participated in a variety of experiments in consumer organization. The concept of the self-conscious organization of consumer power, not the particular form of consumer cooperatives, is central in Gide's thought. In evaluating his contribution it is therefore legitimate to look beyond consumer cooperatives in a narrow sense to consumer cooperation in a broader sense—to other organizations which worked to advance "the reign of the consumer." Two of the groups Gide encouraged will be described to suggest a wider context for consideration of his work.

Cooperative Housing – Like many other reformers of his day, Gide was distressed by the lack of decent housing for ordinary working people. He considered this need second only to food in its importance, yet first in the difficulty of satisfying it under the present economic system. "Of all expenses it is the one whose augmentation is the most certain, the most rapidly increasing, and the most disproportionate to the budget of a working family."[26] Because housing above all other needs calls for collective responsibility, Gide urged consumer cooperatives to include housing in their programs. To do so, however, a society had to possess considerable capital. Since most French consumer cooperatives were not in that fortunate position, Gide also advocated the establishment of special organizations solely to construct housing. In 1908 there were 149 such societies in France, which financed building not only from the deposits of members but also from loans obtained from regular banks. By Gide's admission, this was a small number.

An organization which undertook a more ambitious program of cooperative housing was the Association des Cités-Jardins de France, founded by Georges Benoît-Lévy. Benoît-Lévy was one of the young students who gathered around Gide when in 1898 the latter came from Montpellier to teach at the University of Paris. According to Benoît-Lévy himself, it was while taking a course from Gide that he first dreamed of establishing a housing association.[27] The concept of Garden Cities has already been mentioned as an outgrowth of the decorative arts movement. These cities are based on the assumption that consumer mentality can be altered if well-designed commodities—or, in this case, a well-designed total environment—are provided for it. Benoît-Lévy's approach to housing fits this interpretation. He was convinced that the creation of social evil or prosperity ultimately depends on the architect who designs cities and homes, and that social solidarity can be achieved through architectural design on a preconceived plan. He was especially enthusiastic about the Garden City planned and built by the mining company of Dorgues, which he called "an essay in popular art."[28] Clearly Benoît-Lévy advocated art for the people rather than art by the people.

This was not what Gide had in mind when he advocated solidarity and cooperatively built housing. In particular, he did not advocate the construction of whole cities for workers by corporations raising their own capital. These cities could be marvels of comfort, Gide conceded, and they were indispensable for factories and mines situated far from populated areas where workers could not be hired at all unless housing were provided. But in general he classified such cities with other *"patronal institutions"* of the school of Le Play. They all failed to create genuine solidarity because the workers, "believing themselves exploited, . . . feel little gratitude toward the *patrons* and see [their situation] as a sort of servitude."[29]

Even when a model city was not financed by management, Gide had his doubts about the wisdom of building a wholly new environment on a supposedly rational plan. In 1904 he toured a Garden City in England being built to house thirty thousand people. Upon his return he published an article in the *Semaine littéraire* describing the appeal of the city and then asking the question: how many people would really want to live there?

> It must not be forgotten that those workers [who are supposed to be attracted to Garden Cities] are precisely those who left the country to go to the city . . . . what disgusts us about life in the big city is just what attracts the masses, especially the poor. Many of them, men, women, or even children might prefer their sordid houses, their leprous walls, the promiscuity of neighbors with whom they chat from door to door or across the partitions, the traffic and noise of the street, and especially the café-concert and the "uncontrolled" retailer [of alcohol]— to all the lawns and flowers of the Garden City . . . . It will be necessary to modify in the soul of the people what one moralist has called, in a happy expression, "the order of

enjoyments." Therefore a whole education has to be achieved first: it is not impossible, but it will be long and at the moment I fear that the clientèle of the future city will be recruited mostly from those who are tired of the struggle for life and of noise, . . . or who, disillusioned like Candide, say with him "Cultivate your own garden." But these are already philosophers, and it would certainly be imprudent to count on thirty thousand philosophers to populate the future city.[30]

This is an absorbing passage, and not only because of Gide's prophetic vision of planned retirement villages. He is rejecting the "philosophical" aloofness from the café-concert-loving masses which is so often felt by the planners themselves—their unspoken scorn for the noisy and "promiscuous" sociability that inspires their planned environment. Gide understands how this scorn is communicated through that environment itself, and that the workers might accordingly reject the well-planned "future city."

When Gide concludes that "the order of enjoyments" of ordinary people must be modified before they will live happily in a Garden City, he is echoing Mauclair's conclusion that a preliminary moral education is needed before consumers will reorder their desires. Unlike Mauclair, Gide is confident that he knows how to achieve the necessary conversion. Gide takes very seriously the Biblical admonition "You must be born again." Instead of relying on individual religious experience to achieve that rebirth, however, he relies on the daily experience of cooperative action to transform the personality. The practical action of solidarity "consists of modifying the man by modifying first the environment in which he lives."[31] By "environment" Gide means not physical but social surroundings. He always emphasizes that solidarity in housing means having people associate to plan their housing; he does not rely on design to bring them together. His plans for a future city do not emphasize physical buildings so much as associations of consumption and production altering the social environment.

In his *Semaine littéraire* article Gide underlines the importance of having the consumer society retain ownership, so that it rents the houses rather than sells them. The society must assert its dominance over the buildings because

> the corrosive action of the material and social environment wastes no time in returning to the state of affairs we wish to abolish.
>
> It will be quite otherwise in the future city because, before building the house, we create the environment and because the society retains at once ownership of the houses and of the environment.

In the truly cooperative city "the city would be united not only by the fact of domicile, but by genuine association—a small autonomous world, a microcosm would be created which could teach us now what the future society will be." The new society is that of association, the creation not of a new material environment but of a new human one.

The Social League of Shoppers–In 1901 Mme. Henriette Jean Brunhes, a Parisian housewife who was an avid reader of Ruskin and leader of a women's charitable organization, received from an American friend a clipping about a Social League of Shoppers established in New York about ten years earlier. The American League had had considerable success in persuading New York department stores to improve conditions for employees by publishing "white lists" of stores that adhered to certain standards of working conditions; members were urged to patronize these establishments. Several similar groups had been established in other American cities.

Mme. Brunhes was so intrigued that she spent a year studying the American leagues, and in early 1903 she established the first Ligue Sociale d'Acheteurs ("Social League of Shoppers") in Paris. Membership cost five francs. Most of the members (as was also true of the New York group) were upper-middle-class women. They made four pledges: (1) not to place an order without asking whether it would require work at night or on Sunday; (2) to avoid last-minute orders, especially at busy periods; (3) to refuse any delivery made after seven in the evening or on a Sunday, so as not to be indirectly responsible for longer working hours; and (4) to pay bills promptly. Also in 1903 the League published its first white list of acceptable places to shop, beginning with the names of couturières who had made various pledges regarding their treatment of workers (e.g., no more than nine hours of work a day, and no "homework").

The following year the League extended its scope. It published white lists of bakeries and laundries and began to prepare a series of inquiry sheets informing members of working conditions in various shops and factories. The League also began to issue special bulletins on various topics such as the particularly long and strenuous hours imposed on salespeople by the winter holiday season. The year 1904 also brought the first international conference of Shoppers' Leagues. Held in Geneva, it was attended by representatives from the United States, France, Switzerland, and Germany. In subsequent years the Paris League added more white lists and daughter societies in the provinces, and also intervened in labor disputes and investigated the housing conditions of domestic servants and workers (Georges Benoît-Lévy was a League supporter).[32]

The basic principle of the League was that the shopper is ultimately responsible for working conditions; its basic goal was to use the social and economic power of the consumer wisely to improve working conditions. According to Mme. Bergeron, one of the leaders of the Paris organization, suppliers and consumers share an ultimate interest in eliminating bad working conditions so that everyone can enjoy more well-being and happiness. The "stroke of genius" of the League, she felt, lay in giving an economic advantage to decent treatment of workers. The white lists of the League were a form of free advertising which would increase the business of humane employers. Rather than being asked to make sacrifices, producers could painlessly reach "an equitable entente" with consumers. To reach this goal, Mme. Bergeron stressed, the League had to raise the social consciousness of the shopper. The consumer had to be educated to patronize certain sources of production in preference to others, regardless of price—in other words, to consider moral duty before price or convenience. That moral education consisted of developing the shopper's imagination to foresee the collective results of individual decisions:

> We might better render an account of our responsibility if we could individually ascertain and touch with our fingers in some way the results of our exigencies. But look, we are a multitude; and the evil accomplished in numerous and good company loses three-quarters of its disagreeable aspect. Everyone wants to eat fresh pastry on Sunday; all women order new hats and dresses for Easter; where are they who ask themselves what the result is for the baker, for the cook's boys, for the dressmaker and his workers?

The shopper's lack of awareness of moral responsibility is also due in part to the dissociation of production and consumption—mainly because the producer prefers it that way:

> The League member sees the store but cannot enter the storeroom. She sees the fitting room but cannot enter the workroom. She sees the elegant pastry shop but cannot visit the narrow, overheated rooms where the workers toil, nor the rooming houses where the little scullery boys are lodged and piled up.

Only with the power that comes from unity, concluded Mme. Bergeron, could shoppers inform themselves about conditions which would otherwise "necessarily escape them."[33] For this reason the League demanded rights of intervention, inquiry, and publicity, despite protests from some orthodox liberal economists (like Yves Guyot) that consumers were incompetent to judge the technical organization of labor.

Gide was not wholly comfortable with the Social League of Shoppers. He noted that it was "inspired by social Catholicism." Mme. de la Tour du Pin, wife of one of the most prominent social Catholics, was an early supporter, and the Catholic journal *L'Univers* was one of the first to praise the organization.[34] The League therefore assumed something of the "aristocratic" character that Gide criticized in Le Playist corporations. After all, it was composed of shoppers who could afford to pass up a bargain. Gide felt that a democratically based consumer cooperative could exert more influence in improving conditions of production. Even more significantly, the League reaffirmed the separation of consumer and producer that Gide wanted to overcome: the League aimed to establish harmony between consumers and producers, but only as two distinct groups. Gide also felt that it was the consumer's duty "to put an end at the same time to the consumer's exploitation of man and his pillage of nature,"[35] but the League dealt only with the first of these two responsibilities. Yet the League did advocate the moral responsibility of the consumer and direct contact between producers and consumers—two fundamental principles of "the reign of the consumer," so it is not surprising that one enthusiastic early supporter of the League quoted from Gide's speech by that title at length to explain the purpose of the organization.[36] Nor is it surprising that Gide himself appreciated the congruence of aims. At the end of 1907 he announced his support of the League in an article in the *Semaine littéraire*. This was the first endorsement of the League by a professional economist, and as such was greeted by it as "a great light of hope."[37]

Gide, for his part, considered it immensely hopeful to see an organization addressing itself directly to women as consumers. He had long ago recognized that women usually made most of the purchases for a household, and that the distinction between producer and consumer was largely equivalent to the distinction between male and female. Yet despite their disproportionate role in consumption, it was women who most strongly resisted shopping in consumer cooperatives. Gide understood why women preferred to shop in a corner grocery store. Its convenience "is not of small importance for a housewife who is often fatigued or who has little free time among her chores and errands." Its friendliness and small personal favors—not to mention the availability of credit—were lacking in larger cooperative establishments. Moreover, at a cooperative a housewife had to undergo the trouble and indignity of recording in a notebook every penny she spent.

Gide was unvaryingly and unusually sympathetic about the toil and vexations of running a household—perhaps because he had to run his own during his years alone in Paris—and he urged cooperatives to try to overcome the understandable reluctance of housewives. The stores could be made more attractive and could sponsor gatherings where a woman's desire for sociability could be satisfied. Women could be included on the administrative councils of cooperatives, where their domestic experience could be valuable: "It must not be forgotten that the first cooperative association that existed in the world was the household."[38] Unlike abstractions like socialism or even solidarity, unlike producers' cooperatives, the consumer cooperative was a concrete reality which could directly alter women's lives. One reason Gide retained his optimism about the future of consumer cooperation was the growth of feminism, especially after World War I. He regarded feminism and the consumer movement as natural allies.

Much of the lasting interest of the Social League of Shoppers lies in that alliance. We have seen repeatedly how women have been stereotyped as creatures of consumption par excellence—especially after the decline of the dandy, the prototypical male consumer, a decline which may be attributed in part to the redefinition of women's role in modern society.[39] Women are the ones who crowd into department stores like Au Bonheur des Dames, who urge their henpecked husbands to buy round furniture for chic apartments, who gape at fashion displays in the expositions, who in "La Parisienne" furnish the symbol of the exposition itself. To a large extent the pejorative nature of the concept of consumption itself derives from its association with female submission to organic needs.

The League represents an effort by women to turn their role as consumers into something positive, to raise a peculiarly female activity from the level of shame to that of dignity and responsibility. The League transformed shopping from a utilitarian activity to a moral one, from an occasion for socializing to an occasion for exercising social concern. In the women's sphere it inculcated the habits of moral conduct Louis Weber urged for man's sphere. Explained Mme. Brunhes:

> We force into accord with our principles our daily actions, our little everyday purchases, which are certainly, in appearance, the most trivial, insignificant, and even, it is believed, the most indifferent actions . . . . I ask you, will not the effort shown in the thousand actions of daily life be the most efficacious and extensive means of social work?[40]

The League women claimed that consumer organizations, just as much as institutions of production, disseminate not only technical expertise but also a general social education. Although the League tacitly accepted the dichotomy of male and female, of producer and consumer, its insistence that female consumers had to learn about the realities of production in order to buy wisely meant that the two spheres of sex and economic function would nonetheless be brought closer together. When Guyot complained that the League was incompetent to judge the technical organization of labor, he was resisting not only the meddling of incompetent consumers in the domain of production, but also the meddling of incompetent women in a male domain. It was precisely this incompetence that the League proposed to remedy. It urged women to give up fantasy for reality, to base consumption on the deliberate consideration of facts. The turn to reality, concludes an historian of the League, constitutes the revolutionary character of the organization:

> In place of or beside the romantic woman, nourished by frivolous literature, made wholly of sentimentalism and passionate pseudo-psychology, this revolution forms, educates a woman living in the reality of the world that surrounds her, aware of the sufferings of misery and labor, touched with other sorrows besides those of the fictive heroes of books, . . . and those of torments which are born from conflicts of passions and complications of love.[41]

The emphasis on the reality principle is not just for female consumers. When so much conspires to turn consumption into a dream world, to make it a fantasy realm of fictive pleasures and pseudo-psychology, it is the moral duty of both sexes to face the facts of what our consumer demands extract from man and nature. To be sure, unionization and legislation have done more to regulate labor and environmental conditions than have consumer cooperatives. This does not mean that the consumer is absolved of responsibility, only that he shares it. Some producers and products should be encouraged by consumers, and others should be discouraged. It is as necessary as ever to force the consumer to ask himself, "Whom am I patronizing in purchasing this item?" and "What would be the collective effect of my decision multiplied many times over?"

Today the conscience of the consumer is expressed primarily by boycotts of particular goods produced under unfair labor conditions which happen to come to public attention (recent examples are Farah clothing, or California grapes or lettuce). Abuses of a non-human nature are also resisted by *ad hoc* boycotts (furs, tuna fish). The advantage of the Social League of Shoppers was that it furnished a more permanent and methodical mechanism for investigating the sources of products and for arousing consumer awareness. That mechanism is especially needed today to educate consumers in developed countries about the exploitation of man and nature which their standard of living encourages in less developed countries. At the present there is a profound and to some degree willful ignorance of the cause-and-effect relationship between consumer demand in developed countries and deplorable living conditions in the Third World. "The social responsibility of shoppers! Who among us has seriously thought about it?"[42] asked a League member in 1903. The question still stands.

Concluding Remarks – Because Gide's "reign of the consumer" could take so many institutional forms, the underlying concept should be central in evaluating his contribution. A good place to begin this evaluation is the charge of the maverick French social thinker Georges Sorel (1847–1922) that "the reign of the consumer" is a corrupt bourgeois notion:

> Philanthropists who preach cooperation and ceaselessly repeat that the order established by capitalism must be reversed, that consumption must be rendered its power of direction; such sentiments are natural with people who, receiving rents, salaries, or professional fees, live outside of productive power; they have as an ideal the life of the lettered idler. The socialist ideal is completely different.[43]

Is Gide's theory of the consumer-king as class-bound as Paul Leroy-Beaulieu's theory of luxury? The fact that Gide broke with the Paris group and was later excommunicated by it is not a sufficient rebuttal. Gide kept much in common with economic liberals despite their quarrel. He himself acknowledged their common descent from classical economists like Bastiat and Mill, and his moral bent was perfectly compatible with the traditions of French liberal economics. Gide's collaborator Charles Rist called him "a well-bred liberal" and professed incredulity that orthodox economists did not recognize his kinship with them.[44]

Still, the rift between Gide and the Paris group was far too serious to admit the conclusion that Gide was a sort of closet liberal. His proclamation of "the reign of the consumer" was as alien to the sense of priorities held by the Paris group as it was to Sorel. Beneath the mutual invectives of socialists and liberals lay an unspoken agreement on the supremacy of production. They may have disputed the respective roles of capital and labor in production, but they both were true descendants of Adam Smith in focusing on its laws. The supremacy of the consumer is an idea as foreign to the socialist believer in class struggle and working-class supremacy as to the liberal who lauds entrepreneurs, profits, and competition among producers—despite lip service to Bastiat.

From this perspective it is of little use to label Gide's thought as bourgeois or to expend much energy defending him against this accusation. His originality was in leaving behind such labels. As a social prophet he foresaw that categories of consumption would increasingly gain significance, while categories of production would decrease in importance. "The nineteenth century has been the century of the producers; let us hope that the twentieth century will be that of the consumer." In the twentieth century, whether in praise or disgust, socialists and liberals alike have repeatedly noted the progress of "embourgeoisement." Workers have come to live and think more and more like the middle classes. In Gide's terms this historical development is more appropriately described as a shift in dominance from productive roles to consumptive roles in society. This shift is manifest in concepts of self-identity, allocation of time, expenditure of personal energy, distribution of political power—and, Gide would add, it should also be manifest in ideals of moral and social responsibility.

With Gide the concept of consumption, which for so

long had been only vaguely suggested, became explicit and central. This arrival of self-consciousness meant a reorientation of economic thought and practice alike. When viewed from the perspective of the consumer, familiar economic phenomena are seen in an unfamiliar light. A good example is Gide's response to automobile ownership which became increasingly popular in the middle years of Gide's life. Socialists welcomed automobiles because the industry provided many new jobs, and Paris group economists like Paul Leroy-Beaulieu and Yves Guyot joined in praise because the automobile would increase productivity and national wealth. Gide alone had his doubts. It is true, he remarked in an interview, that the automobile industry would employ thousands and would build many factories, but there were drawbacks. Consumers who bought an auto would not have as much money to spend on other items. Besides,

> each person can taste in his lifetime only a limited sum of sensations; the time consecrated to that of "automobilism"—(and I believe it will be very great)—will be taken at the detriment of certain others: the theatre, museums, reading . . . . There is a proverb that says, "All that glitters is not gold." I think that somewhat with regard to the automobile.[45]

This is not the remark of a corrupt bourgeois, a "lettered idler" who opposes working-class aspirations, but of someone considering the future of consumption as much as the future of production.

Even if we reject the accusation that "the reign of the consumer" is a self-serving bourgeois notion, the question still remains as to the relationship between this concept and that of socialism. Nineteenth-century socialists had difficulty coming to terms with consumption precisely because they identified superfluity with luxury, and luxury with the bourgeoisie. When socialist thought was taking shape in the early nineteenth century, when the abysmal living standards of the many contrasted starkly with the consumer pleasures of the few, these identifications made sense. In this historical context Marx denounced the "unnecessary needs" of the bourgeoisie, meaning frivolous and illusory needs which enslaved workers while their most primary needs went unfulfilled. As the level of production rose and workers began to enjoy higher standards of consumption, these socialist concepts lost some of their force. They tended to hinder understanding of the consumer revolution. Socialists could see it only as a democratization of bourgeois luxury ("embourgeoisement") rather than as an entirely new phenomenon of cheap mass luxury. In the new historical situation terms like *luxury, superfluity,* and *needs* had to be redefined, but few socialists made any attempt at such redefinition. Edmund Wilson has noted that socialists were so intent on seeing consumption in class terms that they had difficulty in comprehending specifically modern modes of consumption. In part this limitation derived from the peculiar personality of Karl Marx himself:

> For Marx, the occupations and habits, the ambitions and desires, of modern man, which he himself had never shared, tended to present themselves as purely class manifestations, the low proclivities of an ignoble bourgeoisie. He could not imagine that the proletariat would take to them. When a proletarian gave any indication of wanting what the bourgeois wanted, Marx regarded him as a renegade and pervert, a miserable victim of petty bourgeois ideas.
>
> . . . The common man, set free from feudal society, seems to do everywhere much the same sort of thing—which is not what Marx had expected him to do because it was not what Marx liked to do himself. The ordinary modern man wants a home with machine-made comforts (where Marx had never cared enough about a home to secure for his wife and his daughters even moderately decent living conditions); he wants amusement parks, movies, sports (Marx claimed that he had once studied horsemanship, but Engels, who had had him on a horse once in Manchester, said that he could never have got

beyond the third lesson); he wants an opportunity to travel in his country: cheap excursions . . . ; he wants social services—hospitals, libraries, roads.[46]

Because socialism so much identifies superfluous consumption with the hated bourgeoisie, at its core is an ethic of austerity. Socialism condemns freedom to consume as an illusory freedom because it only increases subjection at work. The way to attain genuine human freedom is therefore to reduce the proliferation of "unnecessary needs." Once these and the "irrational desires" promoted by capitalism are eliminated, man will cease to be alienated from himself, meaning from his own authentic desires and wishes. Then only "real needs" will be felt. To use other terminology favored by socialists, the self-evident "use value" of objects will triumph over their fantastic, quasi-magical "exchange value." Unfortunately, this tendency toward a no-frills ideal of consumption often became degraded to an unimaginative utilitarianism, by which needs were understood as physical and conscious, to be satisfied by material goods. That kind of reductionism, as Camille Mauclair complained, constituted a Gradgrindian utilitarianism, a brutal factuality uncomprehending of any functionalism above physical maintenance—an example of "thinking in a bourgeois manner" by those who professed to loathe the bourgeoisie. At its best, however, the ascetic strain in socialism can affirm the human freedom to act that comes from material abstinence. Among socialists, as among some bourgeois, there is a yearning, at once nostalgic and prophetic, for the beauty of necessity.

But another strain in socialist thought about consumption, one that became increasingly dominant during the nineteenth century, contradicts the ethic of austerity. More and more the ideal of absolute limitation in consumption became subordinate to the principle of relative equality. The promise of economic justice, of sharing equally in the fruits of human labor, only tended to promote the possibilities of material accumulation. This is what Anatole Leroy-Beaulieu had in mind when he complained that "socialism comes out of Mammonism . . . . It doesn't want to destroy wealth but intends to share it."

Many late nineteenth-century socialist utopias dwell upon the material wonders to be shared under egalitarian regimes. To be sure, the luxuries described are not typically bourgeois luxuries, for they can be enjoyed collectively. Nonetheless, they represent a lavish level of consumption—typically, fleet airships and rapid trains, vast pleasure parks, or highly automated factories, full of comforts and gadgets, that serve as environments of mass production and of mass consumption combined (a good example of the last is found in Zola's utopian *Travail*). This hugely impressive collectivized luxury is a form of that aesthetic of the grandiose which Mauclair detected in iron buildings, in Parisian suburbs, in massive lighting displays and other Babylonian displays of industrial might. Many socialist-inspired futuristic fantasies are reminiscent of the international expositions—landscapes full of marvelous machines, gadgetry, lights and noises, all being enjoyed by happy crowds of people. From this perspective the expositions resemble degenerate utopias.[47]

So in nineteenth-century socialism there is a tension between luxury and asceticism, between a glorification of materialism as the essence of progress and a rejection of it as an impediment to human freedom. This is the same conflict between scientific and moral authorities found in bourgeois thought. Instead of resolving bourgeois ambivalence about consumption, socialism shared that ambivalence.

A good example of the resulting moral confusion is expressed by Zola, who was sympathetic to socialism, in *Au Bonheur des Dames*. On the one hand, Zola extols Octave Mouret's commercial genius. Mouret and the department store are the wave of the future, while poor Uncle Baudu's dusty shop is a relic of the retailing past, justifiably condemned to the scrap heap of history. Only the commercially fit will survive or, what is more, deserve to survive: for Zola the triumph of the department store is a fact of evolution as scientifically determined as the workings of biological evolution. The success of the store depends on Mouret's genius in seducing female shoppers commercially just as he seduces female employees physically. Yet Zola also extols Denise as the heroine of the novel because she resists both Mouret's physical seduction and his commercial seduction. She works hard at the store selling clothes to other women, but she herself is no consumer. She lives simply and puts her money toward her brother's education. Part of Zola's moral confusion arises from the sexual double standard—the man is allowed to seduce but women are not supposed to comply—but he is also ambivalent about the ethics of consumption. The department store would never make money if all women were as thrifty as Denise, yet he admires her thrift. As a moralist Zola praises Denise's self-control; as a scientific socialist he praises Mouret's exploitation of consuming passions. At the end of the book Mouret, realizing that Denise will never submit to him, agrees to marry her—a most incongruous marriage of experience and innocence, of lust and purity, of passion and reason. The marriage, a clumsy device intended to reconcile two opposing moral codes, cannot possibly succeed, just as Zola cannot succeed in reconciling his zeal for social progress— defined as the inevitable evolution of industry, science, and commerce—with his respect for the moral virtues of self-sacrifice and self-restraint.

To extricate ourselves from this muddle we must remind ourselves that the most fundamental socialist ideals have to do with humanitarianism, not futurism. Edmund Wilson has expressed them well:

> [S]omething more important remains that is common to all great Marxists: the desire to get rid of class privilege based on birth and on difference of income; the will to establish a society in which the superior development of some is not paid for by the exploitation, that is, by the deliberate degradation of others—a society which will be homogeneous and cooperative as our commercial society is not, and

directed, to the best of their ability, by the conscious creative minds of its members.[48]

On this level socialism is entirely compatible with Gide's activist solidarism. Both depend on the faith that man can reshape the social world to make it a more just and satisfying place to dwell. Although many decorative arts reformers also claimed sympathy with socialism, they emphasized the reformation of the material environment before reformation of the social environment. Gide never did this. As a result, he never succumbed to that obsession with lifestyle which defeated the decorative arts movement. Similarly, Gide never got trapped in circular debates about luxury, because he always addressed the morality of consumption in a social context. And instead of quarreling with socialists about their theoretical differences, he stressed their common agreement on the necessity of practical cooperative effort.

To overcome the ravages of the capitalist economic system, new forms of practical cooperation are needed above all else. Gide understood this. What is more, he understood the type of organization that would best promote genuine cooperation. Although he was willing to support the Social League of Shoppers, he recognized its inadequacies as a model for consumer organization. Its basic flaw was its ratification of the dichotomy between production and consumption, one of the unfortunate divisions encouraged by capitalism. Because League members were not themselves producers, their sense of solidarity with workers always rested on the somewhat tenuous basis of *noblesse oblige*. As a result, although the Leagues started off with exalted intentions of improving working conditions, they fairly quickly evolved into consumer defense organizations with an adversary relationship to workers. Instead of emphasizing consumer responsibilities, they stressed consumer rights. Before dying out in the 1920s, the Leagues became best known for their campaigns against *la vie chère* (inflation). They tended to blame

workers for rising prices when in fact the causes were far
more massive and global. To some extent, consumer cooperatives also moved to a more adversary relationship with
labor during the stressful wartime and postwar years.
When conditions of shortage encouraged inflation and
profiteering, the consumer cooperatives too battled to
reduce prices and increase supplies. But these organizations were far more democratically based than the
Leagues. In them the principle of cooperation—a principle
which had included both production and consumption,
back in the early days of utopian socialism, and could do
so in the future—was too strong to allow them to become
groups of consumers defending their interests against
producers.

Of the two models of consumer organization that
emerged in turn-of-the-century France, the cooperatives
offered far more creative possibilities than the Leagues.
They still do. Most consumer organizations today are
defensive ones, after the League model, and they run into
resistance on the part of ordinary working-class people
who see these organizations as groups of fuzzy-minded
"elitists", "idealists", and "environmentalists" who lack
appreciation of the need for jobs and productivity. The
charges may be unfair, but the lack of sympathy they
represent is the inevitable liability of a consumer defense
organization. The solution is, not to do more explaining,
but to rehabilitate the cooperative model of organization
that attempts to repair rather than aggravate the modern
separation of production and consumption.

No one should underestimate the difficulties of repair-
ing that division, however, as Gide, for one, tended to do.
In his eagerness to usher in "the reign of the consumer,"
he proclaimed that solidarism, cooperation, *and* consumer
socialism are all really the same thing. But the conflict
between production and consumption, on which the historical distinction between socialism and consumer cooperation rests, is not only a conflict of two groups of people.
In modern times most consumers are also workers. The

deeper conflict is psychological, within the heart and mind of the producer-consumer. He has to weigh the value of time devoted to work against the money he can earn thereby to buy more consumer goods. He must try to find his own private equilibrium between the desire to work productively (for this also is a fundamental human desire) and the desire to consume. The distinction of roles, and the need to achieve a personal balance of them, would not be dispelled by institutional changes such as establishment of consumer cooperatives which would gradually assume production responsibilities.

If Gide neglects the possibilities of self-division within the individual producer-consumer, he also neglects myriad sources of distinction among consumers. He repeats endlessly that consumers all have the same interests, that their unity is the germ of a classless society—but again he is too hasty, overlooking distinctions which cannot be eliminated so easily. There are indeed vast differences among consumers. To take an obvious example, a member of the Social League of Shoppers, willing to pay a premium price for a dress made by a humanitarian couturière, is different from the worker's wife who must hunt for bargains on a department-store rack if she is to enjoy a new dress at all. In this case the distinction between these consumers derives ultimately from their respective incomes, and this distinction in turn derives from their respective relations to the means of production—to their economic class, in traditional Marxist terms. Gide (again like Mauclair) tends to downplay the importance of class lines because he feels himself to be outside them: a bourgeois opposed to the dominantly individualistic bourgeois values, an intellectual unattached to the dominant schools of thought, a Protestant in an overwhelmingly Catholic nation. Gide concludes that everyone could leave behind class categories and attain a view of the universal human interest, but so long as people work as well as consume, the reality of differences based on productive role will endure.

Other significant differences among consumers are not so easily related to their economic class. As we have seen, consumers of approximately the same income and social background can choose strikingly dissimilar lifestyles. They can also indulge in a vast range of somewhat more subtle consumer preferences. Any household furnishes examples. The husband wants to buy a kitchen appliance while the wife wants a pair of skis, or vice versa. One child wants tennis lessons and another prefers a bicycle. Even within brackets of the same age and sex, one person prefers to be a consumer of "automobilism," another of books, another of travel, another of restaurant meals, and so forth. These distinctions are not comprehensible in traditional Marxist terms, nor do they make sense according to the shallow psychological description of a self-interested *homo œconomicus* favored by liberal economists.

They are not differences that Gide, the fervent believer in consumer solidarity, would deem significant. As his nephew André wrote of him, "He could not have been less concerned with the particular and with what differentiates . . . . He lived among entities. [His heart] never beat so strongly as for the collective." Gide's ideal of consumption was entirely "democratic and egalitarian"; he was not a person who could comprehend the attraction of an "aristocratic and individualistic" ideal (to use the phrases of Georges Palante). Yet the attraction of the latter is powerful and widespread. The development of different consumer lifestyles, of different dream worlds, is evidence of the desire of individuals to express their personalities and to act out their fantasies through consumption. Instead of denying this desire, we should find ways for it to be expressed without subverting the claims of social justice. To put the problem another way, we should try to find ways to let consumption be individualistic without being aristocratic. This innovation would require a preliminary understanding of consumer psychology far more subtle than Gide, Marxists, or liberal economists could manage. Only by understanding the sources and implications of psychological differences among consumers, only by defining the relationships between this psychology and society at large could the individualistic ideal of consumption be reconciled with Gide's collective ideal.

In an age accustomed to seeing social and economic life in terms of production, Gide pointed out a new land of thought and action, that of consumption. He compared himself to Christopher Columbus who, instead of searching for the route to a New World from the Near East or around Africa, chose

> to travel in the opposite direction from his predecessors and arrived before them on the banks of the New World. Let us do as he did, change our tack, and heading the bow in the opposite direction, we shall more certainly and more quickly discover our America![49]

He discovered the collective power of consumers and showed how it could promote social justice. The social psychology of the consumer is another new world, one Gide never explored. To investigate this *terra incognita* we shall need other intellectual guides who penetrated further into the strange new lands opened up by the consumer revolution. In this exploration Émile Durkheim (1858–1917) and Gabriel Tarde (1843–1904) were the pioneers.

8 Durkheim, Tarde, and the Emergence of a Sociology of Consumption

Durkheim and the Moral Crisis—Émile Durkheim concluded his first major study, *De la division du travail social* ("The Division of Labor in Society," 1893), with these words:

> It has been said with justice that morality—and by that should be understood not only moral doctrines but customs—is going through a real crisis. . . . Profound changes have been produced in the structure of our societies in a very short time. . . . Our illness is not, . . . as has often been believed, of an intellectual sort; it has more profound causes. . . . it is not a new philosophical system which will relieve the situation. Because certain of our duties are no longer founded in the reality of things, a breakdown has resulted which will be repaired only in so far as a new discipline is established and consolidated. In short, our first duty is to make a moral code for ourselves.[1]

If Durkheim became the father of modern sociology, as he is often labeled, it is because he was convinced that a "new discipline," and not simply a new explanation of traditional duties, had to be "established and consolidated" in order to "make a moral code for ourselves."

Since Durkheim's vocabulary tends to be dry and mechanistic, the moral passion inspiring his vision of sociology may be overlooked. His goal was "to establish the science of ethics" on the principle that "moral facts are phenomena like others; they consist of rules of action recognizable by certain distinctive characteristics. It must, then, be possible to observe them, describe them, classify them, and look for the laws explaining them." The discipline of sociology established on this principle will not only lead to a better understanding of society but also will help reform it. The science of ethics which "teaches us to respect the moral reality [also] furnishes us the means to improve it."[2] The development of sociology as a discipline is therefore Durkheim's contribution to the moral consolidation of the French Third Republic. It has proved more durable than the republic itself.

When his work is seen in this light, Durkheim's kinship with the other, less famous thinkers already mentioned becomes evident. Like them, he was aware of an unprecedented moral crisis in society that made old ideas and verbal exhortations sadly inadequate. Like them, his response was to call for the scrapping of old notions and the framing of a wholly new approach. Finally, Durkheim too appreciated the degree to which the moral crisis involved the need to formulate a modern ethic of consumption. Certainly his achievement goes far beyond analyzing the basis for such an ethic, but the degree to which he is concerned with its necessity has been too little appreciated.

The basis of Durkheim's moral concern is his conviction of an inherent disparity between personal happiness and material progress—a conviction he shares with Rousseau, Balzac, d'Avenel, Anatole Leroy-Beaulieu, and Louis Weber, among others. This theme is sounded repeatedly in *The Division of Labor in Society:* "In fact, is it true that the happiness of the individual increases as man advances? Nothing is more doubtful." The developments of science and industry may satisfy material needs, but they do nothing to satisfy moral ones. "To be sure, once these needs are excited, they cannot be suspended without pain. But our happiness is no greater because they are excited. . . . [C]hanges do not necessarily imply progress." Man's capacity for happiness is severely limited. Each species, whether simple or complex, achieves happiness by attaining a state of equilibrium composed of moderate, stable, regular pleasures. The savage who attains such an equilibrium is quite as happy as the civilized man. The clinching evidence that material progress does not mean moral improvement is the fact that suicide, the ultimate admission of personal unhappiness, becomes increasingly prevalent as society becomes more and more materially civilized.[3]

Durkheim returns to this troubling correlation in his second major study, *Le Suicide, étude de sociologie* ("Suicide: A Study in Sociology," 1897). In this book he presents a more extended analysis of the moral dilemmas of modern consumption in the course of describing the causes of "anomic" (as opposed to egoistic or altruistic) suicide.[4] With concentration and clarity Durkheim discusses themes that other advocates of restraint express more diffusely and vaguely. This part of *Suicide* is worth examining in some detail as a forceful argument against the indefinite proliferation of consumer needs.

Durkheim begins his discussion of anomic suicide by returning to the idea, expressed in *Division of Labor*, that happiness is found in equilibrium rather than accumulation. The equilibrium that must be sought, he now elaborates, involves a balance between the needs of an organism and its means of fulfilling those needs. In an animal this balance is automatically attained, for "its power of reflection is not sufficiently developed to imagine other ends than those implicit in its physical nature." The case is entirely different with human beings. As soon as survival needs are satisfied, man imagines better conditions of life and other desirable goals. This imaginative capacity means that most of man's needs, unlike those of animals, "are not dependent on his body, or not to the same degree." Nothing in man's organic or mental make-up sets a limit to "the quantity of well-being, comfort, or luxury legitimately to be craved by a human being." Durkheim therefore recognizes the power of the imagination, rather than of physical nature, in shaping human needs—and he fears that power. Lacking inherent limits, desires kindled by the imagination become a source of torment rather than of happiness. "They constantly and infinitely surpass the means at their command; they cannot be quenched. Inextinguishable thirst is constantly renewed torture." The person who has no restrictions on his appetites is condemned to "a state of perpetual unhappiness" because partial satisfactions only stimulate more needs.

Since the individual has no internal guide to regulate desires, regulation "must be done by some force exterior to him." That force is society. For Durkheim there is no autonomous self-discipline, only social discipline; no self-restraint, only social restraint. In human life society plays the role that nature fulfills for animals, that of an external regulator enabling the organism to achieve a stable equilibrium between needs and means. Durkheim too is awed by the beauty of necessity—not natural necessity, for man has escaped its domination, but social necessity, which man himself creates in building the social world. Like other admirers of the beauty of necessity, Durkheim believes that genuine liberty is found only in constraint. The isolated and unregulated individual, far from enjoying freedom, finds himself in a restlessly unhappy state of anomie which can eventually drive him to suicide. Moral regulation is as necessary for his survival as his daily bread is.

Durkheim describes in more specific terms in what ways society exercises its authority over the desires of the individual:

> . . . At every moment of history there is a dim perception, in the moral consciousness of societies, of the respective

value of different social services, the relative reward due to each, and the consequent degree of comfort appropriate on the average to workers in each occupation. . . . According to accepted ideas, for example, a certain way of living is considered the upper limit to which a workman may aspire in his efforts to improve his existence, and there is another limit below which he is not willingly permitted to fall unless he has seriously demeaned himself. . . . Likewise the man of wealth is reproved if he lives the life of a poor man, but also if he seeks the refinements of luxury over-much. . . . A genuine regimen exists, therefore, although not always legally formulated, which fixes with relative precision the maximum degree of ease of living to which each social class may legitimately aspire.

This extra-legal regulation is powerful but is neither rigid nor absolute. Within the limits set by social opinion, individual desires have free range and experience a moderate stimulus to improvement. Furthermore, as societies slowly grow richer, standards evolve so that what appears luxurious in one age is deemed necessary in another. This is how society normally limits individual passions and allows the attainment of an equilibrium of happiness.

Durkheim then describes the abnormal situation in which society is so disturbed by crisis that it is no longer able to impose limits on consumers. The crisis may be a sharp one, like a precipitous fall in the stock market, when some individuals suddenly find themselves occupying a lower position than their accustomed one in the hierarchy of consumption. "[T]hey must reduce their requirements, restrain their needs, exercise more self-control . . . their moral education has to be recommenced." The prospect of making such a great adjustment overnight imposes strain and suffering to such an extent that economic crashes are followed by a sharp rise in the suicide rate.

Similar results occur in the wake of a more beneficent and prolonged growth in social wealth. In this case, too, the standard according to which needs are regulated changes drastically, and again the adjustment imposes strain. Collective restraint on individual appetites becomes weak and confused. "The limits are unknown between the possible and the impossible, what is just and what is unjust, legitimate claims and hopes and those which are immoderate." This social state of deregulation, or anomie, is especially dangerous because traditional rules lose their authority at precisely the time when increased prosperity inflames individual desires.

Durkheim concludes that suicides have increased regularly and constantly in modern times because the condition of anomie has become chronic. Until the nineteenth century a network of social forces effectively regulated economic life: religion consoled workers while restraining their masters, politics gave business a relatively subordinate role, and within industry itself occupational groups limited salaries and prices. But during the nineteenth century industry was gradually freed from all such restrictions. Now it is regarded as "the supreme end of individuals and societies alike." Modern civilization only serves to encourage appetites. First in the economic sphere, and finally in all social life,

> the state of crisis and anomie is constant and, so to speak, normal. From top to bottom of the ladder, greed is aroused without knowing where to find ultimate foothold . . . . Reality seems valueless by comparison with the dreams of fevered imaginations.

But all those dreams, novelties, unfamiliar pleasures, and nameless sensations can never form a solid foundation for personal happiness. When the slightest reverse occurs, the individual has no capacity for resignation. He is more likely to resort to suicide than he would in a society that furnished moral regulation. The state of anomie, characterized by society's insufficient ability to restrain individual passions, is a source of acute suffering and distress. This is the moral crisis inevitably engendered by the rapid increase in material prosperity.

Traditionalism, Communism, Socialism: Durkheim's Critique—How can society reestablish its authority? Durkheim holds out no hope for the revival of traditional sources of authority such as those the Le Playists esteemed. The restraining influences of father, religion, and social authorities had deteriorated so seriously, in his opinion, that no amount of exhortation could restore them. Durkheim uses the (French) term *conscience collective* to refer to the mentality that used to make that influence possible. This is a mentality he associates with the social state of mechanical solidarity. This mechanical solidarity of similarity depends on daily, habitual contact with the same concrete environment, so that the mind of the individual is steeped in the outlook of the social group. Society has grown far too large and diversified for that sameness any longer to be possible. The phenomenon of the *conscience collective,* of which religion is the prime expression, is no longer rooted in the reality of things. Attempts to revive it are only indulgence in nostalgia. To frame a moral code for modern times, new sources of authority must be created to replace the *conscience collective.*

This task also preoccupied Durkheim in a series of lectures on communism and socialism he delivered between writing *The Division of Labor* and *Suicide.* He became convinced that the economic dogmas of communism and socialism were only matters of detail, that at the heart of them both was a moral vision. Would that vision suggest a new way for society to restrain the material desires of individuals? To answer this question, Durkheim establishes two ideal types (although this terminology had not been invented when he wrote), one of communism and one of socialism. For the communist type, Durkheim has in mind ideal republics such as those of Plato or Campanella, rather than anything that would today be associated with the term. For the socialist type, he examines the system of Saint-Simon, the early nineteenth-century French utopian socialist. Because the lecture series is, regrettably, incomplete, it does not include later social-isms such as the Marxist variety.

Despite outward similarities, Durkheim proposes, the communist model and the socialist one incarnate oppos-ing moral perspectives on the value of material well-being. In communism, economic interests are perceived as anti-social. Accordingly, communist societies strictly separate industrial from public life, economic interests from those of the state. The role of the state is to constrain economic development so that other, more social types of activity—religious, military, artistic, or moral—may flourish. Com-munist societies are fundamentally ascetic. They encour-age their members to despise material well-being and to be content with material necessities so that non-material ac-tivities may reign supreme. The egalitarianism of com-munism brings everyone down to a Spartan level. Produc-tion remains in private hands because more efficient meth-ods of collective production would only stimulate desires. Consumption, on the contrary, is socialized in order to combat the egoism which results from private ownership. To achieve moral purity by getting rid of egoism is an attractive but impossible ideal, concludes Durkheim. As-cetic communism never has and never can have much practical success:

> [The communist idea] is too speculative to encourage much action. This is the same reason that gives a sentimental and artistic character to all these theories . . . . Egoism is too essential to human nature for it ever to be uprooted, insofar as this would be desirable . . . . Therefore when one wonders under what conditions it could be extirpated, one cannot but be aware that one places oneself outside the conditions of the real, and that one can only end with an idyll of which the poetry may be agreeable to the imagina-tion but which cannot claim to be considered as fact. One feels the charm of representing the world thus regenerated, all the while knowing that this regeneration is impossible.[5]

Socialism is not concerned with eternal questions such as the source of egoism, but with temporal economic questions. Socialism demands not the suppression of economic desires but their rearrangement or socialization. In socialist societies production would be collectivized precisely to make it more efficient so that the highest degree of temporal well-being could be attained. State and industry would effectively be merged, because social interests are seen as equivalent to economic ones. The socialist ideal is a sort of leveling upward so that everyone can satisfy his material appetites as completely as possible.

Durkheim's study of Saint-Simonianism leads him to conclude that the socialist "apotheosis of well-being" is inherently self-defeating. In Saint-Simon's system, earthly possessions are seen not as a means but as "the only possible end of human activity." It therefore fails to address the paradox that material interests can be truly satisfied only when they are subordinate to an end which surpasses them. Men can be content only if making them content is not the self-proclaimed goal of society:

> What is necessary for social order to reign is for the generality of men to be content with their lot; but what is necessary for them to be content with it is not that they have more or less, but that they are convinced they do not have the right to have more. And, for this to be, it is altogether necessary that there be an authority whose superiority they recognize, and which tells them their rights. The individual, abandoned to the pressure of his needs alone, will never admit that he has arrived at the extreme limit of his rights.

Socialism lacks such an authority. Saint-Simon wrongly assumed that desires could be satisfied by a certain quantity of well-being. By sanctifying the passions, he eliminated any hope of restraining them. "If they are sacred things, there is nothing to do but laissez-faire . . . . [W]hen matter and material needs are divinized, by what right can a brake and a rule be imposed on them?" If the only end of society is to prosper economically, there is no higher principle to which to appeal in restraining wants.

The fallacy of Saint-Simon is to try "to construct a stable society on a purely economic basis."[6]

Eventually Saint-Simon did try to provide another basis to society, by establishing a social religion. Durkheim finds the experiment intriguing because it demonstrates that this utopian socialist, however confusedly, "felt the necessity of raising something above the purely economic order which would limit it." Saint-Simon recognized that throughout history religion has been the primary authority limiting material desires and setting social goals above economic ones. He and his disciples did not wish to revive Christianity, for its dogmas anathematize the material world. Their new faith would rehabilitate matter. The religion they devised, however, is purely nominal, theocratic only in appearance, in reality a sort of mystic pantheism where God is simply a name given to the world itself. Logically it could not be otherwise. When terrestrial things are made the end of society, remarks Durkheim, "they take on a value and a dignity that they would not have if the divine were thought of as outside the things of this world." Far from constricting temporal interests, the Saint-Simonian religion only consecrates them. The basis of the religion is purely economic. Its goal is to create social harmony on earth by forging a sense of collective interest out of a mass of disconnected egos. A faith that depends on spontaneous bursts of universal love and a murky sense of cosmic unity can never by effective. Durkheim summarizes Saint-Simon's religious experiment as "a very vigorous attempt of industrialism to succeed at rising above itself, but this attempt aborted. For when one begins with the axiom that there are only economic interests, one is their prisoner and cannot go beyond them."[7]

Occupational Groups: Durkheim's Proposal – Since neither Le Playist traditionalism, ascetic communism, or materialistic socialism offers realistic solutions to the moral crisis, Durkheim ventures another alternative. This is his version of solidarity. He prophesies that the same process of social evolution that has destroyed the *conscience collective* is silently constructing new sources of social authority. His ideas on this subject are developed most fully in *The Division of Labor*. There he describes in some detail the transformation of society from primitive forms of mechanical solidarity to a complex, organic solidarity where distinctive individuals are linked by objective relationships so that the special contribution of each is essential to the success of the whole. The increase of specialization in economic life results in an interdependence far stronger than mechanical similarity. "It is the division of labor which, more and more, fills the role that was formerly filled by the common *conscience*. It is the principal foundation of social aggregates of higher types."[8] While economists praise the division of labor for its greater efficiency in producing goods, Durkheim extols it above all for its moral purpose. The division of labor creates a new social solidarity which at once strengthens individual personality and provides effective restraints upon it.

All this is very abstract, and Durkheim was eager to demonstrate how his concept of organic solidarity could be realized in practical terms. In 1902 he added a preface to the second edition of *The Division of Labor*, titled "Quelques Remarques sur les groupements professionnels" ("Some Remarks on Occupational Groups") to describe the kind of institution that would embody a new organic solidarity. The occupational group, or corporation, would include all the workers in a given profession, from the lowest to the highest. Durkheim emphasizes that he does not advocate the revival of the prerevolutionary corporations, which tended to be parochial, local, and reactionary. His idea of the corporation is far more general. Through most of history, he contends, the occupational group has existed as a quasi-religious, quasi-familial institution providing moral discipline and a sense of community for its members. Revived corporations would have utilitarian functions—mutual assistance, insurance schemes, the fixing of quantities and conditions of production, and remuneration—but they would go beyond these functions to provide a sense of solidarity, a new "moral environment" for their members. As with Gide's concept of consumer cooperatives, Durkheim's proposed organization would be at once economic and moral in its actions. The occupational group would moderate the strong and soothe the protests of the weak; it would enumerate the duties of individuals toward each other and toward the community; and it would decide the share of each so that the appetites of individuals could not exceed certain limits. Its restraint would be omnipresent:

> It follows workers wherever they go, which the family cannot do. Wherever they are, they find it enveloping them, recalling them to their duties, supporting them in need. Finally, since occupational life is almost the whole of life, corporative action makes itself felt in every detail of our occupations, which are thus given a collective orientation. Thus the corporation has everything needed to give the individual a setting, to draw him out of his state of moral isolation.

Durkheim feels that contemporary unions show a "formless and rudimentary" beginning of such occupational groups. They deviate from his ideal in many respects, however, particularly in that workers and employers are not included in the same organization. While Durkheim considers this separation *"legitimate and necessary"* at the present, he hopes the two groups will establish regular contact so that they can eventually establish a common authority to fix their relations and command obedience from both.[9]

Charles Gide predicted "the reign of the consumer": it could be said that Durkheim advocated "the reign of the producer." While Gide proposed a new morality of the consumer, Durkheim prophesied what one of his disciples, Célestin Bouglé (1870–1940), called a "morality of the tool"—a moral code wherein the workplace provides "a sort of *vita nuova* for consciences" and constitutes "the best practical school of solidarity."[10] There were many besides Durkheim who were calling for a "morality of the tool." Bouglé mentions as examples the syndicalist Georges Sorel in France and the Fabian socialist Sidney Webb in England. The enthusiasm of Le Playists for corporations shows that the ethic of the workplace could be as attractive to *patrons* as to workers. The fact that Camille Mauclair also advocated reestablishment of corporations shows how readily this ethic could be grafted onto the decorative arts revival. From all these different perspectives, the idea of a professional association organized around both material and moral goals was highly attractive.

The problem is that by mixing moral and material purposes so intimately in the same institution, they become confused and finally merged. This confusion is present in a general way in Durkheim's thinking about the modern moral crisis. He sees two needs of modern society: the need for an institutionalized, external, stable source of authority to limit individual egoism, and the need for a moral principle to justify that limitation. The occupational group would fill the first need but not the second. Since it is to be based on economic interests, it can provide no goal beyond material ones and thus provide no principle of limitation except to the extent that the material interests of individual members may be restricted to benefit the material interests of the group. In fact, far from serving as a curb to economic interests, the corporation would only emphasize those interests because it would be organized around them. Durkheim himself admits that the occupational group would not "lay too heavy a yoke on industry; it is close enough to the interests it will have to regulate not to restrain them too severely."[11]

Durkheim had criticized Saint-Simonian socialism for positing no higher social goal than "the apotheosis of well-being" and had concluded that this was the basic cause of its failure. His own proposal for corporations would be destined to fail for the same reason. Durkheim wants to confront social reality, to look squarely at the "social facts" of his time. The social fact seems to be that it is no longer possible to propose non-economic goals for social life. The "apotheosis of well-being" is characteristic not only of socialism but of anomic modern society in general.[12] For modern religions to preach asceticism is to indulge in dreams of abnegation with no basis in reality. Religion, which proposes goals beyond terrestrial well-being, is no longer possible:

> [T]he essential principle of the only regulation to which [religion] can subject economic life is contempt for riches . . . . If religion teaches that our duty is to accept with docility our lot as circumstances order it, this is to attach us exclusively to other purposes, worthier of our efforts; and in general religion recommends moderation in desires for the same reason. But this passive resignation is incompatible with the place which earthly interests have now assumed in collective existence. The discipline [those interests] need must not aim at relegating them to second place and reducing them as far as possible, but at giving them an organization in harmony with their importance.[13]

The occupational group provides this "organization" of earthly interests but not their moderation or direction to a superior goal. It therefore subordinates individuals basically because they need subordination. Georges Palante, one of Durkheim's sterner critics, calls this "the tyranny of the group." Palante argues that it seems to be Durkheim's plan for sociology "to take over the function previously assumed by religion, namely, to restrain the individual in the interests of society."[14] Durkheim would respond that the subordination of the individual is precisely what allows him to achieve his full personality: "not only does occupational regulation . . . hinder less than any other the play of individual variation, but it also tends to do so less and less."[15] Yet when Durkheim describes the personality that would be fostered by the occupational group, the ideal sounds bleak and confining:

We can then say that, in higher societies, our duty is not to spread our activity over a large surface, but to concentrate and specialize it. We must contract our horizon, choose a definite task and immerse ourselves in it completely, instead of trying to make ourselves a sort of creative masterpiece, quite complete, which contains its worth in itself and not in the services that it renders.[16]

Just when industrial development was opening up new worlds of experience and liberating people from ancient restraints of geography, education, age, and sex, Durkheim proposes a social world of artificially imposed necessity. In particular, he would not welcome liberation from labor: "Occupational life is almost the whole of life." So it had been in the past, and he would have it only intensified in the future. According to Durkheim, the progress of civilization brings both more specialized work and more continuous work. Animals and savages work only when they must, and even in the Middle Ages many holidays interrupted labor. In advanced societies alone has "work become a permanent occupation, a habit, and indeed, if this habit is sufficiently strengthened, a need."[17] It is not difficult to understand the source of Durkheim's vision of a future of work, so opposed to Gide's vision of "the reign of the consumer." For Durkheim, work is the realm of reality, of social facts. Consumption is the realm of "dreams of fevered imagination" which must be regulated lest an individual degenerate into a state of suicidal anomie. Durkheim's moral vision would eliminate the pathology of a "creative masterpiece" like des Esseintes, who did degenerate in his moral isolation; but it would also eliminate the potential liberation offered when varied experiences of consumption became available to the masses.

Besides the personal costs involved, there are social costs when each person is defined exclusively by the tools he handles, when his thoughts and morality are tightly tied to his occupation. Célestin Bouglé remarks:

To enclose a man too early in a trade is a danger. Not only because such capacities of the individual may merit being cultivated for themselves; but because social life, being in a large part interprofessional and presupposing relations between different types of producers, requires a platform of common notions on which to build.[18]

According to Bouglé, what is needed is a sense of citizenship as well as of professional identity. Only then can the individual envision the general good above the good of the group. Otherwise, social life could be reduced to a series of wars among occupational groups, or between producers and consumers. This is the same reasoning that led Gide to emphasize that the consumer represents the truly universal human interest, as opposed to the necessarily restricted interest of any group of producers.

Certainly Durkheim's proposed organization is by no means universal in its embrace. Like Louis Weber's schools of moral culture, Durkheim's occupational groups would omit the aged, children, and many women. The omission of women is especially serious, because Durkheim himself admits there is one cause of anomic suicide that could not be mitigated by establishing corporations, and this is "the form springing from conjugal anomie." In the institution of marriage the interests of husbands and wives are antagonistic because

the two sexes do not share equally in social life. Man is actively involved in it, while a woman does little more than look on at a distance. His tastes, aspirations, and humor have in large part a collective origin, while his companion's are more directly influenced by her organism. His needs, therefore, are quite different from hers, and so an institution intended to regulate their common life cannot be equitable and simultaneously satisfying to such opposite needs.[19]

Durkheim adds that marriages will become more harmonious only when the psychological differences between the sexes diminish, but the establishment of occupational groups would only intensify those differences, at least in bourgeois marriages where the wife does not work. The husband would become even more identified with his occupational role while the wife, whose occupations of mothering and housework are not encompassed by professional groups, would be even less involved in social life. The division of the sexes, which parallels the division between production and consumption, would be reinforced. The morality of the producer is very much that of the male.

In Durkheim's work as a whole there is a disjunction between the diagnosis of the moral dilemmas of consumption, so cogent and convincing, and the prescription, which is inadequate in many ways. The main reason for this inadequacy is that he analyzes the moral crisis of the consumer and then presents a solution appropriate for a producer. With terms like *anomie* he tries to devise a vocabulary to describe the spiritual cost of unrestricted desires, but then he falls back on the rather more mechanistic vocabulary of an institution to organize desires. Does Durkheim mean to suggest—as Mauclair does at times, but as Gide does not—that people can receive a moral education only as producers, not as consumers? Perhaps the incongruity only tells us how difficult it is to fashion language appropriate to modern consumption. Durkheim is far from alone in his inability to find an adequate vocabulary; indeed, with the term *anomie* he succeeds better than most of his contemporaries. But in suggesting a producers' organization as a prescription for the dilemmas of modern consumers, Durkheim reaches the limits of his intellectual assumptions. The only terminology he knows which would address those dilemmas directly is that of religion. But he is convinced that this terminology is anachronistic. Religion is the preeminent form of the *conscience collective* and is therefore dying as a social fact. Attempts to revive it, whether as communist asceticism or Saint-Simonian pantheism, are only pleasing dreams.

The Role of Religion–Or are they? As Durkheim grew older, he had second thoughts. Although he showed serious interest in the sociology of religion in the 1890s— the same period which saw the writing of *The Division of Labor*, the lectures on socialism, and *Suicide*—only in 1912 did he write a major study with religion at the center rather than at the periphery. This is *Les Formes élémentaires de la vie religieuse: le système totémique en Australie* ("The Elementary Forms of Religious Life: The Totemic System in Australia"). As the sub-title suggests, much of the book is devoted to a summary and discussion of ethnographic studies of native Australian religions. Durkheim felt that the essential outlines of religious faith and practice could be grasped more readily in a primitive state than in a highly developed system like Christianity. Although the totemic beliefs of the Australian tribes seem strange and barbaric to a European, Durkheim argues that in both primitive and civilized form "religion exists; it is a system of given facts; in a word, it is a reality. How could science deny this reality?"[20]

No more does Durkheim speak of religion as an outmoded form of the *conscience collective*. It exists as a social fact and continues to exist because it incarnates some truth of human experience beyond the validity of its specific dogmas. That truth is embedded in the way religious experience symbolizes social experience. Durkheim is as convinced as ever that the individual ego must be limited by the external force of society, but now he adds that God may serve as a metaphor for that force. God "is only a figurative expression of the society." Religious ritual should be interpreted as a dramatization of social relationships, as a sort of mythical sociology. Furthermore, these rituals have a definite social purpose, which is to "strengthen the bonds attaching the individual to the society of which he is a member." Not so much the dogma of the religion but its practice maintains the sense of solidarity necessary for social and therefore for individual life.

From this perspective Durkheim analyzes the function of religious rituals of abstinence. Every religion involves some kind of temporary or permanent prohibition on certain types of consumption, the most obvious example being fasting. "It follows that asceticism is not a rare, exceptional and nearly abnormal fruit of the religious life, as some have supposed it to be; on the contrary, it is one of its essential elements." The strict limitation of consumption is essential because only when the believer loosens his ties to the profane world can he enter into commerce with the sacred. By detaching himself from base and trivial considerations, he sanctifies himself and so prepares himself for access to a higher level of experience than the everyday. To be sure, this effort entails suffering:

> We hold to the profane world by all the fibres of our flesh; our senses attach us to it; our life depends upon it. It is not merely the natural theatre of our activity; it penetrates us from every side, it is a part of ourselves. So we cannot detach ourselves from it without doing violence to our nature and without painfully wounding our instincts.

In primitive religions such as those of the Australians, this need for suffering may be ritualized in repulsive ceremonies of mutilation. Yet the same belief that suffering confers sanctity is at the heart of the Christian faith:

> In both it is admitted that suffering creates exceptional strength [for the believer] . . . . Suffering is the sign that certain of the bonds attaching him to his profane environment are broken; so it testifies that he is partially freed from this environment, and, consequently, it is justly considered the instrument of deliverance. So he who is thus delivered is not the victim of a pure illusion when he believes himself invested with a sort of mastery over things: he really has raised himself above them, by the very act of renouncing them.

These rites demonstrate that religion is valid existentially aside from all considerations of its intellectual validity. As a form of human experience, religion strengthens a person and enables him to rise above the miseries and vexations of life, to endure or even conquer them and, eventually, to feel the force of life more fully. In this way "religious interests are only the symbolic form of social and moral interests." Training in endurance and disinterestedness is eminently necessary for all social life, since society is made possible only through a degree of sacrifice on the part of individuals. Religious rituals symbolize the need for social discipline and, by being performed, reinforce solidarity. Durkheim concludes: "So there is an asceticism which, being inherent in all social life, is destined to survive all the mythologies and all the dogmas; it is an integral part of human culture."

In concluding that religious interests are symbolic of social ones, Durkheim does not have to go far to assert that social bonds are fundamentally religious in character. If the purpose of religion is to create society, then society itself is a religious phenomenon. Religion will not die out but will survive as long as society does. At the same time Durkheim is convinced that religion must be transformed. In particular, it must give up its claims to cognitive validity. Durkheim looks forward to a religious revival, but he also expects to see a different sort of religion than in the past.

By seeing abstinence as an inherently religious attitude, Durkheim transcends his earlier and comparatively superficial solution of imposing moral regulation by establishing occupational groups. In his more mature consideration he takes into account the argument he used in criticizing Saint-Simon, that asceticism is justifiable only with reference to a dimension of experience above that of material well-being. When human experience is restricted to one dimension—when heaven is walled off, to use Anatole Leroy-Beaulieu's expression—there can be no principle of restraint. The question remains, however, whether "society" and "God" can be used interchangeably to describe that higher level of experience. To make society into a divinity is reminiscent of a Saint-Simonian pantheism sanctifying the things of this earth rather than positing another, higher realm of the sacred. Can society in the abstract be understood as a religious being, or does Durkheim's equation of them only lead to a tyranny of the group? Can consumption be regulated with reference to the goal of providing well-being for all society, when that end, while providing a goal above that of the individual ego, is still a material one? Are other, non-material social goals possible, so that consumption may be regulated according to a spiritual goal for human society? God and religion may have to be redefined, but how?

Durkheim does not provide concrete answers in his last book as he had in earlier ones. However, he comes much closer to defining the issues and the social needs involved in making a moral code for ourselves. His acceptance of the truth of religion should not be overstated. Despite being the son of a rabbi, despite the tragic death of his own son in World War I, Durkheim did not become a believer in any conventional sense. His attitude toward religion always remained deeply ambivalent. But in his analysis of the moral price of modern prosperity, in stressing the necessity of religious bonds for social life, he too in a very muted way made the choice between the muzzle of a gun and the foot of the Cross.

Tarde's Place in Intellectual History – Gabriel Tarde failed to heed Durkheim's admonition that the future belongs to specialists. Tarde was a student of economics, sociology, philosophy, ancient and modern history, law, crime, and politics. In his books and articles discussions of all these fields are juxtaposed with allusions to physics, chemistry, music, painting, mathematics, linguistics, and much more. He wrote on topical issues (the moral crisis, solidarity, educational reform, race, alcoholism), as well as on subjects raised only by himself (such as "the social role of joy"), and he also composed short stories and poetry.

This very versatility was one reason why Durkheim was convinced that Tarde pursued "intellectual amusement" rather than serious thought.[21] Durkheim, who led a sober life devoted to work, could only regard as a dilettante someone who dabbled in literary activities and amused the ladies of Parisian salons by reading their palms and analyzing their handwriting. Durkheim wrote in an unadorned, highly organized prose style. Tarde's writing is witty, graceful, vivacious, and often unsystematic—a style which in Durkheim's opinion allowed "the reign of fantasy in the intellectual order,"[22] and many of Durkheim's colleagues agreed with this assessment, shunning Tarde as a sort of intellectual butterfly, charming but inconsequential.

In contrast to Durkheim's central role in the professionalization of the social sciences, Tarde worked in isolation. For much of his life his home was in Dordogne, a remote area of southwestern France. His education was interrupted from the age of nineteen to twenty-four by an eye disease which kept him largely in solitude and drastically curtailed his reading. After recovery, Tarde worked as a local magistrate. He lived the life of a country gentleman, with ample leisure for reading and rumination but with little opportunity for intellectual intercourse with equals. Very slowly he amassed a reputation outside Dordogne through writings on criminology which developed from his judicial duties. He addressed the penological implications of the late nineteenth-century "moral crisis." Only at the age of fifty-one did Tarde go to Paris, and even then he went to a bureaucratic post (director of the Statistical Section in the Ministry of Justice) rather than a university position. Public lectures at the Collège de France came only in the last years of his life.

At the time of his death in 1904, Tarde left no coherent group of disciples. No discipline claims Tarde as its father: as Durkheim foresaw, in modern times versatility is not a solid basis for scholarly influence. Tarde's present reputation rests on his role as a "whipping boy"[23] for Durkheim and as the progenitor of a stillborn sociological theory of imitation.

This unjust fate reveals more about the limitations of contemporary sociology than about the limitations of Gabriel Tarde. Durkheim's suspicions to the contrary, Tarde was no dabbler. He was as deeply and seriously convinced of the validity of his intellectual methods and goals as Durkheim was of his own, but they were much more subtle and elusive than Durkheim's goals and methods, so that Tarde had difficulty finding words to define them. At the outset Tarde used the expression *social psychology* to describe his discipline of sociology. In the course of polemics with Durkheim and others concerning the scientific character of sociology, Tarde came to realize that this formulation was inadequate. He then invented the word *interpsychology* to describe his goal, a new social science which would examine the mental reactions between two people as well as the mental action of a person on a group and the reaction of the collectivity back on the individual. Interpsychology is therefore distinct from classical psychology, which focuses on the individual mind, and also from sociology, "which it goes beyond, and which it explains, but which it does not constitute."[24] The fundamental difference between Tarde's vision of a new social discipline and Durkheim's is that Tarde wanted to detach social science from biology and join it to psychology. For Tarde society is not an organism (Durkheim's favorite metaphor) but a mind, a brain with the same functions as the individual one—memory, imagination, judgment, will, *conscience.*

Although the first and last courses given by Tarde at the Collège de France dealt with interpsychology, he left only a vague outline for this new discipline, in contrast to Durkheim's resounding success in establishing the new discipline of sociology. Still, to do justice to Tarde he should be assessed not as a defeated sociologist but as a pioneer of a still incomplete interpsychology. Tarde and Durkheim took parallel rather than identical routes toward the goal of trying to define a new social science that would be appropriate for an emergent society in a state of moral crisis. And in confronting the moral dilemmas of the modern consumer, in describing the contours of consumer mentality, Tarde's psychological route is superior to any other encountered so far. In modern consumption we have repeatedly noted a crucial component of dream, imagination, reverie, fantasy. To borrow Durkheim's terms, in matters of consumption, fantasy is a social fact.

In this light Durkheim's accusation that Tarde succumbs to a "reign of fantasy in the intellectual order" is as revealing as it is inaccurate. Durkheim himself tries to transcend mechanistic metaphors and terminology, but he never quite succeeds. Consequently he never finds a vocabulary to deal adequately with the imaginative component of social experience. While Durkheim is uncomfortable unless he is absolutely clear on every point, Tarde adopts the maxim that "in social matters, every clear explanation must necessarily be erroneous."[25] Tarde is serious: he takes fantasy seriously. Although he does not at all reject reality, he refuses to limit his thought to it, always insisting on the consideration of possibility as well. "The real is explicable only in connection with the immensity of the possible."[26] The consistent intellectual thread running through Tarde's work is his concern for imagination, change, and potentiality. For him social reality is not self-evident but is a sort of cryptic message which must be decoded by an imaginative observer open to a multitude of possibilities.

This is why Tarde was able to interpret the social language of lifestyles that was emerging in his era—a language incomprehensible to so many others, who are aware only of a babble of commodities. Tarde should be evaluated not as a scientist, not even as a sociologist, but as an interpreter of the future, a social prophet. By this standard he is uniquely perceptive at discerning the implications of the consumer revolution. Also by this standard, his failure to establish an intellectual school becomes less important. Social prophecy is not a vocation that lends itself to accumulating disciples. Durkheim's method could form the basis of an intellectual industry in a way that Tarde's much more individual vision could not.

This difference should not discredit Tarde's ideas. The obvious irony that the theoretician of imitation himself left no imitators can be misleading. If his intellectual construction could not be reproduced as a scale model, so to speak, it has been quarried for raw materials by others for use in constructing their own edifices of thought. In this way Tarde's influence has by no means been negligible. Georges Palante, for example, was a great admirer of Tarde. Above all, Charles Gide seems to have exchanged many ideas with Tarde in developing a new psychological, consumer-oriented economics.

The following presentation of Tarde's ideas is selective rather than exhaustive. Its aim is to highlight his contribution to understanding modern consumption. Although that contribution goes far beyond his theory of imitation, this is still the best place to begin.

Imitation and Invention – Repetition, or self-copying, is the basic tendency of the universe: this is the vision of the cosmos underlying Tarde's vision of society. Imitation in the social world is a form of repetition analogous to wave vibrations in the physical world and to reproduction in the biological world. But unlike the repetition of non-human nature, human imitation involves conscious choice. From birth each individual is surrounded by a multitude of human models whom he can imitate or counter-imitate. ("There are two ways to imitate, in fact: to do exactly like one's model, or to do exactly the contrary.")[27] From all these possibilities a person assembles his own unique set of models (and counter-models) to express his singular personality. His acts of imitation are partly passive and partly active, partly rational and partly intuitive:

> Nothing . . . is less scientific than this absolute separation . . . between the voluntary and the involuntary, between the conscious and the unconscious. Does not one pass by insensible degrees from reflective will to almost

mechanical habit? And what act changes absolutely in nature during this passage?[28]

The best analogy to imitative experience, Tarde proposes, is a hypnotic trance, or, more precisely, the semiconscious and incomplete state of hypnosis preceding a deep trance. (Hypnotism was then a subject of great interest among psychologists.) Tarde argues that the complexities of social interaction can be clarified scientifically by referring to the more elementary interaction between hypnotist and subject (much as Durkheim clarified the complexities of religious faith by examining primitive Australian beliefs):

> The social state, like the hypnotic state, is only a form of dream, a dream of command and a dream of action. To have ideas only suggested and to believe them spontaneous: such is the illusion of the somnambulist [a term then used to refer to a hypnotized person], and of social man as well.[29]

Of course, the hypnotized person is unaware of his propensity to act by suggestion. Contemporary "social man" is similarly unaware of the extent to which his social behavior is rooted in semiconscious entrancement by prestige. It is not by looking at ourselves but at distant civilizations such as ancient Sparta, Egypt, or Israel that we can begin to appreciate how much society is governed by the authority of prestige. The people of those alien civilizations thought themselves independent and rational, as we do, but to us moderns they look like automatons controlled by their ancestors and prophets. Although in modern times the authority of prestige has become much more reciprocal and generalized, we should not flatter ourselves that we are any "less credulous or less docile, in a word less imitative than our ancestors."

In fact, contemporary man is even more prone to imitation, because he is more used to it, just as someone goes into a trance more easily the more he has been hypnotized. The fact that society is still highly susceptible to hypnosis may be seen in the relatively recent career of Napoleon, whose every gesture was obeyed by France. But the most striking contemporary evidence of this susceptibility may be seen when a person who had lived in an environment relatively sparse in models is suddenly thrust into surroundings rich in them. "Not only a freshman who arrives on a college campus, but also a Japanese traveling in Europe, or a country person disembarking in Paris are struck with stupor comparable to a cataleptic state." Memory of the past environment is paralyzed; attention to the new environment is so potent and concentrated that "these stupefied and feverish beings invincibly submit to the magic *charm* of their new surroundings; they believe everything they see." Outward passivity masks their inner state of keen excitation. In less extreme form this trancelike state is chronic among city-dwellers. The abundance of models to imitate renders their minds at once overexcited and numb:

> The movement and the noise of the streets, the store windows, the frenetic and impulsive agitation of their existence, affect them like hypnotic spells. Now urban life, is it not social life concentrated and taken to an extreme? . . . Society is imitation, and imitation is a type of hypnotism.[30]

At last we have found a vocabulary appropriate to the reaction of Denise Baudu and her brothers before Au Bonheur des Dames. They are "country persons disembarking in Paris" who are paralyzed by the "magic *charm* of their new environment," in this case the environment of mass consumption, far richer in models than the one they were used to. By suggesting that this same mental state permeates all of modern urban civilization, Tarde provides the beginnings of a social psychology of the modern consumer, a psychology that incorporates its dreamlike tendencies. This is a complex and mobile vision of social psychology appropriate not only to Denise but also to consumer behavior at expositions, automobile shows, and movies, or even at Fontenay and Samuel

Bing's decorative arts store. When he is faced with such spectacles, in the consumer's mind are mixed emotional hyperactivity and paralysis, envy and scorn, conscious choice and semiconscious obedience, initiative and submission, desire and repulsion. The analogy with hypnosis emphasizes these ambiguities. Hypnosis depends on intimidation, a state where the subject may want to resist entrancement but cannot sufficiently mobilize his inner resources to overcome the force of prestige. The intimidated person becomes malleable "under the gaze of someone else." This is a highly ambivalent state, at once pleasing and disturbing, because "there is a *loving fear* in him who feels it."[31]

Tarde's social psychology rejects a strict dichotomy between rational, conscious behavior and the irrational, unconscious kind. Tarde was writing at the time of the discovery of the unconscious (to use a familiar if imprecise term) by Freud and others. This "discovery" relied to a considerable extent on the use of hypnosis to reveal motivations below the level of consciousness. But Tarde, despite his curiosity about hypnosis, does not conclude that the subconscious rules the conscious mind. Instead he "discovers" the semiconscious, a state between the two. Accordingly, his theory of semiconscious imitative social behavior represents a vast improvement over the model of *homo œconomicus*, who is supposed to be at once rationally choosing and indefinitely desiring, and also over Durkheim's very similar model of an indefinitely desiring individual restrained only by something external to himself, which is called society. In contrast to the classical economists, Tarde suggests that people are not split between rational choice and irrational desire, but act according to a semiconscious imitation that mingles the two. Tarde suggests that the line between the individual and society, between internal feelings and external restraints, is not so rigid and arbitrary. Tarde presents a more "solidarist" psychology than does Durkheim. He sees the mind of the individual as part of an endless social network which in turn contributes to that network, in a dynamic relation of role-setting and role-following.

Tarde's social psychology does leave many unanswered questions. The phenomenon of hypnosis, which provides his central analogy for the workings of imitation, is still a mystery.[32] But he was on the right track because his concepts accurately predict that some suggested solutions to the moral crisis of the modern consumer would prove inadequate. In Tarde's opinion, both preaching and institutionalized programs fail to address the human propensity to imitation. As a result, Tarde has little patience with Durkheim's pedagogy and ideology of duty and patriotism or with his proposal to revive corporations. And although Tarde is mildly optimistic about the future of consumer cooperatives, he does not agree with Gide that the hypnotized consumer can be fully awakened from entrancement by publicity so that he can make reasoned, conscious choices. Tarde is convinced that since "social man" is "a veritable somnambulist,"[33] he will not be wholly delivered from his trance no matter how his social environment is organized. Since in their innermost nature people are believers (*croyants*), there is no point in trying to shake them awake to daylight reason. People will cling to "a dream of command and a dream of action."

For Tarde, this is (to borrow Durkheim's term) a social fact. However, this limited capacity for rational and independent action does not particularly distress him. He is not convinced that deliberate choice among models is superior to imitation based on unreflective impulse or habit derived from traditional concepts of prestige. Indeed, Tarde suggests, the transition from "conscious, difficult, and discussed" imitation to the habitual kind incorporated in social tradition could be the mark of a superior civilization. If people tend to act by faith and habit rather than by reason, this is not cause for alarm, but it should produce an awareness of the importance of instilling desirable habits and beliefs. Instead of lamenting the human propensity to semihypnotic imitation, we should encourage the creation and diffusion of worthy models to copy. Inventions are models that are diffused through repetition, and so Tarde's theory of imitation leads to his theory of invention.

A human invention (or innovation, or discovery, words which Tarde uses nearly interchangeably) is any novel principle, whether grand or nearly imperceptible, usually but not always anonymous, in art, religion, jurisprudence, manners, politics, or any other area of human activity. The principle may be incorporated in a machine or product, but the invention itself is always the idea, the "mental object" rather than the physical one.[34] Just as Tarde's theory of imitation is far broader than a theory of consumer psychology, his concept of invention goes far beyond consumer products—but, again, his ideas are especially illuminating in regard to consumer behavior. His "logical laws of imitation," which describe how inventions proliferate, nearly irresistibly translate themselves into descriptions of the proliferation of consumer goods.

The most basic "logical law" is that once an invention is imitated, it spreads endlessly in all directions in a geometric progression. Tarde himself uses commodities to illustrate this principle, citing statistics on the consumption of coffee and tobacco and on the spread of ownership of bicycles. But some inventions proliferate more successfully than others. In hypothesizing the social mechanisms that select the "fittest" inventions, Tarde seems even more to be describing the workings of the marketplace. One insight is that new inventions or products have to be viewed in the context of others, that they interact actively as people do in imitating each other. Sometimes inventions compete in a "logical duel" where acceptance of one entails rejection of another (for example, the competition between cuneiform and Phoenician writing, which are two inventions serving the same need, or the competition between two different needs, such as aesthetic and patriotic ones). While this dueling is common in politics, religion, and philosophy, in economic life inventions more often unite and strengthen each other through "logical coupling." For example, the discovery of the wheel and the domestication of animals were coupled to form the horse-drawn cart—an example of coupling through integration. Even more common is coupling through accumulation, whereby one invention is superimposed upon another. Tarde speculates that accumulation, rather than substitution or integration, is the most common way inventions interact: they simply pile up in an uncoordinated heap.

In Tarde's terms, the consumer revolution may be interpreted as the unprecedently rapid accumulation of consumer inventions. Even more, it may be defined as an historical epoch in which the activity of invention, which used to be dispersed among many areas of human endeavor, became more and more concentrated in the realm of material goods. Models considered worthy of imitation used to be drawn variously from religious, military, political, and other areas of social activity; during the nineteenth century they were increasingly provided by the marketplace. The general category of invention was transformed into the specific category of commodity.

This process can be explained more precisely if we turn from Tarde's "logical laws" of dueling and coupling to his "extra-logical laws" of imitation. They are "extra-logical" because they refer not to the inherent function or physical utility of inventions but to their *social* function or utility, which encourages their imitation. Tarde's analysis of the "extra-logical" factors involved in the proliferation of inventions constitutes a tentative sociology of consumption.

The Extra-Logical Laws of Imitation—The first of the three extra-logical laws of imitation is at once subtle and crucial. This is the principle of *ab interioribus ad exteriora:* "Imitation . . . proceeds from the inside of man to the outside." The Latin phrase comes from Thomas à Kempis's *The Imitation of Christ,* a devotional book which greatly impressed Tarde and which he often quoted. Like

Durkheim, Tarde suggests that religious experience can serve as a model for social experience in general. The inner spirit of Christ is communicated first, followed only later by imitation of the exterior forms of that spirit. Similarly, inner feelings are copied before exterior things; communion of spirit precedes that of behavior; opinions are borrowed before commodities; and the exchange of souls precedes that of goods.

Once the implications of this principle have been grasped, consumer motivation is enormously clarified, although once again it must be emphasized that Tarde never intended to limit its relevance in this way. He does, however, point out that one deduction from this principle is that an inner desire or need is copied before the specific products that fulfill that need or desire, since imitation of ends precedes that of means.[35] Appearances perhaps to the contrary, the object of the consumer's desire is not so much a material "exterior" object as an internal desire or need incarnated in the commodity.

Tarde further illustrates how this principle operates among consumers by referring to modern "democratized" luxury. According to Tarde, the essence of luxury is not the assemblage of particular items but the idea of spending capriciously on nonessentials. The goods themselves are of secondary, exterior importance next to the pleasure of buying on a whim. Tarde remarks that this idea of spending, formerly reserved for the monarchy and its servants, has now become diffused among the mass of consumers, who all fancy themselves royalty in this respect. (It could be added that the dandies were of crucial importance here in legitimizing and indeed glamorizing the idea of living beyond one's means.)

This analysis of "the democratization of luxury" shows a more profound awareness of consumer psychology than we have seen so far. If nothing else, it is a reminder that the proliferation of cheap and easy credit was as central to the consumer revolution as the proliferation of cheap goods. Even more, Tarde reminds us that while modern technology makes possible the imitation of *goods*, what the consumer fundamentally craves is the imitation of a style of *life*. This is why the democratization of goods alone does not lead to a utopia of social harmony, much as d'Avenel and others hope that it will. To use a geometric analogy (and we shall see that Tarde often used them himself), desire is not a simple line segment that connects a person to a commodity. Instead, the desire of the consumer is mediated through a second person, the model, so that a triangle is formed. The motivating desire is to be like another prestigious person, to adopt that person's desires and needs. This impulse to imitate the model's interior life remains primary and constant, while desire for particular objects is secondary and transient.[36] All the trappings of lifestyle, all the external expressions of luxury, conceal an immaterial respect for someone else's way of life and sense of values.

Then why is respect accorded to certain models rather than to others? Tarde answers this question in his second extra-logical law of imitation, which states that imitation proceeds from superior to inferior. Tarde cannot conceive of a truly egalitarian society without a superior elite. His theory of imitation presupposes a social hierarchy:

> It is fated, since the relationship of model to copier is consequently a relationship of apostle to neophyte, or master to subject. Thus, by the very fact that imitation proceeds from the inside to the outside of the model, it must consist of a *descent* of the example from the superior to the inferior.[37]

However, Tarde's definition of superiority is highly untraditional. The distinguishing mark of the elite is not noble birth, not even wealth, but its ability to generate models which are widely imitated. The underlying source of social prestige in any society is creation and control of crucial inventions—economic, military, cultural, or moral. The character of the elite depends on which inventions are most significant in the society.

This definition of superiority is flexible enough to apply to ancient, to feudal, and to modern societies. Tarde hypothesizes that in the nineteenth century, businessmen formed an elite because they controlled industrial inventions. If the twentieth century is truly that of the consumer, as Gide predicted, then Tarde's definition of social superiority could apply to those who control consumer inventions—"trend-setters" and publicists, for example.

Tarde's concept can even be extended from social entities to geographic ones. In comparison to the country the city is an elite, and the same is true for the relation of provincial centers to the capital. The flood of modern industrial production and consumption, "that is, imitation on an immense scale," presupposes the dominance of certain great cities:

> The course of the Ganges requires the Himalayas. The Himalayas of France is Paris. Paris reigns royally, orientally, over the provinces. . . . Every day, by telegraph or train, it sends into all of France its ideas, its wishes, its conversations, its ready-made revolutions, its ready-made clothing and furniture. This suggestive, imperious fascination that it exercises instantaneously over a vast territory is so profound, so complete, and so continuous that hardly anyone notices it. This hypnotism has become chronic.[38]

Not only cities but whole nations may assume an impersonal but redoubtable elitist status. Although the development of new means of transportation like steamships and railroads may weaken the dominance of traditional hereditary castes within a nation, it gives the nation as a whole the privileges of nobility—to travel widely, to spread its language and products, to indulge in proud self-admiration and ambitious projects.

This national superiority will not last long, however, because of a corollary to the law of imitation from superior to inferior: over time, the nature of the imitation shifts from the unilateral to the reciprocal. As soon as an elite begins to serve as a model, the distance between it and its inferiors begins to diminish:

The march of imitation from top to bottom still goes on, but the inequality which it implies has changed in character. Instead of an aristocratic, intrinsically organic inequality, we have a democratic inequality, of an entirely social origin, which we may call inequality if we wish, but which is really a reciprocity of invariably impersonal prestiges, alternating from individual to individual and from profession to profession. In this way the field of imitation has constantly been growing and freeing itself from heredity.[39]

Although the theory of imitation cannot admit an unstratified society, Tarde can conceive of one in which the various strata have been broken up into small blocs and jumbled together. This is the case in modern times:

There is no longer any man who is imitated in every respect; and he who is imitated the most is himself an imitator with respect to some of his copyists. As a result, imitation is mutualized and specialized in becoming more general.[40]

Since society is composed of beings who imitate each other, the increasing reciprocity of imitation is equivalent to the enlargement of society. Its "magic circle"[41] is being opened to include workers, peasants, women, minors, and other groups formerly excluded. For Tarde, this unseen and mental imitation which lessens psychological distance between superior and inferior constitutes a form of democratization far more genuine than the visible democratization of consumer goods. It is the democratization of the time and inclination to participate in exchange of souls. It is the democratization of the process whereby people come to resemble each other spiritually because they copy each other's inner needs and desires.

The very prevalence of envy in contemporary society indicates to Tarde how rapidly and widely its "magic circle" is expanding. When relations between superior and inferior are rigid and unilateral, the inferior may obey and admire but never thinks of imitating the superior directly, because he has no resources to attempt a copy.

Envy becomes mixed with admiration only when there is the possibility of imitation. Thanks to recent technological progress, the ability to copy has become much more widespread. The reduction of objective inequality has transformed obedience into envy:

> Envy is the symptom of a social transformation which, in bringing together the classes, in diminishing the inequality of their resources, has made possible not only as in the past the transmission of designs and thoughts from the one to the other, their patriotic and religious communion, their participation in the same cult, but also the radiation of luxury and of well-being from one to the other.[42]

Therefore, the opening up of the social circle initially has the effect of increasing social unrest. Workers envy their employers, and peasants new to the city envy the workers. The results are industrial unrest and urban crime caused by those whose desire to consume exceeds their ability to earn. But the demands of the envious will lead to more equality, for envy will achieve its work of assimilation and gradually disappear. Then "a need for individual divergence, for *de-assimilation,*" will emerge, and society will achieve a state in which superiority is ever more often "parceled out" in small pieces rather than stratified in large layers.

The third extra-logical law, which grows out of the second one, describes in more general terms the type of superiority acknowledged by a society—either that of the native and past (the rule of tradition or custom), or that of the foreign and contemporary (the rule of style or fashion). In a society subject to custom, people take pride in their national traditions, which they imitate faithfully, making few innovations. Custom admits of considerable diversity in space but not in time. Consumer goods in a traditional society may vary greatly in different localities, but everywhere they are made to last a long while. A society that accords prestige to fashion, on the contrary, is fertile in invention. The consumer of style is motivated less by group pride than by personal vanity. He favors disposable items since fashion changes quickly over time, but those items tend to be similar everywhere. Far from being parochial, style welcomes foreign models and the process of imitation accordingly reduces geographical diversity.

The ideal type of style brings coherence and comprehensibility to the material characteristics of mass consumption so often decried—lack of durability, foolish and deceptive exoticism, vain self-display, uniformity. Tarde relates all these appearances to the category of style and so finds order in what others often view only as chaos and frivolity. In particular this category clarifies the aims of decorative arts reformers. In Tarde's terms, they were protesting the fashion-imitation that dominates the modern economy and were attempting to revive an art of custom based on craft, country, and profession. The failure of the decorative arts movement to maintain its integrity only confirms the dominance of style in modern times. To reduce that dominance would require massive changes in production as well as in consumption. The artisanal production typical of an age of custom turns out a small number of durable products for local distribution; mass production requires a market based on fashion-imitation, which is to say, on widespread, transient consumption ruled by quantity rather than quality. When a society industrializes, custom-imitation is gradually replaced by fashion-imitation. Attempts, like that of the decorative arts reformers, to resist this transition, are bound to be futile.

On the other hand, Tarde asserts, style will not reign forever in Europe. There are three stages in a complete cycle in any society: a period of custom, one of fashion, and finally a return to custom. In the middle phase, styles compete to become established as part of tradition. Some of them succeed, and so when an age of custom returns, it is an enlarged and enriched custom. Although the reign of fashion can lead to grotesque excesses, it does liberate society from the weight of imitation and it does combat entrenched tradition with reason. But custom is also needed to keep society from a breathless and frantic pursuit of novelty. Neither element is good or bad in itself: it is their alternation that is beneficial. In the cycling of tradition and fashion, only the trend toward geographic uniformity is irreversible. Once spatial unity has been established, the return to spatial fragmentation is inconceivable,

> but we can well conceive . . . that after a period of capricious changes, or rather of hasty experiments, usages might become fixed. Steadfastness in the case of habits is far from contradicting in any respect their universality; the first completes the second.[43]

Economic Psychology – Tarde's logical and extra-logical laws of imitation are explained in his best-known book, *Les Lois de l'imitation* ["The Laws of Imitation"], published in 1890. In the late 1890's Tarde proposed two more social laws, universal opposition and universal adaptation, which complement and complete the earlier theory of universal imitation,[44] and in his next major work, the two-volume *La Psychologie économique* ("Economic Psychology," 1902), he applies these three general laws of imitation, opposition, and adaptation to economic life. This work is Tarde's most extended and explicit treatment of consumption.

Tarde's interest in economics was long-standing. Before the appearance of *Economic Psychology* he had published numerous articles, including his earliest, on economic topics.[45] Here was an area of human behavior where factors of social psychology were of paramount importance but had been ignored entirely or flattened into a ridiculously inadequate model of *homo œconomicus*. Tarde scorned the psychological assumptions of the classical economists. Their abstract economic man was doubly erroneous because it divested individuals not only of spontaneous and sociable emotions but also of associations with any group, corporation, sect, party, or country. "This last simplification is no less mutilating than the other, from which it derives."[46] Classical economists treat goods rather than producers or consumers, abstract riches rather than consciousness. Their cold calculations do not begin to explain the passionate and tumultuous nature of economic behavior. In short, political economy must adopt the viewpoint of interpsychology.

Tarde's contribution to economic thought is part of the late-nineteenth-century intellectual renovation in the field which brought psychic factors to the forefront of inquiry. His speculations, however, are largely independent of the more specialized work of better-known English- and German-speaking economists. What little he knows of their theories (such as the theory of marginal utility) he seems to have picked up from reading Charles Gide's *Principles of Political Economy*, which he praises for its appreciation of the significance of beliefs, ideas, and judgments in economic life. In order to place psychological factors at the center of economics, Tarde rejects the categories of production, distribution, consumption, and circulation found in most contemporary treatises. Instead, he adopts as major headings repetition, opposition, and adaptation. As repetitious elements of economic life he discusses, among other topics, desires and beliefs and their combination in the form of needs. His examination of economic opposition is dominated by a psychological theory of value; his examination of adaptation, by a theory of the harmonizing roles of technological, social, and moral inventions. In *Economic Psychology* the implications of the consumer revolution are handled in a way that reveals all the advantages of Tarde's original and far-ranging mind.

Repetition: Desires, Beliefs, and Needs – Tarde defines consumption as the "reproduction of desires of which certain riches are the object, and judgment as to how those riches will satisfy the desires."[47] To reduce consumption to its simplest terms is thus to reduce it to desire and belief (or judgment). These psychological elements, not material goods, are the primary data of economic inquiry.

Tarde first considers desire. He asks the question that everyone else was raising as a consequence of the consumer revolution: is desire limited, or infinite? Is there any end to wants? Typically, Tarde's response is, "yes and no." He uses geometry to distinguish two major kinds of desires. Periodic desires, which involve organic needs (e.g., desire to eat, to drink, to sleep) form a closed circle. Capricious desires, which arise from more social needs (e.g., the desire to travel, to listen to music, to adorn oneself) form an open-ended parabola. The desires of an individual or of a society may be visualized as the juxtaposition of a circle of periodic desires and a parabola of capricious ones. Left alone, this system of desires tends toward stability. A closed curve tends to stay closed, and even capricious fantasies tend "to enter the round of linked desires, to become fixed there as habit." This self-stabilization indicates that "the human heart is not infinitely elastic, and, beyond a certain number of desires, it comes up against its insurmountable limit."[48]

But the external shock of exposure to a more complex civilization—as when a peasant arrives in the city, or when Europeans establish a colonial settlement—can break open a stable system of desires. Sometimes, once the initial trauma is past, the shock proves beneficial because it has enlarged the system of desires to make a society more civilized. But if a society submits too readily or too quickly to the foreign influence, its old circle of desires may be rent so severely that it cannot be mended. This result destroys personal and social happiness, which is found not in an open-ended succession of desires but in "a rotation . . . of linked desires, periodically renewed and newly satisfied to be renewed again, and so on indefinitely."[49]

This is, in short, Tarde's version of anomie. But unlike Durkheim, Tarde is optimistic that in the long run economic desires will prove self-regulating. In the first place,

the very multiplication of desires ensures their moderation: civilization is a state of numerous but temperate
desires. The ones most capable of expansion in scope are
the least urgent. Desire to eat may be imperious but is
restricted in scope, whereas the less intense desires of
ambition, curiosity, or vanity are so elastic as to seem
virtually unlimited. Furthermore, Tarde distinguishes
positive desires for something from negative desires to
avoid something, and he predicts that the appeal of positive desires will diminish as people learn that they are
self-defeating:

> [In every positive desire] there comes a moment of sudden
> deception where, to their great surprise, as if they had
> returned to earth in some way, or awakened with a start,
> or run aground in their illusory and fantastic port, those
> who not long ago desired look for their desire and no
> longer find it; and this is precisely the moment when they
> expected that it was going to be satisfied at last. . . . The
> profound trap of nature is that the end point where desire
> hopes to find its abatement is or appears to be a pleasure, a
> joy, and that this is impossible, since its abatement implies
> its disappearance or its decrease, while pleasure supposes
> its increase.[50]

After becoming aware of this "trap" through repeated
disappointments, people will turn away from most positive desires in favor of negative ones. The latter are more
rational because their goal, the end of suffering, can in fact
be attained. Art, science, and love, the "three great anes-
thetics of suffering, will flourish."[51]

Finally, Tarde distinguishes passive desires from active ones and predicts that the former, which involve
consumption, will decline relative to the active ones,
which involve production. Tarde does not mean that
people will work more. For him production is by no means
equivalent to labor, which is merely repetition, imitation,
re-production. Only invention is genuinely productive.
The paradox is that invention arises from the liberty of
mind found in leisure, not from the mental constraints

imposed by subjection to an occupation. The desire to produce social and artistic inventions will expand, while inventions responding to organic needs will decline: "spiritual desires offer themselves to us as the great, the immense outlet for human activity in the future, and progress tends to the superiority of their development over those of physical desires." The luxury of the future will not be directed toward bodily comfort or vanity but toward the "interior luxury" of art.[52] By dissociating labor from production and consumption from leisure, Tarde tears apart familiar mental associations to suggest new ones. Production becomes identified not with labor but with creative leisure; consumption is seen as similar to labor because it requires time-consuming, repetitious behavior on the level of life maintenance. Tarde therefore prophesies the decline of *both* labor and consumption satisfying physical desires in order to satisfy more social and artistic desires.

But Tarde does not think that consumers are motivated only by desires, of whatever variety. In the consumer's mind desire and belief are inextricably joined, and in the final analysis belief dominates. Desire for any item becomes a resolution to buy only when the consumer is persuaded that the object will satisfy his desire. In particular, the decision to buy comes down to a sense of confidence, which is to say, of belief or faith, in the utility of the product. There is no objective utility, only a believed utility (*utilité crue*). The consumer is less a creature of desire than one of faith.

This is why advertising plays such a critical role in the modern marketplace. It acts less on desire than on belief; its goal is to elicit both attention and confidence. Advertising backs up its claim to confidence by appealing to the authority of prestigious examples. "It is the example of others which engenders the required degree of confidence in the utility of the thing desired and consequently transforms this desire into will to buy."[53]

As important as advertising may be (and Tarde urges

intensive study of the history of advertising in order to better appreciate its role in economic development) a second stage is required to propagate economic belief. This is conversation. "By conversation I mean any dialogue without direct and immediate utility, where people talk just to talk, out of pleasure, or sport, or politeness." If people did not chat about what they read or heard, advertising would be pointless. Through conversation, diverse desires and beliefs are channeled into a consensus, and without that mental similarity there could be no large industry, because its existence presupposes similar demand over a large region. "Thus the babble of individuals in leisure time, transformed into the consensus of opinion, is the regulator of usages and needs, of tastes, of customs, and, consequently, of industry." Tarde proposes a history of conversation to complement that of advertising. He also suggests studying contemporary talk in all sorts of social groupings—not only in salons, where the habitués pride themselves on their ability to converse in a witty manner, but also in clubs and cafés, which Tarde feels have in fact done more for the art of modern conversation. In any case, as civilization increases, the difference between the talk of the salon and that of the club lessens.[54]

So it is through the interaction of desires and beliefs— the latter propagated by advertising and conversation— that economic needs arise. "We need an article when we *desire* exemption from a certain evil or the acquisition of a certain good and when we *believe* this article to be appropriate to attaining that goal."[55] There is no valid way to distinguish between social and organic needs. Even the most refined needs are founded upon organic demands, and even the most basic needs are expressed according to the specializing refinements of social life. Needs are inevitably "stamped by society." The need to eat, for example, is always expressed in a precise form such as the need to eat rice, or potatoes, or bread. Just as the gradation between organic and social needs is insensible, so is that between luxuries and necessities, or, to use the terminology of classical economists, that between unproductive and productive forms of consumption. Unproductive luxuries make up the whole charm of life, argues Tarde. They are responsible for "all the grandiose or minuscule innovations which have enriched and civilized the world." So-called productive consumptions, on the other hand, did not begin that way: "there is not an object of first necessity, dress, shoes, hat, which did not begin by being a luxury item."[56]

In this way Tarde shrugs off the whole debate about the morality of luxury as pointless and turns instead to an analysis of the geometry of needs, particularly their tendency to become cyclical. Needs which used to be exceptional—the need to smoke, to travel, to buy new furniture or new clothes—have gradually become periodic. Tarde praises Le Play for his work in compiling family budgets and comments that these data demonstrate evolution toward greater regularity of needs. By contrasting ancient budgets with modern ones, it can be seen that expenditures, which is to say, needs, that used to be accidental have become periodic. As more and more formerly extraordinary expenses become cyclical, budgets irresistibly grow larger. This inflation seems so inevitable that if retrenchment is necessary, it appears as an anomaly, while "the peaceable and regular enlargement that had preceded it passes for a healthy and normal development."[57] But while budgets increase over time, each annual one retains its absolute limits. A new need cannot be added without pushing out an old one which struggles to maintain its accustomed place. Budgets are a battleground of contending needs. This observation brings us to the second major division of *Economic Psychology*, which deals with the conflict of values in the mind of the consumer.

Opposition: Value—At the time Tarde wrote, economic thought was dominated by two major theories of value. The Marxist theory held that value was determined by the amount of labor inherent in a product, while classical political economists contended that value was determined by the law of supply and demand. Tarde rejects both theories for the same reason: they propose a supposedly objective standard, when value is actually a subjective judgment. He criticizes the Marxists for claiming they could measure the amount of labor inherent in a product, when labor is not a quantity but a psychological condition definable only in terms of sorrow, boredom, and pain. Tarde is even more intent on unmasking the supposed objectivity of the law of supply and demand. To do so, he imagines a simplified market comprised of a monopolistic seller who is, theoretically, free to fix his price at any level, and buyers with identical desires, beliefs, and incomes, all of which are known precisely by the seller. What does the seller consider in fixing his price? Not *how many* potential consumers there are, but *how much* they want the product. No matter how completely the seller controls the market, he is himself controlled by consumer psychology. The price he sets reflects not a pseudo-objective relationship between number of products and number of consumers, but a psychological relationship between intensity of desire and level of income of the individual buyer.

In the real marketplace, assessment of consumer psychology involves more guesswork. The incomes, desires, and beliefs of buyers differ and are not known precisely by the seller, who must nonetheless set one price for everyone. But the same principle applies: the seller must assess both the hearts and purses of potential buyers, and this is more a matter of intuition and estimation than of mathematical formulae. Thus the origin of value lies in the individual consumer. He invests an object with a particular value as he balances his desires and beliefs against his income. Price, the exterior expression of value, represents the "dénouement" of a "great number of . . . interior combats, of mute and hidden crises" within the consumer's mind.[58] If he has a large income, he does not struggle much in deciding whether to buy, for most expenditures are relatively small compared to his resources. Nor is there much inner conflict if desire is so overwhelming that the consumer is determined to possess an item one way or another.

The real struggles arise in the middle ground, when desire is less urgent and resources less abundant. Then the consumer has to go through a sort of syllogism, weighing what else the money could be spent for or what would have to be sacrificed to possess the item. "The theory of prices is the theory of value understood as a struggle of desires and sacrifice of the lesser desire to the stronger."[59] At the basis of any decision to buy is the following logical affirmation: enunciation of a desire (major statement of the syllogism); confidence in the means which are judged appropriate to realizing the desire (minor statement); and desire to become master of the means (conclusion). The reasoning may be instinctive and unconscious, but it is still the foundation of value decisions. Since value rests on a comparison of mental states in which preference is given to one state over another, it rests on an act of the spirit, of the imagination. Value is a quality like color that we attribute to things but which in truth resides in our own mental activity. It is "a projection of ourselves onto things."[60]

Because people project value in so many different ways, there can be no simple, uniform standard of value. One distinction which must be made is between cost-value, equivalent to price, and use-value, a moral standard unrelated to price. "The more the habits of an individual are regulated and oriented toward a superior end, the more any object whatsoever consumed by him is *worth*, in the sense of use-value, no matter how minuscule its cost-value."[61] Within the general category of use-value there are subdivisions such as value-utility, value-truth, and value-beauty. Value-utility refers to the wealth of a society measured by what have traditionally been regarded as economic goods. Until now economic thinkers have studied mainly value-utility, because this type is the most amenable to quantitative analysis. However, the other two types also deserve consideration by economists because

> there is no agricultural or industrial or any other wealth . . . which cannot be considered from the viewpoint of the *knowledge* it implies, or the *powers* it confers, or the *rights* of which it is the fruit, or of its more or less *aesthetic* or unaesthetic character. . . . The theoretical and aesthetic aspect of all goods is going to become more and more important, not at the expense of, but above and beyond, their utilitarian aspect.[62]

The economics of the future must encompass all types of value to attain a theory of maximum or optimum value. The task is extremely complex because the values that must be coordinated and ordered are heterogeneous, although not incommensurate. Economists must discover how to fit together dissimilar desires in a harmonious hierarchy:

> What [economics] seeks, more laboriously than fruitfully, it must be admitted, is a theory of value that explains the hierarchy of riches in any social state, their height or their depth along the immense scale of human Desire, of human Judgment, and which, by elucidating the causes of their ascent or descent, allows in some measure the modification of their relative values.[63]

The great task of economic thought is therefore a *moral* task, the creation of spiritual harmony so that individuals and societies can live in peace with themselves.

Adaptation: Harmonizing Desires and Beliefs – Tarde is convinced that economic harmony is not achieved through the "invisible hand" of a free marketplace, but through conscious human invention. An age poor in imagination is fertile in conflicts, while an inventive age creates the compromises and solutions necessary to maintain order and peace.

Some harmonizing inventions are material ones. The

introduction of new technologies can reduce conflicts of desire within individuals by cheapening the price of a product (which is equivalent to introducing a new product for certain groups) so that more desires can be satisfied at once. By making it easier to satisfy urgent needs, industrial invention makes them more reconcilable with less urgent, more artistic, "that is to say, social and truly human needs."[64] A similar redirection is achieved when technological progress increases leisure time.

But there are also social, non-material inventions that harmonize, above all the invention of new forms of association: "by association, by federation, contraries become complementary, . . . coadapted to a common end, like the wheels of a single machine."[65] The most fundamental association is the family, which consequently deserves primary attention as a harmonizing agent. Other types of association can also function as harmonizing social inventions. For example, publicity agencies satisfy society's need for information as well as its curiosity, while warning producers and consumers of imminent changes in each other and thereby making possible the adaptation of products to needs.

Tarde is less enthusiastic about the invention of societies to build inexpensive housing for workers. A worker might want to own a home to improve his family life, but this desire cannot be reconciled with his need to move frequently in order to find work. Nor does Tarde see much of a future for production cooperatives. He considers them ill-adapted to mass-production techniques, and he feels they would require more rigorous discipline than an egalitarian age readily permits.

In Tarde's opinion, consumer cooperatives are a more vital and attractive form of association. They could help to settle internal conflicts in the consumer by allowing him more money to spend; instead of having to choose between two complementary needs, he could satisfy both. But—and here Tarde is at once less optimistic and more perceptive than Gide—sometimes a consumer is torn between two contradictory needs, and then a consumer cooperative cannot help to resolve the struggle. No matter how many industrial and social inventions are created, at some point the consumer also requires "moral invention" to help him retain inner harmony. Traditionally, moral invention has been carried out by religious or philosophical sects that propagate a strong faith which in turn forms the basis of a durable morality:

> *Churches*, religious or quasi-religious, confessions of all kind, including certain philosophical schools, Stoic ones for example, should be inscribed at the head of the great procedures of economic adaptation. By their general regulation and hierarchization of desires under the yoke of dogmas, . . . they prevent all possible troubles of consumption, they resolve the question of luxury, and, by imposing predetermined boundaries and forms for production, they oblige the latter to adjust to the former.[66]

Most contemporary economic oppositions could be resolved by a new type of "grand and sovereign free association" for moral regulation, or even by a "number of parallel associations, philosophical churches, peaceable rivals."

The creation of institutions to inculcate morality is not enough, however. They must rest on "a certain number of demonstrable and unshakable truths." Moral invention must include the creation of ideas or, rather, of an ideal. There is no use trying to revive institutions like medieval corporations, cautions Tarde. We lack the common ideal—faith in eternal salvation—which made them effective in fostering earthly solidarity. Modern institutions too will be ineffective unless they are "newly agreed, spontaneously, in a common faith on certain capital points." The modern moral problem is intimately linked to the modern intellectual problem, namely, the relation between science and faith:

> An accord of strong and logical convictions through science, become incontestable in certain regards, and not an equilibrium of opinions made feeble and tolerant through

skepticism; an accord of strong and concurrent passions directed toward a common ideal through lofty social morality, and not an equilibrium of petty needs and petty exchanges through industrialism: this is the aspiration of human evolution.[67]

In order to achieve this aspiration, to articulate such a common ideal, Tarde proposes a new science of "social teleology." This discipline would study the currents of desire in society and their combinations in order to reinforce harmony among them. Economic thought would not be alone in contributing to this science. Morality, law, and politics also are concerned with the whole scale of human values. Along with social logic, social teleology would be the basis of a future general sociology. The basic concept of social teleology must be the distinction between the controlling desire of a society and the industrial means that serve it. In human history industrial means have accumulated while the ends they serve—that is, the controlling desire of the society—have succeeded each other only through elimination of their predecessor. For example, the primitive cart survives in the spring-mounted carriage, and the carriage has been absorbed into the locomotive: these are industrial means which can coexist.

> On the other hand, the Christian's desire for mystical salvation did not absorb, but actually routed, the Roman's desire for civic glory, just as the Copernican theory banished the Ptolemaic system. Industry in this sense is the *matter* of which the *form* is furnished by the reigning concepts of justice and beauty, ideas as to the best direction for conduct.[68]

If unformed by a controlling desire—for spiritual salvation, civic glory, propitiating the gods, or equalizing society—the forces of industry present not a "spectacle of internal harmony" but only chaos.[69]

What is true for society is also true for individuals. Each person finds inner harmony only through a controlling desire

> or, rather, . . . a previous resolution which persists in
> us. . . . This is what is called mental stability in the case of
> individuals, social stability in the case of nations. All social
> or mental stability therefore supposes . . . an ideal . . .
> that morality defends and preserves.[70]

Because personal harmony is the precondition of social
peace, the modern dilemma, at once personal and collective, is once more to relate industrial means to a controlling end. The modern age needs to create form out of
an abundance of matter. At the present it prefers to
accumulate means rather than to make the choices and
sacrifices necessary to order and arrange them:

> It is much easier to pile up neologism on neologism than to
> speak one's language more correctly and thus to introduce
> by degrees grammatical improvements; to collect observa-
> tions and experiments in the sciences than to supply them
> with more general and demonstrable theories; . . . to mul-
> tiply needs, thanks to the ever richer variety of consumer
> goods supplied by the most diversified industries, than to
> substitute for one's dominant need a superior and prefera-
> ble need, one more conducive to the reign of order and
> peace. . . .
> But our modern Europe is somewhat carried away by
> the attraction of deceptive ease. Therefore the striking
> contrast . . . between its industrial exuberance and its aes-
> thetic poverty. . . . Industry has aroused on all sides artifi-
> cial needs that it satisfies pell-mell without taking the
> trouble of selection among them and of their better
> accord. . . . It is necessary . . . for contemporary civiliza-
> tion to liquidate this chaos of heterogeneous needs. . . .
> All these discordant or poorly harmonized needs, which
> flourish at all points on the industrial soil, and their pas-
> sionate worshippers constitute a sort of moral fetishism or
> polytheism which aspires to spread out into a comprehen-
> sive and authoritative moral monotheism, in a new, gener-
> ous, and powerful aesthetic.[71]

To emphasize the tragic dichotomy between grand means
and banal ends which is characteristic of modern industry,

Tarde notes the trouble he had finding a monument characteristic of modern society:

> It is a strange and rarely noticed thing that what industry builds most grandiosely at the present are not products but industrial tools, namely, great factories, immense railroad stations, prodigious machines . . . how shabby are these works of our industry next to their lodgings! How especially do the petty splendors of our private and public luxury pale next to our industrial expositions, where the only utility of products is to display themselves![72]

Tarde does not venture to predict what the controlling desire of the future will be. That outcome rests in the mysterious world of possibilities: "What are the simple and fecund needs that the future will develop, and which are the overgrown and sterile needs that it will prune away? That is the secret. It is difficult to find, but it must be sought."[73] Religion and patriotism, the two ideals which have long dominated society, are quickly fading. Perhaps they may be replaced by love, or ambition, or a cult of pleasure, or a taste for glory. But if some grand ideal does not arrive soon, mankind will have no ideal at all; it will be reduced to a decadent state of unrelated hopes and desires, with nothing to love above life itself. At the moment, instead of seeking a controlling ideal to provide a resolution for economic oppositions, producers are finding a temporary solution in pursuing new markets and stimulating new needs. But they are thereby chasing "an ever-receding mirage of social peace," for production and consumption cannot keep expanding indefinitely. There are limits to growth:

> Is it necessary to recall that the earth is not infinite, and that our civilization is close to having invaded it all?
>
> The *end of the world*, this great terror of the Middle Ages, is destined to become a source of anguish again in another sense. It is no longer in time but in space that this terrestrial globe reveals itself as inextensible; and the deluge of civilized humanity already hurls itself at its limits, at its new Pillars of Hercules, these ones insurmountable.

What are we going to do when soon we will no longer be able to count on external markets, Asian, African, to serve as a palliative or derivative for our discords, as outlets for our merchandise, for our instincts of cruelty, of pillage and of prey, for our criminality as well as for our overflowing birthrate? How will we manage to reestablish among ourselves a relative peace which has had as its condition for so long our conquering projection outside ourselves, far from ourselves?[74]

Tarde responds to his own query: we will manage because society is just entering upon a new phase of adaptation. Having reached its physical limits, the world will turn in on itself, so to speak, to explore its social frontiers and to find harmony in the unprecedented solidarity of the human race.

The Sociability of the Future—Although Tarde uses the term *solidarity*, he prefers to speak of *sociability*. He does not want to confuse his concept with solidarity as a quasi-legal theory or, worse yet, as a biological theory such as Durkheim embraced. To reduce human relations to organic laws, to the utilitarian exchange of services, is in Tarde's opinion an obstacle to genuine sociability based on the free exchange of souls. Tarde is no admirer of the beauty of necessity, and therefore he is no admirer of a solidarity based on association in labor. Unlike Durkheim, who foresees the role of labor as becoming ever more important in the moral life of society, Tarde expects and hopes that the role of labor will diminish radically. "Social evolution begins and ends in games and *fêtes*," he remarks. "Labor is a phase that has to be crossed between the lazy insouciance of primitives and the lively gaiety of future civilized humanity."[75] Our occupations isolate us rather than developing our common humanity. Furthermore, labor often involves a relationship between man and machine which never has the closeness of a relationship between man and man or even between man and nature. Not labor but leisure creates human solidarity.

Leisure allows "spiritual contacts and exchanges, the pleasure of self-instruction and of affecting each other reciprocally, the intensive culture of a sociability at once refined and healthy."[76] Not production but consumption unifies mankind:

> The assimilation of individuals by imitative contagion and their differentiation by cooperation in labor—their assimilation as consumers of books, journals, clothing, food, even of pleasures and of any satisfactions whatsoever, and their differentiation as producers—all these progress in parallel and not at the expense of each other.[77]

But it is as consumers of ideas, which satisfy spiritual desires, not as consumers of material goods, which satisfy physical desires, that humanity will achieve genuine sociability. In fact, "the useless complications of material existence" only divide people, whereas spiritual desires "bring us together [and] make us touch each other at our highest points, like the trees of the forests."[78] For example, the material effect of the railroad is only to increase the disparity among nations and to arouse new antagonisms among them; its moral effect, on the contrary, is to unify them by facilitating the exchange of people and ideas. Eventually the moral unity will predominate over the disunity arising from conflicting material desires. "And then everyone will truly know *la joie de vivre*, when the civilized world will be nothing but . . . an immense salon, a lucid and liberal salon of the eighteenth century open to everyone."[79]

Tarde does not fear that the increasing uniformity of future society will result in undifferentiated "mass society." There will continue to be social groups, but instead of being based on ties of religious or political interest or economic utility, they will be bound together by the disinterested, non-utilitarian, wholly psychological tie of a shared state of mind. Tarde calls this social group of the future a "public." A public is best thought of as a "purely spiritual collectivity, of which the cohesion is entirely mental." Its members are united because they share a controlling desire or faith and because they are aware of their mental unity. Formerly such cohesion was possible only among crowds gathered in the same place at the same time. Now progress in communications technologies (especially the railroad, the telegraph, and the printing press) means that the cohesion of the public, "this spiritualized crowd," is more and more replacing the "grosser and more elementary social life" that depends on physical proximity.[80]

Once again Tarde provides a vocabulary appropriate to the modern consumer mentality. In this case he finds a term to describe the cohesion of those who share a lifestyle, a cohesion not expressed by the more familiar categories of political party, religious sect, or economic class. Tarde himself comments that the mental unity of a dispersed and enormous public is the same as that which unites a commercial clientele. When consumers buy the same products or patronize the same stores or restaurants, they develop a unifying sympathy. "Each of us in buying what responds to his needs is more or less vaguely aware of expressing and developing thereby his union with the social class which eats, dresses, and satisfies itself in a nearly analogous manner. But," Tarde adds, "how much more intimate and deep is the tie that is found among habitual readers of the same newspaper!" There is an element of competition among consumers of similar material goods, but among consumers of similar ideas, "no one would dream of speaking of competition, for there is only a communion of suggested ideas and the consciousness of this communion."[81]

The communion of ideas among a public does more than encourage sociability; it also forms the basis for a new social morality grounded in deference to public opinion. As the soul is to the body, so is public opinion to a public. Public opinion is "a momentary, more or less logical cluster of judgments which, responding to current problems, is reproduced many times over in people of the same country, at the same time, in the same society."[82] Through reading and conversation, a person becomes aware that his judgment resembles that of others, and so individual opinion is transformed into the collective variety. Tarde's concept of public opinion is similar to Durkheim's *conscience collective*. Indeed, Tarde sometimes uses Durkheim's term as a synonym for public opinion. But Durkheim assumes that the *conscience collective* is dying out; that is why it will no longer serve as a basis for morality and will have to be replaced by a "morality of the tool" based on the organic solidarity arising from the division of labor. Tarde, on the contrary, is convinced that in the form of public opinion a new type of *conscience collective* is just being born, and this new type can serve as a future morality. That *morale* will appeal to the sense of honor, "this unconscious and profound respect for opinion which is betrayed in the acts of the most solitary thinkers, despite their illusions about themselves. Now, what is honor except heroic, unreflective, and passive obedience to opinion?" In a very sociable environment the attention of the individual is "exteriorized" so that he is preoccupied with others, and this preoccupation can be a moral force. Even vanity can be seen as

> a sort of superficial honor. . . . [T]he first step toward honor . . . the need to be regarded, to appear, leads to the need to be considered. Consequently, do not mock too bitterly the contagion of vulgar luxury and of vain display, which can bear good fruit.

The new moral authority is the dispersed, collective one of public opinion, and its precondition is "a very intense conformism."[83] Tarde envisions a moral code of conformity among consuming publics rather than a morality of the tool among producing corporations.

According to the laws of imitation, every public will tend to enlarge geometrically and indefinitely. As this happens, the power of public opinion will become more imposing. Its unifying action will accelerate as communications technology becomes ever more efficient. When all humanity is in contact with the same ideas, the same examples will be admired by all. The old groupings that divided mankind will be replaced "by an incomplete and variable segmentation, to indistinct limits, in a path of perpetual renovation and mutual penetration."[84] Along with geographic uniformity will come uniformity in time. The present reign of fashion will give way to the final triumph of custom. Inventiveness will decline because the very social conditions that favor rapid imitation—a busy, dispersed, urban life—are contrary to those which favor innovation—an austere, traditionalist, half-solitary, yet inspiring life among family and countryside. The world is headed for a "reassuring fixity of ideals" in time, along with a "peace-bringing uniformity" in space:[85]

> The progress of civilization is unquestionably manifest in the gradual leveling that it establishes over a territory always more vast, so that someday, perhaps, the same social type, stable and definitive, will cover the entire surface of the globe. . . . But this work of universal uniformization, in which we are taking part, does it reveal in the end a common orientation of diverse societies toward the same pole?—Not at all, for it has as its manifest cause the submersion of the majority of original civilizations under the deluge of one of them, whose rising flood advances in ever larger waves of imitation.[86]

This is the solidarity of universal entropy. The fate of society is not the increasingly complex organization of a living body, but the increasing disorganization of inanimate matter. The hetereogeneous becomes more homogeneous, open curves tend to close, flights of innovation are pulled downward by inertia, energy dissipates, everything simplifies and levels out.

Yet this universal leveling will leave ample room for individualism. As the civilizing action of imitation keeps expanding, each person will have more examples to choose from, and more associations will interlace in a way "particular for him and which will be incarnated in him alone."[87] Universal similarity in dress, law, knowledge, and perhaps even in language may have as its "unique raison d'être" the birth of individual divergences "more true, more intimate, more radical, and more delicate" than all the deceptive distinctions of the past. In the coming era when both personality and sociability will at last be liberated,

> then will unfold the highest flower of social life, the aesthetic life, . . . and social life . . . will finally appear as what it is, as the consequence and complement of organic life; . . . from an infinity of ground-up elements . . . will be extracted this essential principle which is so volatile, the profound and fleeting singularity of people, their manner of being, of thinking, of feeling, which happens only once and only for an instant.[88]

A Fragment of Future History – This is the portrait of the future that emerges from Tarde's major treatises published from 1890 until his death fourteen years later. Before any of them were composed, however, he had written in 1884 an extraordinary short novel, the utopian *Fragment d'histoire future* ("Fragment of Future History"), which was published only in 1896. The French word *histoire* can signify either "history," in the sense of a factual record of the past, or "story," implying an imaginative, even fantastic, tale. Not just this short novel but all of Tarde's works may be regarded as "fragments of future history," poised on an uncertain boundary between tale and history, present and future, reality and possibility. There is a gradual transition, not a sharp break, between the poetic prophecies in his treatises (some of which are quoted above) and the openly fantastic *Fragment*, which nonetheless has a deeply serious purpose in portraying the unfolding of "the highest flower of social life, the aesthetic life." For Tarde, literature is not an alternative to social science, but its complement and completion.[89]

The scene opens five centuries hence. It is an era of

peace following the establishment of a great Asiatic-American-European confederation. Customs, ideas, and even language (Greek) are uniform throughout the world. With only three hours of work a day, everyone enjoys a life of leisure and satisfies his desires for wealth and love. This is a peaceful, stomach-centered society whose noblest monument is the iron statue of a bourgeois king set in the middle of a cabbage garden (we recognize Louis-Philippe).

Just when the universe begins to breath easily—or to yawn a little—the sun begins to go out. As unprecedented cold settles over the earth, long-dormant glaciers revive, expand gigantically, and advance down the Alps like

> a moving cliff made of rocks and overturned locomotives, debris of bridges, railroad stations, hotels, monuments carted along pell-mell, monstrous and heart-breaking bric-à-brac whose triumphant invasion is adorned as if with booty.

The material inventions of civilization are pushed into an incoherent pile; crops freeze; millions die. Mass migrations trek to the warmest parts of the globe, but ice invades even these havens. Finally the last remnants of humanity find themselves huddled near the site of ancient Babylon, facing extinction.

Then arises a hero, the genius Miltiades, who addresses the bedraggled band. We must return to our mother earth, he exhorts his numbed audience. Deep within its bosom are sources of energy and scattered centers of fire which can provide light and heat superior even to that of the sun: "Let us descend into these depths; let us make of these abysses our refuge! The mystics had a sublime presentiment when they said in their Latin: *ab interioribus ad exteriora!*" The fate now being faced by human beings, continues Miltiades, is after all the universal fate. Every star in the universe will eventually lose its heat and bank its fires. Does this mean that life, thought, and love are restricted to the few parts of the universe where there are light and heat?

In that case lifelessness, death, agitated nothingness would be the rule, and life the exception! In that case nine-tenths, maybe ninety-nine/one-hundredths of the solar systems would turn in the void, like absurd and gigantic windmills, useless encumbrances of space! That is impossible and senseless, that is blasphemous; let us have more faith in the unknown! . . . When stars have sown their wild oats, then the serious task of their life begins, and they develop their inner fruit.

With this stirring oration Miltiades inspires his listeners to action. To prepare for their future "neotroglodytism," they gather up all the artistic and intellectual heritage of civilization, "the true capital of humanity." Mining begins. Galleries hollowed out in the earth are methodically filled with masterpieces gleaned from libraries and museums. Then these dilettantes enter the underground galleries, shutting themselves off forever from the surface of the earth.

For the first time a truly social life begins. Left behind are the seasons, the countryside, peasants, flora and fauna, everything living but civilized people. Little had they realized how much organic life had impeded human evolution! "The social environment could reveal and unfold for the first time its own virtue, and the truly social tie could appear in all its force, in all its purity." Far from being bored, people live in a state of

habitual surexcitation maintained by the multiplicity of our relationships and our *social tonics* (shaking the hands of friends, chats, encounters with charming females, etc.) and which, among a number of us, became a state of continued frenzy under the name of troglodytic fever.

The flowering of social life unfolds from a drastic reduction of material needs. People eat meat frozen in the ice and wear hardly any clothing because the climate is so temperate. As for shelter, anyone can drill a hole in the rock and obtain a rent-free home. Technological invention is used not to multiply useless gadgets but to provide necessities—heat from cauldron-volcanoes, lighting from the inner fires of the earth—as well as leisure:

> The part of the necessary being reduced to almost nothing, the part of the superfluous can extend to almost everything. When one lives with so little, there remains much time to think. A minimum of utilitarian labor and a maximum of aesthetic labor: is this not the essence of civilization?

And so aesthetic life flourishes as people produce to serve souls rather than to serve bodies. Instead of a relationship between producer and consumer, based on exchange of services, people enjoy the relationship between artist and art-lover, based on the exchange of admiration and respectful criticism:

> The place that the reduction of needs has left empty in the heart is taken up by talents, artistic and poetic, so that every day talents multiply and become more deeply rooted, become veritable acquired needs, but *needs of production* rather than of consumption. I underline this difference. . . . For the theoretician, for the artist, for the *aesthetician* in all genres, to produce is a passion, to consume is only a taste.

Each vocation develops its "aesthetic" mode of production. Scientists cultivate the intellectual charm of endless polemics about the solar system they never see. Chemists discover the psychology of the atom and the desires of molecules, which appear uniform but turn out to be distinct individuals. "Thanks to [the chemists] we are no longer alone in a frozen world; we feel that these rocks live and take life, we feel these hard metals that protect and warm us swarm fraternally." Painters never weary of metamorphosing traditional images like horses, trees, and flowers, which they make all the more harmonious because they are unhindered by the actual sight of these things. Architects, now called excavators, dig a wanton, picturesque series of burrows, endless like an Oriental epic, an "artificial and truly artistic landscape" which constitutes the "essence and consummation of former nature."

Outside these cities of art there is no countryside, only wilderness. Boundless excursions can be taken through fantastic galleries of crystal that have been pierced in the frozen oceans. In this aquamarine silence, among the reflections from icicles and pearls, tourists gliding on skates or bicycles can glimpse frozen sea creatures, immortalized in death, trapped as if in glass cages; or perhaps a piece of wreckage, or a steeple from a prehistoric town. Locked in perpetual ice, the ocean still conveys a sense of mystery, solitude, and peaceful changelessness.

But in underground life the highest charm is found in a social life ruled by the controlling ideal of love. Patriotism, corporatism, even the family spirit have declined, but love, which used to be hindered by the craving for childish luxuries, finally triumphs: "There is only one [passion], under a thousand names, as there is only one sun above; it is love, soul of our soul, and the source of our art. A genuine and dependable sun, this one." Some heroic lovers who enjoy a Platonic relationship spend their lives wandering together through the cathedral-like cities and producing artistic masterpieces. Most lovers are less ascetic, however, and feel the urges of the flesh. But food supplies are so limited that permission must be obtained before a child may be conceived. The force of public opinion, which threatens banishment for those who disobey, regulates love and restricts procreation to couples where the man has created an artistic masterpiece under the inspiration of the woman.

The wisdom of this regulation is manifest when an excavator happens upon a tribe of Chinese who, it seems, also burrowed underground but let themselves multiply enormously afterward. Although they grow diminutive vegetables in diminutive gardens and raise diminutive pigs, still they must resort to cannibalism to feed themselves. "In what promiscuity, in what a slough of rapacity, of falsehood and theft did these unfortunate ones live! The words of our language are incapable of depicting their filth and grossness." After attempts to civilize the Chinese fail, the tunnel leading to their dens is carefully and permanently sealed.

The underground society does have its malcontents, mainly those displeased with its static purity. Once, when a report comes that the sun is reviving and melting the ice, some people entertain the unhealthy notion of returning to the surface. Luckily, a scholar rummaging in a forgotten corner of the archives comes across some phonograph records and moving pictures of the sights and sounds of earthly nature—thunder, wind, rivers, dawn, and darkness. Even the most passionate advocates of returning to the surface are astonished and disillusioned to find that actual nature is so much less impressive than its depiction by even their most realistic artists. If the sun did ever revive, only the most unruly part of the population would be likely to seek its deceptive advantages. But the possibility of the sun's revival is as unlikely as it is undesirable. As Miltiades said, the blessed stars are the extinct ones: "We . . . continue to believe firmly that among stars as among men the most brilliant are not the best, . . . and that finally, in the heavens as on the earth, happiness lives concealed."

9 A Fragment of Future History: Beyond the Consumer Revolution

Tarde's "fragment of future history" is also a fragment of the past. This underground utopia recreates prerevolutionary French salon society, where courtiers chatted and flirted in an environment of material ease. Tarde ignores the less attractive realities of that past—its bickering and petty quarrels over precedence, its snobbery and *ennui*—to revive the ideal of *civilisation,* the ideal of high intellectual, social, and artistic standards which were to be served rather than smothered by a relatively high standard of material comfort. Tarde's dream is that in the future "everyone will truly know *la joie de vivre,* . . . the civilized world will be nothing but . . . an immense salon, a lucid and liberal salon of the eighteenth century open to everyone."

This too is a dream world of the consumer. By imperceptible degrees Tarde has lured us from social laws to social prophecy to fantasy. His dream of the closed world of courtly consumers becoming universal depends upon an unrealistic reduction of world population and an equally unrealistic conquest of nature by the humanity that remains. In the *Fragment of Future History* the real world that is subject to natural repetition, where human beings depend upon scarce non-human nature for survival—in short, the human condition—all this is obliterated and replaced by a dream world, an "artificial paradise" (the phrase is Baudelaire's) lit by a strange and mysterious sun. Tarde's underground dilettantes enjoy the magical source of indefinite credit Baudelaire said was necessary for dandies. They live off unlimited supplies of energy and food acquired without labor and without pollution. The only reminder of the normal conditions of human life is the bestial Chinese. "In what promiscuity, in what a slough of rapacity, of falsehood and theft did these unfortunate ones live! The words of our language are incapable of depicting their filth and grossness." The courtiers of Versailles probably used similar language to describe the peasants they glimpsed as they traveled from one palace to another in their gilded carriages.

In Tarde's dream world the threats of overpopulation, hunger, disease, and filth are banished permanently by sealing up the entrance to the caves of the Chinese: in reality these threats cannot be eliminated so tidily. The disparity in consumption levels which seems so shocking when we look at prerevolutionary France has not disappeared but has only been extended to a global scale, as a result of "our conquering projection outside ourselves, far from ourselves." Versailles could not have existed without the imposition of crushing taxation upon the rest of France, peasant France. Developed nations today depend on the resources of less developed countries. Dream worlds of the consumer cannot exist without the continued impoverishment of much of the real world.[1] The transcendence of the dialectic of man and nature, a prophecy Tarde and many other nineteenth-century thinkers fervently embraced, has been revealed in the twentieth century as a wishful delusion.

But the dilemmas of modern consumer society involve more than physical limits in a world of many people and scarce resources. They also involve subjective or spiritual limits. Here, too, Tarde indulges in illusion, for he insists that the underground world is one of love, pleasure, and happiness. However, in the background lurks the *ennui* of the malcontents who desire to escape and rediscover a more real level of existence they only half-remember.

Even more ominous, beyond the dream world drifts a nightmare universe of extinct stars. Tarde wants to believe that inside seemingly dead stars a hidden life is sheltered—but if that life is concealed, only faith allows us to believe in its existence. The nightmare thought is that the dead stars are truly dead. What if nothingness *is* the rule, and life the exception? What if the universe is indeed composed of solar systems spinning like absurd and inanimate windmills, useless encumbrances of the void? What if the universal process of entropy will finally cool down the stars to dark and motionless cinders? The theory of universal repetition, to which Tarde keeps returning in cycles of his own, is no dream but a nightmare. Nothing persists, everything repeats endlessly, automatically, with no meaning or goal, in this universe of absurd monotony. Tarde himself asks in one of his poems:

Why the eternity of this inanity?
Why am I? Why are we? What is the use?
The heavens turn, the seas rock back and forth; mystery!
Truth, elegance, voluptuousness—vanity![2]

In universal repetition there is no place for human immortality. The existence of the individual is part of the eternal cycling, and so it happens "only once and only for an instant." There is no more reason to believe that the soul retreats to hidden inner depths to live concealed than to believe that dead stars shelter life within.

This vision of cosmic futility is at the heart of the spiritual dilemma of consumption. Where in the eternal cycles of production and consumption does consumption find a purpose, a meaning as *consommation*, rather than remaining a destruction or *consumation* of matter, a hastening of the universe toward its final, formless state? For the universe to be no more than a process of entropy "is impossible and senseless," cries Miltiades. "That is blasphemous; let us have more faith in the unknown." But this is a plea for religious faith in an age when such faith is hard to find:

> Ah; but my courage fails me, and my heart is sick within me!—Lord, take pity on the Christian who doubts, on the skeptic who would fain believe, on the galley-slave of life who puts out to sea alone, in the darkness of night, beneath a firmament illumined no longer by the consoling beacon-fires of the ancient hope.[3]

Tarde concludes that this nightmare of a dark and empty heaven is so terrifying that illusion is an existential necessity, both for the individual and for society as a whole. "The need for certitude or for stable illusion"[4]—Tarde equates the two—is necessary first of all to make personal existence bearable.

No one can face the prospect of his own death without some degree of self-deception. In one of Tarde's most revealing poems, he asks that he be buried among his ancestors on the plains of Dordogne, that his children and the villagers accompany his bier, and that the local *curé* accord him the last rites of the Church:

> For a divine hope raises itself on our shade.
> Deceptive? perhaps, a lie? perhaps.
> But, after all, among our countless lies,
> One lie more or less matters not.
>
> It is even more a lie, the most hypocritical kind,
> For the false purity of the falsely ambitious
> To be shocked by the hope evoked by the ancient rites,
> The ancient and gentle hope which comes from our
>   forefathers.
>
> If this is lying, I want, after my death, still
> To lie, as the poets always have,
> As do April, youth, and dawn,
> And our toil so long and our triumphs so short![5]

On the collective level as well, Tarde affirms, deceptive hope is necessary. The modern moral crisis will be resolved only by raising up

> some great imaginary object, mystic heaven, patriotic glory, which makes all the desires of all the people who keep colliding against each other on earth converge in the void and accord ideally with each other. Someone who is hallucinated [or an imposter] points out this goal, suggests this vision; it dazzles and blinds and makes them march toward victory in good order. Where their eyes are opened, they will go pell-mell, groping, asking to have their dream back again.[6]

At this point Durkheim's criticism of Tarde for "succumbing to the reign of fantasy in the intellectual order" begins to make more sense. From Durkheim's point of view, Tarde's underground society would be another communist utopia that is "sentimental and artistic," which is to say, completely unrealistic. Durkheim's insistence on confining himself to reality, to the "social facts," by no means ruled out an appreciation of the spiritual dimension of social life, but instead led him to emphasize that this dimension too is a "social fact." Tarde and Durkheim agree that the resolution of the modern moral crisis requires an essentially religious perspective, a collective vision of social good beyond the level of personal desire. But Durkheim would never have called this vision a "dream" that dazzles or blinds. For him the collective goals of society are real, not illusory. Those goals can be explained and defended without resorting to mass hallucination, even if they do depend on the performance of collective rites to express their reality.

Tarde's advantage over Durkheim lies in his appreciation of the human propensity to submit to dreams, to hallucinations, to visions of collective imagination; Tarde's disadvantage lies in his willingness to submit to illusion by indulging in deceptive hopes. If this willingness were confined to a private level—for example, the emotional comfort Tarde finds in ancient Catholic traditions that he cannot accept on intellectual grounds—he could not be faulted. (His attitude does, however, form a telling contrast to Durkheim's refusal to seek emotional comfort in Judaic traditions.) But Tarde's propensity to deceptive hopefulness affects his public role as a thinker. While uniquely prophetic in discerning some basic tendencies at work in the modern consumer society, Tarde interprets the results of those tendencies too benignly. He sees that social behavior is rooted in imitation, but assumes that only the best aspects of civilization, not mediocrity or even barbarism, will be imitated. Tarde describes how the increasingly reciprocal imitation of modern times promotes envy rather than obedience, but he fails to appreciate how destructive, even pathological, this envy can be, how bitter rivalry with one's model can prevent any healthy emulation.[7] Tarde foresees that technological change will vastly alter the relationship of consumption to production, but he assumes that people will prefer leisure to goods and will use leisure creatively rather than passively.

Above all, Tarde ignores the power of economic institutions to impose the type of imitation best suited to their own interests. As a result of this power, the dreams of hypnotized "social man" have tended to be material dreams rather than intellectual or artistic ones. Inventions have tended to be ones of material consumption rather than of culture. Fantasy has been shunted to the realm of consumption, away from other legitimate expressions of the imagination in politics, philosophy, art, religion, and production (in Tarde's sense). Social hypnosis has not led to a quasi-religious polarization of faith around a great central passion or desire of society, but to a fragmented "irreligion of the future" where weary consumers submit to the hypnosis of department stores, expositions, and movie screens, to "look, look, look" with wide and blank eyes at material dreams. Given this situation, why trust that the process of social entropy will usher in a universal aristocracy rather than universal banality, a liberal salon of the eighteenth century rather than a Salon de l'Automobile of the twentieth? Is the rising flood of imitation submerging the various civilizations of the globes not the same foul flood of mass consumption that drowns des Esseintes?

Like the décor of the expositions, Tarde's style of thought is both seductive and intoxicating. And as with fake plaster and false gilt, we should be put on guard. Tarde's poetic facility may lure us into a comfortable acquiescence that avoids harsher interpretations and less pleasing deductions. When does necessary illusion become unnecessary delusion? When do social laws turn into social fantasy, and fantasy into falsehood or madness? If social prophecy includes both reality and possibility, how to distinguish possibility from dream? These questions raised by Tarde's ideas continue to nag no matter how beguiling he is. If this exploration of the dream worlds of the consumer has taught us anything, it is how easily we may be seduced by pleasant illusions and how tenaciously we must fight to retain our lucidity. Because even seemingly harmless and amusing lies can encourage us to acquiesce in larger deceptions, "one lie more or less" *does* matter. This conviction is where we began our quest for an ethic of the consumer, and where we must end.

On the other hand, we should not reject Tarde's valid observations as unreal just because they deal with intangibles. His concepts of a noncontiguous but genuine solidarity found in a public and of the possibility of enlisting public opinion as a moral agent; his understanding of value as a human quality rather than a material quantity; his call for a social teleology to arrange and harmonize disparate values, with the implication that a renovation of material lifestyles will follow rather than precede a renovation of values—in all these ways Tarde's outline of possibilities for inquiry into consumer values speaks directly to the needs of modern society.

But since Tarde's death in 1904, social thought has moved in other directions. In economics, the possibilities for an economic psychology that Tarde raised have been left behind in the rush to quantify aggregate consumer demand or to do banal statistical studies of so-called consumer psychology. These studies all too often serve rather than criticize the assumptions of the prevailing economic system. The notion that economic thought could contribute to a general social teleology, that traditional economic values could be related to other but equally valid ones, has hardly been explored. The broader concept of an ethical economics, such as the French economist-*moralistes* ventured, however inadequately, has also sunk from sight.

In sociology the situation is similar. Its prevailing character reflects the fact that the competition for influence between Tarde and Durkheim was won by Durkheim. He left disciples, methods, and institutions which dominated the young discipline. The professionalization of the social sciences on this basis has had obvious benefits, but it has also meant that many topics are not raised at all or are raised in uninteresting ways. Durkheim's heirs tended to adopt the earlier, more simplistic—which is to say, more mechanistic and positivistic—elements of their master's thought rather than his later, more tentative explorations. In sociology as in economics, the concept of flexible social thought open to moral values has largely been rejected in favor of a supposedly value-neutral system focusing on the quantifiable, aggregate behavior of a static assembly of atomistic individuals.

One great benefit of reexamining late nineteenth-century French thinkers is to rediscover alternative modes of social inquiry which could be considerably more productive. Tarde himself suggested that the implicit metaphysics of individuals as social "atoms" should be replaced by a social monadology. *Monad* is the term used by the German philosopher Gottfried Wilhelm Leibnitz (1646–1716) to describe an autonomous, preexisting entity, "all mirrors and no windows," which he hypothesized as the basic unit of the universe. Each monad shines in its individuality while reflecting the others. When applied to the social universe, the metaphysics of monads implies that the basic elements of society—individual human beings—are far more complicated and interesting than the patterns they form when they interact with each other. Social life goes from heterogeneity and complexity to simplicity and homogeneity, not the other way around. Because monads are diverse from the beginning and ceaselessly increase their diversity through their interaction, "they compose a society where each develops his own individuality and, by a sort of radiation, the individuality of others."[8]

The perspective of monadology would encourage a very different sort of social inquiry from the prevailing assumption of atomism, which posits individual atoms whose reasoning or desiring, or both, takes place in isolation from the external world. The separation of inner self and outside world is the metaphysical assumption behind the image of the solitary *homo œconomicus*. The same assumption lies behind Durkheim's analysis of the infinitely desiring consumer whose wishes are restrained only by a force, external to himself, called society. Tarde's monadology, on the other hand, implies a vision of social and economic reality as a multiplicity of interdependent human beings who live with each other, not separate from each other. Their interaction constitutes a dynamic process, not a static aggregation. Norbert Elias, author of *The Civilizing Process* and himself highly critical of most contemporary sociology, suggests that

> monadology represents an early advance in the direction of precisely the kind of model that is urgently in need of further development in sociology today. The decisive step Leibnitz took was an act of self-distantiation, which enabled him to entertain the idea that one might experience oneself not as an "ego" confronting all other people and things, but as a being among others.[9]

Elias's book demonstrates how fruitful this alternative metaphysics could be for the understanding of consumption as an interactive process.

But contemporary stagnation in social thinking, and especially in thinking about consumption, is not due to metaphysical shortcomings alone. The late nineteenth-century moment of articulation, the moment of discovery of consumption as a concept and as a social role, was a response to the great objective fact of the consumer revolution. Renovation of social thought came about when traditional concepts no longer fit historical reality. Now, a century later, we are confronting another such historical moment and can expect similar intellectual results. During the 1970s new realities began to shake us awake from our dream worlds. In the bleak dawn we scanned the future and discerned not a global salon but what Tarde prophesied in a less sanguine moment: "the end of the world."

We have glimpsed, in the first place, the approaching end of nature's compliance with our demands upon her. The reality of nature's needs has intruded upon our fantasies in the form of polluted air and water, toxic wastes, ever scarcer and therefore more expensive resources, even perhaps in environmentally induced cancers which could be interpreted as the plague of modern consumer society. As des Esseintes learned at Fontenay, nature eventually reasserts herself when outrages are committed against her.

And human beings also reassert themselves. We are witnessing the end of compliance with the insatiable demands of rich nations. Our dreams are coming up against the reality of revolutionary aspirations. Remote and impoverished peoples who used to provide raw materials and cheap labor are now questioning their submissiveness and are imitating our consumer wants. Now that the "democratization of luxury" is being extended globally, we realize that even our moderate versions of luxury cannot possibly be copied by the world's population. Neither natural nor human resources permit the extension of the American way of life to the entire planet.

Given this historical situation, our thinking about consumption is bound to be shaken loose again. "How will we manage to reestablish among ourselves a relative peace which has had as its condition for so long our conquering projection outside ourselves, far from ourselves?" So far our feelings—vague but potent feelings of apprehension, fears of deterioration, or even calamity—have outstripped our ideas. We should now go beyond dread and undertake some social prophecy of our own. So far the concepts that have been ventured to analyze our future as consumers have been banal and unhelpful. The two favorite terms are *narcissism* and *austerity*. The two go together: those who have enjoyed the fruits of the consumer revolution are scolded for their selfish narcissism and are warned that they must submit to a new regime of austerity. No matter how much this analysis is dressed up in twentieth-century psychoanalytic language, it rings of Victorian moralizing and only worsens the prevailing anxiety and despair. Far from suggesting any positive motivation for austerity, the message is that people have to give up pleasures in retribution for past sins of selfish overindulgence. Too often these sermons come from neo-Stoics who convey disdain for the consuming masses in their versions of elitist asceticism. The preaching is most galling when delivered by well-fed government officials with job security, medical benefits, and ample salaries, by visiting lecturers who jet in to deliver appeals to "think small," and businessmen who disembark from large company-owned cars to call for belt-tightening.

Surely we can do better than this. Surely we can go beyond hypocritical Calvinism in confronting profound historical change. If the 1970s were a narcissistic "Me Decade," the reason is not that human self-centeredness suddenly blossomed, but that we who are accustomed to consuming in certain patterns responded in predictable fashion when familiar goods and services began to slip from our grasp. We try to hang on to the familiar, and no amount of preaching will alter that entirely human reaction to loss and change. What will enable us to adapt to the loss of the old is, as Tarde reminds us, invention of the new. We need a positive *morale*. For so long our imaginative capacities have been directed to fantasies of escape, adventure, eroticism, and wealth incarnated in commodities that we have neglected other uses of inventiveness. To supersede the dream worlds of the consumer will require not the stifling of imagination but its expansion and redirection.

Some of the needed inventions are technological ones of alternative sources of energy, new products, and improved methods of production and conservation. Already there is a good deal of activity of this sort, which promises to ease our demands on natural resources without altering drastically our present living conditions. What is too often forgotten is that the success of such technological innovations will be related inextricably to what Tarde so happily calls "social inventions." In the realm of social invention, more than anywhere else, we now have a chance to exercise creativity.

For too long our social inventiveness has been confined by assumptions of individualism. Just as the pleasures of consumption have been defended by extolling the supposed liberty of the individual consumer, now the need to reduce consumption is viewed in terms of narcissism and austerity. From the perspective of individual responsibility, reducing consumption is a grim task. Each person, or at the most each family, must bow to harsh necessity and hack away at its budgetary circle, slashing wants in order to slash expenditures. The private, passive concept of austerity faithfully reflects the private, passive forms of consumption that have become habitual with us in our prosperity. The two symbols of mid-twentieth-century American consumer society, the television and the automobile, incarnate those habitual forms. Driving alone in a car or watching television, we are cut off from effective social exchanges. Our eyes are fixed straight ahead and our minds close in on private reveries. Instead of acting spontaneously, we react to messages directed at us from the roadways and airways.[10] Although these technologies of transportation and communication severely damage our sense of community, they continue to prevail because furnishing privately owned commodities is profitable under our economic system, while other means of serving human needs are not. Private austerity does not recast our assumptions as consumers; it only turns them upside down. We who have consumed separately and passively are now expected to deny ourselves with the same isolated resignation.

But when responsibility for reducing consumption is seen in terms of social solidarity, the prospect is immensely hopeful for attaining more fulfillment, fairness, and freedom. As Durkheim suggested in *The Elementary Forms of Religious Life,* a radical reduction in consumption levels does not have to be an accidental cause of suicidal despair but can be a deliberate means of strengthening social bonds. To make an asset of austerity, however, we must recognize that social ties are not and cannot be based primarily on a search for personal gratification calculated in utilitarian terms of profits and losses, costs and benefits. People have claims on society and make contributions to it that cannot be weighed on these scales. As Durkheim recognized, an indispensable element of social life is the self-restraint, the self-sacrifice, of individuals. At the same time, self-denial strengthens the individual in a way that cannot be measured by a utilitarian calculus.

That is why a creative, active, shared austerity—not the destructive, passive, individualistic type—can augment both our sense of personal worth and our sense of community. The fundamental premise must be that the sufferings of austerity are to be shared by all. Those who preach the virtues of enduring economic hardship cannot be the last to feel it themselves. The pains of unemployment and inflation should not be allowed to fall disproportionately on minorities, the underprivileged, the elderly, the disabled, and those who lack an organization to voice their needs. If asceticism is, in Durkheim's words, "inherent in all social life," then all society should participate in its rites.

Solidarist austerity also entails rejecting the moral assumption that the individual consumer has the right, if not the duty, to maximize his own material self-interest. In more concrete terms, this means discarding the notion that any form of consumption is permitted if a person can afford it. The concept of sumptuary laws should be revived. We have already made a collective decision that no one, no matter how wealthy, should be able to wear the pelts of endangered species. We should make other such decisions regarding scarce natural resources—for example, that no one should be allowed to own a car with an engine over a certain size because the shared social costs in pollution, energy, and materials are too high.

In the long run, however, a solidarist austerity opens up far more choices in consumption than it eliminates. Again the automobile furnishes a good example. For the individual an automobile may indeed be a necessity if it is his only dependable means of transportation to work or school. There is little he can do to cut back on this form of consumption. But if society as a whole decides that certain types of automobiles, at least, constitute a collective luxury—which is to say, a superfluity society no longer can afford—then all sorts of alternatives become possible in organizing other choices of transportation. Once we free ourselves from the dominance of privately owned commodities, we can experiment with many new modes of consumption. Right now the consumer enjoys a deceptive liberty of choice among commodities on the market, all the while being subject to the overarching tyranny of the market itself. The consumer should be able to go to attractive parks for recreation, rather than feeling constrained to purchase a second home or install his own swimming pool; to use a bicycle for commuting, instead of risking life and limb by cycling on automobile-infested highways; to live in smaller, shared, but still pleasant housing rather than resigning himself to single-family dwellings as the only desirable type.

Divesting ourselves of old forms of consumption will require technological invention, but even more it will require social invention. For all forms of consumption, society as a whole must reconsider its priorities and reallocate its wealth. Once we recognize that our luxuries are far more collective than personal in character, we can deal with them much more creatively. This type of social invention goes far beyond the concept of consumer activist groups in which consumers unite to assert their rights. Too often this is only the right to gripe. The need is to control and direct consumption, not simply to demand redress for grievances. Of the two models of consumer organizations which emerged in France around the turn of the century, the cooperative model deserves more attention now than consumer leagues. Only by assuming active control of consumption will consumers achieve genuine liberty, which is to say, liberty expressive of the long-term general will (to use Rousseau's famous if imprecise term) rather than of transitory personal wishes. Rousseau's fundamental argument against luxury, it should be recalled, is that it constitutes a subtle, hardly noticeable, but highly effective form of tyranny. The history of consumption demonstrates that alterations in prevailing patterns of material consumption are inseparable from alterations in the quality of social relationships. If we are going to reduce consumption seriously, fundamental social changes are inevitable. The role of social invention is to see that these changes are in the direction of increased equity and democracy.

However, as Tarde would again remind us, social invention is not enough. Moral invention is also required. The problems of consumption that have emerged in recent years are not only those engendered by quantitative limits to economic growth but are also subjective ones arising from an awareness of the limits to personal satisfaction afforded by consumption. Somehow our many comforts do not add up to genuine enjoyment. Even as we enjoy the pleasures and rewards of democratized luxury, we are troubled by suspicions of its purposelessness, of our own confusion about priorities, and of our loss of freedom when so much time and attention are devoted to purchasing and maintenance. Most of all, we sense our diversion from life's realities—the realities of hunger, unhappiness, loneliness, sickness, death, imprisonment, disappointment. Suffering has no place in a dream world: "famine is not and never can be an exposition attraction." Yet suffering remains part of the human condition. To be sure, the spiritual void of a "disenchanted world" is not the fault of the consumer revolution alone. Religious faith was weakening for many reasons. But because of the consumer revolution, we have been encouraged to compensate for the vision of a dark and empty heaven by indulging in material fantasies.

Now that we face "the end of the world" in the sense of an end to indefinitely expanding consumerism, our capacity for moral invention may emerge again. Just because our consumer choices are being restricted, we have to reconsider ultimate priorities; just because consumer lifestyles are becoming untenable, we have to invent other moral codes; and just because we face limits to growth as traditionally defined in quantitative economic terms, we may evolve new definitions of growth less dependent on commodities. Until now what we have defined as a "high standard of living" (as John Kenneth Galbraith remarks with his usual dry succinctness) "consists, in considerable measure, in arrangements for avoiding muscular energy, increasing sensual pleasure and for enhancing caloric intake above any conceivable nutritional requirement."[11] The role of moral invention now is to devise other definitions of a high standard of living.

This does not mean a rejection of materialism reminiscent of the pillar saints. This reversal of values is as unlikely as it is unnecessary. Creative, collective austerity means not regression to past values but emergence to new ones. Our moral task is to distinguish valid pleasures and uses of commodities from trivial and inauthentic ones. To begin, we must sort out the values that can arise only from human associations from those which can legitimately be afforded by inanimate objects. Things can delight us with their beauty. They can console us by enduring over time and reminding us of people we love—this is their "sentimental value." Consumer goods can give pleasures of familiarity and of novelty. All these values can be best appreciated, however, only when false ones—especially over-reliance on commodities as a means of personal self-expression and as indicators of social standing—are seen as what they are, as manipulation by and for the benefit of the economic system.

Moral invention cannot be limited to the realm of consumer values alone. We must consider how consumption should relate to other human activities in order to devise a valid hierarchy of values or a social teleology. We need to put material goods in their place, so to speak, to award them a worthy but not overly dominant position in our scale of values. So far this effort has led to an emphasis on "interpersonal relationships." Personal counseling, group therapies, awareness training, marriage encounters, and other experiments have proliferated in response to declining opportunities for material consumption. All this activity is laudable in that it emphasizes the importance of non-material, human interactions, but its shortcomings are enormous. The quest for better interpersonal relationships all too easily becomes another species of consumerism when it is packaged in the form of courses, managerial seminars, how-to books, and other salable items. And far from overcoming our corrosive individualism, these techniques only aggravate it. The lone "inner self" is entrusted with the responsibility for improving relations with external "others."

Personal relations arise in a social context, and so the quest for a private sense of meaning and feeling of relatedness cannot be separated from a sense of social purpose.

The enduring importance of the concept of *la morale*, and especially of the *morale* of solidarity, is that it affirms this link. In order to put consumption in its proper place in our scale of moral values, we should concentrate less on interpersonal relations and more on social relations— above all, on our relations as producers. One of Tarde's most valid social prophecies is that in "future history" active needs of production must be expanded if passive needs of consumption are to contract. This is not just another "morality of the tool." Tarde clearly defines production as creative, non-specialized, non-repetitive activity that affords a sense of personal identity and of communication with the larger community. This is certainly not the kind of activity that predominates in the workplace now. Indeed, John Kenneth Galbraith has argued that the important contemporary class division is not between a leisure class and a working class, but between an educated "New Class" of workers who enjoy painless, imaginative labor in attractive surroundings, and those whose only reward from their labor is their paycheck.[12] For too long the supposed joys of consumption have been used as an excuse for maintaining the latter conditions of undemocratic and unfulfilling work. The job may be dull (so goes the argument), but it pays well. Now that paychecks buy fewer consumer goods and leisure activities, that argument is going to be less persuasive. Fortunately, the pleasures of the kind of work enjoyed by the New Class, unlike many consumer pleasures, can be expanded vastly without simultaneously becoming less attractive. The best motivation for reducing consumption lies in increasing the pleasures of production.

If it seems strange to think of production in terms of pleasure, the reason is that the pressures of capitalism have so exclusively directed our desires toward commodities. We need to restore the ties between work and desire; this would go far toward healing the separations between production and consumption and between work and leisure which have become so profound and rigid. One great benefit of Tarde's underground utopia is that it portrays a society in which these separations have been healed and the ties between production and desire been restored. Accordingly, like other utopias, Tarde's *Fragment of Future History* provides a moral education, and specifically (in the wonderful phrase of M.-H. Abensour) "the education of desire."[13]

Such moral invention in the realm of production depends on social invention: the two cannot be disjoined, and the ethic of solidarity provides the common link. As Gide emphasized, the natural extension of democratic consumer cooperation is democratic cooperation in production. All sorts of social inventions besides cooperatives are possible for achieving this general goal: flexibility in work schedules, opportunities for part-time work, self-management rather than the prevailing authoritarianism, not to mention ownership by workers themselves. Such possibilities have barely begun to be explored. The reason is obvious. The economic powers-that-be profit directly by encouraging us to think of community in terms of consumption, and especially in terms of common lifestyles. They can also encourage, or at least tolerate, experiments in interpersonal relations that are non-threatening or even diversionary. There is also a community of shared work which is far more genuine—but this involves a direct challenge to those who presently hold economic power. Still, the challenge is coming. Gide looked forward to an alliance of feminism and consumerism: the entry of large numbers of women into the work force may mean an alliance of feminism and a new labor movement. If women refuse to submit to the habitual procedures and ingrained values of the workplace, if they adhere to the principle of solidarity rather than chasing personal "success," they can play a major role in reshaping us from a society of consumers to one of producers, in Tarde's sense.

In all these ways the concept of solidarity provides a basis for moral and social invention far more promising than the utilitarian formula of "the greatest happiness of the greatest number." The utilitarian ethic has prevailed for so long because it is fundamentally an ethic of the individual consumer, who has been courted assiduously by our economic system. In this ethical view, people as well as commodities are things to be used by the self-aggrandizing individual. The real objection to consumer society is that it encourages the same attitude toward human beings as toward commodities. In contrast, the ethic of solidarity recognizes collective, long-term interests beyond short-term majority rule, and the reality of a sense of community as well as an element of personal happiness.

At the same time that it provides a basis for a new social ethic, solidarity also offers a spiritual dimension. It suggests a sense of meaning beyond the maintenance of personal life and of purpose transcending possessions and publicity. This is especially true for Tarde's monadological version of solidarity. If a person is thought of as a living monad, then his influence as a model, although it may be anonymous, reverberates endlessly. At the present the sense of self-importance as a model is limited, for the most part, to details of lifestyle. We are self-consciously aware of how others esteem our clothes, furnishings, cars, and recreations, and we in turn regard and emulate the consumer habits of others. But this human propensity to emulation, which is a central lesson of consumer society, can be turned to many other purposes. In far more subtle and significant ways we serve as models for others. Because we are always teaching by example, we are not tiny and insignificant atoms lost in a vast social universe outside ourselves; instead, we are at the center of a universe of imitation. We may exist "only once and only for an instant," but the waves of imitation we initiate endure far from us and long after us. Solidarity instills a sense of coexistence with all humanity in space—the many as opposed to the self—and of continuity in time—the long-term as well as the short-term. None of this will restore unquestioning faith in life after death, nor does it erase the nightmare vision of dead stars in an empty sky. But it is a basically religious affirmation that we are all members of humanity and share a collective destiny beyond individual life. The *morale* of solidarity echoes the religious imperative to love one another.

All these possibilities for technological, social, and moral invention lie before us, our new Pacific to explore. As Tarde cautions, however, these are only possibilities, not predictabilities. "The real is explicable only in connection with the immensity of the possible."[14] As we survey that immensity, we can allow ourselves hope but not optimism. The present could just as well open out upon a future of increasing anomie and frustration, of the breakdown of solidarity rather than its strengthening, of more *ennui* and envy and guilt rather than less. The growing awareness of scarcity may not lead to a more equitable distribution of resources but to an even more unjust one. Like the courtiers of prerevolutionary France, we may not prove inventive enough to escape a collective destiny of exile, impoverishment, and execution.

Prerevolutionary France is past history. Future history is still being shaped, and all we know for certain is that the history of the consumer is entering a new phase. As Gide said of himself, we are explorers destined to set sail on uncharted seas of thought and action. Like him, like the other social prophets of his time, we should muster the courage to move in an unfamiliar direction. Until now we moderns have assumed that the promised land of global social harmony lies in the direction of an ever-increasing standard of material well-being. Now we should try to sail toward the future on the opposite tack, in quest of a creative, shared austerity that will emphasize equity among men and harmony with nature. If we change our course and brave the unknown, we too may arrive on the banks of a new world.

Notes

CHAPTER 1

1. Hannah Arendt, *The Human Condition: A Study of the Central Dilemmas Facing Modern Man* (Garden City, N.Y.: Doubleday Anchor Books, 1959 [1958]), pp. 72–83, 108–10. Her distinction between consumer goods and use objects parallels her distinction between labor and work—the first performed by people in order to live, the second so they may make a home for themselves in the world.

Any reader who requires more detailed citations should consult Rosalind Williams, *The Dream World of Consumption: Its Emergence in French Thought, 1880–1914* (Ph.D. dissertation, University of Massachusetts, 1978).

2. Raymond Williams, "Consumer," in *Keywords: A Vocabulary of Culture and Society* (New York: Oxford University Press, 1976), pp. 68–70. Williams echoes Arendt's distinction between consumer goods and use objects when he notes: "to say *user* rather than **consumer** is still to express a relevant distinction" (p. 70).

3. Vance Packard, *The Hidden Persuaders* (New York: Donald McKay, 1957), and J. K. Galbraith, *The Affluent Society* (Boston: Houghton Mifflin, 1958). A social scientist who has specialized in the implications of modern consumption but who remains less well known to the general public is George Katona: see his *The Mass Consumption Society* (New York: McGraw-Hill, 1964).

4. Jean Fourastié, *Machinisme et bien-être* (Paris: Éditions de Minuit, 1951), on the general problem of tracing changes in standards of living; Fourastié, *Le Grand Espoir du XXᵉ siècle: progrès technique, progrès économique, progrès social* (Paris: Presses Universitaires de France, 1949), pp. 46–47, 124–25, 199; and Pierre Sorlin, in *La Société française 1840–1914* in *Sociétés contemporaines*, ed. François Bedarida, (2 vols., Paris: B. Arthaud, 1969), Vol.1, pp. 140–44, 189–92. For more on credit and income, see Theodore Zeldin, *France 1848–1945*, Vol. II, pp. 627–28, 644–45.

5. Sorlin, *Société française*, pp. 237–38. To be sure, in rural areas the arrival of mass consumption was far slower than in cities and towns. See Eugen Weber, *Peasants into Frenchman: The Modernization of Rural France 1870–1914* (Stanford, Calif.: Stanford University Press, 1976).

CHAPTER 2

1. Saint-Simon, quoted in Frantz Funck-Brentano, *La Cour du roi soleil* (Paris: Éditions B. Grasset, 1938), p. 75.

2. Ibid., p. 77.

3. Henri Sée, *La France économique et sociale au XVIIIᵉ siècle* (Paris: Librairie Armand Colin, 1925), pp. 81, 162.

4. Funck-Brentano, *Cour*, p. 232.

5. Georges Duby and Robert Mandrou, *A History of French Civilization*, trans. James Blakely Atkinson (New York: Random House, 1965 [1958]), p. 339.

6. The complete poem is printed (with a very helpful critical study) in André Morize, *L'Apologie du luxe au XVIIIᵉ siècle, et "Le Mondain" de Voltaire, étude critique sur "Le Mondain" et ses sources* (Geneva: Slatkine Reprints, 1970 [1909]). Morize notes that Voltaire originally ended the poem with the phrase "The true terrestrial Paradise is in Paris."

7. Quoted in Norbert Elias, *The Civilizing Process*, p. 36.

8. Quoted in Morize, *L'Apologie*, p. 47, from Voltaire's poem "La Défense du Mondain," in which the *philosophe* replied to critical attacks on "Le Mondain."

9. Morize covers this debate in considerable detail: ibid., pp. 177–89. His bibliography of the debate is exhaustive.

10. Elias, *The Civilizing Process*, p. 45.

11. Quoted in the *Encyclopaedia Britannica*, Macropaedia, vol. 15 (15th ed., 1978), p. 1171.

12. Quoted (from *Mémoires d'un touriste*) by René Girard, *Mensonge romantique et vérité romanesque* (Paris: Bernard Grasset, 1961), p. 129.

13. Quoted by Bernard Guyon, *La Pensée politique et sociale de Balzac* (2nd ed., Paris: Librairie Armand Colin, 1967), p. 353.

14. Ibid., p. 314n.

15. Honoré de Balzac, *Cousin Bette*, in *La Comédie humaine de Honoré de Balzac*, trans. Katharine Prescott Wormeley (New York: Athenaeum Society, 1888), pp. 457–59.

16. Honoré de Balzac, *Old Goriot: A Marriage Settlement*, intro. by George Saintsbury, n.t. (New York: The Review of Reviews, n.d.), vol. 2, p.2.

17. Quoted by Guyon, *Pensée politique*, p. 456.

18. Quoted by E. J. Oliver, *Honoré de Balzac*, Masters of World Literature Series, ed. Louis Kronenberger (New York: Macmillan; London: Collier-Macmillan, 1964), p. 126. See also Oliver's discussion of Balzac's early novelette *La Peau de chagrin* (1831), which is especially relevant to our subject (pp. 48–51).

19. Heinrich Heine, quoted in ibid., p. 123.

20. Girard, *Mensonge*, pp. 75–142 passim.

21. On the endurance of courtly modes of consumption, see Lewis Mumford's penetrating discussion of "the Country House myth" in *The Story of Utopias*, intro. by Hendrik Willem van Loon (New York: Boni and Liveright, 1922), pp. 193–211.

CHAPTER 3

1. Many of these details are from Richard D. Mandell, *Paris 1900: The Great World's Fair* (n.p.: University of Toronto Press, 1967), chapter 1. For an excellent short summary of the French universal expositions, see Raymond Isay, *Panorama des expositions universelles* (3rd ed., Paris: Gallimard, 1937).

2. Henri Chardon, "L'Exposition de 1900," *Revue de Paris* 1 (February 1, 1896): 644. Chardon was participating in a debate as to whether another exposition should be held in 1900. Because of the commercialism of the 1889

event, there was strong opposition to the proposal. On the debate see Mandell, *Paris 1900*, pp. 25–51.

3. This description is from Paul Morand, *1900 A.D.*, trans. Mrs. Romilly Fedden (New York: William Farquhar Payson, 1931), p. 66. See also pp. 65–66 and the photograph facing p. 67.

4. Eugène-Melchior de Vogüé, "La Défunte Exposition," *Revue des deux mondes*, 4th per., 162 (November 15, 1900): 384–85.

5. Michel Corday [Louis-Léonard Pollet], "La Force à l'Exposition," *Revue de Paris* 1 (January 15, 1900): 439.

6. Maurice Talmeyr, "L'École du Trocadéro," *Revue des deux mondes*. All quotations from Talmeyr are from this article unless otherwise noted. He also wrote a series "Notes sur l'Exposition" that appeared in *Le Correspondant* between April 10, 1899, and April 25, 1900. Altogether the series included thirteen articles.

7. Richard D. Sennett, *The Fall of Public Man* (New York: Alfred A. Knopf, 1976), pp. 141–49.

8. Émile Zola, *Au Bonheur des Dames* (Lausanne: Éditions Rencontre, n.d.), pp. 122–23.

9. Ibid., p. 153.

10. Ibid., p. 288.

11. Ibid., pp. 472–73.

12. Roger de Félice, "Le Salon de l'Automobile," *Les Arts de la vie* 3 (January, 1905): 12.

13. These quotations from Talmeyr about exposition décor are from his "Notes sur l'Exposition," *Le Correspondant* 199 (April 25, 1900): 401.

14. Michel Corday, "À l'Exposition.—Visions lointaines," *Revue de Paris* 2 (March 15, 1900): 422–38. Quotations from Corday are from this article unless otherwise noted. Corday's reports on the exposition are summarized in his book *Comment on a fait l'Exposition* (Paris: E. Flammarion, 1900).

15. For information on the capital investments and profits of expositions, see Charles Gide, "La Liquidation de l'Exposition universelle," *Revue d'économie politique* 15 (June, 1901): 674–77; Louis Joubert, "Fin de rêve. L'Exposition universelle de 1900," *Le Correspondant* 201 (November 24, 1900): 771–84; and Paul Leroy-Beaulieu, "Les Grands Inconvénients des foires universelles et la nécessité d'y renoncer," *L'Économiste français* 2 (December 7, 1895): 729–31.

16. See Zeldin, *France*, vol. 2, p. 389. See also the general histories of the cinema cited by Zeldin.

17. Louis Haugmard, "L' 'Esthétique' du cinématographie," pp. 762–71. Quotations from Haugmard are from this article.

18. By Jean-Marie Guyau (1854–1888).

19. Michel Corday, "À l'Exposition.—La Force à l'Exposition," *Revue de Paris* 1 (January 15, 1900): 438–39. See his note at the bottom of p. 438 regarding the number of kilowatts involved in this display.

20. In Villiers de l'Isle-Adam, *Oeuvres*, ed. Jacques-Henry Bornecque (n.p.: Le Club Français du Livre, 1957), p. 57. The short story was first published in *La Renaissance littéraire et artistique* (November 30, 1873) and was republished in 1883 as part of Villiers's *Contes cruels*.

21. Robert de La Sizeranne, "La Beauté des machines, à propos du Salon de l'Automobile," *Revue des deux mondes*, 5th per., 42 (December 1, 1907):

657; Camille Mauclair, "La Décoration lumineuse," *Revue bleue* 8 (November 23, 1907): 656; and Émile Berr, "Une Exposition parisienne.—Le 'Salon' des chauffeurs," *Revue bleu* 11 (December 24, 1904): 829.

22. De Félice, "Le Salon de l'Automobile," pp. 11–12.

23. Ibid.

24. Ibid.

25. La Sizeranne, "La Beauté," pp. 657–58.

26. Georges d'Avenel, "Le Mécanisme de la vie moderne: la publicité," *Revue des deux mondes*, 5th per., 1 (February 1, 1901): 657, 659.

27. This scene is amusingly, and pathetically, described by Berr, "Exposition parisienne," p. 829.

28. Zeldin, *France*, vol. 2, pp. 627–29.

29. Pierre Calmettes, "The 'Big Store' of Paris," *Architectural Record* 12 (September, 1902): 431–44.

30. Zeldin, *France*, vol. 2, p. 628.

31. The *Revue des deux mondes* series ran from July 15, 1894, to August 1, 1905, and included twenty-eight installments. The book *Le Mécanisme de la vie moderne* was published in five editions, plus several reprintings, from 1896 to 1905. D'Avenel was president of the Supervisory Board and editor of the Political Chronicle of the *Revue des deux mondes*.

32. In a review of d'Avenel's *Le Mécanisme de la vie moderne* by Paul Dudon, S.J., in *Études publiées par les pères de la Compagnie de Jésus* 83 (June, 1900): 703.

33. D'Avenel, *Les Français de mon temps*, intro. Charles Sardea (Paris: Plon-Nourrit, 1904), p. 1.

34. D'Avenel, *Le Nivellement des jouissances*, pp. 303–4.

35. Quoted by Ernest Seillière in "Georges d'Avenel, historien et moraliste," *Revue des deux mondes*, 8th per., 53 (September 15, 1939): 445.

36. Ibid., p.446.

37. D'Avenel, *Nivellement*, p. 4. D'Avenel's research into the history of consumption resulted in the monumental four-volume *Histoire économique de la propriété, des salaires, des denrées, et de tous les prix en générale, depuis l'an 1200 jusqu'en l'an 1800* (1894–1898), later condensed for a more general audience in *La Fortune privée à travers sept siècles* (1895), *Paysans et ouvriers depuis sept cent ans* (1889), and *Les Riches depuis sept cent ans* (1909).

38. D'Avenel, "Mécanisme: la soie," *Revue des deux mondes*, 4th per., 138 (December 15, 1896): 790–91.

39. Ibid., p. 820.

40. D'Avenel, "Mécanisme: la maison parisienne.—L'Intérieur," *Revue des deux mondes*, 4th per., 140 (April 15, 1897): 800–801.

41. Ibid, p. 800.

42. D'Avenel, "Mécanisme: la soie," p. 805. The quotation is from a poem by Alfred de Musset titled "La Coupe et les lèvres": "Aimer est le grand point, qu'importe la maîtresse? / Qu'importe le flacon pourvu qu'on ait l'ivresse?"

43. Quoted by Seillière, "Georges d'Avenel," p. 448.

44. D'Avenel, *Nivellement*, p. 313.

45. Ibid., p. 315.

46. Ibid., p. 310.

47. D'Avenel, "Mécanisme: L'alcool et les liqueurs," *Revue des deux mondes*, 4th per., 151 (January 1, 1899): 129–30.

48. D'Avenel, *Nivellement*, p. 151. In his recent book *Social Limits to Growth*, A Twentieth Century Fund Study (Cambridge, Mass., and London: Harvard University Press, 1976), Fred Hirsch uses the terms "material economy" and "positional economy" to distinguish goods that can be multiplied indefinitely without losing any of their desirability from those that cannot.

49. D'Avenel, *Les Français*, pp. 256–57.

50. Talmeyr, "L'École," pp. 212–13.

51. Ibid., p. 213. The laws to which Talmeyr refers had recently been promulgated by the French national assembly.

CHAPTER 4

1. Thorstein Veblen, *The Theory of the Leisure Class: An Economic Study of Institutions* (New York: New American Library, 1899, 1912), p. 79.

2. The term *genteel* is used by John E. Kasson in *Amusing the Millions: Coney Island at the Turn of the Century* (New York: Hill and Wang, 1978) to describe what I have more often referred to as a "bourgeois" consumption style.

3. See Raymond Williams, "Dominant, Residual and Emergent," in *Marxism and Literature* (London: Oxford University Press, 1977), pp. 121–27.

4. Ellen Moers, *The Dandy: Brummell to Beerbohm* (New York: Viking Press, 1960), pp. 20–21.

5. Émilien Carassus, *Le Mythe du dandy* (Paris: A. Colin, 1971), p. 108, quoting Barbey.

6. Moers, *Dandy*, p. 256.

7. Ibid., p. 264.

8. Ibid.

9. Ibid., p. 265; cf. pp. 262–65.

10. Carassus, *Mythe*, p. 249.

11. Ibid., pp. 251–52.

12. Moers, *Dandy*, p. 38.

13. Carassus, *Mythe*, p. 82.

14. Ibid.

15. Quoted by George D. Painter, *Proust: The Early Years* (Boston and Toronto: Little, Brown and Company, 1959), p. 209; see pp. 155–57 on Montesquiou.

16. Richard A. Grant, *The Goncourt Brothers*, no. 183 in Twayne's World Authors Series, gen. ed. Sylvia E. Bowman (New York: Twayne Publishers, 1972), pp. 144–45 (trans. by Grant).

17. Painter, *Proust*, pp. 155–56, 162.

18. One example of the view of decadents as curiosities is Alfred Edward Carter, *The Idea of Decadence in French Literature 1830–1900* (Toronto: University of Toronto Press, 1958), who recounts at unnecessary length the admittedly ludicrous plots of second-rate decadent novels. Their dismissal as irrelevant is expressed by H. Stuart Hughes in *Consciousness and Society: The Reorientation of European Social Thought 1890–1930* (New York: Random House, Vintage Books, 1958), p. 34.

19. F. W. Hemmings, *Culture and Society in France 1848–1898: Dissi-*

dents and Philistines (London: B. T. Batsford, 1971), p. 217. On the relations between Huysmans and Montesquiou, see Painter, *Proust*, pp. 155, 161.

20. J.-K. Huysmans, *Against the Grain [À Rebours]*, intro. Havelock Ellis (New York: Illustrated Editions, 1931), p. 84. I have generally followed this translation (no name given) but have tidied it up at points.

21. Ibid., p. 308.

22. Ibid., p. 339.

23. Ibid., p. 107.

24. Ibid., pp. 162–63.

25. Ibid., p. 164.

26. Huysmans' remarks are found in ibid., pp. 271, 316; d'Avenel's comments are from his article "Mécanisme: l'alcool," pp. 120–21.

27. Huysmans, *Against the Grain*, pp. 103–4.

28. Ibid., p. 281.

29. This is the general interpretation advanced by Wylie Sypher in *Literature and Technology: The Alien Vision* (New York: Random House, 1968), especially in the chapter "The Pathos of Consuming" (pp. 151–59).

30. Huysmans, *Against the Grain*, p. 128.

31. Ibid., p. 196.

32. D'Avenel, *Nivellement*, p. 313 (italics in the original).

33. The former opposition is expressed by César Graña in *Bohemian vs. Bourgeois: French Society and the French Man of Letters in the Nineteenth Century* (New York and London: Basic Books, 1964), also published by Basic Books under the title *Modernity and Its Discontents* (New York, 1964). The latter opposition is discussed by Daniel Bell in *The Cultural Contradictions of Capitalism* (New York: Basic Books, 1976).

34. Huysmans, *Against the Grain*, p. 282.

35. Ibid., p. 283.

36. Ibid.

37. Ibid, pp. 284–85.

38. Ibid.

39. Ibid, pp. 102–3.

40. Ibid., pp. 224–25.

41. Ibid., p. 285.

42. Ibid., p. 336.

43. Ibid.

44. Ibid., p. 188.

45. Ibid., p. 193.

46. Ibid., p. 338.

47. Joseph Conrad, *Youth, a Narrative: And Two Other Stories, Heart of Darkness and The End of the Tether*, ed. Morton Dauwen Zabel (Garden City, N.Y.: Doubleday Anchor Books, 1959), p. 143. (*Heart of Darkness* was originally published in 1902.)

48. Lucien Goldmann, *Pour un sociologie du roman* (Paris: Gallimard, 1964), p. 187.

49. Sypher, *Literature and Technology*, p. 191.

50. Quoted by Carter, *Idea of Decadence*, p. 14.

51. Quoted by Bonner Mitchell, *Les Manifestes littéraires de la Belle Époque* (Paris: Seghers, 1966), p. 19.

52. Quoted by Huysmans himself in his 1903 preface to *À Rebours*,

written twenty years after its initial publication: Huysmans, *Against the Grain*, p. 73. See also Moers, *Dandy*, p. 268.

53. This is the analysis presented by Edmund Wilson in *Axel's Castle: A Study in the Imaginative Literature of 1870–1930* (New York: Charles Scribner's Sons, 1931), written to introduce English-speaking readers to French decadents and symbolists. For a more recent book (in French) on the subject of the symbolists and subsequent writers, see Michel Décaudin, *La Crise des valeurs symbolistes: vingt ans de poésie française* (Toulouse: Privat, 1960).

54. Quoted by Décaudin, *Crise*, p. 23.

CHAPTER 5

1. Camille Mauclair, *Servitude et grandeur littéraires*, p. 15. The title alludes to Alfred de Vigny's *Servitude et grandeur militaires* (1835).

2. Mauclair, *Servitude*, pp. 86–87.

3. Ibid., pp. 23, 38.

4. Ibid., p. 112.

5. Ibid, p. 115.

6. Ibid.

7. Ibid., pp. 116–21.

8. Ibid, pp. 19–20, 45–47. The symbolist referred to is Charles-Henry Hirsch.

9. Ibid., pp. 244, 249. See pp. 231–37 for a very Proustian description of a party attended by Mauclair, at which the emptiness of "careerism" was revealed to him.

10. Camille Mauclair, "L'Oeuvre sociale de l'art moderne," *Revue socialiste* 33 (1901): 678, 681, 683.

11. H. A. Needham, *Le Développement de l'esthétique sociologique en France et en Angleterre au XIXᵉ siècle*, p. 100, cites this quotation from Gautier's preface to *Mademoiselle de Maupin*. Needham remarks that Gautier later changed his mind and admitted that art might be applied to industrial and consumer objects, but it is Gautier's manifesto that has been remembered, not his second thoughts. Needham's book is a valuable source on a subject that has received much more attention in England than in France.

12. Camille Mauclair, "L'Artiste moderne et son attitude sociologique," *Grande revue* 21 (March 1, 1902): 625.

13. Mauclair, *Servitude*, pp. 64–70.

14. Camille Mauclair, "La Réforme de l'art décoratif en France," *Nouvelle revue* 98 (February 15, 1896): 730, 742, 746.

15. Mauclair discusses these terms, and explains his reasons for coming to prefer *applied art* to *decorative art*, in "La Crise des arts décoratifs," p. 755.

16. Camille Mauclair, "Où en est notre 'Art décoratif,' " p. 522.

17. *Grand Larousse de la langue française* (1973), vol. 3, p. 2009, defines *fonctionnalisme* or *fonctionalisme* as "the tendency to submit the forms of an object or of a building to the function it must serve, in abstraction from every other preoccupation" (my translation). Paul Robert, ed., *Dictionnaire alphabétique et analogique de la langue française*, fasc. 19 (1955), p. 85, says that the noun *fonction* was used in a biological sense from the sixteenth century. Robert, p. 85, and *Grand Larousse*, p. 2009, agree on the date 1845 as that of the introduction into French of the adjectival form *fonctionnal*.

18. Camille Mauclair, "L'Artiste moderne et son attitude sociologique," *Grande revue* 22 (April 1, 1902): 141. (The first part of this illuminating article is cited in note 12.)

19. Mauclair, "Crise," p. 755.

20. Mauclair, "Réforme," p. 740.

21. Mauclair, "L'Artiste moderne" (April 1, 1902): 141.

22. Mauclair, "Crise," pp. 742–43.

23. The term *sociological aesthetic* comes from H. A. Needham, *Développement.*

24. Mauclair, *Servitude,* p. 121.

25. Mauclair, "L'Artiste moderne" (April 1, 1902): 141.

26. Mauclair, *Servitude,* p. 177.

27. Mauclair, "Crise," p. 755.

28. Camille Mauclair, "Le Besoin d'art du peuple," p. 308.

29. Mauclair, "Crise," p. 756.

30. Ibid.

31. For example, Octave Mourey, "Nécrologie: Émile Gallé," *L'Art moderne,* no. 40 (October 2, 1904): 322; and Gaston Varenne, "La Pensée et l'art d'Émile Gallé," *Mercure de France* 86 (July 1, 1910): 44.

32. Varenne, "Pensée," p. 44. On the School of Nancy, see ibid., p. 43, and Mario Amaya, *Art Nouveau* (London: Studio Vista, 1966), pp. 100–105. There is also a special issue of *La Plume* devoted to "Le Nouvel Art décoratif et l'École lorraine," no. 157 (November 1, 1895).

33. Varenne, "Pensée," pp. 34–35.

34. Quoted in ibid., pp. 36–37.

35. Mauclair, "Crise," p. 755.

36. Ibid., pp. 755–56.

37. Sorlin, *Société française,* vol. 1, p. 154.

38. Mauclair, "Besoin," p. 308.

39. Mauclair, "Crise," p. 755.

40. Ibid.

41. Mauclair, "Où en," p. 520.

42. Amaya, *Art Nouveau,* pp. 101–4, and Martin Battersby, *The World of Art Nouveau* (London: Arlington Books, 1968), pp. 146–48. See the description of the submarine style by Robert de La Sizeranne, "L'Art à l'Exposition de 1900: avons-nous un style moderne?" *Revue des deux mondes,* 4th per., 161 (October 15, 1900): 873.

43. Mauclair, "Besoin," p. 308.

44. Mauclair, *Servitude,* pp. 177–78.

45. Mauclair, "Besoin," pp. 306, 308. Mauclair is probably alluding here to Jean Lahor, who was a strong advocate of free admission for the poor to libraries and museums.

46. Ibid., pp. 307–8.

47. Ibid., p. 307.

48. Ibid.

49. Mauclair, "Crise," p. 757.

50. Ibid., pp. 758–59.

51. Mauclair, "L'Artiste moderne" (March 1, 1902): 637–38.

52. Mauclair discusses this subject in "La Psychologie du bijou," *Revue bleue* 5 (April 7, 1906): 435–37.

53. See "Sur le programme des néo-classiques d'Henri Clouard, 10 février, 1914," in Bonner Mitchell, *Les Manifestes littéraires de la Belle Époque,* pp. 179–85. Mitchell argues that the importance of the classical revival has been seriously underrated by cultural and literary historians.

For derogatory remarks about Mauclair, see Eugène Montfort in *Les Marges,* no. 6 (February, 1905): 231, as well as the issue of *Les Marges,* no. 5 (October, 1904), in which there is an *enquête* on the topic of social art, which Montfort seems to equate with preachiness. See also Francis de Miomandre, "Camille Mauclair," *Mercure de France* 142 (June, 1902): 641–54, in which the author defends Mauclair against the charge that he had abandoned "l'art de l'élite pour l'art social" (p. 651).

54. Camille Mauclair, "Le Nouveau Paris du peuple," pp. 79–80, 82–83. He names some of the suburbs he has in mind: Pantin, Charonne, La Butte-aux-Cailles, Malakoff, Pont de Flandre, Quartier du Combat, Saint-Ouen, La Rapée, and Vaugirard.

55. Camille Mauclair, "Le Style de la rue moderne," pp. 719, 722.

56. Mauclair, "Nouveau Paris," p. 82.

57. Mauclair, "Style," p. 721.

58. Mauclair, "Nouveau Paris," p. 82. For similar remarks see Mauclair, "Style," p. 722.

59. For this analysis I have drawn upon Raymond Williams, *The Country and the City* (London: Chatto and Windus, 1973), especially p. 121.

60. Mauclair, "Style," p. 721.

61. Camille Mauclair, "L'Architecture du fer," *Revue bleue* 8 (August 31, 1907): 278–79.

62. Camille Mauclair, "La Décoration lumineuse," *Revue bleue* 8 (November 23, 1907): 656.

63. Ibid.

64. Ibid., pp. 656–57.

65. Ibid., pp. 657–58.

66. Mauclair, "L'Architecture," p. 279.

67. Mauclair, "Décoration," p. 658.

68. Ibid., p. 657.

69. Camille Mauclair, "La Réaction nationaliste en art et l'ignorance de l'homme des lettres," *Revue des revues* 54 (January 15, 1905): 151–53. For a similar homage to this generation, see Eugène Montfort, ed. *Vingt-cinq ans de littérature française: tableau de la vie littéraire de 1895 à 1920* (2 vols., Paris: Librairie de France, n.d.), vol. 1, p. 257.

70. Ibid., p. 154.

71. Ibid., p. 164.

72. Mauclair, "Où en," p. 521.

73. Ibid., pp. 523–24.

74. Lahor established the Société d'art populaire et d'hygiène, first proposed in his *L'Art pour le peuple à défaut de l'art par le peuple* (Paris: Larousse, 1903). His activities in getting cheap housing for workers contributed to the establishment of the Société Française des Habitations à Bon Marché. See also his proposal for "Une Société à créer pour la protection des paysages français," *La Revue* 36 (March 1, 1901): 526–32.

The head of the Association des Cités-Jardins de France was Georges Benoît-Lévy, who imported the idea from England. See his *La Cité-Jardin* (3 vols.,

Paris: Éditions des Cités-Jardins de France, 1911 [1903]). Lahor refers to Benoît-Lévy in *L'Art pour le peuple*, p. 29, as president of the Société Populaire des Beaux-Arts, which distributed engravings of artistic masterpieces to the masses in order to make beauty accessible to all. Benoît-Lévy was also active in the Ligue des Espaces Libres (see *Cité-Jardin*, vol. 3, p. 193).

75. Benoît-Lévy, vol. 3, pp. 25, 176, 195–213. The workers rented houses from the company.

76. Émile Zola, *Travail (Labor): A Novel*, n.t. (New York and London: Harper and Brothers, 1901), pp. 183–84, 562–64.

77. This is a reference to the book by Robert Venturi, Denise Scott Brown, and Steven Izenour, *Learning from Las Vegas* (Cambridge, Mass.: MIT Press, 1972).

78. Georges Palante, *Les Antinomies entre l'individu et la société* (Paris: Félix Alcan, 1913), pp. 176, 178–79.

79. Ibid., p. 179.

80. Charles Andler, *La Civilisation socialiste [Sténographie d'une leçon de clôture prononcée à l'École Socialiste le 3 juin 1910]* (Paris: Marcel Rivière, 1911), pp. 11–12.

81. J.-K. Huysmans, "Chronique d'art.—Fantaisie sur le Musée des arts décoratifs et sur l'architecture cuite," *Revue indépendante*, n.s. 1 (November, 1886): 30–33. In *Servitude*, pp. 17–18, Mauclair describes the *Revue indépendante* as "an organ of liaison between emerging symbolism and the literature which preceded it."

82. See the comment by Mauclair, "L'Art décoratif," pp. 742.

83. Quoted by Varenne, "Pensée," p. 33.

84. Mauclair, "Psychologie de la nature morte," in his *La Beauté des formes* (Paris: Albin Michel, 1909), pp. 150–59. I have not been able to discover where the article was originally published (the book is a collection of previously published essays).

85. Émile Magne, "Les Métiers d'art dans le roman contemporain," *Mercure de France* 102 (March 1, 1913): 5–34.

86. Mauclair, "L'Artiste moderne" (April 1, 1902): 142.

CHAPTER 6

1. *Séances et travaux de l'Académie des sciences morales et politiques*, n.s. 130 (July 30, 1888): 401–3.

2. The article is "Les Apologistes du luxe et ses détracteurs," *Revue des deux mondes* 42 (November 1, 1880): 95–128. The only copy of the book I could obtain was the second edition, published in London by Swan Sonnenschein and Co. in 1891.

3. *Séances et travaux*, n.s. 130 (August 6, 1888): 719. For other Académie discussions of the subject, see the listings under "Luxe" in Henri Vergé and Paul de Boutarel, eds. *Table alphabétique et bibliographique des matières et des auteurs figurant dans les cent trente premiers volumes du compte rendu, Séances et travaux de l'Académie des sciences morales et politiques, Institut de France* (Paris: Alphonse Picard, 1889).

4. See Paul Leroy-Beaulieu, "Études sociales.—Le Luxe, la fonction de la richesse. 1. Caractère et variété du luxe. Son Rôle économique," *Revue des*

deux mondes 126 (November 1, 1894): 72–100, and "2. La Législation et le luxe.—
La Fonction sociale de la fortune," 126 (December 1, 1894): 547–73. The book
was published in Paris by Guillaumin in 1896.

5. Charles Secrétan (1815–1895), a Swiss correspondent of the Institut who was widely read in France, followed the discussions closely and was
inspired by them to write an essay on luxury for the *Revue philosophique*
(September, 1888), which was reprinted in his *Études sociales* (Paris: Félix Alcan,
1889). Secrétan, a Protestant, was an important influence on Charles Gide,
another Protestant and then an economist at the University of Montpellier,
who presented his response to the debate in subsequent editions of his popular
treatise *Principes d'économie politique*. (Gide will be discussed at length in
Chapter 7.)

6. Schumpeter's book is quoted in French by Luc Bourcier de Car-
bon, *Essai sur l'histoire de la pensée et des doctrines économiques* (Paris: Éditions
Montchrétien, 1972), pp. 124–25. I have retranslated the text.

7. *La Morale économique* was written by Gustave de Molinari (1819–
1912); *La Morale de la concurrence* by Yves Guyot (1843–1928); and *Les Rapports* by
Baudrillart.

8. G.-H. Bousquet, *Essai sur l'évolution de la pensée économique* (Paris:
Marcel Biard, 1927), pp. 191–92.

9. Henri Baudrillart, *Des rapports de l'économie politique et de la morale*
(2nd ed., Paris: Guillaumin, 1883 [1860]), p. 470.

10. Henri Baudrillart, *Histoire du luxe privé et public depuis l'antiquité
jusqu'à nos jours* (4 vols., Paris: Hachette, 1878–1880), vol. 1, p. 2.

11. Paul Leroy-Beaulieu in *Séances et travaux* (August 6, 1888): 724.

12. Ibid, p. 725; see also Paul Leroy-Beaulieu, *Traité théorique et pratique d'économie politique* (5 vols., Paris: Guillaumin, 1896), vol. 4, pp. 203–4.

13. Paul Leroy-Beaulieu in *Séances et travaux* (August 6, 1888): 725; see
also his "Études sociales" (December 1, 1894): 554.

14. Paul Leroy-Beaulieu, *Traité*, vol. 4, p. 239; see also his remarks in
Séances et travaux (August 6, 1888): 719–20, and in "Études sociales" (November
1, 1894): 73.

15. Paul Leroy-Beaulieu, *Traité*, vol. 4, p. 241; see also his remarks in
Séances et travaux (August 6, 1888): 720.

16. Paul Leroy-Beaulieu, *Traité*, vol. 1, pp. 104–7; vol. 4, p. 236.

17. Paul Leroy-Beaulieu, "Études sociales" (November 1, 1894): 79–88.

18. Paul Leroy-Beaulieu, *Traité*, vol. 1, p. 389. In 1881 he published his
Essai sur la répartition des richesses et la tendance à une moindre inégalité des conditions
(Paris: Guillaumin) to demonstrate that material inequalities were being re-
duced: workers' salaries were rising while interest rates were falling, and so
wealth was being more and more equally distributed by natural economic forces.
See also his *Traité*, vol. 4, pp. 209–13, 254, 257–58.

19. Ibid., vol. 4, p. 281. See also his "Études sociales" (November 1,
1894): 75.

20. Paul Leroy-Beaulieu in *Séances et travaux* (August 6, 1888): 720.

21. Paul Leroy-Beaulieu, *Traité*, vol. 1, p. 390.

22. Ibid., vol. 4, p. 248.

23. On Bukharin, see William M. Johnston, *The Austrian Mind: An
Intellectual and Social History 1848–1938* (Berkeley, Los Angeles, and London:

University of California Press, 1972), pp. 85–86; and Eric Roll, *A History of Economic Thought* (New York: Prentice-Hall, 1942), p. 405n.

24. Paul Leroy-Beaulieu, *Traité*, vol. 1, pp. 104–5. He further argues that from an economic point of view it is a good thing that the human race as a whole does not practice self-denial; the laws of economics would not change even if moral behavior did.

25. Gordon Wright, *France in Modern Times: 1760 to the Present* (Chicago: Rand McNally, 1960), pp. 300–318.

26. Examples of Catholic liberals (not to be confused with liberal Catholics, who are defined by their liberalism in religious matters) are Joseph Rambaud (1849–1919), member of the Catholic Faculty of Lyon and author of *Cours d'économie politique* and *Histoire des doctrines économiques*, and Charles Périn (1815–1908), professor of political economy at the Catholic University of Louvain, whose major work is *De la richesse dans les sociétés chrétiennes* (2 vols., Paris: V. Lecoffre, 1861). For general information on the École d'Angers (as Catholic economic liberals were called) see René Gonnard, *Histoire des doctrines économiques depuis les physiocrates* (5th ed., Paris: R. Pichon et R. Durand-Auzias, 1947), pp. 460–61.

Examples of Social Catholics and Christian Democrats are Marc Sangnier (1873–1950) and the Marquis de la Tour du Pin (1834–1924). For a list of other people connected with this group and an enumeration of their principles, see Gonnard, *Histoire*, pp. 461–68.

27. Z. Strat, *Le Rôle du consommateur dans l'économie moderne* (Paris: Éditions de la Vie Universitaire, 1922), p. 105; see also pp. 103–7.

28. See, for example, the annual reports of Abt Associates, Inc., 55 Wheeler Street, Cambridge, Massachusetts.

29. Anatole Leroy-Beaulieu, *La Papauté, le socialisme et la démocratie* (3rd ed., Paris: Calmann-Lévy, 1892), p. 99. (Most of the contents of this book originally appeared as articles in the *Revue des deux mondes*.)

30. Anatole Leroy-Beaulieu, *La Révolution et le libéralisme: essais de critique et d'histoire* (Paris: Hachette, 1890), p. 84.

31. Comment made by Charles Secrétan, "Questions sociales, II.—Le Luxe," *Revue philosophique*, no. 9 (September, 1888): 243. The interchange is recorded in *Séances et travaux*, n.s. 130 (August 13, 1888): 735.

32. Anatole Leroy-Beaulieu, "Le Règne de l'argent," pp. 721–42. Subsequent quotations from Anatole Leroy-Beaulieu are taken from this article passim.

33. Published in Paris by Calmann-Lévy.

34. Jules Delvaille, "La Crise morale," *Nouvelle revue*, n.s. 33 (March 1, 1905): 5–6. For a list of some of the more important books on the topic, see ibid., p. 7n. On Académie discussions, see M. A. Darlu, "Classification des idées morales du temps présent," in G. Belot et al., eds., *Morale sociale: leçons professées au Collège libre des sciences sociales* (Paris: Félix Alcan, 1899), pp. 17–26.

35. See Chapter V, n. 80.

36. Delvaille, "Crise morale," pp. 5–7.

37. Ibid., p. 7, referring to Darlu in Belot et al., *Morale sociale*, p. 18.

38. Delvaille, "Crise morale," p. 8.

39. J. G. Courcelle-Seneuil, *Séances et travaux*, n.s. 130 (August 13, 1888): 730–31, and n.s. 130 (July 30, 1888): 404.

40. The articles appear in the issues no. 6 (November, 1905): 836–58; no. 3 (May, 1906): 342–60; no. 3 (May, 1907): 327–47; and no. 2 (March, 1909): 207–30. Unless otherwise noted, quotes from Weber are taken from these articles passim.

41. Henri Baudrillart, *Histoire du luxe,* vol. 4, pp. 678–79.

42. Anatole Leroy-Beaulieu, "Nos hôtes," *La Révolution et le libéralisme,* pp. 325–28. The article first appeared in the *Nouvelle Revue* 61 (December 15, 1889) under the title "Nos hôtes de 1889."

43. Baudrillart, *Histoire du luxe,* vol. 4, pp. 591–94.

44. Georges d'Avenel, "Le Mécanisme de la vie moderne.—Le Prêt populaire, monts-de-piété,—Bons Crespin,—Crédit mutuel," *Revue des deux mondes,* 5th per., 1 (January 1, 1901): 196.

45. Georges d'Avenel, "Le Mécanisme de la vie moderne.—Les grands magasins," *Revue des deux mondes,* 4th per., 124 (July 15, 1894): 367–368. See also a similar passage in his *Les Français de mon temps* (Paris: Plon-Nourrit, 1904), pp. 348–49.

46. Louis Weber, *Le Rhythme du progrès: étude sociologique* (Paris: Félix Alcan, 1913), pp. ix–x.

47. Arendt, *The Human Condition,* pp. 13–18, 262–68.

48. This tendency to a political interpretation is the main weakness of Theodore Zeldin's otherwise useful discussion in his *France 1848–1945,* vol. 1, chapter 21, "Solidarism." This chapter appears in the section of the book devoted to French politics, and it presents solidarism as one of four doctrines shaping the French political life of that era (the other three being opportunism, radicalism, and socialism). Large portions of the chapter on solidarism are devoted to much more familiar political subjects, which are evidently discussed to establish a frame of reference: Boulangism, the *Ralliement,* the careers of Méline and Waldeck-Rousseau, and the Dreyfus Affair. The portion of the chapter that does deal directly with solidarist principles treats them in a political context and (rather unconvincingly, at times) tries to demonstrate that mutualism and the social legislation of the Third Republic resulted specifically from solidarist ideas. Although the chapter promises more than it delivers, it does rightly call attention to the importance of solidarist thought in France at that time.

49. The phrase of Ziegler was popularized by Alfred Fouillée in his article "La Question morale est-elle une question sociale?" *Revue des deux mondes,* 4th per., 160 (August 1, 1900): 481–512. The phrase "social technology" appears in E. de Roberty, "Morale et politique," in Belot et al., eds., *Morale sociale,* p. 275, and in Gustave Belot, "En quête d'une morale positive," *Revue de métaphysique et de morale,* no. 2 (March, 1906): 165. Louis Weber often refers to morality as a technique (e.g., "La Morale d'Épictète" [March, 1909]: 223, 234).

50. Strat, *Rôle du consommateur,* p. 109. Also on the general subject of solidarity, see J. E. S. Hayward, "The Official Social Philosophy of the French Third Republic: Léon Bourgeois and Solidarism," *International Review of Social History* 6 (1961): 19–48, and J. Scott, *Republican Ideas and the Liberal Tradition in France, 1870–1914* (New York: Columbia University Press, 1951), pp. 157–86 (part 2, chapter 2, "Solidarité: An Official Philosophy"). See also A. Darlu, "Réflexions d'un philosophe sur une question du jour: la solidarité," *Revue de métaphysique et de morale* 5 (1897): 120–28, and Maurice

Zablet, "Le Solidarisme," *Grande Revue* 16 (March 1, 1901): 675–96, and 17 (April 1, 1901): 120–38.

51. Célestin Bouglé, *Du Sage antique au citoyen moderne: études sur la culture morale* (Paris: Armand Colin, 1921), pp. 200–202, citing Benjamin Constant, who notes that individual liberty is typical of modern liberalism, while collective liberty was typical of ancient political systems.

For a recent and stimulating discussion of the collective aspects of consumption see Hirsch, *Social Limits to Growth*. Hirsch also emphasizes the importance of social morality in understanding and changing consumer behavior.

52. See Elias's "Introduction to the 1968 Edition," reproduced as Appendix 1 in *The Civilizing Process*, pp. 219–63.

53. Émile Durkheim, *The Division of Labor in Society*, pp. 109, 130–31. See book 1, chapter 2, "Mechanical Solidarity through Likeness," pp. 70–110, and book 1, chapter 3, "Organic Solidarity due to the Division of Labor," pp. 111–32.

CHAPTER 7

1. Charles Gide, *L'École nouvelle* (n.p., [1890?]), p. 79.

2. Ibid., p. 103.

3. Bernard Lavergne, *L'Ordre coopératif: étude générale de la coopération de consommation* (2 vols., Paris: Félix Alcan, 1926), vol. 1, pp. 84–87.

4. Charles Gide, *La Coopération: conférences de propagande*, p. 145.

5. Gide, *École nouvelle*, pp. 137–38.

6. Tsunao Miyajima, *Souvenirs sur Charles Gide, 1847–1932* (Paris: Librairie du Recueil Sirey, 1934), p. 64; and A. Lavondès, *Charles Gide: un précurseur de l'Europe unie et de l'ONU.—Un apôtre de la coopération entre les hommes*, preface by Bernard Lavergne [Uzès (Gard): La Capitehe, 1953], pp. 121–22.

7. Cited by Miyajima, *Souvenirs*, pp. 58–59 (the obituary appeared in the *Nouvelle revue française* in August and October, 1932).

8. Gide, *Coopération*, p. 147. The speech, titled "L'Idée de solidarité en tant que programme économique," was delivered to the Cercle des Étudiants Protestants de Paris in March, 1893. It was originally published in the *Revue internationale de sociologie* (October, 1893).

9. Ibid., pp. 149–50.

10. Charles Gide and Charles Rist, *Histoire des doctrines économiques* (7th ed., 2 vols., Paris: Librairie du Recueil Sirey, 1947), vol. 2, pp. 616–17.

11. Gide, *Coopération*, p. 152.

12. Strat, *Rôle du consommateur*, p. 114.

13. Gide, *Coopération*, p. 229; see also p. 162.

14. The speech is printed in Gide, *Coopération*, pp. 207–27. All subsequent quotations in this section are from that speech.

15. Charles Gide, *Cours d'économie politique* (Paris: L. Larose et L. Tenin, 1909), p. 738; see also pp. 736–40, and Charles Gide, *Principes d'économie politique*, pp. 569–73.

16. Quoted in Derrick Leon, *Ruskin: The Great Victorian* (London: Routledge and Kegan Paul, 1949), pp. 451–52.

17. Charles Gide, *Les Sociétés coopératives de consommation* (2nd ed., Paris: Armand Colin, 1910), pp. 264–76.

18. Charles Gide, *L'École de Nîmes*, p. 82.

19. Quoted in ibid.

20. Gide, *Coopération*, p. 138, quoting from Claudio Janet's *Le Socialisme d'état*.

21. Charles Gide, *Du rôle pratique du pasteur dans les questions sociales [Rapport présenté à l'assemblée générale de l'Association Protestante pour l'Étude Pratique des Questions Sociales tenue à Nîmes le 18 et 19 octobre 1888]* (La Vigan: Société Anonyme de l'Imprimerie Viganaise, 1888), pp. 28–29. This speech to a circle of young Protestant students is especially revealing of Gide's religious convictions.

For his general comments on the school of Le Play and the evolution of the *patronat*, see Gide, *Cours*, pp. 671–74.

22. Gide, *Coopération*, p. 138.

23. Gide, *École de Nîmes*, p. 91.

24. Ibid., p. 110.

25. Ibid., p. 282.

26. Gide, *Sociétés coopératives*, p. 120.

27. Lavondès, *Charles Gide*, pp. 119–20; Georges Benoît-Lévy, *La Cité-Jardin*, vol. 3, p. 165.

28. Benoît-Lévy, *Cité-Jardin*, vol. 3., pp. 20, 26–27, 198.

29. Gide, *Cours*, pp. 730, 730n; see also pp. 728–33 and Gide, *Principes*, pp. 578–81.

30. Charles Gide, "La Cité-Jardin," *Semaine littéraire*, no. 523 (January 9, 1904): 17.

31. Gide, *École nouvelle*, p. 152. See also Gide and Rist, *Histoire*, pp. 621–22, on the subjects of art for the people and of garden cities.

32. On the New York group, see Maurice Deslandres, *L'Acheteur, son rôle économique et social: les ligues sociales d'acheteurs* (Paris: Félix Alcan, 1911), pp. 1–26. On French organizations, see ibid., pp. 27–92, and H. La Coudraie, "La Ligue sociale des acheteurs," *Semaine littéraire*, no. 518 (December 9, 1903): 588.

33. These quotes are from La Coudraie, "Ligue sociale," p. 588.

34. Gide and Rist, *Histoire*, p. 607n; Deslandres, *Acheteur*, p. 33. The Leagues' constitution of 1904 took a position of religious and political neutrality, however (ibid., p. 39).

35. Gide, *Coopération*, p. 220.

36. La Coudraie, "Ligue sociale," p. 588.

37. Deslandres, *Acheteur*, p. 63.

38. Gide, *Coopération*, pp. 195–96.

39. This thesis is advanced by Ellen Moers at the end of her book *The Dandy*.

40. La Coudraie, "Ligue sociale," p. 588.

41. Deslandres, *Acheteur*, pp. 60–61.

42. La Coudraie, "Ligue sociale," p. 588.

43. Georges Sorel, *Introduction à l'économie moderne* (2nd rev. ed., Paris: Marcel Rivière, 1922), p. 131. See also pp. 165–82 on what Sorel calls "charlatanisme coopérative." Gide himself cites the passage quoted here and says it is directed at his book *Coopération* and especially at his lecture in it titled "Le Règne du consommateur": Gide, *Cours*, p. 722n.

44. Charles Rist in *Revue des études coopératives* (April, 1932): 213–14, cited by Lavondès, *Charles Gide*, p. 13.

45. Gustave de Molinari, "L'Automobile est-elle une richesse?" in *Ultima verba, mon dernier ouvrage* (Paris: V. Giard et E. Brière, 1911), pp. 161–62.

46. Edmund Wilson, *To the Finland Station: A Study in the Writing and Acting of History* (Garden City, New York: Doubleday Anchor Books, 1953 [1940]), pp. 322–23.

47. I borrowed this phrase from Louis Marin, "Disneyland: A Degenerate Utopia," *Glyph I* (Baltimore and London: Johns Hopkins University Press, 1977), pp. 50–66.

48. Wilson, *Finland Station*, p. 484.

49. Gide, *Coopération*, p. 104.

CHAPTER 8

1. Émile Durkheim, *Division of Labor*, pp. 408–9. The book was first published in 1893 under the title *La Division du travail social: étude sur l'organisation des sociétés supérieures* (Paris: Félix Alcan).

2. Durkheim, *Division of Labor*, pp. 32, 36 (from preface to the first edition). Durkheim's moral passion is certainly not overlooked by his most recent and exhaustive biographer in English: Steven Lukes, *Emile Durkheim: His Life and Works, a Historical and Critical Study* (London: Allen Lane, Penguin Press, 1973).

3. Durkheim, *Division of Labor*, pp. 27, 241, 244, 246–51.

4. Émile Durkheim, *Suicide: A Study in Sociology*, trans. John A. Spaulding and George Simpson, pp. 246–58. All subsequent quotations in this section are from this part of the book, in which Durkheim discusses anomic suicide. The book was originally published in Paris by Félix Alcan. Durkheim had introduced and defined the key term *anomie* in *Division of Labor*, pp. 353–73.

5. Émile Durkheim, *Le Socialisme*, p. 68. This book, compiled from lectures Durkheim wrote in 1895–1896, was published posthumously. See also Lukes, *Emile Durkheim*, pp. 245–54, and H. Stuart Hughes, *Consciousness and Society*, pp. 75–78, for information on these lectures and analyses of them.

6. Durkheim, *Socialisme*, pp. 226, 256, 260.

7. Ibid., p. 221, 229, 260.

8. Durkheim, *Division of Labor*, p. 173. For his summary of the differences between the two types of solidarity, see pp. 226–27.

9. Ibid., pp. 6–31; see also Durkheim, *Suicide*, pp. 378–79.

10. Célestin Bouglé, "La Morale de l'outil.—Le Rôle moral des associations professionelles," *Revue bleue*, 5th ser., 5 (June 16, 1906): 754.

11. Durkheim, *Socialisme*, p. 229.

12. In *Suicide*, p. 56, and in *Socialisme*, p. 261, Durkheim uses this phrase to characterize modern civilization.

13. Durkheim, *Suicide*, p. 383.

14. See especially Palante's article "L'Impunité du groupe," *La Plume*, no. 310 (March 15, 1902): 353–58, and his *Les Antinomies entre l'individu et la société*, p. 280.

15. Durkheim, *Division of Labor*, p. 303.

16. Ibid., p. 401.

17. Ibid., p. 394.

18. Célestin Bouglé, *Du sage antique au citoyen moderne*, p. 244.

19. Durkheim, *Suicide*, p. 385.

20. Émile Durkheim, *Les Formes élémentaires de la vie religieuse*, p. 478. Subsequent quotations in this section are also from this book: pp. 285, 323, 351, 355, 356, 464, 475, and 478.

21. The phrase is used by Durkheim in a letter cited by Lukes, *Emile Durkheim*, p. 310.

22. Ibid.

23. Terry N. Clark, "Gabriel Tarde," in *International Encyclopedia of the Social Sciences*, ed. David L. Sills (1968), vol. 15, pp. 509–14. In his book *Prophets and Patrons: The French University and the Emergence of the Social Sciences* (Cambridge, Mass.: Harvard University Press, 1973), p. ?, Clark admits that his own efforts to demonstrate the importance of Tarde and other non-Durkheimian sociologists "have not been particularly convincing." Clark has done the most extensive studies of Tarde in English.

The quarrel between Durkheim and Tarde is well described by Lukes, *Emile Durkheim*, pp. 302–13 (narrative treatment) and by Jean Milet, *Gabriel Tarde et la philosophie de l'histoire* (Paris: Librairie Philosophique J. Vrin, 1970), pp. 247–57 (analytical treatment).

24. Milet, *Gabriel Tarde*, p. 396; see also pp. 396–99 for a previously unpublished manuscript in which Tarde outlines his plans for the discipline of interpsychology.

25. Quoted by Lukes, *Emile Durkheim*, p. 306.

26. Gabriel Tarde, *Les Lois de l'imitation, étude sociologique* (3rd ed., Paris: Félix Alcan, 1900), p. *xxiii*.

27. Ibid., p. *xi*.

28. Ibid., p. *viii*.

29. Ibid., p. 85.

30. Ibid., pp. 91, 95.

31. Ibid., p. 94.

32. See Ernest R. Hilgard, "Hypnotic Phenomena: The Struggle for Scientific Acceptance," *American Scientist* 59, no. 5 (September-October, 1971): 567–77.

33. Tarde, *Lois*, p. 83. The importance of French psychologists such as Hippolyte Bernheim (1840–1919) and his colleagues composing the "school of Nancy" (which has no connection except geographical proximity with Gallé's School of Nancy) who were students of hypnotic phenomena is too often little appreciated for its influence on the future development of Freud in particular and of psychoanalysis in general. See Michael D. Biddiss, *The Age of the Masses: Ideas and Society in Europe since 1870* (New York: Harper Colophon Books, 1977), pp. 57–58.

34. René Worms, "La Philosophie sociale de G. Tarde," *Revue philosophique* 60 (August, 1905): 138.

35. Tarde, *Lois*, p. 225.

36. This is the central thesis of René Girard's fascinating and highly relevant study of nineteenth-century literature, *Mensonge romantique et vérité romanesque*.

37. Tarde, *Lois*, p. 232.

38. Ibid., pp. 245–46.

39. Gabriel Tarde, *The Laws of Imitation*, trans. from the second French edition by Elsie Clews Parsons (New York: Henry Holt, 1903), pp. 367–38.

40. Tarde, *Lois*, p. 252.

41. Tarde, *Laws*, p. 348.

42. Tarde, *Lois*, p. 219.

43. Tarde, *Laws*, p. 324.

44. The theory of opposition is explained most fully in *L'Opposition universelle* (Paris: Félix Alcan, 1897) and the theory of adaptation (with a summary of the three major concepts—imitation, opposition, and adaptation) in *Les Lois sociales* (Paris: Félix Alcan, 1898).

45. See especially his "La Croyance et le désir: possibilité de leur mesure," *Revue philosophique* 10 (August, 1880): 150–80, and (September, 1880): 264–83; and his "La Psychologie en économie politique," *Revue philosophique* 12 (September, 1881): 232–50, and (October, 1881): 401–18.

46. Gabriel Tarde, *La Psychologie économique*, vol. 1, p. 115.

47. Ibid., vol. 1, p. 149.

48. Ibid., vol. 1, p. 158, and vol. 2, p. 114.

49. Ibid., vol. 1, p. 155.

50. Tarde, "Psychologie en économie politique," p. 416.

51. Ibid., p. 417.

52. Tarde, *Psychologie économique*, vol. 1, pp. 295–96, and vol. 2, p. 117.

53. Ibid., vol. 1, p. 189.

54. Gabriel Tarde, *L'Opinion et la foule* (2nd ed., Paris: Félix Alcan, 1904 [1901]), pp. *vi–vii*, 83, 115–16; and Tarde, *Psychologie économique*, vol. 1, p. 197. The more thorough examination of the topic is in *L'Opinion*.

55. Tarde, *Psychologie économique*, vol. 1, p. 202.

56. Ibid., vol. 1, pp. 169–70. Tarde's definition of luxury depends on the psychological motivation of the consumer, not on the cost or character of the object involved. The luxurious character of objects appears when they no longer serve to maintain the physical or social being of an individual in its integrity, but, rather, "extend it, swell it by vanity." The example that inspires Tarde's definition of luxury is not one of the conventional ones (expensive clothing, jewels, etc.) but that of national military spending. Such spending, says Tarde, is certainly an unproductive, costly form of consumption that cannot be understood in rational or objective terms. Like any other form of consumption, it must be approached on a psychological level. How can we make sense of the fact that each nation feels it must keep buying submarines, no matter how ruinous the expense? The answer lies in motivation. A nation feels it must maintain its existence at any price. Military expenditure becomes a genuine luxury only when inspired by national megalomania rather than by legitimate self-defense. *Psychologie économique*, vol. 2, p. 106.

57. Ibid., vol. 1, pp. 118–19.

58. Quoted by Auguste Dupont, *Gabriel Tarde et l'économie politique (un essai d'introduction du point de vue psychologique dans le domaine économique)* (Paris: V. Giard et E. Brière, 1910), p. 223.

59. Ibid., p. 210.

60. Tarde, *Psychologie économique*, vol. 1, p. 63.

61. Ibid., vol. 2, p. 256.

62. Ibid., vol. 1, p. 678.

63. Tarde, "Lettre à M. Espinas," *Revue philosophique* 60 (1901): 678.

64. Tarde, *Psychologie économique*, vol. 2, p. 254.

65. Tarde, *L'Opposition universelle*, p. 428.
66. Tarde, *Psychologie économique*, vol. 2, p. 413.
67. Ibid., vol. 2, pp. 413, 417; Gabriel Tarde, *La Logique sociale* (Paris: Félix Alcan, 1895), p. 384.
68. Tarde, *Lois*, pp. 195–96.
69. Ibid., p. 196.
70. Ibid., p. 172.
71. Ibid., pp. 198–99.
72. Ibid., p. 200.
73. Ibid., p. 199.
74. Tarde, *Psychologie économique*, vol. 2, pp. 418–19.
75. Quoted in Dupont, *Gabriel Tarde*, p. 254.
76. Tarde, *Psychologie économique*, vol. 2, p. 264.
77. Gabriel Tarde, "Questions sociales," *Revue philosophique* 35 (1893): 629.
78. Tarde, *Psychologie économique*, vol. 1, p. 187.
79. Tarde, "La Psychologie en économie politique," p. 418.
80. Tarde, *L'Opinion*, pp. 6, 18–19.
81. Ibid., pp. 18–19.
82. Ibid., p. 68. On pp. 64–67, Tarde suggests that there are three elements to the public mind: tradition (opinion of the dead, incorporated into custom); reason (from an elite); and opinion. The last has developed most recently but is growing much faster than the other two. The interaction of the three makes up the history of the public mind. The positive mission of public opinion is to turn the reason of today into the tradition of tommorow.
83. Gabriel Tarde, "L'Avenir de la moralité," *Revue philosophique* 22 (1886): 404, 406; see also Tarde, *Lois*, p. 387.
84. Tarde, *L'Opinion*, p. 60.
85. Tarde, *Laws*, p. 346.
86. Tarde, *Lois*, pp. 66–67.
87. Tarde, *Psychologie économique*, vol. 2, p. 421.
88. Tarde, *Lois*, pp. 422, 424.
89. See Milet, *Gabriel Tarde*, p. 21n, for information on the writing and publication of *Fragment*. In 1896 the work first appeared in the *Revue internationale de sociologie*, and in the same year it was published in Paris as a brochure (V. Giard et E. Brière). In 1904 a costly posthumous edition appeared, and the following year an English translation was published, with a foreword by H. G. Wells, under the unfortunate title *Underground Man*. Quotations in the rest of this chapter are from the 1904 edition (Lyon and Paris: A. Storck).

CHAPTER 9

1. On this general subject see Richard J. Barnet, *The Lean Years: Politics in the Age of Scarcity* (New York: Simon and Schuster, 1980).
2. *Gabriel Tarde: introduction et pages choisies par ses fils* (Paris: Louis-Michaud, 1909), p. 32.
3. See Chapter 3, p. 128.
4. Tarde, "La Psychologie en économie politique," p. 417.
5. Dupont, *Gabriel Tarde*, p. 64. The poem was published posthumously in 1904. Tarde's funeral was conducted according to its directions.

6. In Gabriel Tarde, *La Criminalité comparée* (Paris: Félix Alcan, 1886), pp. 208–10, cited by Dupont, *Gabriel Tarde*, p. 84.

7. Such are the warnings of René Girard in *Mensonge romantique et vérité romanesque*. Girard generally agrees with Tarde on the mechanisms of imitative desire but comes to much more pessimistic conclusions about their probable results.

8. *Gabriel Tarde*, p. 5 (preface). See Gabriel Tarde, "Les Monades et la science sociale," in *Essais et mélanges sociologiques*, Bibliothèque de criminologie (Paris: G. Masson; Lyon: A. Storck, 1900), pp. 371–79. See also the stimulating discussion by Milet, *Gabriel Tarde*, pp. 145–90.

9. Elias, *The Civilizing Process*, p. 251 (from his introduction to the 1968 edition).

10. For an analysis of "mobile privatization" as a dominant form of modern consumer technology, see Raymond Williams, *Television: Technology and Cultural Form* (New York: Schocken Books, 1974), especially p. 26; and his comments on "traffic" as a concept of modern consciousness and social relations in *The Country and the City*, especially p. 296.

11. J. K. Galbraith, *The New Industrial State* (New York: New American Library, 1967), p. 174.

12. J. K. Galbraith, *The Affluent Society* (Boston: Houghton Mifflin, 1958), pp. 340–45.

13. Quoted by Edward P. Thompson in *William Morris: Romantic to Revolutionary* (1st American ed., New York: Pantheon Books, 1977 [1955]), p. 791.

14. Tarde, *Lois*, p. *xxiii*.

Selected Bibliography

Because the field of consumer history is so ill-defined, there is no standard bibliography to draw upon, nor even the beginnings of one. Consequently, any attempt to present a complete list of relevant sources would be hopeless. This highly selective list includes only those primary sources I found most pertinent. Most secondary sources are listed in the notes. However, I have included here a few secondary sources of general utility which deserve special attention.

Avenel, Georges d'. *Le Mécanisme de la vie moderne*. Paris: A. Colin, 1896 [and other editions].

———. *Le Nivellement des jouissances*. Paris: Ernest Flammarion, 1913.

Balzac, Honoré de. *La Comédie humaine*. Available in English translations.

Deslandres, Maurice, *L'Acheteur, son rôle économique et social: les ligues sociales d'acheteurs*. Paris: Félix Alcan, 1911.

Durkheim, Émile. *The Division of Labor in Society*. Trans. George Simpson. New York: Free Press, 1965.

———. *Les Formes élémentaires de la vie religieuse: le système totémique en Australie*. Bibliothèque de Philosophie Contemporaine. 5th ed., Paris: Presses Universitaires de France, 1968. Available in English translations.

———. *Le Socialisme: sa définition, ses débuts, la doctrine Saint-Simonienne*. Paris: Presses Universitaires de France, 1971.

———. *Suicide: A Study in Sociology*. Trans. John A. Spaulding and George Simpson. New York: Free Press; London: Collier Macmillan, 1951.

Elias, Norbert. *The Civilizing Process: The Development of Manners—Changes in the Code of Conduct and Feeling in Early Modern Times*. Trans. Edmund Jephcott. New York: Urizen Books, 1978 (1939).

Gaumont, J. *Histoire générale de la coopération en France, les idées et les faits*. 2 vols. Paris: Fédération Nationale des Coopératives de Consommation, 1923–1924.

Gide, Charles. *La Coopération; conférences de propagande.* Paris: Librairie de la Société du Recueil Général des Lois et des Arrêts, 1900.

————. *L'École de Nîmes: cours sur la coopération au Collège de France [Décembre 1925–Avril 1926].* Paris: Association pour l'Enseignement de la Coopération, 1927.

————. *Principes d'économie politique.* 9th ed., Paris: L. Larose et L. Tenin, 1905.

Haugmard, Louis. "L' 'Esthétique' du cinématographie." *Le Correspondant* 251 (May 25, 1913): 762–71.

Huysmans, Joris-Karl. *À Rebours* (1884). Available in English translations under the title *Against the Grain.*

Lavergne, Bernard. *Les Coopératives de consommation en France.* Paris: Librairie Armand Colin, 1923.

Leroy-Beaulieu, Anatole. "Le Règne de l'argent." *Revue des deux mondes,* 4th per., 122 (March 15, 1894): 241–60; 122 (April 15, 1894): 721–42.

Leroy-Beaulieu, Paul. "Études sociales—Le luxe, la fonction de la richesse." *Revue des deux mondes,* 4th per., 126 (November 1, 1894): 72–100; 126 (December 1, 1894): 547–73.

Mauclair, Camille. "Le Besoin d'art du peuple." *Revue bleue* 4 (September 2, 1905): 306–10.

————. "La Crise des arts décoratifs." *Revue bleue* 5 (June 16, 1906): 755–59.

————. "Le Nouveau Paris du peuple." *Revue bleue* 5 (January 20, 1906): 79–83.

————. "Où en est notre 'Art décoratif?' " *Revue bleue* 8 (April 24, 1909): 520–24.

————. *Servitude et grandeur littéraires.* Paris: Librairie Ollendorff (1922?).

————. "Le Style de la rue moderne." *Revue bleue* 4 (December 2, 1905): 719–22.

Mustoxidi, T. M. *Histoire de l'esthétique française, 1700–1900.* Paris: Librairie Ancienne Honoré Champion, 1920.

Needham, H. A. *Le Développement de l'esthétique sociologique en France et en Angleterre au XIXe siècle.* Paris: Librairie Ancienne Honoré Champion, 1926.

Strat, Z. *Le Rôle du consommateur dans l'économie moderne.* Paris: Éditions de la Vie Universitaire, 1922.

Talmeyr, Maurice. "L'École du Trocadéro." *Revue des deux mondes,* 4th per., 162 (November 1, 1900): 198–213.

Tarde, Gabriel. *Fragment d'histoire future.* Lyon and Paris: A. Storck, 1904. Available in English under the title *Underground Man.*

————. *Les Lois de l'imitation, étude sociologique.* 3rd ed., Paris: Félix Alcan, 1900. Available in English translation as *The Laws of Imitation.*

————. *On Communication and Social Influence: Selected Papers.* Ed. and with intro. by Terry N. Clark. Chicago and London: University of Chicago Press, 1969.

————. *L'Opinion et la foule.* 2nd ed., Paris: Félix Alcan, 1904.

————. *La Psychologie économique.* 2 vols. Paris: Félix Alcan, 1902.

Weber, Louis. "La Morale d'Épictète et les besoins présents de l'enseignement moral." *Revue de métaphysique et de morale.* No. 6 (November, 1905): 836–58; no. 3 (May, 1906): 432–60; no. 3 (May, 1907): 327–47; no. 2 (March, 1909): 207–29.

Zeldin, Theodore. *France 1848–1945.* Vol. I: *Ambition, Love and Politics.* Oxford: Clarendon Press, 1973. Vol. II: *Intellect, Taste and Anxiety.* Oxford: Clarendon Press, 1977. In *Oxford History of Modern Europe,* ed. Lord Bullock and Sir William Deakin.

Zola, Émile. *Au Bonheur des Dames.* Lausanne: Edihons Rencontre, n.d.

INDEX

Designer: Jane Rockwell
Compositor: Huron Valley Graphics, Inc.
Printer: Thomson-Shore, Inc.
Binder: John H. Dekker & Sons
Text: 11/13 Palatino
Display: Palatino